Selected Sermons, Prayers,

and Devotions

Selected Sermons, Prayers, *and* Devotions

BY

John Henry Newman

PREFACE BY

Peter J. Gomes

EDITED BY

John F. Thornton and *Susan B. Varenne*

VINTAGE SPIRITUAL CLASSICS

VINTAGE BOOKS
A DIVISION OF RANDOM HOUSE, INC.
NEW YORK

A VINTAGE SPIRITUAL CLASSICS ORIGINAL, MAY 1999
First Edition

Editing and arrangement of the texts, About the Vintage Spiritual Classics,
Preface to the Vintage Spiritual Classics, Chronology of the Life of John
Henry Newman, and Suggestions for Further Reading copyright © 1999 by
Random House, Inc.

Library of Congress Cataloging-in-Publication Data
Newman, John Henry, 1801–1890.
[Selections, 1999]
Selected sermons, prayers, and devotions / John Henry Newman ;
preface by Peter J. Gomes ; edited by John F. Thornton
and Susan B. Varenne. — 1st ed.
p. cm. — (Vintage spiritual classics)
Includes bibliographical references.
ISBN 0-375-70551-1
1. Church of England — Sermons. 2. Sermons, English — 19th century.
3. Prayers. 4. Meditations. I. Thornton, John F., 1942–
II. Varenne, Susan B. III. Title. IV. Series.
BX5133.N4S352 1999
252'.03 — dc21   98-54136
CIP

www.vintagebooks.com

Book design by Fritz Metsch

Printed in the United States of America.
10 9 8 7 6 5 4 3 2 1

CONTENTS

ABOUT THE
VINTAGE SPIRITUAL CLASSICS

by John F. Thornton and Susan B. Varenne, General Editors

A turn or shift of sorts is becoming evident in the reflections of men and women today on their life experiences. Not quite as adamantly secular and, perhaps, a little less insistent on material satisfactions, the reading public has recently developed a certain attraction to testimonies that human life is leavened by a Presence that blesses and sanctifies. Recovery, whether from addictions or personal traumas, illness, or even painful misalignments in human affairs, is evolving from the standard therapeutic goal of enhanced self-esteem. Many now seek a deeper healing that embraces the whole person, including the soul. Contemporary books provide accounts of the invisible assistance of angels. The laying on of hands in prayer has made an appearance at the hospital bedside. Guides for the spiritually perplexed have risen to the top of best-seller lists. The darkest shadows of skepticism and unbelief, which have eclipsed the presence of the Divine in our rational age, are beginning to lighten and part.

If the power and presence of God are real and effective, what do they mean for human experience? What does He offer to men and women, and what does He ask in return? How do we recognize Him? Know Him? Respond to Him? God has a reputation for being both benevolent and wrathful. Which will He be for me and when? Can these aspects of the Divine somehow be reconciled? Where is God when I suffer? Can I lose Him? Is God truthful, and are His promises to be trusted?

Are we really as precious to God as we are to ourselves and our loved ones? Do His providence and amazing grace guide our faltering steps toward Him, even in spite of ourselves? Will God abandon us if the sin is serious enough, or if we have episodes of resistance and forgetfulness? These are fundamental questions any person might address to God during a lifetime. They are pressing and difficult, often becoming wounds in the soul of the person who yearns for the power and courage of hope, especially in stressful times.

The Vintage Spiritual Classics present the testimony of writers across the centuries who have considered all these difficulties and who have pondered the mysterious ways, unfathomable mercies, and deep consolations afforded by God to those who call upon Him from out of the depths of their lives. These writers, then, are our companions, even our champions, in a common effort to discern the meaning of God in personal experience. For God is personal to us. To whom does He speak if not to us, provided we have the desire to hear Him deep within our hearts?

Each volume opens with a specially commissioned essay by a well-known contemporary writer that offers the reader an appreciation of its intrinsic value. A chronology of the general historical context of each author and his work is provided, as are suggestions for further reading.

We offer a final word about the act of reading these spiritual classics. From the very earliest accounts of monastic practice—dating back to the fourth century—it is evident that a form of reading called *lectio divina* ("divine" or "spiritual reading") was essential to any deliberate spiritual life. This kind of reading is quite different from that of scanning a text for useful facts and bits of information, or advancing along an exciting plot line to a climax in the action. It is, rather, a meditative approach, by which the reader seeks to taste and savor the beauty and truth of every phrase and passage. This process of contemplative reading has the effect of enkindling in the reader compunction for past behavior that has been less than beautiful and true. At the same time, it increases the desire to seek a realm where all that is lovely and unspoiled may be found. There are four steps in *lectio divina*: first, to read, next to meditate, then to rest in the sense of God's nearness, and, ultimately, to resolve to govern one's actions in the light of new understanding. This kind of reading is itself an act of prayer. And, indeed, it is in prayer that God manifests His Presence to us.

by Peter J. Gomes

These last years of the twentieth century have found the preaching of doctrinal theology in a very low estate. In an age that prides itself upon the efficiency and effectiveness of communication, in which words and images hold unprecedented influence over the minds and emotions of vast audiences, words about the Word made flesh appear less and less credible. It is a commonplace that preaching no longer works and that communication about religious things must find new forms of expression. Preachers are encouraged to take their cues from the secular format of the television talk show, which caters to fast-track celebrity or sensational sound bites, and they are told that congregations should be thought of as audiences with short attention spans, no capacity for complexity or analysis, and no appetite for anything that demands or confronts.

Preaching, in our contemporary perception of it, is "authoritarian," and people are annoyed by the notion that they are to be instructed in matters from on high by someone who knows more than they. Preaching as self-affirmation, in the current antiintellectual, antiauthority, and antielitist climate, exists to affirm *my* situation, *my* interests, and *my* anxieties, and it is the preacher's task to discern those perceived needs, and to cater to them. Thus contemporary preaching often amounts to an ecumenical exercise in which the bland lead the bland. Pop psychology, spiritual consumerism, and the talk-show sensibility have become the contentless forms which today pass for public preaching. It is no wonder that the religion sections of the bookstores are overwhelmed with self-help books on the quickest route to painless, nondidactic spiritual satisfaction. No one any longer expects the preaching of sermons to meet any serious need.

Thus this appearance of a collection of the sermons of John Henry Newman could not come at a more propitious moment. At this lowest point in the credibility of the written word, at this moment of supreme self-satisfaction with the secular status quo, we are confronted with the magisterial power of the authority of the spoken and written word, and it is not the case that the power of these words consists in the artful devices of rhetoric and oratory, although they are splendid examples of both. Rather, their power consists in that about which these words speak: the word of God, and God Himself. In these sermons we do not so much see Cardinal Newman as we see what Cardinal Newman knew and saw of God. It is in this sense that Newman is an incarnational preacher, showing not himself but the one who is revealed in his words. Newman accomplishes the sublime ambition of every honest, consecrated preacher: he allows his words to reveal *the* Word made flesh, and filled with grace and truth. These sermons and meditations are not only exemplary models of the preacher's art for preachers, they are, perhaps, of even greater importance in their impact upon those faithful who seek to better understand that faith to which they have committed themselves.

The title that Newman gave to his original collection says it all: *Plain and Parochial Sermons.* They are written in what the seventeenth-century English Puritans would have called the "plain stile," shunning the rhetorical artifices much favored by the rhetoricians and Court preachers of the day. They were meant to exhibit piety, not learning, and while they are profoundly learned, the learning is a means and not an end in itself. The end, of course, is the accomplishment of a transaction in which the human media of thought and word are meant to affect the contemplation of holy things. In the plain style, anything that does not contribute directly to this end is shunned. Nothing extraneous to the transaction is permitted. We are not meant to "know" the preacher through his discourse by means of clever analysis or self-revealing anecdotes. We are not meant to see the preacher as "just one of us," and thus "identify" with his human struggles or achievements. While all preaching is self-revealing, authentic preaching is not about the self. In these sermons it is clear that we are meant to see what Newman saw and that we are not meant to see Newman. The plain style is meant to be transparent. We are meant to be able to see through it to the objective of the exercise. The sermon is not the light but the means which allows us to see the light. In the plain style neither the preacher nor even the words themselves are meant to stand in the way of the light or to cast a shadow, however felicitous or euphonious, on the light. The words, then, are meant to be servants of the Word.

Newman's plain style, his lean and efficient use of language, is all the more remarkable in an age in which orotundity flourished in public speech, and language itself was exercised as a florid art form, particularly in the service of religion. The nineteenth century cultivated the high art of verbal expression, with preaching, like parliamentary debate and the discourse of advocates in the law courts, a form of public entertainment with high expectations. It was said of the eighteenth-century English evangelist George Whitefield, a contemporary of the Wesleys, that he could make grown men weep at the mere pronunciation of "Mesopotamia"; and in the High Victorian era, of which Newman was so conspicuous a part, the great prime ministers Disraeli and Gladstone were also accounted the greatest orators of the day. Today their best prose seems bloated and over the top; Newman, however, reads with a clarity and focus as refreshing today as it was out of fashion yesterday. As it has been said of enduring classical architecture and the favored physiognomy of classical portraiture, Newman's prose has good bones.

Another revealing aspect of these sermons of Newman is found in his title for them: "parochial." Newman's preaching is not abstract but is grounded in pastoral concerns for the needs of the parish, the gathered people of God who are meant to be not simply edified but fed. Newman's parish was the University Church of St. Mary the Virgin in Oxford, and his auditors, while they included the great and the good of the university, were most particularly the young undergraduate members, for whom faith was at the very least conventional and perfunctory. Newman's mission was to make these young fops interested in effective piety and in the ultimate destiny of their souls: his was indeed the cure of souls in a soulless age and place. John Milton, in his poem *Lycidas*, described the "hungry sheep" who looked up to be fed, and who were met by the "blind mouths" of clergy indifferent to spiritual nourishment.

Newman was no blind-mouthed preacher but rather one determined to feed his people on the nourishing teachings of Holy Mother Church. He understood preaching to be the instruction of the people in the words and ways of God so that they might better fit themselves on earth for their eventual place in heaven. Preaching thus was a primer in the way of the heavenly life on earth, and for Newman it proceeded from the invincible assumption that earth is a tutorial of heaven, or, in St. Augustine's words, that earth is but a colony of heaven. "Parochial," for Newman, does not mean small-minded or locally bound, but quite the contrary: for Newman the local is the place in which we prepare for the eternal, and, indeed, the two must not be confused.

What strikes the contemporary reader in these sermons is the profound sense that Newman is grounded not so much in this life as in the life to come. By this I do not mean to suggest that Newman was some life-denying mystic or ascetic who lived in a realm of shadowy expectations. Not at all. We get the sense of Newman's stability, indeed, serenity, in the world of which he was a part because of his security in the world that is to come. He is able to cope with *here* because he is convinced of *there* and understands with St. Paul that his true citizenship and allegiance are in heaven. Thus while he is not world-denying in the sense of denigrating creation, he is heaven-affirming, for it is for heaven that the faithful have been created. He understands what St. Augustine meant when he said in his famous prayer, "Thou hast made us for Thyself, and our hearts are restless until they find their rest in Thee."

It may be argued that the nineteenth century was possibly the first thoroughly materialistic century in the history of Western Christendom. Even the so-called Dark Ages of the medieval period consisted of a struggle between the spiritual sensitivity of the old paganism and the maturing faith of Christianity. The belief in inevitable human progress and the self-sufficiency of rational discourse, with the technological skills to prove it and the economic success to sustain it, were not given assumption on either side of these premodern cultural wars. Newman was born in 1801 and died in 1890 and flourished at the high noon of that most self-sufficient and arrogant of centuries. It was thus given to him to wage spiritual warfare *contra mundum*. He understood by the power of his own experience the meaning of St. Paul's indictment of the powers and principalities in his Epistle to the Ephesians. He was engaged in spiritual warfare with the prevailing ideology of the secular and the material. He knew that he was living in an age of what might be called the new paganism, a world described by the crazed poet-seer William Blake as one dominated by dark, satanic mills. Newman knew that the enemies of true religion were a thoughtless conformity to the value of a materialistic culture, a self-satisfied sense of comfort, the impoverishment of the religious imagination, and a loss of the sense of sin, and hence of the promise of redemption.

Furthermore, Newman understood that this was not a new phenomenon but a contemporary manifestation of an old one. This was the formative context of the primitive Church, and it would be to the primitive Church that he would turn for the spiritual and intellectual resource with which to combat the spirit of the age. Increasingly, contemporary Anglicanism was for Newman a part of the problem and not a part of the solution, and it was for this reason that he resigned his Anglican orders in 1843 and was received into the Catholic Church in 1845.

It is important to realize that his *Plain and Parochial Sermons*, the first volume of which was published in 1834, were both preached and published while Newman was still an Anglican. They represent his growing struggle to reconcile his experience of Anglicanism with what he was discovering of the nature of the Church through his study of the early Church Fathers. In 1827, two years after his ordination to the Anglican priesthood, he began an intensive study of the Church Fathers, which brought him to the conclusions that the authentic foundations of the Christian Church were to be found there and that those foundations were revealed, apostolic, and Catholic. By his appointment in 1828 as vicar of St. Mary the Virgin, he was given a forum in which to pursue and express his views that the Church of England could be reinvorgorated only by a renewed appeal to the spirit and discipline of the early Church. In 1838 he moved in his studies from the ancient Church to the New Testament itself and published *Lectures on the Doctrine of Justification*, in which he discussed the New Testament's teaching of the divine indwelling of

God in the individual soul. In this year there also appeared three more volumes of his sermons. Two years later he published his essays, *The Church of the Fathers*, in which he discussed revealed religion in the early Church.

It was his reading of St. Augustine which forced him to reconsider the catholicity of the English Church, and it was his study of St. Athanasius and his writings against the Arian heresy which led him to conclude that the traditional Anglican sympathy toward the Arian position, which compromises the divinity of Christ, placed the English Church outside Catholic orthodoxy. Thus in the period from 1838 to 1843, by his careful study of the early Church, Newman was drawn to the conclusion that the continuity of the apostolic faith depended upon the authority of the Roman Catholic Church. On September 18, 1843, he preached his last sermon as an Anglican.

Newman's collected sermons, in eight volumes, proved to be popular and went through many editions. In 1868, over twenty years after he became England's most famous convert to Roman Catholicism, these sermons from his Anglican period were republished. In them we find the themes which provide a sense of deep spiritual continuity in the development of Newman's thought, themes made accessible to a lay audience which increasingly transcended the differences between Anglicans and Roman Catholics. They have this appeal not because they are without specificity but because their aim transcends the partisan polemic which would tempt one to classify them with the superficial labels of "Protestant" or "Catholic." For Newman the issue was not primarily which of these forms of Christianity was right but rather which one would offer the stronger and more authentic resources for waging mortal combat with the devil and all his works. Newman's struggle was not so much an ecclesiastical one as a moral one, a mortal struggle between religious truth and secular, godless power. His movement to Rome is often seen as a rejection of Protestantism in its Anglican form. What is more important is to understand this movement as an embrace of the only legitimate force available with which to wage holy war against the seductions of the world.

These sermons stake out the claims of the spiritually minded in the face of the worldly. The themes embrace the importance of revealed religion, the presence and providence of God, the divine indwelling of God in the soul, the reality of things unseen, the importance of faith and obedience in the life of the believer. For Newman the only security in this world of tribulation is the unseen reality of the spiritual world, a world which is ruled by Christ, and for which Christ gave himself for our redemption, which act is recapitulated in the sacramental life of the believer. Word and sacrament, faith and obedience are the means of grace and the hope of glory for the believer. These are, in the words of the Epistle to the Hebrews, "Those things which cannot be shaken" (12:27), and the believer who holds to these things will never stagger at the uneven motions of this life and world.

For Newman the sermon is a form of argument, the statement of a proposition that is to be demonstrated and applied for the well-being of the believer. The basis for his arguments invariably is the teaching of the Fathers of the early Church, who inhabited a world threatened with many of the same secular assumptions prevalent in Newman's day. The Fathers provide the basis for a devout and serious life, and hence they provide the foundation for Newman's sermons and teachings. Such apostolic teaching and preaching do not depend for their verification upon the personal experience of the believer, but the personal experience of the believer will confirm the validity of the apostolic teaching and preaching. Thus, revealed religion is not the result of a personal discovery or encounter as so much of experimental Protestantism insists: revealed religion is the divine self-disclosure of God by God, and as such, like the Incarnation itself, is an act of divine condescension which the believer apprehends and receives.

The believer is called first to obedience, not to understanding, for it is in obedience that the habits of the heart are formed, and one is led to holiness by repeating the pattern of holiness. Newman asks, "Is not holiness the result of many patient, repeated efforts after obedience, gradually working on us, and first modifying and then changing our hearts?" Holiness is conformity to the will of God, and thus obedience, and even good works themselves, are means to that sublime end rather than ends in themselves. "Outward acts, done on principle, create inward habits. I repeat, the separate acts of obedience to the will of God, good works as they are called, are of service to us, as gradually severing us from this world of sense, and impressing our hearts with a heavenly character." This is from the very first sermon of this volume, "Holiness Necessary for Future Blessedness" (see p. 3). To obtain this holiness, he reminds his listeners, is the work of a lifetime, and thus after the fashion of the great eighteenth-century devotional writer William Law, he invites the believer to the contemplation of a devout and holy life.

There are practical ways of achieving this holiness. In his sermon "Love of Relations and Friends" on the feast day of St. John the Evangelist, he writes:

Now I shall here maintain, in opposition to such notions of Christian love, and with our Savior's pattern before me, that the best preparation for loving the world at large, and loving it duly and wisely, is to cultivate an intimate friendship and affection towards those who are immediately about us. (p. 74)

It is the example of Jesus and John of which he speaks, and he argues:

What we are towards our earthly friends in the instincts and wishes of our infancy, such we are to become at length toward God and man in the extended field of our duties as accountable beings. (p. 74)

This is not the mere elevation of friendship to a spiritual virtue, a point which would easily be embraced by the secular classical authors who would have been well known to his Oxford University parishioners; "but again," as he goes on to say, "the love of our private friends is the only preparatory exercise for the love of all men." Love for Newman in this context was affection concentrated and then expanded not only to the whole of humankind but to the Author of humankind itself, God.

How do we know that we know God? To respond to this perennially perplexing question Newman turns in his sermon "Saving Knowledge" to the text from John 2:3, "Hereby do we know that we know Him if we keep His commandments." Obedience for Newman is the test of faith, and thus the two parts which constitute the whole of the Christian's duty are faith and obedience. The knowledge of God proceeds from doing what it is that God requires.

In the sermon "Moral Effects of Communion with God," Newman takes up the subject of prayer from Psalm 27:4: "One thing have I desired of the Lord, which I will require; even that I may dwell in the house of the Lord all the days of my life, to behold the fair beauty of the Lord, and to visit His temple."

What the psalmist desires, says Newman, the Christian enjoys to the full, what he calls "the liberty of holding communion with God in His Temple all through our life." The form of that communion is prayer, which he describes as "conversing with God." Prayer is divine converse, and it differs from human conversation as God differs from man. "He who does not pray, does not claim his citizenship with heaven, but lives, though an heir of the kingdom, as if he were a child of earth." Prayer is a gift linking the earthly realm to the heavenly realm. It is the means of the one who abides in the earthly realm to claim his true citizenship in the heavenly one: "He who does not use a gift, loses it," says Newman in anticipation of the twentieth-century slogan "Use it or lose it." He goes on to say:

> He who neglects to pray, not only suspends the enjoyment, but is in a way to lose the possession, of his divine citizenship. . . . As speech is the organ of human society, and the means of human civilization, so is prayer the instrument of divine fellowship and divine training. (p. 171)

The effect of divine meditation is to admit us into the next world and to withdraw us from the claims of this one: it makes us children of God. It is prayer, or communion, with God which makes the desirable possible.

Among the most persistent of Newman's pastoral themes in these sermons is the Christian paradox of being in the world but not of the world. It is implicit in every sermon and exposition of doctrine. In his sermon "Watching," from the text "Take ye heed, watch and pray; for ye know not when the time is" (Mark 13:33), he takes up the question of what it is to watch for Christ:

He watches for Christ who has a sensitive, eager, apprehensive mind; who is awake, alive, quick-sighted, zealous in seeking and honoring Him; who looks out for Him in all that happens, and who would not be surprised, who would not be overagitated or overwhelmed, if he found that He was coming at once. (p. 182)

Newman here is not indulging in eschatological shock therapy, which had been the stock-in-trade of certain forms of rabid Protestantism that culminated in the American-driven Second-Advent movement, which predicted the coming of the Lord on October 31, 1844. Instead he here is arguing that Christian watchfulness is a steady state of readiness, not a panic state. The believer should not be surprised by the future nor intimidated by the present. He goes on to say:

This then is to watch; to be detached from what is present, and to live in what is unseen; to live in the thought of Christ as He came once, and as He will come again; to desire His second coming, from our affectionate and grateful remembrance of His first. (p. 182)

The idolatrous are those who mistake the temporary for the permanent, and in so doing identify God with this world and the things of this world. Such do not watch for God, for they have made a god of the things that are and were in the goods of this world. Many "good" Christians like things as they are and where they were: "They are satisfied to remain on earth; they do not wish to move; they do not wish to change."

Newman does not choose to speculate on the when and the how of the coming of the Lord, following the godly counsel of St. Paul and St. Augustine, who dismiss such calculations as foolish and presumptuous. He does say, "Year passes after year silently; Christ's coming is ever nearer than it was. Oh that, as He comes nearer earth, we may approach nearer heaven!"

The final sentence of this sermon might well be the whole summary of Newman's thought in all of these sermons: "Life is short; death is certain; and the world to come is everlasting."

In his sermon "The Eucharistic Presence," preached on Easter

from the text "This is the Bread which cometh down from
heaven, that a man may eat thereof and not die" (John 6:50), we
are again reminded that these sermons were delivered while
Newman was still an Anglican. He began by noting that the
quarter of the year from Ash Wednesday to Trinity Sunday is
called "The Sacramental Season," and thus a consideration of
Christ in the Eucharist is most appropriate. Christ's presence in
the Eucharist he acknowledges as a mystery: "All that we know
or need to know is that He *is* given to us, and that in the Sacrament of Holy Communion." How this is the case he does not try
to demonstrate, arguing only that the mystery has increased
rather than decreased our reverence for the sacrament; and then
he writes with reference to the Roman Catholic Church:

> We know that one very large portion of Christendom holds
> more than we [Anglicans] hold. That belief, which goes
> beyond ours, shows how great the gift is really. I allude to
> the doctrine of what is called Transubstantiation, which we
> do not admit; or that the Bread and Wine cease to be, and
> that Christ's sacred Body and Blood are directly seen,
> touched, and handled under the *appearances* of Bread and
> Wine. This our Church considers there is no ground for
> saying, and our Lord's own words contain marvel enough,
> even without adding anything to them by way of explana-
> tion. (p. 259)

He would, of course, change his mind on this in not too many
years to come. Newman understands the miracle of the feeding of
the five thousand with the loaves and fishes as a means by which
the Lord's Supper is to be understood.

One miracle helps us identify the other as a miracle, a supernatural work of God as well: "The feeding then of the multitude
with the loaves interprets the Lord's Supper; and as the one is a
supernatural work, so is the other also."

In "Religion Pleasant to the Religious," from Psalm 34:8, Newman is almost playful in his argument, and reminiscent of a book
review attributed to Abraham Lincoln: "Those who like this sort
of thing will like this." Of religion, that is, God's service, Newman says, "Alas! this is the very thing I lament—that God's ser-

vice is not pleasant to you. It is not pleasant to those who do not like it: true; but it *is* pleasant to those who *do*."

Noting that "the pleasures of holiness are far more pleasant to the holy than the pleasures of sin to the sinner," he encourages his listeners to undertake an experiment in holiness, to "taste and see," in the words of the text. "Men know what sin is, by experience. They do not know what holiness is; and they cannot obtain the knowledge of its secret pleasure, till they join themselves truly and heartily to Christ, and devote themselves to His service"— until they "taste," and thereby try. It is a challenge, the sort of thing designed to appeal to the experimental nature of his young undergraduate listeners, men interested in novelty and competition. "Think of all this, my brethren, and rouse yourselves, and run forward with a good courage on your way towards heaven."

Preaching is both pastoral and systematic theology, and for Newman it was also sacramental theology. His preaching on the Eucharist, and the presence of Christ within it, is the foundation upon which he will build the structure within which to receive the eucharistic doctrines of the Roman Catholic Church. The pastoral sympathies of his eucharistic sermon, however, are not hedged about by doctrinal conceits, and we can imagine that many, particularly the unformed and uninformed young, were drawn to a closer consideration of holy things. In his sermon "Divine Calls," in which he speaks of the calls of Samuel and St. Paul, he translates those heroic calls into the calls made of God upon all believers, in baptism. He reminds his hearers that they have already been called: "Calling is not a thing future with us, but a thing past."

Calling, however, is not a one-time thing for Newman. Regeneration occurs over and over again, and he would have little sympathy with the once "born again," which has become such a litmus test for evangelical piety. He writes:

> For in truth we are not called once only, but many times; all through our life Christ is calling us. He called us first in Baptism; but afterwards also; whether we obey His voice or not, He graciously calls us still. If we fall from our Baptism, He calls us to repent; if we are striving to fulfill our calling, He calls us on from grace to grace, and from holiness to holiness, while life is given us. (p. 298)

In case we don't get it, he says, "He calls us again and again, in order to justify us again and again—and again and again, and more and more, to sanctify and glorify us." Protestantism knew much of the perseverance of the saints. It would be in this sermon and others like it that Newman would preach of the equally pervasive notion of the persistence of God.

Newman was not simply a thinking believer, he was also a devout one, and his prayers, verses, and devotions reveal the passionate piety of one who chose to express his convictions in a variety of literary forms. The musical world knows Newman through his poem "The Dream of Gerontius," set in oratorio form by Sir Edward Elgar, and one of the great wonders of the choral world. Church people, particularly of an older generation, know Newman because of his hymn once universally popular at funerals, "Lead, Kindly Light, amid the encircling gloom." Less well known are his so-called "Loretto Meditations," devotional commentaries concerning aspects of the reverence due the Virgin Mary, and the title of a sermon that he gave in Oxford on the feast of the Annunciation, March 25, 1832. This collection contains eight meditations, two each on the Immaculate Conception, the Annunciation, Our Lady's Dolors, and the Assumption.

Of his prayers and poems, two may be chosen as representative of Newman's spiritual struggle. In his prayer to St. Philip Neri, whom he regarded as his patron saint, Newman asks for the sevenfold gifts of wisdom, understanding, counsel, fortitude, knowledge, religion, and holy fear:

> Beg for me the gift of Wisdom, that I may prefer heaven to earth, and know truth from falsehood:
> The gift of Understanding, of which I may have imprinted upon my mind the mysteries of His Word:
> The gift of Counsel, that I may see my way in all perplexities:
> The gift of Fortitude, that with bravery and stubbornness I may battle with my foe:
> The gift of Knowledge, to enable me to direct all my doings with a pure intention to the glory of God:

The gift of Religion, to make me devout and conscientious:
And the gift of Holy Fear, to make me feel awe,
     reverence, and sobriety amid all my spiritual blessings.

In December 1832, Newman and his friend Hurrell Froude
decided to visit the Mediterranean and spend the winter of 1833
touring Sicily and the south of Italy. Leaving St. Mary's to the care
of his curate, Newman set forth, intending to return to his duties
in April for the Easter Term. He had agreed with Froude and
some other friends to produce a volume of religious poetry to be
called *Lyra Apostolica* and to consist of a "mixture," in the words
of Froude: "some fierce and some meek—the plan is to have none
above twenty lines." This holiday would give Newman an opportunity to produce his share of the work. He was not unfamiliar
with his own muse, was easily given to versification, and as he set
out aboard the *Hermes* for this idyll, he wrote:

I went afar; the world unroll'd
     Her many-pictured page;
I stored the marvels which she told,
     And trusted to her gage.

Her pleasures quaff'd I sought awhile
     The scenes I priz'd before;
But parent's praise and sister's smile
     Stirr'd my cold heart no more.

While on this trip he recorded his impressions and experiences
in verse, keeping, as it were, a poetical diary or daybook. These
poems, together with his letters and journal entries, record a sensitive, anxious, and intense young man for whom a holiday was
occasion for more rather than for less introspection; and later in
life, when writing his celebrated *Apologia Pro Vita Sua*, he would
depend upon the written record of his Mediterranean sojourn to
explicate the life of his soul and mind at this critical preconversion
period. When he visited Naples and Rome, he did so with a
decided anti-Roman bias, as his letters reveal. Rome's pagan past
and its triumphant present offended the devout Anglican's sensi-
bilities, and of the Eternal City he wrote:

How shall I name thee, light of the wide west,
    Or heinous error-seat?
O Mother best, close tracing Jesus' feet,
    Do not thy titles glow
In those stern judgement-fires which shall complete
    Earth's strife with heaven, and ope the eternal woe?

Yet his emotions were mixed, one might even say conflicted, as he tried to analyze the mixture of good and evil that he saw in Rome, a church in a dual "Babylonian captivity" to corrupted Christianity and secular tyranny. This intellectual and spiritual struggle, together with a significant physical and even mental affliction on this journey, would be the context for some of his most significant preconversion poetry and devotional writing.

One might call Newman's illness in Sicily at Easter 1833 the preoccupation of his preconverted self-understanding. Fever, nightmares, hallucinations, anxieties of body and of spirit in a foreign place at the holiest time of the Christian year, and on the eve of his return to the rigors of an Oxford about to be aroused by John Keble's Assize sermon,* all conspired to excite his muse and stimulate within him a spiritual crisis of which the fever was but the outward and visible manifestation. He was ill for nearly three weeks of a virulent form of fever described by some as "gastric" fever and by others as the scarlet fever, which was epidemic at that time in Sicily. He was near death and would recall the experience in the memorandum "My Illness in Sicily," which he wrote between 1834 and 1840. The old wives' tale is that such a fever will either kill or cure, and Newman understood his affliction to be both a judgment and a renewal. It is out of the fever that he writes, "Now in all this seems something remarkable and providential,"

---

*John Keble's famous Assize sermon, "National Apostasy," given in 1833, marked the start of the Oxford Movement (1833–1845). In it Keble had pointed out the miserable condition of the Church of England at the time. The Oxford Movement asserted independence of the Church from the claims of the State, which had moved to regulate certain Church affairs. The movement insisted on the apostolic authority of the Church to govern its own affairs and tried to recover the ideals and high standards that had previously characterized the Church of England. (The term *assize* simply refers to the sermon's external occasion, the seasonal appearance for hearings in Oxford of the court of assize.)

and he concluded that he was spared and restored because "God has still work for me to do." This is the setting in which he writes the poem "Consolation," which alludes to Matthew 14:22–32, the account of Peter's attempt to walk on water and the fear that he would sink, which caused him nearly to do so until rescued by Jesus. The text is Matthew 14:27, "It is I; be not afraid." The voice is that of Peter, through whom, of course, Newman speaks:

> When I sink down in gloom or fear,
>   Hope blighted or delay'd,
> Thy whisper, Lord, my heart shall cheer.
>   " 'Tis I; be not afraid!"
>
> Or, startled at some sudden blow,
>   If fretful thoughts I feel,
> "Fear not, it is but I!" shall flow,
>   As balm my wound to heal.
>
> Nor will I quit Thy way, though foes
>   Some onward pass defend;
> From each rough voice the watchword goes,
>   Be not afraid! . . . a friend!"
>
> And oh! when judgment's trumpet clear
>   Awakes me from the grave,
> Still in its echo may I hear,
>   " 'Tis Christ; he comes to save."

The homeward journey was not an easy one. Newman left Italy on the thirteenth of June, a passenger on an orange boat destined for Marseilles, which for nearly a week was becalmed in the Strait of Bonifacio. Unable to do much or go anywhere, still a convalescent and anxious for home, he wrote what is perhaps his most famous verse, which he titled "The Pillar of the Cloud," but which is more familiarly known as "Lead, Kindly Light," a hymn of spiritual resignation, pilgrimage, and subordination. Here, after the rigors of the trip, a chastened and weary pilgrim, one who "loved the garish day" and who had been filled with the fears of self-will, submits himself to be guided and directed even as the

children of Israel were led through the wilderness by the cloudy
pillar and the fire toward the Promised Land. For Newman this
land was now England. The poem's lines are described as the
"supreme expression, simple and beautiful and haunting, of spiritual surrender." On the ninth of July he arrived home and went
to his mother's house. On the following Sunday John Keble
preached his sermon "National Apostasy," and of it the rejuve-
nated Newman wrote, "I have ever considered, and kept the day,
as the start of the religious movement of 1833."

The world in which we live would have been all too familiar to
Newman. He would have known of its arrogance and its petti-
ness. He would recognize the apparent triumph of the material
over the spiritual, and the preference for secular explanation to
Christian experience. Holiness of life, he would note, remains as
elusive as ever, and men and women prefer the form of religion to
its substance. It was to just such a world that Newman preached
and wrote, and for such a world that his sermons were published,
responding as they did to that fundamental hunger and thirst for
righteousness which becomes all the more apparent the more
unrighteous we are. Incarnational preaching then, as now, is the
means toward holiness of life. Once again, in an accessible form in
this collection and in a clear voice, we are able to take the benefit
of Newman's preaching. All we need to know he has told us:

Life is short;
　Death is certain:
　　　and the world to come is everlasting.

Sparks House, Cambridge
Epiphany 1998

1801 John Henry Newman was born February 21, in London, the eldest of six children of John Newman and Jemima Fourdrinier. He was baptized a few weeks after his birth and enjoyed a happy, pious childhood with a moderate Anglican background of moral precepts, prayers, and hymns.

1807 Newman recalled in his early forties that by the age of six "God put it into my heart ... to ask *What* and *Why* I was." It seemed to him that from early on an inner Voice spoke to his soul and was a loving presence to him.

1808 Newman was sent to Ealing to boarding school, where he excelled in his studies and showed himself to be a leader of the other boys. At twelve he could read Virgil, Homer, and Herodotus and at fifteen had mastered the curriculum.

1815 After reading Paine, Hume, and Voltaire, Newman fell into a state of unbelief and a pride of worldly independence, with the sense of God very much dimmed in his soul.

1816 A decisive year. His father's business failed, and Newman himself suffered a serious illness. Both together brought about a spiritual crisis for him. Walter Mayers, master of classics at Ealing, comforted him with teachings about God's mercy and the hope of eternal salvation. He recovered his sense of God's divine influence on his life. Newman always regarded this inner conversion as one of the most profound and important moments of his life.

1816   Newman arrived at the insight that "it would be the will of God" that he "should lead a single life." He was accepted at Trinity College, Oxford.

1817   Made his first communion in the college chapel.

1818   Because of fatigue and overexcitement, Newman failed his examination and received his B.A. degree without distinction.

1822   Newman stood for exams at Oriel, in which he was successful, and was elected a fellow of Oriel College. This gave him an assured income with which to help his family. He had made up his mind to seek ordination in the Anglican Church.

1824   On Trinity Sunday, Newman was ordained deacon. He was able to comfort his father as he died. Newman then assumed the full burden of his mother and brothers and sisters.

1825   Newman was ordained a priest of the Church of England by the bishop of Oxford on Trinity Sunday.

1827   Newman began his serious study of the early Church Fathers. Eventually he became convinced that full Christian Revelation emanated from these sources.

1828   Newman's beloved younger sister, Mary, died after a brief illness, causing him tremendous grief. From this moment "the heavenly vision" and the understanding of "holiness as the only thing of eternal worth" were uppermost in his mind. He was appointed vicar of St. Mary the Virgin, Oxford, where he began to preach his deeply earnest, still famous sermons.

1833   John Keble preached his sermon "National Apostasy" to draw attention to the decline of the Church of England. Newman saw this as the start of the Oxford Movement to reform the Church by reinvigorating it with the spirit and discipline of early Christianity. The movement lasted through 1841.

1834   The first volume of *Parochial Sermons* was published.

1836   Newman's mother died; his two surviving sisters were married. His great friend, Hurrell Froude, died of consumption. Newman was given Froude's Roman Breviary, which he began to recite daily.

1838   *Lectures on the Doctrine of Justification*, Newman's description of the New Testament teaching of the divine indwelling of God in the individual soul, was published. The fourth, fifth, and sixth volumes of the *Sermons* reflect this profound Christian humanism. This period marked the height of Newman's influence in the Anglican Church.

1840   Newman published *The Church of the Fathers*, his essays on revealed religion in the early Church. His reading of St. Augustine moved him to reconsider the Catholicity of the English Church. He retired to Littlemore, where he bought ten acres and established a place of retreat for himself and friends who occasionally joined him there.

1841   Newman translated the writings of St. Athanasius, which led him to investigate Arianism and, hence, to recognize the semi-Arian tendencies of the Anglican Church. He concluded that Rome was the true Church of the Apostles. Because of the resulting painful controversies with his Anglican friends, Newman determined to stay on at Littlemore, where he would live for six years.

1842   Six volumes of *Parochial Sermons* were in print by this time; each had been through several large editions.

1843   *Sermons Preached Before the University of Oxford*, on the relation between faith and reason, appeared in print. Newman publicly withdrew his anti-Catholic statements from print.

1843   On September 7, Newman wrote to his bishop to resign from St. Mary's. On September 18, he preached his last sermon at Littlemore. He had returned to the state of a layman.

1844   Newman wrote *An Essay on the Development of Christian Doctrine*, in which he set forth that salvation history requires a living authority in charge to reject error. He was convinced that this power resided in the Roman Church, which is heir to the Church of the Fathers.

1845   Newman was received into the Catholic Church on October 9.

1846   Newman left Littlemore in February for Old Oscott College, henceforth called Maryvale. In September he traveled to Rome to study Catholic theology.

1847   Newman received Holy Orders in the Catholic Church on May 30.

1848   Newman inaugurated the English Oratory on February 2 at Maryvale.

1849   Newman preached his first Catholic sermons, *Discourse Addressed to a Mixed Congregation*.

1852   Newman began the foundation of Catholic University in Dublin. He delivered, then published, ten discourses on university education. These later formed the first part of *The Idea of a University*.

1854   Newman was installed as rector of Catholic University on June 3.

1858   Newman retired as rector in October and left Ireland. He returned to England and founded the Birmingham Oratory School for Catholic boys.

1859   Newman became, briefly, editor of the *Rambler*, a literary magazine for educated Catholics. The July issue, his last, contained his famous article "On Consulting the Faithful in Matters of Doctrine."

1864   Newman wrote his *Apologia Pro Vita Sua*, a spiritual autobiography, to counter the charge that he had secretly tried to undermine the Church of England while still a member of it.

1865   Newman wrote *The Dream of Gerontius*, a poem describing death, judgment, and purgatory.

1868   *Parochial and Plain Sermons* was republished.

BX 5135.N4 P32
1987

1870   Newman wrote *A Grammar of Assent* to clarify the ideas of certitude in religious matters and the importance of doctrinal statements.

1879   Newman was made a cardinal by Pope Leo XIII.

1890   Newman died at Birmingham on August 11, surrounded by his Oratorian friends.

Prayers Poems Meditations (AN Wilson)
BV 4811. N525 1990

The thirty-five sermons of John Henry Newman selected for the first part of this book may be found in the eight-volume series published as *Parochial and Plain Sermons* (London, 1882–1889). They comprise the bulk of the sermons from the period when he was an Anglican priest. For the reader's reference, in brackets at the end of each sermon included in the present book, the original volume and sermon number are given, e.g. [I, 1].

For the reader in search of more from these volumes, they are presently available from Ignatius Press (San Francisco, 1997), gathered as eight-volumes-in-one.

Selections appearing in the second part of this book were published in *Meditations and Devotions of the Late Cardinal Newman* (London, 1893), *Verses on Various Occasions* (London, 1903), and *The Dream of Gerontius* (London, 1907).

These volumes are now combined in the reprint collection *Prayers, Verses, and Devotions* (San Francisco: Ignatius Press, 1989).

The last item in this book, "Prayer," is taken from Newman's sermon "Wisdom and Innocence," first given in 1844 and later published as Sermon 20 in the volume *Sermons Bearing on Subjects of the Day* (London, 1879), pp. 11–12.

Selected Sermons

Chapter 1

HOLINESS NECESSARY FOR FUTURE
BLESSEDNESS

Holiness, without which no man shall see the Lord.
—Heb. 12:14

In this text it has seemed good to the Holy Spirit to convey a chief truth of religion in a few words. It is this circumstance which makes it especially impressive; for the truth itself is declared in one form or other in every part of Scripture. It is told us again and again, that to make sinful creatures holy was the great end which our Lord had in view in taking upon Him our nature, and thus none but the holy will be accepted for His sake at the last day. The whole history of redemption, the covenant of mercy in all its parts and provisions, attests the necessity of holiness in order to salvation; as indeed even our natural conscience bears witness also. But in the text what is elsewhere implied in history, and enjoined by precept, is stated doctrinally, as a momentous and necessary fact, the result of some awful irreversible law in the nature of things, and the inscrutable determination of the Divine Will.

Now someone may ask, "Why is it that holiness is a necessary qualification for our being received into heaven? why is it that the Bible enjoins upon us so strictly to love, fear, and obey God, to be just, honest, meek, pure in heart, forgiving, heavenly-minded, self-denying, humble, and resigned? Man is confessedly weak and corrupt; *why* then is he enjoined to be so religious, so unearthly? *why* is he required (in the strong language of Scripture) to become 'a new creature'? Since he is by nature what he is, would it not be an act of greater mercy in God to save him altogether without this holiness, which it is so difficult, yet (as it appears) so necessary for him to possess?"

Now we have no right to ask this question. Surely it is quite enough for a sinner to know, that a way has been opened through God's grace for his salvation, without being informed why that way, and not another way, was chosen by Divine Wisdom. Eternal life is "the *gift* of God." Undoubtedly He may prescribe the terms on which He will give it; and if He has determined holiness to be the way of life, it is enough; it is not for us to inquire why He has so determined.

Yet the question may be asked reverently, and with a view to enlarge our insight into our own condition and prospects; and in that case the attempt to answer it will be profitable, if it be made soberly. I proceed, therefore, to state one of the reasons, assigned in Scripture, why present holiness is necessary, as the text declares to us, for future happiness.

To be holy is, in our Church's words, to have "the true circumcision of the Spirit"; that is, to be separate from sin, to hate the works of the world, the flesh, and the devil; to take pleasure in keeping God's commandments; to do things as He would have us do them; to live habitually as in the sight of the world to come, as if we had broken the ties of this life, and were dead already. Why cannot we be saved without possessing such a frame and temper of mind?

I answer as follows: That, even supposing a man of unholy life were suffered to enter heaven, *he would not be happy there;* so that it would be no mercy to permit him to enter.

We are apt to deceive ourselves, and to consider heaven a place like this earth; I mean, a place where everyone may choose and take his *own* pleasure. We see that in this world, active men have their own enjoyments, and domestic men have theirs; men of literature, of science, of political talent, have their respective pursuits and pleasures. Hence we are led to act as if it will be the same in another world. The only difference we put between this world and the next, is that *here* (as we know well) men are *not always sure,* but *there,* we suppose they *will be always sure,* of obtaining what they seek after. And accordingly we conclude, that *any man,* whatever his habits, tastes, or manner of life, if *once admitted* into heaven, would be happy there. Not that we altogether deny, that some preparation is necessary for the next world; but we do not estimate its real extent and importance. We think we can reconcile ourselves to God when we will; as if nothing were required in the case of men in general, but some temporary attention, more than ordinary, to our religious duties—some strictness, during our last sickness, in the Services of the Church, as men of business arrange their letters and papers on taking a journey or balancing an account. But an opinion like this, though commonly acted on, is refuted as soon as put into words. For heaven, it is plain from Scripture, is not a place where many different and discordant pursuits can be carried on at once, as is the case in this world. Here every man can do his *own* pleasure, but there he must do *God's* pleasure. It would be presumption to attempt to determine the employments of that eternal life which good men are to pass in God's presence, or to deny that that state which eye hath not seen, nor ear heard, nor mind conceived, may comprise an infinite variety of pursuits and occupations. Still so far we are distinctly told, that the future life will be spent in God's *presence,* in a sense which does not apply to our present life; so that it may be best described as an endless and uninterrupted worship of the Eternal Father, Son, and Spirit. "They serve Him day and night in His temple, and He that sitteth on the throne shall dwell among them. . . . The Lamb which is in the midst of the throne shall feed them, and shall lead them unto living fountains of waters." Again, "The city had no need of the sun, neither of the moon to shine in it, for the glory of God did lighten it, and the Lamb is the light thereof. And the nations of them which are saved shall walk in the light of it, and the kings of the earth do bring their glory and honor into it."[1] These passages from St. John are sufficient to remind us of many others.

Heaven then is not like this world; I will say what it is much more like—*a church.* For in a place of public worship no language of this world is heard; there are no schemes brought forward for temporal objects, great or small; no information how to strengthen our worldly interests, extend our influence, or establish our credit. These things indeed may be right in their way, so that we do not set our hearts upon them; still (I repeat), it is certain that we hear nothing of them in a church. Here we hear solely and entirely of *God.* We praise Him, worship Him, sing to Him, thank Him, confess to Him, give ourselves up to Him, and ask His blessing. And *therefore,* a church is like heaven; viz. because both in the one and the other, there is one single sovereign subject—religion—brought before us.

Supposing, then, instead of it being said that no irreligious man could serve and attend on God in heaven (or see Him, as the text expresses it), we were told that no irreligious man could worship, or spiritually see Him in church; should we not at once perceive the meaning of the doctrine? viz. that, were a man to come hither, who had suffered his mind to grow up in its own way, as nature or chance determined, without any deliberate habitual effort after truth and purity, he would find no real pleasure here, but would soon get weary of the place; because, in this house of God, he would hear only of that one subject which he cared little or nothing about, and nothing at all of those things which excited his hopes and fears, his sympathies and energies. If then a man without religion (supposing it possible) were admitted into heaven, doubtless he would sustain a great disappointment. Before, indeed he fancied that he could be happy there; but when he arrived there, he would find no discourse but that which he had shunned on earth, no pursuits but those he had disliked or despised, nothing which bound him to aught *else* in the universe, and made him feel at home, nothing which he could enter into and rest upon. He would perceive himself to be an isolated being, cut away by Supreme Power from those objects which were still entwined around his heart. Nay, he would be in the presence of that Supreme Power, whom he never on earth could bring himself steadily to think upon, and whom now he regarded only as the destroyer of all that was precious and dear to him. Ah! he could not *bear* the face of the Living God; the Holy God would be no object of joy to him. "Let us alone! What have we to do with thee?" is the sole thought and desire of unclean souls, even while they acknowledge His Majesty. None but the holy can look upon the Holy One; without holiness no man can endure to see the Lord.

When, then, we think to take part in the joys of heaven without holiness, we are as inconsiderate as if we supposed we could take an interest in the worship of Christians here below without possessing it in our measure. A careless, a sensual, an unbelieving mind, a mind destitute of the love and fear of God, with narrow views and earthly aims, a low standard of duty, and a benighted conscience, a mind contented with itself, and unresigned to God's will, would feel as little pleasure, at the last day, at the words, "Enter into the joy of thy Lord," as it does now at the words, "Let us pray." Nay, much less, because, while we are in a church, we may turn our thoughts to other subjects, and contrive to forget that God is looking on us; but that will not be possible in heaven.

We see, then, that holiness, or inward separation from the world, is necessary to our admission into heaven, because heaven is *not* heaven, is not a place of happiness *except* to the holy. There are bodily indispositions which affect the taste, so that the sweetest flavors become ungrateful to the palate; and indispositions which impair the sight, tingeing the fair face of nature with some sickly hue. In like manner, there is a moral malady which disorders the inward sight and taste; and no man laboring under it is in a condition to enjoy what Scripture calls "the fullness of joy in God's presence, and pleasures at His right hand forevermore."

Nay, I will venture to say more than this—it is fearful, but it is right to say it—that if we wished to imagine a punishment for an unholy, reprobate soul, we perhaps could not fancy a greater than to *summon it to heaven.* Heaven would be hell to an irreligious man. We know how unhappy we are apt to feel at present, when alone in the midst of strangers, or of men of different tastes and habits from ourselves. How miserable, for example, would it be to have to live in a foreign land, among a people whose faces we never saw before, and whose language we could not learn. And this is but a faint illustration of the loneliness of a man of earthly dispositions and tastes, thrust into the society of saints and angels. How forlorn would he wander through the courts of heaven! He would find no one like himself; he would see in every direction the marks of God's holiness, and these would make him shudder. He would feel himself always in His presence. He could no longer turn his thoughts another way, as he does now, when conscience reproaches him. He would know that the Eternal Eye was ever upon him; and that Eye of holiness, which is joy and life to holy creatures, would seem to him an Eye of wrath and punishment. God cannot change His nature. Holy He must ever be. But while He is holy, no unholy soul can be happy in heaven. Fire does not inflame iron, but it inflames straw. It would cease to be fire if it did not. And so heaven itself would be fire to those who would fain escape across the great gulf from the torments of hell. The finger of Lazarus would but increase their thirst. The very "heaven that is over their head" will be "brass" to them.

And now I have partly explained why it is that holiness is prescribed to us as the condition on our part for our admission into heaven. It seems to be necessary from the very nature of things. We do not see how it could be otherwise. Now then I will mention two important truths which seem to follow from what has been said.

1. If a certain character of mind, a certain state of the heart and affections, be necessary for entering heaven, our *actions* will avail for our salvation, chiefly as they tend to produce or evidence this frame of mind. Good works (as they are called) are required, not as if they had anything of merit in them, not as if they could of themselves turn away God's anger for our sins, or purchase heaven for us, but because they are the means, under God's grace, of strengthening and showing forth that holy principle which God implants in the heart, and without which (as the text tells us) we cannot see Him. The more numerous are our acts of charity, self-denial, and forbearance, of course the more will our minds be schooled into a charitable, self-denying, and forbearing temper. The more frequent are our prayers, the more humble, patient, and religious are our daily deeds, this communion with God, these holy works, will be the means of making our hearts holy, and of preparing us for the future presence of God. Outward acts, done on principle, create inward habits. I repeat, the separate acts of obedience to the will of God, good works as they are called, are of service to us, as gradually severing us from this world of sense, and impressing our hearts with a heavenly character.

It is plain, then, what works are *not* of service to our salvation—all those which either have no effect upon the heart to change it, or which have a bad effect. What then must be said of those who think it an easy thing to please God, and to recommend themselves to Him; who do a few scanty services, call these the walk of faith, and are satisfied with them? Such men, it is too evident, instead of being themselves profited by their acts, such as they are, of benevolence, honesty, or justice, may be (I might even say) injured by them. For these very acts, even though good in themselves, are made to foster in these persons a bad spirit, a corrupt state of heart; viz. self-love, self-conceit, self-reliance, instead of tending to turn them from this world to the Father of spirits. In like manner, the mere outward acts of coming to church, and saying prayers, which are, of course, duties imperative upon all of us,

are really serviceable to those only who do them in a heavenward
spirit. Because such men only use these good deeds to the
improvement of the heart; whereas even the most exact outward
devotion avails not a man, if it does not improve it.

2. But observe what follows from this. If holiness be not
merely the doing of a certain number of good actions, but is an
inward character which follows, under God's grace, from doing
them, how far distant from that holiness are the multitude of
men! They are not yet even obedient in outward deeds, which is
the first step towards possessing it. They have even to learn to
practice good works, as the means of changing their hearts, which
is the end. It follows at once, even though Scripture did not
plainly tell us so, that no one is able to prepare himself for heaven,
that is, make himself holy, in a short time—at least we do not see
how it is possible; and this, viewed merely as a deduction of the
reason, is a serious thought. Yet, alas! as there are persons who
think to be saved by a few scanty performances, so there are others who suppose they may be saved all at once by a sudden and
easily acquired faith. Most men who are living in neglect of God,
silence their consciences, when troublesome, with the promise of
repenting some future day. How often are they thus led on till
death surprises them! But we will suppose they *do* begin to repent
when that future day comes. Nay, we will even suppose that
Almighty God were to forgive them, and to admit them into His
holy heaven. Well, but is nothing more requisite? are they in a fit
state to *do Him service in heaven*? is not this the very point I have
been so insisting on, that they are *not* in a fit state? has it not been
shown that, even if admitted there without a change of heart, they
would find no pleasure in heaven? and is a change of heart
wrought in a day? Which of our tastes or likings can we change at
our will in a moment? Not the most superficial. Can we then at a
word change the whole frame and character of our minds? Is not
holiness the result of many patient, repeated efforts after obedience, gradually working on us, and first modifying and then
changing our hearts? We dare not, of course, set bounds to God's
mercy and power in cases of repentance late in life, even where
He has revealed to us the general rule of His moral governance;
yet, surely, it is our duty ever to keep steadily before us, and act
upon, those general truths which His Holy Word has declared.

His Holy Word in various ways warns us, that, as no one will find happiness in heaven, who is not holy, so no one can learn to be so, in a short time, and when he will. It implies it in the text, which names a qualification, which we know in matter of fact does ordinarily take time to gain. It propounds it clearly, though in figure, in the parable of the wedding garment, in which inward sanctification is made a condition distinct from our acceptance of the proffer of mercy, and not negligently to be passed over in our thoughts as if a necessary consequence of it; and in that of the ten virgins, which shows us that we must meet the bridegroom with the oil of holiness, and that it takes time to procure it. And it solemnly assures us in St. Paul's Epistles, that it is possible so to presume on Divine grace, as to let slip the accepted time, and be sealed even before the end of life to a reprobate mind.[2]

I wish to speak to you, my brethren, not as if aliens from God's mercies, but as partakers of His gracious Covenant in Christ; and for this reason in especial peril, since those only can incur the sin of making void His Covenant, who have the privilege of it. Yet neither on the other hand do I speak to you as willful and obstinate sinners, exposed to the imminent risk of forfeiting, or the chance of having forfeited, your hope of heaven. But I fear there are those, who, if they dealt faithfully with their consciences, would be obliged to own that they had not made the service of God their first and great concern; that their obedience, so to call it, has been a matter of course, in which the heart has had no part; that they have acted uprightly in worldly matters chiefly for the sake of their worldly interest. I fear there are those, who, whatever be their sense of religion, still have such misgivings about themselves, as lead them to make resolve to obey God more exactly some future day, such misgivings as convict them of sin, though not enough to bring home to them its heinousness or its peril. Such men are trifling with the appointed season of mercy. To obtain the gift of holiness is the work of *a life*. No man will ever be perfect here, so sinful is our nature. Thus, in putting off the day of repentance, these men are reserving for a few chance years, when strength and vigor are gone, that WORK for which a *whole* life would not be enough. That work is great and arduous beyond expression. There is much of sin remaining even in the best of men, and "if the righteous scarcely be saved, where shall the ungodly and the sinner appear?"[3] Their doom may be fixed any moment; and though this thought should not make a man despair today, yet it should ever make him tremble for tomorrow.

Perhaps, however, others may say: "We know something of the power of religion—we love it in a measure—we have many right thoughts—we come to church to pray; this is a proof that we are prepared for heaven: we are safe, and what has been said does not apply to us." But be not you, my brethren, in the number of these. One principal test of our being true servants of God is our wishing to serve Him better; and be quite sure that a man who is contented with his own proficiency in Christian holiness, is at best in a dark state, or rather in great peril. If we are really imbued with the grace of holiness, we shall abhor sin as something base, irrational, and polluting. Many men, it is true, are contented with partial and indistinct views of religion, and mixed motives. Be you content with nothing short of perfection; exert yourselves day by day to grow in knowledge and grace; that, if so be, you may at length attain to the presence of Almighty God.

Lastly; while we thus labor to mold our hearts after the pattern of the holiness of our Heavenly Father, it is our comfort to know, what I have already implied, that we are not left to ourselves, but that the Holy Ghost is graciously present with us, and enables us to triumph over, and to change our own minds. It is a comfort and encouragement, while it is an anxious and awful thing, to know that God works in and through us.[4] We are the instruments, but we are only the instruments, of our own salvation. Let no one say that I discourage him, and propose to him a task beyond his strength. All of us have the gifts of grace pledged to us from our youth up. We know this well; but we do not use our privilege. We form mean ideas of the difficulty, and in consequence never enter into the greatness of the gifts given us to meet it. Then afterwards, if perchance we gain a deeper insight into the work we have to do, we think God a hard master, who commands much from a sinful race. Narrow, indeed, is the way of life, but infinite is His love and power who is with the Church, in Christ's place, to guide us along it.

[I, 1]

Chapter 2

THE IMMORTALITY OF THE SOUL

What shall a man give in exchange for his soul?
—Matt. 16:26

I suppose there is no tolerably informed Christian but considers he has a correct notion of the difference between our religion and the paganism which it supplanted. Everyone, if asked what it is we have gained by the Gospel, will promptly answer, that we have gained the knowledge of our immortality, of our having souls which will live forever; that the heathen did not know this, but that Christ taught it, and that His disciples know it. Everyone will say, and say truly, that this was the great and solemn doctrine which gave the Gospel a claim to be heard when first preached, which arrested the thoughtless multitudes, who were busied in the pleasures and pursuits of this life, awed them with the vision of the life to come, and sobered them till they turned to God with a true heart. It will be said, and said truly, that this doctrine of a future life was the doctrine which broke the power and the fascination of paganism. The poor benighted heathen were engaged in all the frivolities and absurdities of a false ritual, which had obscured the light of nature. They knew God, but they forsook Him for the inventions of men; they made protectors and guardians for themselves; and had "gods many and lords many."5 They had their profane worship, their gaudy processions, their indulgent creed, their easy observances, their sensual festivities, their childish extravagances, such as might suitably be the religion of beings who were to live for seventy or eighty years, and then die once for all, never to live again. "Let us eat and drink, for tomorrow we die," was their doctrine and their rule of life. "Tomorrow we die"—this the Holy Apostles admitted. They taught so far *as* the heathen; "Tomorrow we die," but then they added, "And after death *the Judgment*"—judgment upon the eternal soul, which lives in spite of the death of the body. And this was the truth, which awakened men to the necessity of having a better and deeper religion than that which had spread over the earth, when Christ came, which so wrought upon them that they left that old false worship of theirs, and it fell. Yes! though throned in all the power of the world, a sight such as eye had never before seen, though supported by the great and the many, the magnificence of kings, and the stubbornness of people, it fell. Its ruins remain scattered over the face of the earth; the shattered works of its great upholder, that fierce enemy of God, the Pagan Roman Empire. Those ruins are found even among themselves, and show how marvelously great was its power, and therefore how much more powerful was that which broke its power; and this was the doctrine of the immortality of the soul. So entire is the revolution which is produced among men, wherever this high truth is really received.

I have said that every one of us is able fluently to speak of this doctrine, and is aware that the knowledge of it forms the fundamental difference between our state and that of the heathen. And yet, in spite of our being able to speak about it and our "form of knowledge"[6] (as St. Paul terms it), there seems scarcely room to doubt, that the greater number of those who are called Christians in no true sense realize it in their own minds at all. Indeed, it is a very difficult thing to bring home to us, and to feel, that we have souls; and there cannot be a more fatal mistake than to suppose we see what the doctrine means, as soon as we can use the words which signify it. So great a thing is it to understand that we have souls, that the knowing it, taken in connection with its results, is all one with *being serious,* i.e., truly religious. To discern our immortality is necessarily connected with fear and trembling and repentance, in the case of every Christian. Who is there but would be sobered by an actual sight of the flames of hell fire and the souls therein hopelessly enclosed? Would not all his thoughts be drawn to that awful sight, so that he would stand still gazing fixedly upon it, and forgetting everything else; seeing nothing else, hearing nothing, engrossed with the contemplation of it; and when the sight was withdrawn, still having it fixed in his memory, so that he would be henceforth dead to the pleasures and employments of this world, considered in themselves, thinking of them only in their reference to that fearful vision? This would be the overpowering effect of such a disclosure, whether it actually led a man to repentance or not. And thus absorbed in the thought of the life to come are they who really and heartily receive the words of Christ and His Apostles. Yet to this state of mind, and therefore to this true knowledge, the multitude of men called Christians are certainly strangers; a thick veil is drawn over their eyes; and in spite of their being able to talk of the doctrine, they are as if they never had heard of it. They go on just as the heathen did of old: they eat, they drink; or they amuse themselves in vanities, and live in the world, without fear and without sorrow, just as if God had not declared that their conduct in this life would decide their destiny in the next; just as if they either had no souls, or had nothing or little to do with the saving of them, which was the creed of the heathen.

Now let us consider what it is to bring home to ourselves that we have souls, and in what the especial difficulty of it lies; for this may be of use to us in our attempt to realize that awful truth.

We are from our birth apparently dependent on things about us. We see and feel that we could not live or go forward without the aid of man. To a child this world is everything: he seems to himself a part of this world—a part of this world, in the same sense in which a branch is part of a tree; he has little notion of his own separate and independent existence: that is, he has no just idea he has a soul. And if he goes through life with his notions unchanged, he has no just notion, even to the end of life, that he has a soul. He views himself merely in his connection with this world, which is his all; he looks to this world for his good, as to an idol; and when he tries to look beyond this life, he is able to discern nothing in prospect, because he has no idea of anything, nor can fancy anything, *but* this life. And if he is obliged to fancy something, he fancies this life over again; just as the heathen, when they reflected on those traditions of another life, which were floating among them, could but fancy the happiness of the blessed to consist in the enjoyment of the sun, and the sky, and the earth, as before, only as if these were to be more splendid than they are now.

To understand that we have souls, is to feel our separation from things visible, our independence of them, our distinct existence in ourselves, our individuality, our power of acting for ourselves this way or that way, our accountableness for what we do. These are the great truths which lie wrapped up indeed even in a child's mind, and which God's grace can unfold there in spite of the influence of the external world; but at first this outward world prevails. We look off from self to the things around us, and forget ourselves in them. Such is our state—a depending for support on the reeds which are no stay, and overlooking our real strength— at the time when God begins His process of reclaiming us to a truer view of our place in His great system of Providence. And when He visits us, then in a little while there is a stirring within us. The unprofitableness and feebleness of the things of this world are forced upon our minds; they promise but cannot perform, they disappoint us. Or, if they do perform what they promise, still (so it is) they do not satisfy us. We still crave for something, we do not well know what; but we are sure it is something which the world has not given us. And then its changes are so many, so sudden, so silent, so continual. It never leaves changing; it goes on to change, till we are quite sick at heart—then it is that our reliance on it is broken. It is plain we cannot continue to depend upon it, unless we keep pace with it, and go on changing too; but this we cannot do. We feel that, while it changes, we are one and the same; and thus, under God's blessing, we come to have some glimpse of the meaning of our independence of things temporal, and our immortality. And should it so happen that misfortunes come upon us (as they often do) then still more are we led to understand the nothingness of this world; then still more are we led to distrust it, and are weaned from the love of it, till at length it floats before our eyes merely as some idle veil, which, notwithstanding its many tints, cannot hide the view of what is beyond it—and we begin, by degrees, to perceive that there are but two beings in the whole universe, our own soul, and the God who made it.

Sublime, unlooked-for doctrine, yet most true! To everyone of us there are but two beings in the whole world, himself and God; for, as to this outward scene, its pleasures and pursuits, its honors and cares, its contrivances, its personages, its kingdoms, its multitude of busy slaves, what are they to us? nothing—no more than a show: "The world passeth away and the lust thereof." And as to those others nearer to us, who are not to be classed with the vain world, I mean our friends and relations, whom we are right in loving, these, too, after all, are nothing to us here. They cannot really help or profit us; we see them, and they act upon us, only (as it were) at a distance, through the medium of sense; they cannot get at our souls; they cannot enter into our thoughts, or really be companions to us. In the next world it will, through God's mercy, be otherwise; but here we enjoy, not their presence, but the anticipation of what one day shall be; so that, after all, they vanish before the clear vision we have, first, of our own existence, next of the presence of the great God in us, and over us, as our Governor and Judge, who dwells in us by our conscience, which is His representative.

And now consider what a revolution will take place in the mind that is not utterly reprobate, in proportion as it realizes this relation between itself and the most high God. We never in this life can fully understand what is meant by our living forever, but we can understand what is meant by this world's *not* living forever, by its dying never to rise again. And learning this, we learn that we owe it no service, no allegiance; it has no claim over us, and can do us no material good nor harm. On the other hand, the law of God written on our hearts bids us serve Him, and partly tells us how to serve Him, and Scripture completes the precepts which nature began. And both Scripture and conscience tell us we are answerable for what we do, and that God is a righteous Judge; and above all, our Savior, as our visible Lord God, takes the place of the world as the Only-begotten of the Father, having shown Himself openly, that we may not say that God is hidden. And thus a man is drawn forward by all manner of powerful influences to turn from things temporal to things eternal, to deny himself, to take up his cross and follow Christ. For there are Christ's awful threats and warnings to make him serious, His precepts to attract and elevate him, His promises to cheer him, His gracious deeds and sufferings to humble him to the dust, and to bind his heart once and forever in gratitude to Him who is so surpassing in mercy. All these things act upon him; and, as truly as St. Matthew rose from the receipt of custom when Christ called, heedless what bystanders would say of him, so they who, through grace, obey the secret voice of God, move onward contrary to the world's way, and careless what mankind may say of them, as understanding that they have souls, which is the one thing they have to care about.

I am well aware that there are indiscreet teachers gone forth into the world, who use language such as I have used, but mean something very different. Such are they who deny the grace of Baptism, and think that a man is converted to God all at once. But I have no need now to mention the difference between their teaching and that of Scripture. Whatever their peculiar errors are, so far as they say that we are by nature blind and sinful, and must, through God's grace, and our own endeavors, learn that we have souls and rise to a new life, severing ourselves from the world that is, and walking by faith in what is unseen and future, so far as they say true, for they speak the words of Scripture; which says, "Awake thou that sleepest, and arise from the dead, and Christ shall give thee light. See then that ye walk circumspectly, not as fools, but as wise, redeeming the time, because the days are evil; wherefore be ye not unwise, but understanding what the will of the Lord is."[7]

Let us, then, seriously question ourselves, and beg of God grace to do so honestly, whether we are loosened from the world, or whether, living as dependent on it, and not on the Eternal Author of our being, we are in fact taking our portion with this perishing outward scene, and ignorant of our having souls. I know very well that such thoughts are distasteful to the minds of men in general. Doubtless many a one there is, who, on hearing doctrines such as I have been insisting on, says in his heart, that religion is thus made gloomy and repulsive; that he would attend to a teacher who spoke in a less severe way; and that in fact Christianity was not intended to be a dark, burdensome law, but a religion of cheerfulness and joy. This is what young people think, though they do not express it in this argumentative form. They view a strict life as something offensive and hateful; they turn from the notion of it. And then, as they get older and see more of the world, they learn to defend their opinion, and express it more or less in the way in which I have just put it. They hate and oppose the truth, as it were upon principle; and the more they are told that they have souls, the more resolved they are to live as if they had not souls. But let us take it as a clear point from the first, and not to be disputed, that religion must ever be difficult to those who neglect it. All things that we have to learn are difficult at first; and our duties to God, and to man for His sake, are peculiarly difficult, because they call upon us to take up a new life, and quit the love of this world for the next. It cannot be avoided; we must fear and be in sorrow, before we can rejoice. The Gospel must be a burden before it comforts and brings us peace. No one can have his heart cut away from the natural objects of its love, without pain during the process and throbbings afterwards. This is plain from the nature of the case; and, however true it be, that this or that teacher may be harsh and repulsive, yet he cannot materially alter things. Religion is in itself at first a weariness to the worldly mind, and it requires an effort and a self-denial in everyone who honestly determines to be religious.

But there are other persons who are far more hopeful than those I have been speaking of, who, when they hear repentance and newness of life urged on them, are frightened at the thought of the greatness of the work; they are disheartened at being told to do so much. Now let it be well understood, that to realize our individual accountableness and immortality, of which I have been speaking, is not required of them all at once. I never said a person was not in a hopeful way who did not thus fully discern the world's vanity and the worth of his soul. But a man is truly in a very desperate way who does not wish, who does not try, to discern and feel all this. I want a man, on the one hand, to confess his immortality with his lips, and, on the other, to live as if he tried to understand his own words, and then he is in the way of salvation; he is in the way towards heaven, even though he has not yet fully emancipated himself from the fetters of this world. Indeed none of us (of course) are entirely loosened from this world. We all use words, in speaking of our duties, higher and fuller than we really understand. No one entirely realizes what is meant by his having a soul; even the best of men is but in a state of progress towards the simple truth; and the most weak and ignorant of those who seek after it cannot but be in progress. And therefore no one need be alarmed at hearing that he has much to do before he arrives at a right view of his own condition in God's sight, i.e., at *faith;* for we all have much to do, and the great point is, are we willing to do it?

Oh that there were such a heart in us, to put aside this visible world, to desire to look at it as a mere screen between us and God, and to think of Him who has entered in beyond the veil, and who is watching us, trying us, yes, and blessing, and influencing, and encouraging us towards good, day by day! Yet, alas, how do we suffer the mere varying circumstances of every day to sway us! How difficult it is to remain firm and in one mind under the seductions or terrors of the world! We feel variously according to the place, time, and people we are with. We are serious on Sunday, and we sin deliberately on Monday. We rise in the morning with remorse at our offenses and resolutions of amendment, yet before night we have transgressed again. The mere change of society puts us into a new frame of mind; nor do we sufficiently understand this great weakness of ours, or seek for strength where alone it can be found, in the Unchangeable God. What will be our thoughts in that day, when at length this outward world drops away altogether, and we find ourselves where we ever have been, in His presence, with Christ standing at His right hand!

On the contrary, what a blessed discovery is it to those who make it, that this world is but vanity and without substance; and that really they are ever in their Savior's presence. This is a thought which it is scarcely right to enlarge upon in a mixed congregation, where there may be some who have not given their hearts to God; for why should the privileges of the true Christian be disclosed to mankind at large, and sacred subjects, which are his peculiar treasure, be made common to the careless liver? He knows his blessedness, and needs not another to tell it him. He knows in whom he has believed; and in the hour of danger or trouble he knows what is meant by that peace, which Christ did not explain when He gave it to His Apostles, but merely said it was not as the world could give.

"Thou wilt keep him in perfect peace whose mind is stayed on Thee, because he trusteth in Thee. Trust ye in the Lord forever, for in the Lord Jehovah is everlasting strength."[8]

[I, 2]

KNOWLEDGE OF GOD'S WILL WITHOUT OBEDIENCE

If ye know these things, happy are ye if ye do them.
—John 13:17

There never was a people or an age to which these words could be more suitably addressed than to this country at this time; because we know more of the way to serve God, of our duties, our privileges, and our reward, than any other people hitherto, as far as we have the means of judging. To us then especially our Savior says, "If ye know these things, happy are ye if ye do them."

Now, doubtless, many of us think we know this very well. It seems a very trite thing to say, that it is nothing to *know* what is right, unless we *do* it; an old subject about which nothing new can be said. When we read such passages in Scripture, we pass over them as admitting them without dispute; and thus we contrive practically to forget them. Knowledge is nothing compared with doing; but the *knowing* that knowledge is nothing, we make to be *something,* we make it count, and thus we cheat ourselves.

This we do in parallel cases also. Many a man instead of *learning* humility in practice, confesses himself a poor sinner, and next *prides* himself upon the confession; he ascribes the glory of his redemption to God, and then becomes in a manner *proud* that he is redeemed. He is proud of his so-called humility.

Doubtless Christ spoke no words in vain. The Eternal Wisdom of God did not utter His voice that we might at once catch up His words in an irreverent manner, think we understand them at a glance, and pass them over. But His word endureth forever; it has a depth of meaning suited to all times and places, and hardly and painfully to be understood in any. They, who think they enter into it easily, may be quite sure they do not enter into it at all.

Now then let us try, by His grace, to make the text a living word to the benefit of our souls. Our Lord says, "If ye know, happy are ye, if ye do." Let us consider *how* we commonly read Scripture.

We read a passage in the Gospels, for instance, a parable perhaps, or the account of a miracle; or we read a chapter in the Prophets, or a Psalm. Who is not struck with the beauty of what he reads? I do not wish to speak of those who read the Bible only now and then, and who will in consequence generally find its sacred pages dull and uninteresting; but of those who study it. Who of such persons does not see the beauty of it? For instance, take the passage which introduces the text. Christ had been washing His disciples' feet. He did so at a season of great mental suffering; it was just before He was seized by His enemies to be put to death. The traitor, His familiar friend, was in the room. All of His disciples, even the most devoted of them, loved Him much less than they thought they did. In a little while they were all to forsake Him and flee. This He foresaw; yet He calmly washed their feet, and then He told them that He did so by way of an example; that they should be full of lowly services one to the other, as He to them; that He among them was in fact the highest who put himself the lowest. This He had said before; and His disciples must have recollected it. Perhaps they might wonder in their secret hearts *why* He repeated the lesson; they might say to themselves, "We have heard this before." They might be surprised that His significant action, His washing their feet, issued in nothing else than a precept already delivered, the command to be humble. At the same time they would not be able to deny, or rather they would deeply feel, the beauty of His action. Nay, as loving Him (after all) above all things, and reverencing Him as their Lord and Teacher, they would feel an admiration and awe of Him; but their minds would not rest sufficiently on the *practical* direction of the instruction vouchsafed to them. They knew the truth, and they admired it; they did not observe what it was they lacked. Such may be considered their frame of mind; and hence the force of the text, delivered primarily against Judas Iscariot, who knew and sinned deliberately against the truth; secondarily referring to all the Apostles, and St. Peter chiefly, who promised to be faithful, but failed under the trial; lastly, to us all, all of us here assembled, who hear the word of life continually, know it, admire it, do all but obey it.

Is it not so? is not Scripture altogether pleasant except in its strictness? do not we try to persuade ourselves, that to *feel* religiously, to confess our love of religion, and to be able to talk of religion, will stand in the place of careful obedience, of that *self-denial* which is the very substance of true practical religion? Alas! that religion, which is so delightful as a vision, should be so distasteful as a reality. Yet so it is, whether we are aware of the fact or not.

1. The multitude of men even who profess religion are in this state of mind. We will take the case of those who are in better circumstances than the mass of the community. They are well educated and taught; they have few distresses in life, or are able to get over them by the variety of their occupations, by the spirits which attend good health, or at least by the lapse of time. They go on respectably and happily, with the same general tastes and habits which they would have had if the Gospel had not been given them. They have an eye to what the world thinks of them; are charitable when it is expected. They are polished in their manners, kind from natural disposition or a feeling of propriety. Thus their religion is based upon self and the world, a mere *civilization;* the same (I say), as it would have been in the main (taking the state of society as they find it), even supposing Christianity were not the religion of the land. But it is; and let us go on to ask, how do they in consequence feel towards it? They accept it, they add it to what they *are,* they ingraft it upon the selfish and worldly habits of an unrenewed heart. They have been taught to revere it, and to believe it to come from God; so they admire it, and accept it as a rule of life, so far forth as it agrees with the carnal principles which govern them. So far as it does *not* agree, they are blind to its excellence and its claims. They overlook or explain away its precepts. They in no sense obey *because* it commands. They do right when they *would* have done right had it not commanded; however, they speak well of it, and think they understand it. Sometimes, if I may continue the description, they adopt it into a certain refined elegance of sentiments and manners, and then the irreligion is all that is graceful, fastidious, and luxurious. They love religious poetry and eloquent preaching. They desire to have their feelings roused and soothed, and to secure a variety and relief in that eternal subject which is unchangeable. They tire of

its simplicity, and perhaps seek to keep up their interest in it by means of religious narratives, fictitious or embellished, or of news from foreign countries, or of the history of the prospects or successes of the Gospel; thus perverting what is in itself good and innocent. This is their state of mind at best; for more commonly they think it enough merely to show some slight regard for the subject of religion; to attend its services on the Lord's day, and then only once, and coldly to express an approbation of it. But of course every description of such persons can be but general; for the shades of character are so varied and blended in individuals, as to make it impossible to give an accurate picture, and often very estimable persons and truly good Christians are partly infected with this bad and earthly spirit.

2. Take again another description of them. They have perhaps turned their attention to the means of promoting the happiness of their fellow creatures, and have formed a system of morality and religion of their own; then they come to Scripture. They are much struck with the high tone of its precepts, and the beauty of its teaching. It is true, they find many things in it which they do not understand or do not approve; many things they would not have said themselves. But they pass these by; they fancy that these do not apply to the present day (which is an easy way of removing anything we do not like), and *on the whole* they receive the Bible, and they think it highly serviceable for the lower classes. Therefore, they recommend it, and support the institutions which are the channels of teaching it. But as to their own case, it never comes into their minds to apply its precepts seriously to themselves; they *know* them already, they consider. They *know* them and that is enough; but as for *doing* them, by which I mean, going forward to obey them, with an unaffected earnestness and an honest faith *acting upon* them, receiving them as they are, and not as their own previously formed opinions would have them be, they have nothing of this right spirit. They do not contemplate such a mode of acting. To recommend and affect a moral and decent conduct (on *whatever* principles) seems to them to be enough. The spread of knowledge bringing in its train a selfish temperance, a selfish peaceableness, a selfish benevolence, the morality of expedience, this satisfies them. They care for none of the truths of the Scripture, *on the ground* of their being in Scrip-

ture; these scarcely become more valuable in their eyes for being there written. They do not obey *because* they are told to obey, on faith; and the need of this divine principle of conduct they do not comprehend. Why will it not answer (they seem to say) to make men good in one way as well as another? "Abana and Pharpar, rivers of Damascus, are they not better than all the waters of Israel?" as if all the knowledge and the training that books ever gave had power to unloose one sinner from the bonds of Satan, or to effect more than an outward reformation, an *appearance* of obedience; as if it were not a far different principle, a principle independent of knowledge, above it and before it, which leads to *real* obedience, that principle of divine faith, given from above, which has life in itself, and has power really to use knowledge to the soul's welfare; in the hand of which knowledge is (as it were) the torch lighting us on our way, but not teaching or strengthening us to walk.

3. Or take another view of the subject. Is it not one of the most common excuses made by the poor for being irreligious, that they have had no education? as if to know much was a necessary step for right practice. Again, they are apt to think it *enough* to know and to talk of religion, to make a man religious. Why have you come hither today, my brethren?—not as a matter of course, I will hope; not merely because friends or superiors told you to come. I will suppose you have come to church *as a religious act;* but beware of supposing that all is done and over by the act of coming. It is not enough to be *present* here; though many men act as if they forgot they must attend to what is going on, as well as come. It is not enough to listen to what is preached; though many think they have gone a great way when they do this. You *must pray;* now this is very hard in itself to anyone who tries (and this is the reason why so many men prefer the sermon to the prayers, because the former is merely the getting *knowledge,* and the latter is to do a *deed* of obedience); you must *pray;* and this I say is very difficult, because our thoughts are so apt to wander. But even this is not all—you must, as you pray, really intend to *try to practice* what you pray for. When you say, "Lead us not into temptation," you must in good earnest mean to avoid in your daily conduct those temptations which you have already suffered from. When you say, "Deliver us from evil," you must mean to struggle against

that evil in your hearts, which you are conscious of, and which you pray to be forgiven. This is difficult; still more is behind. You must actually carry your good intentions into effect during the week, and in truth and reality war against the world, the flesh, and the devil. And anyone here present who falls short of this, that is, who thinks it enough to come to church to *learn* God's will, but does not bear in mind to do it in his daily conduct, be he high or be he low, know he mysteries and all knowledge, or be he unlettered and busily occupied in active life, he is a fool in His sight, who maketh the wisdom of this world foolishness. Surely he is but a trifler, as substituting a formal outward service for the religion of the heart; and he reverses our Lord's words in the text, "because he knows these things, most unhappy is he, because he does them not."

4. But someone may say, "It is so very *difficult* to serve God, it is so much against my own mind, such an effort, such a strain upon my strength to bear Christ's yoke, I must give it over, or I must delay it at least. Can nothing be taken instead? I acknowledge His law to be most holy and true, and the accounts I read about good men are most delightful. I wish I were like them with all my heart; and for a little while I feel in a mind to set about imitating them. I have begun several times, I have had seasons of repentance, and set rules to myself; but for some reason or other, I fell back after a while, and was even worse than before. I know, but I cannot do. O wretched man that I am!"

Now to such a one I say, You are in a much more promising state than if you were contented with yourself, and thought that knowledge was everything, which is the grievous blindness which I have hitherto been speaking of; that is, you are in a better state, if you do not feel too much comfort or confidence in your confession. For *this* is the fault of many men; they make such an acknowledgment as I have described a *substitute* for real repentance; or allow themselves, after making it, to *put off* repentance, as if they could be suffered to give a word of promise which did not become due (so to say) for many days. You are, I admit, in a better state than if you were satisfied with yourself, *but you are not in a safe state*. If you were now to die, you would have no hope of salvation: no hope, that is, if your own showing be true, for I am taking your own words. Go before God's judgment seat, and there plead that you know the Truth and have not done it. This is what you frankly own—how will it there be taken? "Out of thine own mouth will I judge thee," says our Judge Himself, and who shall reverse His judgment? Therefore such a one must make the confession with great and real terror and shame, if it is to be considered a promising sign in him; else it is mere hardness of heart. For instance: I have heard persons say lightly (everyone must have heard them) that they own it would be a wretched thing indeed for them or their companions to be taken off suddenly. The young are especially apt to say this; that is, before they have come to an age to be callous, or have formed excuses to overcome the natural true sense of their conscience. They say they hope someday to repent. This is their own witness against themselves, like that bad prophet at Bethel who was constrained with his own mouth to utter God's judgments while he sat at his sinful meat. But let not such a one think that he will receive anything of the Lord; he does not speak in faith.

When, then, a man complains of his hardness of heart or weakness of purpose, let him see to it whether this complaint is more than a mere pretense to quiet his conscience, which is frightened at his putting off repentance; or, again, more than a mere idle word, said half in jest and half in compunction. But, should he be earnest in his complaint, then let him consider he has no need to complain. Everything is plain and easy to the earnest; it is the double-minded who find difficulties. If you hate your own corruption in sincerity and truth, if you are really pierced to the heart that you do not do what you know you should do, if you *would* love God if you could, then the Gospel speaks to you words of peace and hope. It is a very different thing indolently to say, "I would I were a different man," and to close with God's offer to make you different, when it is put before you. Here is the test between earnestness and insincerity. You say you wish to be a different man; Christ takes you at your word, so to speak; He offers to make you different. He says, "I will take away from you the heart of stone, the love of this world and its pleasures, if you will submit to My discipline." Here a man draws back. No; he cannot bear to *lose* the love of the world, to part with his present desires and tastes; he cannot *consent* to be changed. After all he is well satisfied at the bottom of his heart to remain as he is, only he wants his conscience taken out of the way. Did Christ offer to do this for him, if He would but make bitter sweet and sweet bitter, darkness light and light darkness, *then* he would hail the glad tidings of peace—till then he needs Him not.

But if a man is in earnest in wishing to get at the depths of his own heart, to expel the evil, to purify the good, and to gain power over himself, so as to do as well as know the Truth, what is the difficulty?—a matter of time indeed, but not of uncertainty is the recovery of such a man. So simple is the rule which he must follow, and so trite, that at first he will be surprised to hear it. God does great things by plain methods; and men start from them through pride, *because* they are plain. This was the conduct of Naaman the Syrian. Christ says, "Watch and pray"; herein lies our cure. To watch and to pray are surely in our power, and by these means we are certain of getting strength. You feel your weakness; you fear to be overcome by temptation: then keep out of the way of it. This is watching. Avoid society which is likely to mislead you; flee from the very shadow of evil; you cannot be too careful; better be a little too strict than a little too easy—it is the safer side. Abstain from reading books which are dangerous to you. Turn from bad thoughts when they arise, set about some business, begin conversing with some friend, or say to yourself the Lord's Prayer reverently. When you are urged by temptation, whether it be by the threats of the world, false shame, self-interest, provoking conduct on the part of another, or the world's sinful pleasures, urged to be cowardly, or covetous, or unforgiving, or sensual, shut your eyes and think of Christ's precious blood shedding. Do not dare to say you cannot help sinning; a little attention to these points will go far (through God's grace) to keep you in the right way. And again, pray as well as watch. You must know that you can do nothing of yourself; your past experience has taught you this; therefore look to God for the will and the power; ask Him earnestly in His Son's Name; seek His holy ordinances. Is not *this* in your power? Have you not power at least over the limbs of your body, so as to attend the means of grace constantly? Have you literally not the power to come hither; to observe the Fasts and Festivals of the Church; to come to His Holy Altar and receive the Bread of Life? Get yourself, at least, to do this; to put out the hand, to take His gracious Body and Blood;

this is no arduous work—and you say you really *wish* to gain the blessings He offers. What would you have more than a free gift, vouchsafed "without money and without price"? So, make no more excuses; murmur not about your own bad heart, your knowing and resolving, and not doing. Here is your remedy.

Well were it if men could be persuaded to be in earnest; but few are thus minded. The many go on with a double aim, trying to serve both God and mammon. Few can get themselves to do what is right, *because* God tells them; they have another aim; they desire to please self or men. When they can obey God without offending the bad master that rules them, then, and then only, they obey. Thus religion, instead of being the *first* thing in their estimation, is but the second. They differ, indeed, one from another what to put foremost: one man loves to be at ease, another to be busy, another to enjoy domestic comfort: but they agree in converting the truth of God, which they know to be Truth, into a mere instrument of secular aims; not discarding the Truth, but degrading it.

When He, the Lord of hosts, comes to shake terribly the earth, what number will He find of the remnant of the true Israel? We live in an educated age. The false gloss of a mere worldly refinement makes us decent and amiable. We all know and profess. We think ourselves wise; we flatter each other; we make excuses for ourselves when we are conscious we sin, and thus we gradually lose the consciousness that we are sinning. We think our own times superior to all others. "Thou blind Pharisee!" This was the fatal charge brought by our Blessed Lord against the falsely enlightened teachers of His own day. As then we desire to enter into life, let us come to Christ continually for the two foundations of true Christian faith—humbleness of mind and earnestness!

[I, 3]

Chapter 4

THE SPIRITUAL MIND

The kingdom of God is not in word, but in power.
—1 Cor. 4:20

How are we the better for being members of the Christian Church? This is a question which has ever claims on our attention; but it is right from time to time to examine our hearts with more than usual care, to try them by the standard of that divinely enlightened temper in the Church, and in the Saints, the work of the Holy Ghost, called by St. Paul "the spirit." I ask then, how are we the better for being Christ's disciples? what reason have we for thinking that our lives are very different from what they would have been if we had been heathens? Have we, in the words of the text, received the kingdom of God in word or in power? I will make some remarks in explanation of this question, which may (through God's grace) assist you, my brethren, in answering it.

1. Now first, if we would form a just notion how far we are influenced by the power of the Gospel, we must evidently put aside everything which we do merely in imitation of others, and not from religious principle. Not that we can actually separate our good words and works into two classes, and say, what is done from faith, and what is done only by accident, and in a random way; but without being able to draw the line, it is quite evident that so very much of our apparent obedience to God arises from mere obedience to the world and its fashions; or rather, that it is so difficult to say what *is* done in the spirit of faith, as to lead us, on reflection, to be very much dissatisfied with ourselves, and quite out of conceit with our past lives. Let a person merely reflect on the number and variety of bad or foolish thoughts which he suffers, and dwells on in private, which he would be ashamed to put into words, and he will at once see, how very poor a test his outward demeanor in life is of his real holiness in the sight of God. Or again, let him consider the number of times he has attended public worship as a matter of course because others do, and with-

out seriousness of mind; or the number of times he has found himself unequal to temptations when they came, which beforehand he and others made light of in conversation, blaming those perhaps who had been overcome by them, and he must own that his outward conduct shapes itself unconsciously by the manners of those with whom he lives, being acted upon by external impulses, apart from any right influence proceeding from the heart. Now, when I say this, am I condemning all that we do without thinking expressly of the duty of obedience at the *very time* we are doing it? Far from it; a religious man, in proportion as obedience becomes more and more easy to him, *will* doubtless do his duty unconsciously. It will be *natural* to him to obey, and therefore he will *do* it *naturally,* i.e., without effort or deliberation. It is difficult things which we are obliged to think about before doing them. When we have mastered our hearts in any matter (it is true) we no more think of the duty while we obey, than we think how to walk when we walk, or by what rules to exercise any art which we have thoroughly acquired. *Separate acts* of faith aid us only while we are *unstable.* As we get strength, but one extended act of faith (so to call it) influences us all through the day, and our whole day is but one act of obedience also. Then there is no minute distribution of our faith among our particular deeds. Our will runs parallel to God's will. This is the very privilege of confirmed Christians; and it is comparatively but a sordid way of serving God, to be thinking when we do a deed, "if I do not do this, I shall risk my salvation; or, if I do it, I have a chance of being saved"; *comparatively* a groveling way, for it is the best, the only way for sinners such as we are, to *begin* to serve God in. Still as we grow in grace, we throw away childish things; then we are able to stand upright like grown men, without the props and aids which our infancy required. This is the noble manner of serving God, to do good without thinking about it, without any calculation or reasoning, from love of the good, and hatred of the evil—though cautiously and with prayer and watching, yet so generously, that if we were suddenly asked why we so act, we could only reply "because it is our way," or "because Christ so acted"; so spontaneously as not to know so much that we *are* doing right, as that we are *not* doing wrong; I mean, with more of instinctive fear of sinning, than of minute and careful apprecia-

tion of the *degrees* of our obedience. Hence it is that the best men
are ever the most humble; as for other reasons, so especially
because they *are accustomed* to be religious. They surprise *others,*
but not themselves; they surprise others at their very calmness
and freedom from thought about themselves. This is to have a
great mind, to have within us that "princely heart of innocence"9
of which David speaks. Common men see God at a distance; in
their attempts to be religious they feebly guide themselves as by a
distant light, and are obliged to calculate and search about for the
path. But the long-practiced Christian, who, through God's
mercy, has brought God's presence near to him, the elect of God,
in whom the Blessed Spirit dwells, he does not look out of doors
for the traces of God; he is moved by God dwelling in him, and
need not but act on instinct. I do not say there is any man altogether such, for this is an angelic life; but it is the state of mind to
which vigorous prayer and watching tend.

How different is this high obedience from that random
unawares way of doing right, which to so many men seems to
constitute a religious life! The excellent obedience I have been
describing is obedience *on habit*. Now the obedience I condemn as
untrue, may be called obedience *on custom*. The one is of the
heart, the other of the lips; the one is in power, the other in word;
the one cannot be acquired without much and constant vigilance,
generally not without much pain and trouble; the other is the
result of a mere passive imitation of those whom we fall in with.
Why need I describe what every man's experience bears witness
to? Why do children learn their mother tongue, and not a foreign
language? Do they think about it? Are they better or worse for
acquiring one language and not another? Their character, of
course, is just what it would have been otherwise. How then are
we better or worse, if we have but in the same passive way admitted into our minds certain religious opinions; and have but accustomed ourselves to the words and actions of the world around us?
Supposing we had never heard of the Gospel, should we not do
just what we do, even in a heathen country, were the manners of
the place, from one cause or another, as decent and outwardly
religious? This is the question we have to ask ourselves. And if
we are conscious to ourselves that we are not greatly concerned
about the question itself, and have no fears worth mentioning of

being in the wrong, and no anxiety to find what is right, is it not evident that we are living to the world, not to God, and that whatever virtue we may actually have, still the Gospel of Christ has come to us not in power, but in word only?

I have now suggested one subject for consideration concerning our reception of the kingdom of God; viz. to inquire whether we have received it more than *externally;* but,

2. I will go on to affirm that we may have received it in a higher sense than in word merely, and yet in no real sense in *power;* in other words, that our obedience may be in some sort religious, and yet hardly deserve the title of Christian. This may be at first sight a startling assertion. It may seem to some of us as if there were no difference between being religious and being Christian; and that to insist on a difference is to perplex people. But listen to me. Do you not think it possible for men to do their duty, i.e., be religious, in a heathen country? Doubtless it is. St. Peter says that in every nation he that feareth God and worketh righteousness is accepted with Him.[10] Now are such persons, therefore, Christians? Certainly *not*. It would seem, then, it *is* possible to fear God and work righteousness, yet without being Christians; for (if we would know the truth of it) to be a Christian is to do this, and to do *much more* than this. Here, then, is a fresh subject for self-examination. Is it not the way of men to dwell with satisfaction on their good deeds, particularly when, for some reason or other, their conscience smites them? Or when they are led to the consideration of death, then they begin to turn in their minds how they shall acquit themselves before the judgment seat. And then it is they feel a relief in being able to detect, in their past lives, any deeds which may be regarded in any sense religious. You may hear some persons comforting themselves that they never harmed anyone; and that they have not given in to an openly profligate and riotous life. Others are able to say more; they can speak of their honesty, their industry, or their general conscientiousness. We will say they have taken good care of their families; they have never defrauded or deceived anyone; and they have a good name in the world; nay, they have in one sense lived in the fear of God. I will grant them this and more; yet possibly they are not altogether Christians in their obedience. I will grant

that these virtuous and religious deeds are really fruits of faith, not external merely, done without thought, but proceeding from the heart. I will grant they are really praiseworthy, and, when a man from want of opportunity knows no more, really acceptable to God; yet they determine nothing about his having received the Gospel of Christ in power. Why? for the simple reason that they are *not enough*. A Christian's faith and obedience is *built* on all this, but is only built on it. It is not the same as it. To be Christians, surely it is not enough to be that which we are enjoined to be, and must be, even without Christ; not enough to be no better than good heathens; not enough to be, in some slight measure, just, honest, temperate, and religious. We must indeed be just, honest, temperate, and religious, before we can rise to Christian graces, and to *be* practiced in justice and the like virtues is the way, the ordinary way, in which we receive the fullness of the kingdom of God; and, doubtless, any man who despises those who try to practice them (I mean conscientious men, who notwithstanding have not yet clearly seen and welcomed the Gospel system), and slightingly calls them "mere moral men" in disparagement, such a man knows not what spirit he is of, and had best take heed how he speaks against the workings of the inscrutable Spirit of God. I am not wishing to frighten these imperfect Christians, but to lead them on; to open their minds to the greatness of the work before them, to dissipate the meager and carnal views in which the Gospel has come to them, to warn them that they must never be contented with themselves, or stand still and relax their efforts, but not go on *unto perfection;* that till they are much more than they are at present, they have received the kingdom of God in word, not in power; that they are not spiritual men, and can have no comfortable sense of Christ's presence in their souls; for to whom much is given, of him is much required.

What is it, then, that they lack? I will read several passages of Scripture which will make it plain. St. Paul says, "If any man be in Christ, he is a new creature: old things are passed away; behold, all things are become new." Again: "The life which I now live in the flesh, I live by the faith of the Son of God, who loved me, and gave Himself for me." "The love of Christ constraineth us." "Put on, therefore, as the elect of God, holy and beloved, bowels of mercies, kindness, humbleness of mind, meekness, long-suffering, forbearing one another, and forgiving one another, if any man have a quarrel against any, even as Christ forgave you, so also do ye; and above all these things, put on charity, which is the bond of perfectness. And let the peace of God rule in your hearts, to that which also ye are called in one body, and be ye thankful. Let the word of Christ dwell in you richly in all wisdom." "God hath sent forth the Spirit of His Son into your hearts." Lastly, our Savior's own memorable words, "If any man will come after Me, let him deny himself, and take up his cross daily and follow Me."[11] Now it is plain that this is a very different mode of obedience from any which natural reason and conscience tell us of—different, *not in its nature,* but *in its excellence and peculiarity.* It is much more than honesty, justice, and temperance; and *this* is to be a Christian. Observe in what respect it is different from that lower degree of religion which we may possess without entering into the mind of the Gospel. First of all in its faith; which is placed, not simply in God, but in God as manifested in Christ, according to His own words, "Ye believe in God, believe also in Me."[12] Next, we must adore Christ as our Lord and Master, and love Him as our most gracious Redeemer. We must have a deep sense of our guilt, and of the difficulty of securing heaven; we must live as in His presence, daily pleading His Cross and Passion, thinking of His holy commandments, imitating His sinless pattern, and depending on the gracious aids of His Spirit; that we may really and truly be servants of Father, Son, and Holy Ghost, in whose name we were baptized. Further, we must, for His sake, aim at a noble and unusual strictness of life, perfecting holiness in His fear, destroying our sins, mastering our whole soul, and bringing it into captivity to His Law, denying ourselves lawful things, in order to do Him service, exercising a profound humility, and an unbounded, never-failing love, giving away much of our substance in religious and charitable works, and discountenancing and shunning irreligious men. This is to be a Christian; a gift easily described, and in a few words, but attainable only with fear and much trembling; promised, indeed, and in a measure accorded at once to everyone who asks for it, but not secured till after many years, and never in this life fully realized. But be sure of this, that every one of us, who has had the opportunities of instruction and sufficient time, and yet does not in some good measure possess it, everyone, who, when death comes, has not gained his portion of that gift which it requires a course of years to gain, and which he might have gained, is in a peril so great and fearful, that I do not like to speak about it. As to the notion of a partial and ordinary fulfillment of the duties of honesty, industry, sobriety, and kindness, "avail- ing"[13] him, it has no Scriptural encouragement. We must stand or fall by another and higher rule. We must have become what St. Paul calls "new creatures"; [14] that is, we must have lived and worshiped God as the redeemed of Jesus Christ, in all faith and humbleness of mind, in reverence towards His word and ordi- nances, in thankfulness, in resignation, in mercifulness, gentle- ness, purity, patience, and love.

Now, considering the obligation of obedience which lies upon us Christians, in these two respects, first, as contrasted with a mere outward and nominal profession, and next contrasted with that more ordinary obedience which is required of those even who have not the Gospel, how evident is it that we are far from the kingdom of God! Let each in his own conscience apply this to himself. I will grant he has *some* real Christian principle in his heart; but I wish him to observe *how little* that is likely to be. Here is a thought not to keep us from rejoicing in the Lord Christ, but to make us "rejoice with trembling,"[15] wait diligently on God, pray Him earnestly to teach us more of our duty, and to impress the love of it on our hearts, to enable us to obey both in that free spirit, which can act right without reasoning and calculation, and yet with the caution of those who know their salvation depends on obedience in little things, from love of the truth as manifested in Him who is the Living Trust come upon earth, "the Way, the Truth, and the Life."[16]

With others we have no concern; we do not know what their opportunities are. There may be thousands in this populous land who never had the means of hearing Christ's voice fully, and in whom virtues short of evangelical will hereafter be accepted as the fruit of faith. Nor can we know the *hearts* of *any* men, or tell what is the degree in which they have improved their talents. It is enough to keep to ourselves. We dwell in the full light of the

Gospel, and the full grace of the Sacraments. We ought to have the holiness of Apostles. There is no reason except our own willful corruption, that we are not by this time walking in the steps of St. Paul or St. John, and following them as they followed Christ. What a thought is this! Do not cast it from you, my brethren, but take it to your homes, and may God give you grace to profit by it!

[I, 6]

Chapter 5

THE CHRISTIAN MYSTERIES

How can these things be?
—1 John 3:9

There is much instruction conveyed in the circumstance, that the Feast of the Holy Trinity immediately succeeds that of Whitsunday. On the latter Festival we commemorate the coming of the Spirit of God, who is promised to us as the source of all spiritual knowledge and discernment. But lest we should forget the nature of that illumination which He imparts, Trinity Sunday follows, to tell us what it is not; not a light accorded to the reason, the gifts of the intellect; inasmuch as the Gospel has its mysteries, its difficulties, and secret things, which the Holy Spirit does not remove.

The grace promised us is given, not that we may know more, but that we may do better. It is given to influence, guide, and strengthen us in performing our duty towards God and man; it is given to us as creatures, as sinners, as men, as immortal beings, not as mere reasoners, disputers, or philosophical inquirers. It teaches what we are, whither we are going, what we must do, how we must do it; it enables us to change our fallen nature from evil to good, "to make ourselves a new heart and a new spirit." But it tells us nothing for the *sake* of telling it; neither in His Holy Word, nor through our consciences, has the Blessed Spirit thought fit so to act. Not that the desire of knowing sacred things for the sake of knowing them is wrong. As knowledge about earth, sky, and sea, and the wonders they contain, is in itself valuable, and in its place desirable, so doubtless there is nothing sinful in gazing wistfully at the marvelous providence of God's moral governance, and wishing to understand them. But still God has not given us such knowledge in the Bible, and therefore to look into the Bible for such knowledge, or to expect it in any way from the inward teaching of the Holy Ghost, is a dangerous mistake, and (it may be) a sin. And since men are apt to prize knowledge above holiness, therefore it is most suitably provided, that Trinity

Sunday should succeed Whitsunday; to warn us that the enlightening vouchsafed to us is not an understanding of "all mysteries and all knowledge," but that love or charity which is "the fulfilling of the Law."

And in matter of fact there have been very grievous mistakes respecting the nature of Christian knowledge. There have been at all times men so ignorant of the object of Christ's coming, as to consider mysteries inconsistent with the light of the Gospel. They have thought the darkness of Judaism, of which Scripture speaks, to be a state of intellectual ignorance; and Christianity to be, what they term, a "rational religion." And hence they have argued, that no doctrine which was *mysterious,* i.e., too deep for human reason, or inconsistent with their self-devised notions, could be contained in Scripture; as if it were honoring Christ to maintain that when He said a thing, He could not have meant what He said, because *they* would not have said it. Nicodemus, though a sincere inquirer, and (as the event shows) a true follower of Christ, yet at first was startled at the mysteries of the Gospel. He said to Christ, "How can these things be?" He felt the temptation, and overcame it. But there are others who are altogether offended and fall away on being exposed to it; as those mentioned in the sixth chapter of St. John's Gospel, who went back and walked no more with Him.

The Feast of Trinity succeeds Pentecost; the light of the Gospel does not remove mysteries in religion. This is our subject. Let us enlarge upon it.

1. Let us consider such difficulties of religion, as press upon us independently of the Scriptures. Now we shall find the Gospel has not removed these; they remain as great as before Christ came. How excellent is this world! how very good and fair is the face of nature! how pleasant it is to walk into the green country, and "to meditate in the field at the eventide."[17] As we look around, we cannot but be persuaded that God is most good, and loves His creatures; yet amid all the splendor we see around us, and the happy beings, thousands and ten thousands, which live in the air and water, the question comes upon us, "But *why is there pain in the world*?" We see that the brutes prey on each other, inflicting violent, unnatural deaths. Some of them, too, are enemies of man, and harm us when they have an opportunity. And

man tortures others unrelentingly, nay, condemns some of them to a life of suffering. Much more do pain and misery show themselves in the history of man—the numberless diseases and casualties of human life, and our sorrows of mind—then, further, the evils we inflict on each other, our sins and their awful consequences. Now why does God permit so much evil in His own world? This is a difficulty, I say, which we feel at once, before we open the Bible; and which we are quite unable to solve. We open the Bible; the fact is acknowledged there, but it is not explained at all. We are told that sin entered the world *through the devil,* who tempted Adam to disobedience; so that God created the world good, *though* evil is in it. But why He thought fit to *suffer* this, we are not told. We know no more on the subject than we did before opening the Bible. It was a mystery before God gave His revelation, it is as great a mystery now; and doubtless for this reason, because knowledge about it would do us no good, it would merely satisfy curiosity. It is not practical knowledge.

2. Nor, again, are the difficulties of Judaism removed by Christianity. The Jews were told, that if they put to death certain animals, they should be admitted by way of consequence into God's favor, which their continual transgressions were ever forfeiting. Now there was something mysterious here. How should the death of unoffending creatures make God gracious to the Jews? They could not tell, of course. All that could be said to the point was, that in the daily course of human affairs the unoffending constantly suffer instead of the offenders. One man is ever suffering for the fault of another. But this experience did not lighten the difficulty of so mysterious a provision. It was still a mystery that God's favor should depend on the death of brute animals. Does Christianity solve this difficulty? No; it continues it. The Jewish sacrifices indeed are done away, but still there remains One Great Sacrifice for sin, infinitely higher and more sacred than all other conceivable sacrifices. According to the Gospel message, Christ has voluntarily suffered, "the just for the unjust, to bring us to God." Here is the mystery continued. Why was this suffering necessary to procure for us the blessings which we were in ourselves unworthy of? We do not know. We should not be better men for knowing why God did not pardon us with-

out Christ's death; so He has not told us. One suffers for another in the ordinary course of things; and under the Jewish Law, too; and in the Christian scheme; and why all this, is still a mystery.

Another difficulty to a thoughtful Israelite would arise from considering the state of the heathen world. Why did not Almighty God bring all nations into His Church, and teach them, by direct revelation, the sin of idol worship? He would not be able to answer. God had chosen one nation. It is true the same principle of preferring one to another is seen in the system of the whole world. God gives men unequal advantages, comforts, education, talents, health. Yet this does not satisfy us, *why* He has thought fit to do so at all. Here, again, the Gospel recognizes and confirms the mysterious fact. *We* are born in a Christian country, others are not; *we* are baptized; *we* are educated; others are not. We are favored *above* others. But why? We cannot tell; no more than the Jews could tell why they were favored—and for this reason, because to know it is nothing to us; it would not make us better men to know it. It is intended that we should look to ourselves, and rather consider why we have privileges given us, than why others have not the same. Our Savior repels such curious questions more than once. "Lord, and what shall this man do?"[18] St. Peter asked about St. John. Christ replied, "If I will that he tarry till I come, *what is that to thee? Follow thou Me.*"

Thus the Gospel gives us no advantages in respect to mere *barren knowledge,* above the Jew, or above the unenlightened heathen.

3. Nay, we may proceed to say, further than this, *that it increases our difficulties.* It is indeed a remarkable circumstance, that the very revelation that brings us *practical and useful knowledge* about our souls, in the very *act of doing* so, nay (as it would seem), in *consequence of* doing so, brings us mysteries. We gain spiritual light at the price of intellectual perplexity; a blessed exchange doubtless (for which is better, to be well and happy within ourselves, or to know what is going on at the world's end?), still at the price of perplexity. For instance, how infinitely important and blessed is the news of eternal happiness? but we learn in connection with this joyful truth, that there is *a state of endless misery* too. Now, how great a mystery is this! yet the difficulty goes hand in hand with the spiritual blessing. It is still more

strikingly to the point to refer to the message of mercy itself. We are saved by the death of Christ; but who is Christ? Christ is the Very Son of God, Begotten of God and One with God from everlasting, God incarnate. This is our inexpressible comfort, and a most sanctifying truth if we receive it rightly; but how stupendous a mystery *is* the incarnation and sufferings of the Son of God! Here, not merely do the good tidings and the mystery go together, as in the revelation of eternal life and eternal death, but the very doctrine which *is* the mystery, brings to comfort also. Weak, ignorant, sinful, desponding, sorrowful man gains the knowledge of an infinitely merciful Protector, a Giver of all good, most powerful, the Worker of all righteousness within him; at what price? at the price of a mystery. "The Word was made flesh, and dwelt among us, and we beheld His glory"; and He laid down His life for the world. What rightly disposed mind but will gladly make the exchange, and exclaim, in the language of one whose words are almost sacred among us, "Let it be counted folly, or frenzy, or fury whatsoever; it is our comfort and our wisdom. We care for no *knowledge* in the world but this, that man hath sinned, and God hath suffered; that God hath made Himself the Son of Man, and that men are made the righteousness of God."[19]

   The same singular connection between religious light and comfort, and intellectual darkness, is also seen in the doctrine of the Trinity. Frail man requires pardon and sanctification; can he do otherwise than gratefully devote himself to, and trust implicitly in, his Redeemer and his Sanctifier? But if our Redeemer were not God, and our Sanctifier were not God, how great would have been our danger of preferring creatures to the Creator! What a source of light, freedom, and comfort is it, to know we cannot love Them too much, or humble ourselves before Them too reverently, for both Son and Spirit are separately God! Such is the *practical* effect of the doctrine; but what a mystery also is therein involved! What a source of perplexity and darkness (I say) to the reason, is the doctrine which immediately results from it! for if Christ be by Himself God, and the Spirit be by Himself God, and yet there be but One God, here is plainly something altogether beyond our comprehension; and, though we might have antecedently supposed there were numberless truths relating to Almighty God which we could neither know nor understand, yet certain as this is, it does not make this mystery at all less overpowering when it *is* revealed.

And it is important to observe, that this doctrine of the Trinity *is not proposed in Scripture as a mystery.* It seems then that, as we draw forth many remarkable facts concerning the natural world which do not lie on its surface, so by meditation we detect in Revelation this remarkable principle, which is not openly propounded, *that religious light is intellectual darkness.* As if our gracious Lord had said to us, "Scripture does not *aim* at making mysteries, but they are as shadows brought out by the Sun of Truth. When you knew nothing of revealed light, you knew not revealed darkness. Religious truth requires you should be told *something,* your own imperfect nature prevents your knowing *all;* and to know *something,* and *not all—partial knowledge—*must of course perplex; doctrines imperfectly revealed must be mysterious."

4. Such being the necessary mysteriousness of Scripture doctrine, how can we best turn it to account in the contest which we are engaged in with our evil hearts? Now we are given to see how to do this in part, and, as far as we see, let us be thankful for the gift. It seems, then, that difficulties in revelation are especially given to prove *the reality of our faith.* What shall separate the insincere from the sincere follower of Christ? When the many own Christ with their lips, what shall try and discipline His true servant, and detect the self-deceiver? Difficulties in revelation mainly contribute to this end. They are stumbling blocks to proud and unhumbled minds, and were intended to be such. Faith is unassuming, modest, thankful, obedient. It receives with reverence and love whatever God gives, when convinced it is His gift. But when men do not feel rightly their need of His redeeming mercy, their lost condition and their inward sinfulness, when, in fact, they do not seek Christ in good earnest, in order to gain something, and do something, but as a matter of curiosity, or speculation, or form, *of course* these difficulties will become great objections in the way of their receiving His word simply. And I say these difficulties were intended to be such by Him who "scattereth the proud in the imagination of their hearts." St. Peter assures us, that that same cornerstone which is unto them that believe *"precious,"* is "unto them which be disobedient, a stone of

stumbling, and a rock of offense," "whereunto also (he adds) *they were appointed.*"[20] And our Lord's conduct through His ministry is a continued example of this. He spoke in parables,[21] that they might see and hear, yet not understand—a righteous detection of insincerity; whereas the same difficulties and obscurities, which offended irreligious men, would but lead the humble and meek to seek for more light, for information as far as it was to be obtained, and for resignation and contentedness, where it was not given. When Jesus said, "Except ye eat the flesh of the Son of man, drink His blood, ye have no life in you. . . . Many of His disciples . . . said, This is a hard saying: who can bear it? . . . and from that time many . . . went back, and walked no more with Him. . . . Then said Jesus unto the twelve, Will ye also go away? Then Simon Peter answered Him, Lord, to whom shall we go? Thou hast the words of eternal life." Here is the trial of faith, *a difficulty.* Those "that believe not" fall away; the true disciples remain firm, for they feel their *eternal interests* at stake, and ask the very plain and practical, as well as affectionate question, *"To whom* shall we go,"[22] if we leave Christ?

At another time our Lord says, "I thank Thee, O Father, Lord of heaven and earth, that Thou hast hid these things from the wise and prudent (those who trust reason rather than Scripture and conscience), and hast revealed them unto babes (those who humbly walk by faith). Even so, Father, for so it seemed good in Thy sight."[23]

5. Now what do we gain from thoughts such as these? Our Savior gives us the conclusion, in the words, which follow a passage I have just read. "Therefore said I unto you, that no man can come unto Me, except it were given him of My Father." Or again, "No man can come to Me, except the Father, which hath sent Me, draw him." Therefore, if we feel the necessity of coming to Christ, yet the difficulty, let us recollect that the gift of coming is in God's hands, and that we must pray Him to give it to us. Christ does not merely tell us that we cannot come of ourselves (though this He does tell us), but He tells us also with whom the power of coming is lodged, with His Father, that we may seek it of Him. It is true, religion has an austere appearance to those who never have tried it; its doctrines full of mystery, its precepts of harshness; so that it is uninviting, offending different men in different ways,

but in some way offending all. When then we feel within us the rising of this opposition to Christ, proud aversion to His Gospel, or a low-minded longing after this world, let us pray God to draw us; and though we cannot move a step without Him, at least let us try to move. He looks into our hearts and sees our strivings even before we strive, and He blesses and strengthens even our feebleness. Let us get rid of curious and presumptuous thoughts by going about our business, whatever it is; and let us mock and baffle the doubts which Satan whispers to us by *acting* against them. No matter whether we believe doubtingly or not, or know clearly or not, so that *we act* upon our belief. The rest will follow in time; part in this world, part in the next. Doubts may pain, but they cannot harm, unless we give way to them; and that we *ought not* to give way, our conscience tells us, so that our course is plain. And the more we are in earnest to "work out our salvation," the less shall we care to know how those things really are, which perplex us. At length, when our hearts are in our work, we shall be indisposed to take the trouble of listening to curious truths (if they are but curious), though we might have them explained to us. For what says the Holy Scripture? that of speculations "there is no end," and they are "a weariness of the flesh"; but that we must "fear God and keep His commandments; for this is the whole duty of man."[24]

[I, 16]

Chapter 6

CHRISTIAN REVERENCE

Serve the Lord with fear, and rejoice with trembling.
—Ps. 2:11

Why did Christ show Himself to so few witnesses after He rose from the dead? Because *He was a King,* a King exalted upon God's "Holy hill of Zion"; as the Psalm says which contains the text. Kings do not court the multitude, or show themselves as a spectacle at the will of others. They are the rulers of their people, and have their state as such, and are reverently waited on by their great men: and when they show themselves, they do so out of their condescension. They act by means of their servants, and must be *sought* by those who would gain favors from them.

Christ, in like manner, when exalted as the Only-begotten Son of God, did not mix with the Jewish people, as in the days of His humiliation. He rose from the grave in secret, and taught in secret for forty days, because "the government was upon His shoulder." He was no longer a servant washing His disciples' feet, and dependent on the wayward will of the multitude. He was the acknowledged Heir of all things. His throne was established by a Divine decree; and those who desired His salvation, were bound to *seek* His face. Yet not even by those who sought was He at once found. He did not permit the world to approach Him rashly, or curiously to gaze on Him. Those only did He call beside Him who had been His friends, who loved Him. Those only He bade "ascend the hill of the Lord," who had "clean hands and a pure heart, who had not worshiped vanity nor sworn deceitfully." These drew near, and "saw the Lord God of Israel," and so were fitted to bear the news of Him to the people at large. *He* remained "in His holy temple"; *they* from Him proclaimed the tidings of His Resurrection, and of His mercy, His free pardon offered to all men, and the promises of grace and glory which His death had procured for all who believe.

Thus are we taught to serve our risen Lord with fear, and

rejoice with trembling. Let us pursue the subject thus opened upon us—Christ's second sojourn on earth (after His Resurrection) was *in secret*. The time had been when He "preached openly in the synagogues," and in the public ways; and openly wrought miracles such as man never did. Was there to be no end of His labors in our behalf? His *death* "finished" them; afterwards He taught His *followers* only. Who shall complain of His withdrawing Himself at last from the world, when it was of His own spontaneous loving-kindness that He ever showed Himself at all?

Yet it must be borne in mind, that even before He entered into His glory, Christ spoke and acted as a King. It must not be supposed that, even in the days of His flesh, He could forget who He was, or "behave Himself unseemly" by any weak submission to the will of the Jewish people. Even in the lowest acts of His self-abasement, still He showed His greatness. Consider His conduct when He washed St. Peter's feet, and see if it were not calculated (assuredly it was) to humble, to awe, and subdue the very person to whom He ministered. When He taught, warned, pitied, prayed for, His ignorant hearers, He never allowed them to relax their reverence or to overlook His condescension. Nay, He did not allow them to praise Him aloud, and publish His acts of grace; as if what is called popularity would be a dishonor to His holy Name, and the applause of men would imply their right to censure. The world's praise is akin to contempt. Our Lord delights in the tribute of the secret heart. Such was His conduct in the days of His flesh. Does it not interpret His dealings with us after His Resurrection? He who was so reserved in His communications of Himself, even when He came to minister, much more would withdraw Himself from the eyes of men when He was exalted over all things.

I have said, that even when a servant, Christ spoke with the authority of a king; and have given you some proof of it. But it may be well to dwell upon this. Observe then, the difference between His promises, stated doctrinally and generally, and His mode of addressing those who came actually before Him. While He announced God's willingness to forgive *all* repentant sinners, in all the fullness of loving-kindness and tender mercy, yet He did not use supplication to these persons or those, whatever their number or their rank might be. He spoke as one who knew He had great favors to confer, and had nothing to gain from those who received them. Far from urging them to accept His bounty, He showed Himself even backward to confer it, inquired into their knowledge and motives, and cautioned them against entering His service without counting the cost of it. Thus sometimes He even repelled men from Him.

For instance: When there went "great multitudes with Him . . . He turned and said unto them, If any man come to Me, and hate not his father and mother, and wife and children, and brothers and sisters, yea, and his own life also, he cannot be My disciple." These were not the words of one who courted popularity. He proceeds—"Which of you intending to build a tower, sitteth not down first, and counteth the cost, whether he have sufficient to finish it? . . . So likewise, whosoever he be of you, that forsaketh not all that he hath, he cannot be My disciple."[25] On the other hand, observe His conduct to the powerful men, and the learned Scribes and Pharisees. There are persons who look up to human power, and who are pleased to associate their names with the accomplished and cultivated of this world. Our blessed Lord was as inflexible towards these, as towards the crowds which followed Him. They asked for a sign; He named them "an evil and adulterous generation," who refused to profit by what they had already received.[26] They asked Him, whether He did not confess Himself to be One with God; but He, rather than tell such proud disputers, seemed even to abandon His own real claim, and made His former clear words ambiguous.[27] Such was the King of Israel in the eyes both of the multitude and of their rulers; a "hard saying," a "rock of offense even to the disobedient," who came to Him "with their lips, while their hearts were far from Him." Continue this survey to the case of individuals, and it will still appear, that, loving and merciful as He was most abundantly, yet still He showed both His power and His grace with reserve, even to them, as well as to the fickle many, or the unbelieving Pharisees.

One instance is preserved to us of a person addressing Him, with some notions, indeed, of His greatness, but in a light and careless tone. The narrative is instructive from the mixture of good and bad which the inquirer's character displays.[28] He was young, and wealthy, and is called "a ruler"; yet was anxious for

Christ's favor. So far was well. Nay, he "came running and kneeling to Him." And he *seemed* to address Him in what would generally be considered as respectful terms: "Good Master," he said. Yet our Savior saw in his conduct a deficiency—"One thing thou lackest": viz. *devotion* in the true sense of the word, a giving himself up to Christ. This young man seems to have considered religion as an easy work, and thought he could live as the world, and yet serve God acceptably. In consequence, we may suppose, he had little right notion of the dignity of a Messenger from God. He did not associate the Ministers of religion with awful prospects beyond the grave, in which he was interested; nor *reverence* them accordingly, though he was not without some kind of *respect* for them. Doubtless he thought he was *honoring* our Lord when he had called Him *"Good Master"*; and would have been surprised to hear his attachment to sacred subjects and appointments called in question. Yet our Savior rejected such half homage, and rebuked what even seemed piteously offered. *"Why* callest thou Me good?" He asked; "There is none good but One, that is, God": as if He said, "Observest thou *what* words thou art using as if words of course? [*sic*] 'Good Master'—am I accounted by thee as a teacher of man's creation, and over whom man has power, and to be accosted by a form of honor, which, through length of time, has lost its meaning; or am I acknowledged to come and have authority from Him who is the only source of goodness?" Nor did our Lord relax His severity even after this reproof. Expressly as it is told us, *"He loved him,"* and spoke to him therefore in great compassion and mercy, yet He strictly charged him to sell all he had and give it away, if he would show he was in earnest, and He sent him away "sorrowful."

You may recollect, too, our Lord's frequent inquiry into *the faith* of those who came to Him. This arose, doubtless, from the same rule, a regard to His own Majesty as a King. "If thou canst believe, all things are possible to him that believeth."[29] He did not work miracles as a mere display of power; or allow the world profanely to look on as at some exhibition of art. In this respect, as in others, even Moses and Elias stand in contrast with Him. Moses wrought miracles before Pharaoh to rival the magicians of Egypt. Elijah challenged the prophets of Baal to bring down fire from heaven. The Son of God deigned not to exert His power before

Herod, after Moses' pattern; nor to be judged by the multitude, as Elijah. He subdued the power of Satan at His own appointed seasons; but when the devil tempted Him and demanded a miracle in proof of His Divinity, He would do none.

Further, even when an inquirer showed earnestness, still He did not try to gain him over by smooth representations of His doctrine. He declared, indeed, the general characteristic of His doctrine, "My yoke is easy"; but "He made Himself strange and spake roughly" to those who came to Him. Nicodemus was another ruler of the Jews, who sought Him, and he professed his belief in His miracles and Divine mission. Our Savior answered in these severe words—"Verily, verily, I say unto thee, Except a man be born again, he cannot see the kingdom of God."

Such was our Savior's conduct even during the period of His ministry; much more might we expect it to be such, when He had risen from His state of servitude, and such we find it.

No man saw Him rise from the grave. His Angels indeed beheld it; but His earthly followers were away, and the heathen soldiers were not worthy. They saw, indeed, the great Angel, who rolled away the stone from the opening of the tomb. This was Christ's servant; but Him they saw not. *He* was on His way to see His own faithful and mourning followers. To these He had revealed His doctrine during His humiliation, and called them "His friends."[30] First of all, He appeared to Mary Magdalene in the garden itself where He had been buried; then to the other women who ministered unto Him; then to the two disciples traveling to Emmaus; then to all the Apostles separately; besides, to Peter and to James; and to Thomas in the presence of them all. Yet not even these, His friends, had free access to Him. He said to Mary, "Touch Me not." He came and left them according to His own pleasure. When they saw Him, they felt an awe which they had not felt during His ministry. While they doubted if it were He, "None of them," St. John says, "durst ask Him, Who art Thou? believing that it was the Lord."[31] However, as kings have their days of state, on which they show themselves publicly to their subjects, so our Lord appointed a meeting of His disciples, when they might see Him. He had determined this even before His Crucifixion; and the Angels reminded them of it. "He goeth before you into Galilee; there shall ye see Him, as He said unto you."[32] The place of meeting was a mountain; the same (it is supposed) as that on which He had been transfigured; and the number who saw Him there was five hundred at once, if we join St. Paul's account to that in the Gospels. At length, after forty days, He was taken from them; He ascended up, "and a cloud received Him out of their sight."

Are *we* to feel less humble veneration for Him now, than His Apostles then? Though He is our Savior, and has removed all slavish fear of death and judgment, are we, therefore, to make light of the prospect before us, as if we were sure of that reward which He bids us struggle for? Assuredly, we are still to "serve the Lord with fear, and rejoice with reverence," to "kiss the Son, lest He be angry, and so we perish from the right way, if His wrath be kindled, yea but a little." In a Christian's course, *fear and love must go together*. And this is the lesson to be deduced from our Savior's withdrawing from the world after His Resurrection. He showed His love for men by dying for them, and rising again. He maintained His honor and great glory by retiring from them when His merciful purpose was attained, that they might seek Him if they would find Him. He ascended to His Father out of our sight. Sinners would be ill company for the exalted King of Saints. When we have been duly prepared to see Him, we shall be given to approach Him.

In heaven, love will absorb fear; but in this world, *fear and love must go together*. No one can love God aright without fearing Him; though many fear Him, and yet do not love Him. Self-confident men, who do not know their own hearts, or the reasons they have for being dissatisfied with themselves, do not fear God, and they think this bold freedom is to love Him. Deliberate sinners fear but cannot love Him. But devotion to Him consists in love and fear, as we may understand from our ordinary attachment to each other. No one really loves another, who does not feel a certain reverence towards him. When friends transgress this sobriety of affection, they may indeed continue associates for a time, but they have broken the bond of union. It is mutual respect which makes friendship lasting. So again, in the feelings of inferiors towards superiors. Fear must go before love. Till he who has authority shows he has it and can use it, his forbearance will not be valued duly; his kindness will look like weakness. We learn to condemn what we do not fear; and we cannot love what we condemn. So in religion also. We cannot understand Christ's mercies till we understand His power, His glory, His unspeakable holiness, and our demerits; that is, until we first fear Him. Not that fear comes first, and then love; for the most part they will proceed together. Fear is allayed by the love of Him, and our love sobered by our fear of Him. Thus He draws us on with encouraging voice amid the terrors of His threatenings. As in the young ruler's case, He loves us, yet speaks harshly to us that we may learn to cherish mixed feelings towards Him. He hides Himself from us, and yet calls us on, that we may hear His voice as Samuel did, and, believing, approach Him with trembling. This may seem strange to those who do not study the Scriptures, and to those who do not know what it is earnestly to seek after God. But in proportion as the state of mind is strange, so is there in it, therefore, untold and surpassing pleasure to those who partake it. The bitter and the sweet, strangely tempered, thus leave upon the mind the lasting taste of Divine Truth, and satisfy it; not so harsh as to be loathed; nor of that insipid sweetness which attends enthusiastic feelings, and is wearisome when it becomes familiar. Such is the feeling of conscience too, God's original gift; how painful! yet who would lose it? "I opened my mouth and panted, for I longed for Thy commandments."33 This is David's account of it. Ezekiel describes something of the same feeling when the Spirit lifted him up and took him away "and he went in bitterness, in the heat of his spirit," "the hand of the Lord" being "strong upon him."34

Now how does this apply to us here assembled? Are we in danger of speaking or thinking of Christ irreverently? I do not think we are in any immediate danger of deliberate profaneness; but we are in great danger of this, viz. first, of allowing ourselves to appear profane, and secondly, of gradually becoming irreverent, while we are pretending to be so. Men do not begin by *intending* to dishonor God; but they are afraid of the ridicule of others: they are ashamed of appearing religious; and thus are led to pretend that they are worse than they really are. They say things which they do not mean; and, by a miserable weakness, allow actions and habits to be imputed to them which they dare not really indulge in. Hence, they affect a liberty of speech which only befits the companions of evil spirits. They take God's name in vain, to show that they can do what devils do, and they invoke the evil spirit, or speak familiarly of all that pertains to him, and deal about curses wantonly, as though they were not firebrands—as if acknowledging the Author of Evil to be their great master and lord. Yes! he *is* a master who allows himself to be served without trembling. It is his very art to lead men to be at ease with him, to think lightly of him, and to trifle with him. He will submit to their ridicule, take (as it were) their blows, and pretend to be their slave, that he may ensnare them. *He* has no dignity to maintain, and he waits his time when his malice shall be gratified. So it has ever been all over the earth. Among all nations it has been his aim to make men laugh at him; going to and fro upon the earth, and walking up and down in it, hearing and rejoicing in that light perpetual talk about him which is his *worship*.

Now, it is not to be supposed that all this careless language can be continued without its affecting a man's heart at last; and this is the second danger I spoke of. Through a false shame, we disown religion with our lips, and next our words affect our thoughts. Men at last become the cold, indifferent, profane characters they professed themselves to be. They think contemptuously of God's Ministers, Sacraments, and Worship; they slight His Word, rarely looking into it, and never studying it. They undervalue all religious profession, and judging of others by themselves, impute the conscientious conduct they witness to bad motives. Thus they are in heart infidels; though they may not formally be such, and may attempt to disguise their own unbelief under pretense of objecting to one or other of the doctrines or ordinances of religion. And should a time of temptation come, when it would be *safe* to show themselves as they really are, they will (almost unawares) throw off their profession of Christianity, and join themselves to the scoffing world.

And how must Christians, on the other hand, treat such heartless men? They have our Lord's example to imitate. Not that they dare precisely follow the conduct of Him who had no sin. They dare not assume to themselves any honor on their own account; and they are bound, especially if they are His Ministers, to humble themselves as the Apostles did and "going out to the highways and hedges (as it were), compel"[35] men to be saved. Yet, while they use greater earnestness of entreaty than their Lord, they must not forget His dignity the while, who sends them. He manifested His love towards us, "in deed and in truth," and we, His Ministers, declare it in word; yet for the very reason that it is so abundant, we must in very gratitude learn reverence towards Him. We must not take advantage (so to say) of His goodness; or misuse the powers committed to us. Never must we solicitously press the truth upon those who do not profit by what they already possess. It dishonors Christ, while it does the scorner harm, not good. It is casting pearls before swine. We must wait for all opportunities of being useful to men, but beware of attempting too much at once. We must impart the Scripture doctrines, in measure and season, as they can bear them; not being eager to recount them all, rather, hiding them from the world. Seldom must we engage in controversy or dispute; for it lowers the sacred truths to make them a subject for ordinary debate. Common propriety suggests rules like these at once. Who would speak freely about some revered friend in the presence of those who did not value him? or who would think he could with a few words overcome their indifference towards him? or who would hastily dispute about him when his hearers had no desire to be made to love him?

Rather, shunning all intemperate words, let us show our light before men by our *works*. Here we must be safe. In doing justice, showing mercy, speaking the truth, resisting sin, obeying the Church—in thus glorifying God, there can be no irreverence. And, above all, let us look at home, check all bad thoughts, presumptuous imaginings, vain desires, discontented murmurings, self-complacent reflections, and so in our hearts ever honor Him in secret, whom we reverence by open profession.

May God guide us in a dangerous world; and deliver us from evil. And may He rouse to serious thought, by the power of His Spirit, all who are living in profaneness or unconcern!

[I, 23]

Chapter 7
CHRISTIAN MANHOOD

When I was a child, I spake as a child, I understood as a child, I thought as a child; but when I became a man, I put away childish things.
— 1 Cor. 13:11

When our Lord was going to leave the world and return to his Father, He called His disciples *orphans;* children, as it were, whom He had been rearing, who were still unable to direct themselves, and who were soon to lose their Protector; but He said, "I will not leave you comfortless orphans, I will come to you";[36] meaning to say, He would come again to them in the power of His Holy Spirit, who should be their present all-sufficient Guide, though He Himself was away. And we know, from the sacred history, that when the Holy Spirit came, they ceased to be the defenseless children they had been before. He breathed into them a divine life, and gifted them with spiritual manhood, or *perfection,* as it is called in Scripture. From that time forth, they put away childish things; they spake, they understood, they thought, as those who had been taught to govern themselves; and who, having "an unction from the Holy One, knew all things."

That such a change was wrought in the Apostles, according to Christ's promise, is evident from comparing their conduct *before* the day of Pentecost, when the Holy Spirit descended on them, and *after.* I need not enlarge on their wonderful firmness and zeal in their Master's cause afterwards. On the other hand, it is plain from the Gospels, that before the Holy Ghost came down, that is, while Christ was still with them, they were as helpless and ignorant as children; had no clear notion what they ought to seek after, and how; and were carried astray by their accidental feelings and their long-cherished prejudices. What was it but to act the child, to ask how many times a fellow Christian should offend against us, and we forgive him, as St. Peter did? or to ask to see the Father, with St. Philip? or to propose to build tabernacles on the mount, as if they were not to return to the troubles of the world? or to dispute who should be the greatest?[37] or to look for Christ's restoring at that time the temporal kingdom to Israel?[38] Natural as such views were in the case of half-instructed Jews, they were evidently unworthy of those whom Christ had made His, that He might "present them perfect" before the throne of God.

Yet the first disciples of Christ at least put off their vanities once for all, when the Spirit came upon them; but as to ourselves, the Spirit has long since been poured upon us, even from our earliest years; yet it is a serious question, whether multitudes of us, even of those among us who make a profession of religion, are even so far advanced in a knowledge of the Truth as the Apostles were before the day of Pentecost. It may be a profitable employment today to consider this question, as suggested by the text, to inquire how far we have proceeded in putting off such childish things as are inconsistent with a manly, honest profession of the Gospel.

Now, observe, I am not inquiring whether we are plainly living in sin, in willful disobedience; nor even whether we are yielding through thoughtlessness to sinful practices and habits. The condition of those who act against their conscience, or who act without conscience, that is, lightly and carelessly, is far indeed from bearing any resemblance to that of the Apostles in the years of their early discipleship. I am supposing you, my brethren, to be on the whole followers of Christ, to profess to obey Him; and I address you as those who seem to themselves to have a fair hope of salvation. I am directing your attention, not to your sins, not to those faults and failings which you know to be such, and are trying to conquer, as being confessedly evil in themselves, but to such of your views, wishes, and tastes, as resemble those which the Apostles cherished, true believers though they were, before they attained their manhood in the Gospel: and I ask, how far you have dismissed these from your minds as vain and trifling; that is, how far you have made what St. Paul in the text seems to consider the first step in the true spiritual course of a Christian, on whom the Holy Ghost has descended.

1. For example, let us consider our love of the pleasures of life. I am willing to allow there is an innocent love of the world, innocent in itself. God made the world, and has sanctioned the general form of human society, and has given us abundant pleasures in it;

I do not say *lasting* pleasures, but still, while they are present, really pleasures. It is natural that the young should look with hope to the prospect before them. They cannot help forming schemes about what they will do when they come into active life, or what they would wish to be, had they their choice. They indulge themselves in fancyings about the future, which they know at the time cannot come true. At other times they confine themselves to what is possible; and then their hearts burn, while they dream of quiet happiness, domestic comfort, independence. Or, with bolder views, they push forward their fortunes into public life, and indulge ambitious hopes. They fancy themselves rising in the world, distinguished, courted, admired; securing influence over others, and rewarded with high station. James and John had such a dream when they besought Christ that they might sit at His side in the most honorable places in His kingdom.

Now such dreams can hardly be called sinful in themselves, and without reference to the particular case; for the gifts of wealth, power, and influence, and much more of domestic comfort, come from God, and may be religiously improved. But, though not directly censurable, they are *childish;* childish either in themselves, or at least when cherished and indulged; childish in a Christian, who has infinitely higher views to engross his mind; and, as being childish, excusable only in the young. They *are* an offense when retained as life goes on; but in the young we may regard them after the pattern of our Savior's judgment upon the young man who was rich and noble. He is said to have "loved him"; pitying (that is) and not harshly denouncing the anticipations which he had formed of happiness from wealth and power, yet withal not concealing from him the sacrifice of all these which he must make, "if he would be perfect," that is, a man, and not a mere child in the Gospel.

2. But there are other childish views and habits besides, which must be put off while we take on ourselves the full profession of a Christian; and these, not so free from intrinsic guilt as those which have been already noticed—such as the love of display, greediness of the world's praise, and the love of the comforts and luxuries of life. These, though wrong tempers of mind, still I do not now call by their hardest names, because I would lead persons, if I could, rather to turn away from them as unworthy a

Christian, with a sort of contempt, outgrowing them as they grow in grace, and laying them aside as a matter of course, while they are gradually learning to "set their affections on things above, not on things of the earth."

Children have evil tempers and idle ways which we do not deign to speak seriously of. Not that we, in any degree, approve them or endure them on their own account; nay, we punish some of them; but we bear them *in* children, and look for their disappearing as the mind becomes more mature. And so in religious matters there are many habits and views, which we bear with in the unformed Christian, but which we account disgraceful and contemptible should they survive that time when a man's character may be supposed to be settled. Love of display is one of these; whether we are vain of our abilities, or our acquirements, or our wealth, or our personal appearance; whether we discover our weakness in talking much, or in love of managing, or again in love of dress. Vanity, indeed, and conceit are always disagreeable, for the reason that they interfere with the comfort of other persons, and vex them; but I am here observing, that they are *in themselves* odious, when discerned in those who enjoy the full privileges of the Church, and are by profession men in Christ Jesus, odious from their inconsistency with Christian faith and earnestness.

And so with respect to the love of worldly comforts and luxuries (which, unhappily, often grows upon us rather than disappears, as we get old), whether or not it be natural in youth, at least, it is (if I may so say) *shocking* in those who profess to be "perfect," if we would estimate things aright; and this from its great incongruity with the spirit of the Gospel. Is it not something beyond measure strange and monstrous (if we could train our hearts to possess a right judgment in all things), to profess that our treasure is not here, but in heaven with Him who is ascended thither, and to own that we have a cross to bear after Him, who first suffered before He triumphed; and yet to set ourselves *deliberately* to study our own comfort as some great and sufficient end, to go much out of our way to promote it, to sacrifice anything considerable to guard it, and to be downcast at the prospect of the loss of it? Is it possible for a true son of the Church militant, while "the ark, and Israel, and Judah abide in tents," and the "servants of his Lord are encamped in the open field," to "eat and drink" securely, to wrap himself in the furniture of wealth, to feed his eyes with the "pride of life," and complete for himself the measure of this world's elegancies?

Again, all timidity, irresolution, fear of ridicule, weakness of purpose, such as the Apostles showed when they deserted Christ, and Peter especially when he denied Him, are to be numbered among the tempers of mind which are childish as well as sinful; which we must learn to despise—to be ashamed at ourselves if we are influenced by them, and, instead of thinking the conquest of them a great thing, to account it as one of the very first steps towards being but an ordinary true believer; just as the Apostles, in spite of their former discipleship, only commenced (surely) their Christian course at the day of Pentecost, and then took to themselves a good measure of faith, boldness, zeal, and self-mastery, not as some great proficiency and as a boast, but as the very condition of their being Christians at all, as the elements of spiritual life, as a mere outfitting, and a small attainment indeed in that extended course of sanctification through which the Blessed Spirit is willing to lead every Christian.

Now in this last remark I have given a chief reason for dwelling on the subject before us. It is very common for Christians to make much of what are but petty services; first to place the very substance of religious obedience in a few meager observances, or particular moral precepts which are easily complied with, and which they think fit to call giving up the world; and then to make a great vaunting about their having done what, in truth, everyone who is not a mere child in Christ ought to be able to do, to congratulate themselves upon their success, ostentatiously to return thanks for it, to condemn others who do not happen to move exactly along the very same line of minute practices in detail which they have adopted, and in consequence to forget that, after all, by such poor obedience, right though it be, still they have not approached even to a distant view of that point in their Christian course, at which they may consider themselves, in St. Paul's words, to have "attained" a sure hope of salvation; just as little children, when they first have strength to move their limbs, triumph in every exertion of their newly acquired power, as in some great victory. To put off idle hopes of earthly good, to be sick of flattery and the world's praise, to see the emptiness of tem-

poral greatness, and to be watchful against self-indulgence—
these are but the beginnings of religion; these are but the preparation of heart, which religious earnestness implies; without a good
share of them, how can a Christian move a step? How could
Abraham, when called of God, have even set out from his native
place, unless he had left off to think much of this world, and cared
not for its ridicule? Surely these attainments are but our first
manly robe, showing that childhood is gone; and, if we feel the
love and fear of the world still active within our hearts, deeply
must we be humbled, yes, and alarmed; and humbled even
though but the traces remain of former weaknesses. But even if
otherwise, what thanks have we? See what the Apostles were, by
way of contrast, and then you will see what is the true life of the
Spirit, the substance and full fruit of holiness. To love our
brethren with a resolution which no obstacles can overcome, so as
almost to consent to an anathema on ourselves, if so be we may
save those who hate us; to labor in God's cause against hope, and
in the midst of sufferings; to read the events of life, as they occur,
by the interpretation which Scripture gives them, and that, not as
if the language were strange to us, but to do it promptly; to perform all our relative daily duties most watchfully; to check every
evil thought, and bring the whole mind into captivity to the law
of Christ; to be patient, cheerful, forgiving, meek, honest, and
true; to persevere in this good work till death, making fresh and
fresh advances towards perfection; and after all, even to the end,
to confess ourselves unprofitable servants, nay, to feel ourselves
corrupt and sinful creatures, who (with all our proficiency) would
still be lost unless God bestowed on us His mercy in Christ—
these are some of the difficult realities of religious obedience,
which we must pursue, and which the Apostles in high measure
attained, and which we may well bless God's holy Name, if He
enables us to make our own.

Let us then take it for granted, as a truth which cannot be gain-
said, that to break with the world, and make religion our first
concern, is only to cease to be children; and, again, that in consequence, those Christians who have come to mature years, and yet
do not even so much as this, are "in the presence of the Angels of
God" an odious and unnatural spectacle, a mockery of Christianity. I do not say what such men are in God's sight, and what

are their prospects for the next world, for that is a fearful thought—and we ought to be influenced by motives far higher than that mere slavish dread of future punishment to which such a consideration would lead us.

But here someone may ask, whether I am not speaking severely in urging so many sacrifices at the beginning of true Christian obedience. In conclusion, then, I observe, in the first place, that I have not said a word against the moderate and thankful enjoyment of this life's goods, *when* they actually come in our way; but against the wishing earnestly for them, seeking them, and preferring them to God's righteousness, which is commonly done. Further, I am not excluding from the company of Christians all who cannot at once make up their minds thus vigorously to reject the world, when its goods are dangerous, inexpedient, or unsuitable; but excluding them from the company of mature, manly Christians. Doubtless our Lord deals gently with us. He has put His two Sacraments apart from each other. Baptism first admits us to His favor; His Holy Supper brings us among His perfect ones. He has put from fourteen to twenty years between them, in the ordinary course of things, that we may have time to count the cost, and make our decision calmly. Only there must be no standing still—there cannot be; time goes slowly, yet surely, from birth to the age of manhood, and in like manner, our minds, though slowly formed to love Christ, must still be forming. It is when men are mature in years, and yet are "children in understanding," then they are intolerable, because they have exceeded their season, and are out of place. Then it is that ambitious thoughts, trifling pursuits and amusements, passionate wishes and keen hopes, and the love of display, are directly sinful, because they are by that time deliberate sins. While they were children, "they spake as children, understood, thought as children"; but when they became men, "it was high time to awake out of sleep"; and "put away childish things." And if they have continued children instead of "having their senses exercised to discriminate between the excellent and the base," alas! what deep repentance must be theirs, before they can know what true peace is!—what self-reproach and sharp self-discipline, before their eyes can be opened, to see effectually those truths which are "spiritually discerned"!

So much on the case of those who neglect to grow betimes into the hope of their calling. As to the young themselves, it is plain that nothing I have said can give encouragement to them to acquiesce in their present incomplete devotion of themselves to God, because it will be as much as they can do, even with their best efforts, to make their growth of wisdom and of stature keep pace with each other. And if there be anyone who, as thinking the enjoyments of youth must soon be relinquished, deliberately resolves to make the most of them before the duties of manhood come upon him, such a one, in doing so, is rendering it impossible for him to give them up, when he is called to do so. As for those who allow themselves in what, even in youth, is clearly sinful—the deliberate neglect of prayer, profaneness, riotous living, or other immorality—the case of such persons has not even entered into my mind, when I spoke of youthful thoughtlessness. They, of course, have no "inheritance in the kingdom of Christ and of God."

But if there be those among us, and such there well may be, who, like the young ruler, "worshiping Christ," and "loved" by Him, and obeying His commandments from their youth up, yet cannot but be "sorrowful" at the thought of giving up their pleasant visions, their childish idolatries, and their bright hopes of earthly happiness, such I bid be of good cheer, and take courage. What is it your Savior requires of you, more than will also be exacted from you by that hard and evil master, who desires your ruin? Christ bids you give up the world; but will not, at any rate, the world soon give up you? Can you keep it, by being its slave? Will not he, whose creature of temptation it is, the prince of the world, take it from you, whatever he at present promises? What does your Lord require of you, but to look at all things as they really are, to account them merely as His instruments, and to believe that good is good because He wills it, that He can bless as easily by hard stone as by bread, in the desert as in the fruitful field, if we have faith in Him who gives us the true bread from heaven? Daniel and his friends were princes of the royal house of David; they were "children well-favored, and skillful in all wisdom, cunning in knowledge, and understanding science";[39] yet they had faith to refuse even the literal meat and drink given them, because it was an idol's sacrifice, and God sustained them without it. For ten days of trial they lived on pulse and water; yet "at the end," says the sacred record, "their countenances appeared fairer and fatter in flesh than all the children which did eat the portion of the king's meat." Doubt not, then, His power to bring you through any difficulties, who gives you the command to encounter them. He has showed you the way; He gave up the home of His Mother Mary to "be about His Father's business," and now He but bids you take up after Him the Cross which He bore for you, and "fill up what is wanting of His afflictions in your flesh." Be not afraid—it is but a pang now and then, and a struggle; a covenant with your eyes, and a fasting in the wilderness, some calm habitual watchfulness, and the hearty effort to obey, and all will be well. Be not afraid. He is most gracious, and will bring you on by little and little. He does not show you whither He is leading you; you might be frightened did you see the whole prospect at once. Sufficient for the day is its own evil. Follow His plan; look not on anxiously; look down at your present footing "lest it be turned out of the way," but speculate not about the future. I can well believe that you have hopes now, which you cannot give up, and even which support you in your present course. Be it so; whether they will be fulfilled, or not, is in His hand. He may be pleased to grant the desires of your heart; if so, thank Him for His mercy; only be sure, that all will be for your highest good, and "as thy days, so shall thy strength be. There is none like unto the God of Jeshurun, who rideth upon the heaven in thy help, and in His excellency on the sky. The Eternal God is thy refuge, and underneath are the everlasting arms."[40] He knows no variableness, neither shadow of turning; and when we outgrow our childhood, we but approach, however feebly, to His likeness, who has no youth nor age, who has no passions, no hopes, nor fears, but who loves truth, purity, and mercy, and who is supremely blessed, because He is supremely holy.

Lastly, while we thus think of Him, let us not forget to be up and doing. Let us beware of indulging a mere barren faith and love, which dreams instead of working, and is fastidious when it should be hardy. This is only spiritual childhood in another form; for the Holy Ghost is the Author of active good works, and leads us to the observance of all lowly deeds of ordinary obedience as the most pleasing sacrifice to God.

[I, 26]

Chapter 8

THE INCARNATION

(THE FEAST OF THE NATIVITY OF OUR LORD)

The Word was made flesh, and dwelt among us.
—John 1:14

Thus does the favored Apostle and Evangelist announce to us that Sacred Mystery, which we this day especially commemorate, the incarnation of the Eternal Word. Thus briefly and simply does he speak as if fearing he should fail in fitting reverence. If any there was who might seem to have permission to indulge in words on this subject, it was the beloved disciple, who had heard and seen, and looked upon, and handled the Word of Life; yet, in proportion to the height of his privilege, was his discernment of the infinite distance between him and his Creator. Such too was the temper of the Holy Angels, when the Father "brought in the First-begotten into the world":[41] they straightway worshiped Him. And such was the feeling of awe and love mingled together, which remained for a while in the Church after Angels had announced His coming, and Evangelists had recorded His sojourn here, and His departure; "there was silence as it were for half an hour."[42] Around the Church, indeed, the voices of blasphemy were heard, even as when He hung on the cross; but in the Church there was light and peace, fear, joy, and holy meditation. Lawless doubtings, importunate inquirings, confident reasonings were not. A heartfelt adoration, a practical devotion to the Ever-blessed Son, precluded difficulties in faith, and sheltered the Church from the necessity of speaking.

He who had seen the Lord Jesus with a pure mind, attending Him from the Lake of Gennesareth to Calvary, and from the Sepulchre to Mount Olivet, where He left this scene of His humiliation; he who had been put in charge with His Virgin Mother, and heard from her what she alone could tell of the Mystery to which she had ministered; and they who had heard it from his mouth, and those again whom these had taught, the first generations of the Church, needed no explicit declarations concerning His Sacred Person. Sight and hearing superseded the multitude of words; faith dispensed with the aid of lengthened Creeds and Confessions. There was silence. "The Word was made flesh"; "I believe in Jesus Christ His only Son our Lord"; sentences such as these conveyed everything, yet were officious in nothing. But when the light of His advent faded, and love waxed cold, then there was an opening for objection and discussion, and a difficulty in answering. Then misconceptions had to be explained, doubts allayed, questions set at rest, innovators silenced. Christians were forced to speak against their will, lest heretics should speak instead of them.

Such is the difference between our own state and that of the early Church, which the present Festival especially brings to mind. In the New Testament we find the doctrine of the Incarnation announced clearly indeed, but with a reverent brevity. "The Word was made flesh." "God was manifest in the flesh." "God was in Christ." "Unto us a Child is born, the mighty God." "Christ, over all, God, blessed forever." "My Lord and my God." "I am Alpha and Omega, the beginning and the ending, the Almighty." "The Son of God, the brightness of His glory, and the express image of His person."[43] But we are obliged to speak more at length in the Creeds and in our teaching, to meet the perverse ingenuity of those who, when the Apostles were removed, could with impunity insult and misinterpret the letter of their writings.

Nay, further, so circumstanced are we, as to be obliged not only thus to guard the Truth, but even to give the reason of our guarding it. For they who would steal away the Lord from us, not content with forcing us to measures of protection, even go on to bring us to account for adopting them; and demand that we should put aside whatever stands between them and their heretical purposes. Therefore it is necessary to state clearly, as I have already done, why the Church has lengthened her statements of Christian doctrine. Another reason of these statements is as follows: time having proceeded, and the true traditions of our Lord's ministry being lost to us, the Object of our faith is but faintly reflected on our minds, compared with the vivid picture which His presence impressed upon the early Christians. True is it the Gospels will do very much by way of realizing for us the incarnation of the Son of

God, if studied in faith and love. But the Creeds are an additional help this way. The declarations made in them, the distinctions, cautions, and the like, supported and illuminated by Scripture, draw down, as it were, from heaven, the image of Him who is on God's right hand, preserve us from an indolent use of words without apprehending them, and rouse in us those mingled feelings of fear and confidence, affection and devotion towards Him, which are implied in the belief of a personal advent of God in our nature, and which were originally derived to the Church from the very sight of Him.

And we may say further still, these statements—such, for instance, as occur in the Te Deum and Athanasian Creed—are especially suitable in divine worship, inasmuch as they kindle and elevate the religious affections. They are hymns of praise and thanksgiving; they give glory to God as revealed in the Gospel, just as David's Psalms magnify His Attributes as displayed in nature, His wonderful works in the creation of the world, and His mercies towards the house of Israel.

With these objects, then, it may be useful, on today's Festival, to call your attention to the Catholic doctrine of the Incarnation.

The Word was from the beginning, the Only-begotten Son of God. Before all worlds were created, while as yet time was not, He was in existence, in the bosom of the Eternal Father, God from God, and Light from Light, supremely blessed in knowing and being known of Him, and receiving all divine perfections from Him, yet ever One with Him who begat Him. As it is said in the opening of the Gospel: "In the beginning was the Word, and the Word was with God, and the Word was God." If we may dare conjecture, He is called the Word of God, as mediating between the Father and all creatures; bringing them into being, fashioning them, giving the world its laws, imparting reason and conscience to creatures of a higher order, and revealing to them in due season the knowledge of God's will. And to us Christians He is especially the Word in that great mystery commemorated today, whereby He became flesh, and redeemed us from a state of sin.

He, indeed, when man fell, might have remained in the glory which He had with the Father before the world was. But that unsearchable Love, which showed itself in our original creation, rested not content with a frustrated work, but brought Him down again from His Father's bosom to do His will, and repair the evil which sin had caused. And with a wonderful condescension He came, not as before in power, but in weakness, in the form of a servant, in the likeness of that fallen creature whom He purposed to restore. So He humbled Himself; suffering all the infirmities of our nature in the likeness of sinful flesh, all but a sinner—pure from all sin, yet subjected to all temptation—and at length becoming obedient unto death, even the death of the Cross.

I have said that when the Only-begotten Son stooped to take upon Him our nature, He had no fellowship with sin. It was impossible that He should. Therefore, since our nature was corrupt since Adam's fall, He did not come in the way of nature, He did not clothe Himself in that corrupt flesh which Adam's race inherits. He came by miracle, so as to take on Him our imperfection without having any share in our sinfulness. He was not born as other men are; for "that which is born of the flesh is flesh."[44]

All Adam's children are children of wrath; so our Lord came as the Son of Man, but not the son of sinful Adam. He had no earthly father; He abhorred to have one. The thought may not be suffered that He should have been the son of shame and guilt. He came by a new and living way; not, indeed, formed out of the ground, as Adam was at the first, lest He should miss the participation of our nature, but selecting and purifying unto Himself a tabernacle out of that which existed. As in the beginning, woman was formed out of man by Almighty power, so now, by a like mystery, but a reverse order, the new Adam was fashioned from the woman. He was, as had been foretold, the immaculate "seed of the woman," deriving His manhood from the substance of the Virgin Mary; as it is expressed in the articles of the Creed, "conceived by the Holy Ghost, born of the Virgin Mary."

Thus the Son of God became the Son of Man; mortal, but not a sinner; heir of our infirmities, not of our guiltiness; the offspring of the old race, yet "the beginning of the" new "creation of God." Mary, His Mother, was a sinner as others, and born of sinners; but she was set apart, "as a garden enclosed, a spring shut up, a fountain sealed," to yield a created nature to Him who was her Creator. Thus He came into this world, not in the clouds of heaven, but born into it, born of a woman; He, the Son of Mary, and she (if it may be said), the mother of God. Thus He came, selecting and setting apart for Himself the elements of body and soul; then, uniting them to Himself from their first origin of existence, pervading them, hallowing them by His own Divinity, spiritualizing them, and filling them with light and purity, the while they continued to be human, and for a time mortal and exposed to infirmity. And, as they grow from day to day in their holy union, His Eternal Essence still was one with them, exalting them, acting in them, manifesting Itself through them, so that He was truly God and Man, One Person—as we are soul and body, yet one man, so truly God and man are not two, but One Christ. Thus did the Son of God enter this mortal world; and when He had reached man's estate, He began His ministry, preached the Gospel, chose His Apostles, suffered on the Cross, died, and was buried, rose again, and ascended on high, there to reign till the day when He comes again to judge the world. This is the All-gracious Mystery of the Incarnation, good to look into, good to adore; according to the saying in the text, "The Word was made flesh, and dwelt among us."

The brief account thus given of the Catholic doctrine of the Incarnation of the Eternal Word, may be made more distinct by referring to some of those modes mentioned in Scripture, in which God has at diverse times condescended to manifest Himself in His creatures, which come short of it.

1. God was in the Prophets, but not as He was in Christ. The divine authority, and in one sense, name, may be given to His Ministers, considered as His representatives. Moses says to the Israelites, "Your murmurings are not against us, but against the Lord." And St. Paul, "He therefore that despiseth, despiseth not man, but God."[45] In this sense, Rulers and Judges are sometimes called gods, as our Lord Himself says.

And further, the Prophets were inspired. Thus John the Baptist is said to have been filled with the Holy Ghost from his mother's womb. Zacharias was filled with the Holy Ghost, and prophesied. In like manner the Holy Ghost came on the Apostles at Pentecost and at other times; and so wonderfully gifted was St. Paul, that "from his body were brought unto the sick handkerchiefs or aprons, and the diseases departed from them, and the evil spirits went out of them."[46] Now the characteristic of this miraculous inspiration was, that the presence of God came and went. Thus we read, in the aforementioned and similar narratives, of the Prophet or Apostle being *filled* with the Spirit on particular occasions; as again of "the Spirit of the Lord departing from Saul," and an evil spirit troubling him. Thus this divine inspiration was so far parallel to demoniacal possession. We find in the Gospels the devil speaking with the voice of his victim, so that the tormentor and the tormented could not be distinguished from each other. They seemed to be one and the same, though they were not; as appeared when Christ and His Apostles cast the devil out. And so again the Jewish Temple was in one sense inhabited by the presence of God, which came down upon it at Solomon's Prayer. This was a type of our Lord's manhood dwelt in by the Word of God as a Temple; still, with this essential difference, that the Jewish Temple was perishable, and again the Divine Presence might recede from it. There was no real unity between the one and the other; they were separable. But Christ says to the Jews of His own body, "Destroy this Temple and I will raise it in three days," implying in these words such a unity between the Godhead and the manhood, that there could be no real separation, no dissolution. Even when His body was dead, the Divine Nature was one with it; in like manner it was one with His soul in paradise. Soul and body were really one with the Eternal Word—not one in name only—one never to be divided. Therefore Scripture says that He rose again "according to the Spirit of holiness"; and "that it was not possible that He should be holden of death."47

2. Again, the Gospel teaches us another mode in which man may be said to be united with Almighty God. It is the peculiar blessedness of the Christian, as St. Peter tells us, to be "partaker of the Divine Nature."48 We believe, and have joy in believing, that the grace of Christ renews our carnal souls, repairing the effects of Adam's fall. Where Adam brought in impurity and unbelief, the power of God infuses faith and holiness. Thus we have God's perfections communicated to us anew, and, as being under immediate heavenly influences, are said to be one with God. And further, we are assured of some real though mystical fellowship with the Father, Son, and Holy Spirit, in order to this: so that both by a real presence in the soul, and by the fruits of grace, God is one with every believer, as in a consecrated Temple. But still, inex-

pressible as is this gift of Divine Mercy, it were blasphemy not to
say that the indwelling of the Father in the Son is infinitely above
this, being quite different in kind; for He is not merely of a divine
nature, divine by participation of holiness and perfection, but Life
and Holiness itself, such as the Father is, the Co-eternal Son
incarnate, God clothed with our nature, the Word made flesh.

3. And lastly, we read in the Patriarchal History of various
appearances of Angels so remarkable that we can scarcely hesitate
to suppose them to be gracious visions of the Eternal Son. For
instance, it is said that "the Angel of the Lord appeared unto"
Moses "in a flame of fire out of the midst of a bush"; yet presently
this supernatural Presence is called "the Lord," and afterwards
reveals His name to Moses, as the "God of Abraham, Isaac, and
Jacob." On the other hand, St. Stephen speaks of Him as "the
Angel which appeared to Moses in the bush." Again, he says soon
after, that Moses was "in the Church in the wilderness with the
Angel which spake to him in the mount Sinai"; yet in the Book of
Exodus we read, "Moses went up unto God, and the Lord called
unto him out of the mountain"; "God spake all these words saying";[49] and the like. Now, assuming, as we seem to have reason to
assume, that the Son of God is herein revealed to us as graciously
ministering to the Patriarchs, Moses, and others, in angelic form,
the question arises, what was the nature of this appearance? We
are not informed, nor may we venture to determine; still, anyhow, the Angel was but the temporary outward form which the
Eternal Word assumed, whether it was of a material nature, or a
vision. Whether or not it was really an Angel, or but an appearance existing only for the immediate purpose, still, anyhow, we
could not with propriety say that our Lord "took upon Him the
nature of Angels."

Now these instances of the indwelling of Almighty God in a
created substance, which I have given by way of contrast to that
infinitely higher and mysterious union which is called the Incarnation, actually supply the senses in which heretics at various
times have perverted our holy and comfortable doctrine, and
which have obliged us to have recourse to Creeds and Confessions. Rejecting the teaching of the Church, and dealing rudely
with the Word of God, they have ventured to deny that "Jesus
Christ is come in the flesh," pretending He merely showed Him-

self as a vision or phantom; or they have said that the Word of God merely dwelt in the man Christ Jesus, as the Shechinah in the Temple, having no real union with the Son of Mary (as if there were two distinct Beings, the Word and Jesus, even as the blessed Spirit is distinct from a man's soul); or that Christ was called God for His great spiritual perfections, and that He gradually attained them by long practice. All these are words not to be uttered, except to show what the true doctrine is, and what is the meaning of the language of the Church concerning it. For instance, the Athanasian Creed confesses that Christ is "God of the substance of the Father, begotten before the worlds, perfect God," lest we should consider His Divine Nature, like ours, as merely a nature resembling God's holiness: that He is "Man of the substance of His Mother, born in the world, perfect man," lest we should think of Him as "not come in the flesh," a mere Angelic vision; and that "although He be God and man, yet He is not two, but one Christ," lest we should fancy that the Word of God entered into Him and then departed, as the Holy Ghost in the Prophets.

Such are the terms in which we are constrained to speak of our Lord and Savior, by the craftiness of His enemies and our own infirmity; and we entreat His leave to do so. We entreat His leave, not as if forgetting that a reverent silence is best on so sacred a subject; but, when evil men and seducers abound on every side, and our own apprehensions of the Truth are dull, using zealous David's argument, "Is there not a cause" for words? We entreat His leave, and we humbly pray that what was first our defense against pride and indolence, may become an outlet of devotion, a service of worship. Nay, we surely trust that He will accept mercifully what we offer in faith, "doing what we can"; though the ointment of spikenard which we pour out is nothing to that true Divine Glory which manifested itself in Him, when the Holy Ghost singled Him out from other men, and the Father's voice acknowledged Him as His dearly beloved Son. Surely He will mercifully accept it, if faith offers what the intellect provides; if love kindles the sacrifice, zeal fans it, and reverence guards it. He will illuminate our earthly words from His own Divine Holiness, till they become saving truths to the souls which trust in Him. He who turned water into wine, and (did He so choose) could make bread of the hard stone, will sustain us for a brief season on this mortal fare. And we, while we make use of it, will never so forget its imperfection, as not to look out constantly for the True Beatific Vision; never so perversely remember that imperfection as to reject what is necessary for our present need. The time will come, if we be found worthy, when we, who now see in a glass darkly, shall see our Lord and Savior face to face; shall behold His countenance beaming with the fullness of Divine Perfections, and bearing its own witness that He is the Son of God. We shall see Him as He is.

Let us then, according to the light given us, praise and bless Him in the Church below, whom Angels in heaven see and adore. Let us bless Him for His surpassing loving-kindness in taking upon Him our infirmities to redeem us, when He dwelt in the innermost love of the Everlasting Father, in the glory which He had with Him before the world was. He came in lowliness and want; born amid the tumults of a mixed and busy multitude, cast aside into the outhouse of a crowded inn, laid to His first rest among the brute cattle. He grew up, as if the native of a despised city, and was bred to a humble craft. He bore to live in a world that slighted Him, for He lived in it, in order in due time to die for it. He came as the appointed Priest, to offer sacrifice for those who took no part in the act of worship; He came to offer up for sinners that precious blood which was meritorious by virtue of His Divine Anointing. He died, to rise again the third day, the Sun of Righteousness, fully displaying that splendor which had hitherto been concealed by the morning clouds. He rose again, to ascend to the right hand of God, there to plead His sacred wounds in token of our forgiveness, to rule and guide His ransomed people, and from His pierced side to pour forth His choicest blessings upon them. He ascended, thence to descend again in due season to judge the world which He has redeemed. Great is our Lord, and great is His power, Jesus the Son of God and Son of Man. Ten thousand times more dazzling bright than the highest Archangel, is our Lord and Christ. By birth the Only-begotten and Express image of God; and in taking our flesh, not sullied thereby, but raising human nature with Him, as He rose from the lowly manger to the right hand of power, raising human nature, for Man has redeemed us, Man is set above all creatures, as one with the Creator, Man shall judge man at the last day. So honored is this earth, that no stranger shall judge us, but He who is our fellow, who will sustain our interests, and has full sympathy in all our imperfections. He who loved us, even to die for us, is graciously appointed to assign the final measurement and price upon His own work. He who best knows by infirmity to take the part of the infirm, He who would fain reap the full fruit of His Passion, He will separate the wheat from the chaff, so that not a grain shall fall to the ground. He who has given us to share His own spiritual nature, He from whom we have drawn the life's blood of our souls, He our brother will decide about His brethren. In that His second coming, may He in His grace and loving pity remember us, who is our only hope, our only salvation!

[II, 3]

Chapter 9

LOVE OF RELATIONS AND FRIENDS

(FEAST OF ST. JOHN THE EVANGELIST)

Beloved, let us love one another, for love is of God.
—1 John 4:7

St. John the Apostle and Evangelist is chiefly and most familiarly known to us as "the disciple whom Jesus loved." He was one of the three or four who always attended our Blessed Lord, and had the privilege of the most intimate intercourse with Him; and, more favored than Peter, James, and Andrew, he was His bosom friend, as we commonly express ourselves. At the solemn supper before Christ suffered, he took his place next [to] Him, and leaned on His breast. As the other three communicated between the multitude and Christ, so St. John communicated between Christ and them. At that Last Supper, Peter dared not ask Jesus a question himself, but bade John put it to Him—who it was that should betray Him. Thus St. John was the private and intimate friend of Christ. Again, it was to St. John that our Lord committed His Mother, when He was dying on the Cross; it was to St. John that He revealed in vision after His departure the fortunes of His Church.

Much might be said on this remarkable circumstance. I say *remarkable,* because it might be supposed that the Son of God Most High could not have loved one man more than another; or again, if so, that He would not have had only one friend, but, as being All-holy, He would have loved all men more or less, in proportion to their holiness. Yet we find our Savior had a private friend; and this shows us, first, how entirely He was a man, as much as any of us, in His wants and feelings; and next, that there is nothing contrary to the spirit of the Gospel, nothing inconsistent with the fullness of Christian love, in having our affections directed in an especial way towards certain objects, towards those whom the circumstances of our past life, or some peculiarities of character, have endeared to us.

There have been men before now, who have supposed Christian love was so diffusive as not to admit of concentration upon individuals; so that we ought to love all men equally. And many there are, who, without bringing forward any theory, yet consider practically that the love of many is something superior to the love of one or two; and neglect the charities of private life, while busy in the schemes of an expansive benevolence, or of effecting a general union and conciliation among Christians. Now I shall here maintain, in opposition to such notions of Christian love, and with our Savior's pattern before me, that the best preparation for loving the world at large, and loving it duly and wisely, is to cultivate an intimate friendship and affection towards those who are immediately about us.

It has been the plan of Divine Providence to ground what is good and true in religion and morals, on the basis of our good natural feelings. What we are towards our earthly friends in the instincts and wishes of our infancy, such we are to become at length towards God and man in the extended field of our duties as accountable beings. To honor our parents is the first step towards honoring God; to love our brethren according to the flesh, the first step towards considering all men our brethren. Hence our Lord says, we must become as little children, if we would be saved; we must become in His Church, as men, what we were once in the small circle of our youthful homes. Consider how many other virtues are grafted upon natural feelings. What is Christian high-mindedness, generous self-denial, contempt of wealth, endurance of suffering, and earnest striving after perfection, but an improvement and transformation, under the influence of the Holy Spirit, of that natural character of mind which we call romantic? On the other hand, what is the instinctive hatred and abomination of sin (which confirmed Christians possess), their dissatisfaction with themselves, their general refinement, discrimination, and caution, but an improvement, under the same Spirit, of their natural sensitiveness and delicacy, fear of pain, and sense of shame? They have been chastised into self-government, by a fitting discipline, and now associate an acute sense of discomfort and annoyance with the notion of sinning. And so of the love of our fellow Christians and of the world at large, it is the love of kindred and friends in a fresh shape, which has this use, if it had no other, that it is the natural branch on which a spiritual fruit is grafted.

But again, the love of our private friends is the only preparatory exercise for the love of all men. The love of God is not the same thing as the love of our parents, though parallel to it; but the love of mankind in general should be in the main the same habit as the love of our friends, only exercised towards different objects. The great difficulty in our religious duties is their extent. This frightens and perplexes men—naturally; those especially who have neglected religion for a while, and on whom its obligations disclose themselves all at once. This, for example, is the great misery of leaving repentance till a man is in weakness or sickness; he does not know how to set about it. Now God's merciful Providence has in the natural course of things narrowed for us at first this large field of duty; He has given us a clue. We are to begin with loving our friends about us, and gradually to enlarge the circle of our affections, till it reaches all Christians, and then all men. Besides, it is obviously impossible to love all men in any strict and true sense. What is meant by loving all men, is, to feel well-disposed to all men, to be ready to assist them, and to act towards those who come in our way, as if we loved them. We cannot love those about whom we know nothing; except indeed we view them in Christ, as the objects of His Atonement, that is, rather in faith than in love. And love, besides, is a habit, and cannot be attained without actual *practice,* which on so large a scale is impossible. We see then how absurd it is when writers (as is the manner of some who slight the Gospel) talk magnificently about loving the whole human race with a comprehensive affection, of being the friends of all mankind, and the like. Such vaunting professions, what do they come to? that such men have certain benevolent *feelings* towards the world, feelings and nothing more; nothing more than unstable feelings, the mere offspring of an indulged imagination, which exist only when their minds are wrought upon, and are sure to fail them in the hour of need. This is not to love men, it is but to talk about love. The real love of man *must* depend on practice, and therefore, must begin by exercising itself on our friends around us, otherwise it will have no existence. By trying to love our relations and friends, by submitting to their wishes, though contrary to our own, by bearing with their infirmities, by overcoming their occasional waywardness by kindness, by dwelling on their excellences, and trying to copy them, thus it is that we form in our hearts that root of charity, which, though small at first, may, like the mustard seed, at last even overshadow the earth. The vain talkers about philanthropy, just spoken of, usually show the emptiness of their profession, by being morose and cruel in the private relations of life, which they seem to account as subjects beneath their notice. Far different indeed, far different (unless it be a sort of irreverence to contrast such dreamers with the great Apostle, whose memory we are today celebrating), utterly the reverse of this fictitious benevolence was his elevated and enlightened sympathy for all men. We know he is celebrated for his declarations about Christian love. "Beloved, let us love one another, for love is of God. If we love one another, God dwelleth in us, and His love is perfected in us. God is love, and he that dwelleth in love dwelleth in God, and God in him."[50] Now did he begin with some vast effort at loving on a large scale? Nay, he had the unspeakable privilege of being the *friend of Christ*. Thus he was taught to love others; first his affection was concentrated, then it was expanded. Next he had the solemn and comfortable charge of tending our Lord's Mother, the Blessed Virgin, after His departure. Do we not here discern the secret sources of his especial love of the brethren? Could he, who first was favored with his Savior's affection, then trusted with a son's office towards His Mother, could he be other than a memorial and pattern (as far as man can be), of love, deep, contemplative, fervent, unruffled, unbounded?

Further, that love of friends and relations, which nature prescribes, is also of use to the Christian, in giving form and direction to his love of mankind at large, and making it intelligent and discriminating. A man, who would fain begin by a general love of all men, necessarily puts them all on a level, and, instead of being cautious, prudent, and sympathizing in his benevolence, is hasty and rude; does harm, perhaps, when he means to do good, discourages the virtuous and well-meaning, and wounds the feelings of the gentle. Men of ambitious and ardent minds, for example, desirous of doing good on a large scale, are especially exposed to the temptation of sacrificing individual to general good in their plans of charity. Ill-instructed men, who have strong abstract notions about the necessity of showing generosity and candor towards opponents, often forget to take any thought of those who are associated with themselves; and commence their (so-called) liberal treatment of their enemies by an unkind desertion of their friends. This can hardly be the case when men cultivate the private charities as an introduction to more enlarged ones. By laying a foundation of social amiableness, we insensibly learn to observe a due harmony and order in our charity; we learn that all men are not on a level; that the interests of truth and holiness must be religiously observed; and that the Church has claims on us before the world. We can easily afford to be liberal on a large scale, when we have no affections to stand in the way. Those who have not accustomed themselves to love their neighbors whom they have seen, will have nothing to lose or gain, nothing to grieve at or rejoice in, in their larger plans of benevolence. They will take no interest in them for their own sake; rather, they will engage in them because expedience demands, or credit is gained, or an excuse found for being busy. Hence too we discern how it is, that private virtue is the only sure foundation of public virtue; and that no national good is to be expected (though it may now and then accrue), from men who have not the fear of God before their eyes.

I have hitherto considered the cultivation of domestic affections as the *source* of more extended Christian love. Did time permit, I might now go on to show, besides, that they involve a real and difficult exercise of it. Nothing is more likely to engender selfish habits (which is the direct opposite and negation of charity), than *independence* in our worldly circumstances. Men who have no tie on them, who have no calls on their daily sympathy and tenderness, who have no one's comfort to consult, who can move about as they please, and indulge the love of variety and the restless humors which are so congenial to the minds of most men, are very unfavorably situated for obtaining that heavenly gift, which is described in our Liturgy, as being "the very bond of peace and of all virtues." On the other hand, I cannot fancy any state of life more favorable for the exercise of high Christian principle, and the matured and refined Christian spirit (that is, where the parties really seek to do their duty), than that of persons who differ in tastes and general character, being obliged by circumstances to live together, and mutually to accommodate to each other their respective wishes and pursuits. And this is one among the many providential benefits (to those who will receive them) arising out of the Holy Estate of Matrimony; which not only calls out the tenderest and gentlest feelings of our nature, but, where persons do their duty, must be in various ways more or less a state of self-denial.

Or, again, I might go on to consider the private charities, which have been my subject, not only as the sources and as the discipline of Christian love, but further, as the *perfection* of it; which they are in some cases. The Ancients thought so much of friendship, that they made it a *virtue*. In a Christian view, it is not quite this; but it is often accidentally a special *test* of our virtue. For consider: let us say that this man, and that, not bound by any very necessary tie, find their greatest pleasure in living together; say that this continues for years, and that they love each other's society the more, the longer they enjoy it. Now observe what is implied in this. Young people, indeed, readily love each other, for they are cheerful and innocent; more easily yield to each other, and are full of hope— types, as Christ says, of His true converts. But this happiness does not last; their tastes change. Again, grown persons go on for years as friends; but these do not live together; and, if any accident throws them into familiarity for a while, they find it difficult to restrain their tempers and keep on terms, and discover that they are best friends at a distance. But what is it that can bind two friends together in intimate converse for a course of years, but the participation in something that is Unchangeable and essentially Good, and what is this but religion? Religious tastes alone are unalterable. The Saints of God continue in one way, while the fashions of the world change; and a faithful indestructible friendship may thus be a test of the parties, so loving each other, having the love of God seated deep in their hearts. Not an infallible test certainly; for they may have dispositions remarkably the same, or some engrossing object of this world, literary or other; they may be removed from the temptation to change, or they may have a natural sobriety of temper, which remains contented wherever it finds itself. However, under certain circumstances, it is a lively token of the presence of Divine grace in them; and it is always a sort of symbol of it, for there is at first sight something of the nature of virtue in the very notion of constancy, dislike of change being not only the characteristic of a virtuous mind, but in some sense a virtue itself.

And now I have suggested to you a subject of thought for today's Festival, and surely a very practical subject, when we consider how large a portion of our duties lies at home. Should God call upon us to preach to the world, surely we must obey His call; but at present, let us do what lies before us. Little children, let us love one another. Let us be meek and gentle; let us think before we speak; let us try to improve our talents in private life; let us do good, not hoping for a return, and avoiding all display before men. Well may I so exhort you at this season, when we have so lately partaken together the Blessed Sacrament which binds us to mutual love, and gives us strength to practice it. Let us not forget the promise we then made, or the grace we then received. We are not our own; we are bought with the blood of Christ; we are consecrated to be temples of the Holy Spirit, an unutterable privilege, which is weighty enough to sink us with shame at our unworthiness, did it not the while strengthen us by the aid itself imparts, to bear its extreme costliness. May we live worthy of our calling, and realize in our own persons the Church's prayers and professions for us!

[II, 5]

Chapter 10

CHRIST, A QUICKENING SPIRIT

(The Feast of the Resurrection of Our Lord)

Why seek ye the living among the dead? He is not here, but is risen.
—Luke 24:5, 6

Such is the triumphant question with which the Holy Angels put to flight the sadness of the women on the morning of Christ's resurrection. "O ye of little faith," less faith than love, more dutiful than understanding, why come ye to anoint His Body on the third day? Why seek ye the Living Savior in the tomb? The time of sorrow is run out; victory has come, according to His Word, and ye recollect it not. "He is not here, but is risen!"

These were deeds done and words spoken eighteen hundred years since; so long ago, that in the world's thought they are as though they never had been; yet they hold good to this day. Christ is to us now, just what He was in all His glorious Attributes on the morning of the Resurrection; and we are blessed in knowing it, even more than the women to whom the Angels spoke, according to His own assurance, "Blessed are they that have not seen, and yet have believed."

On this highest of Festivals, I will attempt to set before you one out of the many comfortable subjects of reflection which it suggests.

1. First, then, observe how Christ's resurrection harmonizes with the history of His birth. David had foretold that His "soul should not be left in hell" (that is, the unseen state), neither should "the Holy One of God see corruption." And with a reference to this prophecy, St. Peter says, that it "was not possible that He should be holden of death;"[51] as if there were some hidden inherent vigor in Him, which secured His manhood from dissolution. The greatest infliction of pain and violence could only destroy its powers for a season; but nothing could make it decay. "Thou wilt

not suffer Thy *Holy* One to see corruption"; so says the Scripture, and elsewhere calls Him the "*Holy* child Jesus."⁵² These expressions carry our minds back to the Angels' announcement of His birth, in which His incorruptible and immortal nature is implied. "That *Holy* Thing" which was born of Mary, was "the Son," not of man, but "of God." Others have been born in sin, "after Adam's own likeness, in His image,"⁵³ and, being born in sin, they are heirs to corruption. "By one man sin entered into the world, and death," and all its consequences, "by sin." Not one human being comes into existence without God's discerning evidences of sin attendant on his birth. But when the Word of Life was manifested in our flesh, the Holy Ghost displayed that creative hand by which, in the beginning, Eve was formed; and the Holy Child, thus conceived by the power of the Highest, was (as the history shows) immortal even in His mortal nature, clear from all infection of the forbidden fruit, so far as to be sinless and incorruptible. Therefore, though He was liable to death, "it was impossible He should be *holden*" of it. Death might overpower, but it could not keep possession; "it had no dominion over Him."⁵⁴ He was, in the words of the text, "*the Living* among the dead."

And hence His rising from the dead may be said to have evinced His Divine original. He was "*declared* to be the Son of God with power, according to the Spirit of Holiness"; that is, His essential Godhead, "by the resurrection of the dead."⁵⁵ He had been condemned as a blasphemer by the Jewish rulers, "because He made Himself the Son of God"; and He was brought to the death of the Cross, not only as a punishment, but as a practical refutation of His claim. He was challenged by His enemies on this score: "If thou be the Son of God, come down from the cross." Thus His Crucifixion was as though a trial, a new experiment on the part of Satan, who had before tempted Him, whether he was like other men, or the Son of God. Observe the event. He was obedient unto death, fulfilling the law of that disinherited nature which He had assumed; and in order, by undergoing it, to atone for our sins. So far was permitted by God's "determinate counsel and foreknowledge"; but there the triumph of His enemies, so to account it, ended—ended with what was necessary for our redemption. He said, "It is finished"; for His humiliation was at its lowest depth when He expired. Immediately some incipient tokens showed themselves, that the real victory was with Him; first, the earthquake and other wonders in heaven and earth. These even were enough to justify His claim in the judgment of the heathen centurion, who said at once, "Truly this *was* the Son of God." Then followed His descent into hell, and triumph in the unseen world, whatever that was. Lastly, that glorious deed of power on the third morning which we now commemorate. The dead arose. The grave could not detain Him who "had life in Himself." He rose as a man awakes in the morning, when sleep flies from him as a thing of course. Corruption had no power over that Sacred Body, the fruit of a miraculous conception. The bonds of death were broken as "green withes," witnessing by their feebleness that He was the Son of God.

Such is the connection between Christ's birth and resurrection; and more than this might be ventured concerning His incorrupt nature, were it not better to avoid all risk of trespassing upon that reverence with which we are bound to regard it. Something might be said concerning His personal appearance, which seems to have borne the marks of one who was not tainted with birth sin. Men could scarce keep from worshiping Him. When the Pharisees sent to seize Him, all the officers, on His merely acknowledging Himself to be Him whom they sought, fell backwards from His presence to the ground. They were scared as brutes are said to be by the voice of man. Thus, being created in God's image, He was the second Adam; and much more than Adam in His secret nature, which beamed through His tabernacle of flesh with awful purity and brightness even in the days of His humiliation. "The first man was of the earth, earthy; the second man was the Lord from heaven."[56]

2. And if such was His visible Majesty, while He yet was subject to temptation, infirmity, and pain, much more abundant was the manifestation of His Godhead, when He was risen from the dead. Then the Divine Essence streamed forth (so to say) on every side, and environed His Manhood, as in a cloud of glory. So transfigured was His Sacred Body, that He who had deigned to be born of a woman, and to hang upon the Cross, had subtle virtue in Him, like a spirit, to pass through the closed doors to His assembled followers; while, by condescending to the trial of their

senses, He showed that it was no mere spirit, but He Himself, as before, with wounded hands and pierced side, who spoke to them. He manifested Himself to them, in this His exalted state, that they might be His witnesses to the people; witnesses of those separate truths which man's reason cannot combine, that He had a real human body, that it was partaker in the properties of His Soul, and that it was inhabited by the Eternal Word. They handled Him; they saw Him come and go, when the doors were shut; they felt, what they could not see, but could witness even unto death, that He was "their Lord and their God"—a triple evidence, first, of His Atonement; next of their own resurrection unto glory; lastly, of His Divine Power to conduct them safely to it. Thus manifested as perfect God and perfect man, in the fullness of His sovereignty, and the immortality of His holiness, He ascended up on high to take possession of His kingdom. There He remains till the last day, "Wonderful, Counselor, the Mighty God, the Everlasting Father, the Prince of Peace."[57]

3. He ascended into heaven, that He might plead our cause with the Father; as it is said, "He ever liveth to make intercession for us."[58] Yet we must not suppose, that in leaving us He closed the gracious economy of His Incarnation, and withdrew the ministration of His incorruptible Manhood from His work of loving mercy towards us. "The Holy One of God" was ordained, not only to die for us, but also to be "the beginning" of a new "creation" unto holiness, in our sinful race; to refashion soul and body after His own likeness, that they might be "raised up together, and sit together in heavenly places in Christ Jesus." Blessed forever be His Holy Name! before He went away, He remembered our necessity, and completed His work, bequeathing to us a special mode of approaching Him, a Holy Mystery, in which we receive (we know not how) the virtue of that Heavenly Body, which is the life of all that believe. This is the blessed Sacrament of the Eucharist, in which "Christ is evidently set forth crucified among us"; that we, feasting upon the Sacrifice, may be "partakers of the Divine Nature." Let us give heed lest we be in the number of those who "discern not the Lord's Body," and the "exceeding great and precious promises" which are made to those who partake it. And since there is some danger of this, I will here make some brief remarks concerning this great gift; and, pray

God that our words and thoughts may accord to its unspeakable sacredness.

Christ says, "As the Father hath life in Himself; so hath He given also to the Son to have life in Himself"; and afterwards He says, "Because I live, ye shall live also."[59] It would seem then, that as Adam is the author of death to the whole race of men, so is Christ the Origin of immortality. When Adam ate the forbidden fruit, it was as a poison spreading through his whole nature, soul and body; and thence through every one of his descendants. It was said to him, when he was placed in the garden, "In the day that thou eatest thereof, thou shalt surely die"; and we are told expressly, "in Adam *all* die." We all are born heirs to that infection of nature which followed upon his fall. But we are also told, "As in Adam all die, even so in Christ shall all be made alive"; and the same law of God's Providence is maintained in both cases. Adam spreads poison; Christ diffuses life eternal. Christ communicates life to us, one by one, by means of that holy and incorrupt nature which He assumed for our redemption; how, we know not; still, though by an unseen, surely by a real communication of Himself. Therefore St. Paul says, that "the last Adam was made" not merely "a living soul," but "a *quickening*" or life-giving "Spirit," as being "the Lord from heaven."[60] Again, in his own gracious words, He is "the Bread of Life." "The Bread of God is He which cometh down from heaven, and giveth life unto the world"; or, as He says more plainly, "I am the Bread which came down from heaven"; "I am that Bread of Life"; "I am the living Bread which came down from heaven; if any man eat of this bread, he shall live forever: and the Bread that I will give is My flesh, which I will give for the life of the world." And again, still more clearly, "Whoso eateth My flesh, and drinketh My blood, hath eternal life; and I will raise him up at the last day."[61] Why should this communion with Him be thought incredible, mysterious and sacred as it is, when we know from the Gospel how marvelously He wrought, in the days of His humiliation, towards those who approached Him? We are told on one occasion, "the whole multitude sought to touch Him; for there went *virtue* out of Him, and healed them all." Again, when the woman with the issue of blood touched Him, He "immediately knew that virtue had gone out of Him."[62] Such grace was invisible, known only by the cure it effected, as in the case of the woman. Let us not doubt, though we do not sensibly approach Him, that He can still give us the virtue of His purity and incorruption, as He has promised, and in a more heavenly and spiritual manner, than "in the days of His flesh"; in a way which does not remove the mere ailments of this temporal state, but sows the seed of eternal life in body and soul. Let us not deny Him the glory of His life-giving holiness, that diffusive grace which is the renovation of our whole race, a spirit quick and powerful and piercing, so as to leaven the whole mass of human corruption, and make it live. He is the first fruits of the Resurrection: we follow Him each in his own order, as we are hallowed by His inward presence. And in this sense, among others, Christ, in the Scripture phrase, is "formed in us"; that is, the communication is made to us of His new nature, which sanctifies the soul, and makes the body immortal. In like manner we pray in the Service of the Communion that "our sinful bodies may be made clean by His body, and our souls washed through His most precious blood; and that we may evermore dwell in Him and He in us."

Such then is our risen Savior in Himself and towards us: conceived by the Holy Ghost; holy from the womb; dying, but abhorring corruption; rising again the third day by His own inherent life; exalted as the Son of God and Son of Man, to raise us after Him; and filling us incomprehensibly with His immortal nature, till we become like Him; filling us with a spiritual life which may expel the poison of the tree of knowledge, and restore us to God. How wonderful a work of grace! Strange it was that Adam should be our death, but stranger still and very gracious, that God Himself should be our life, by means of that human tabernacle which He has taken on Himself.

O blessed day of the Resurrection, which of old time was called the Queen of Festivals, and raised among Christians an anxious, nay contentious diligence duly to honor it! Blessed day, once only passed in sorrow, when the Lord actually rose, and the disciples believed not; but ever since a day of joy to the faith and love of the Church! In ancient times, Christians all over the world began it with a morning salutation. Each man said to his neighbor, "Christ is risen"; and his neighbor answered him, "Christ is risen indeed, and hath appeared unto Simon." Even to Simon, the coward disciple who denied Him thrice, Christ is risen; even to us, who long ago vowed to obey Him, and have yet so often denied Him before men, so often taken part with sin, and followed the world, when Christ called us another way. "Christ is risen indeed, and hath appeared to Simon!" to Simon Peter the favored Apostle, on whom the Church is built Christ has appeared. He has appeared to His Holy Church first of all, and in the Church He dispenses blessings, such as the world knows not of. Blessed are they if they knew their blessedness, who are allowed, as we are, week after week, and Festival after Festival, to seek and find in that Holy Church the Savior of their souls! Blessed are they beyond language or thought, to whom it is vouchsafed to receive those tokens of His love, which cannot otherwise be gained by man, the pledges and means of His special presence, in the Sacrament of His Supper; who are allowed to eat and drink the food of immortality, and receive life from the bleeding side of the Son of God! Alas! by what strange coldness of heart, or perverse superstition is it, that anyone called Christian keeps away from that heavenly ordinance? Is it not very grievous that there should be anyone who fears to share in the greatest conceivable blessing which could come upon sinful men? What in truth is that fear, but unbelief, a slavish sin-loving obstinacy, if it leads a man to go year after year without the spiritual sustenance which God has provided for him? Is it wonderful that, as time goes on, he should learn deliberately to doubt of the grace therein given? that he should no longer look upon the Lord's Supper as a heavenly feast, or the Lord's Minister who consecrates it as a chosen vessel, or that Holy Church in which he ministers as a Divine ordinance, to be cherished as the parting legacy of Christ to a sinful world? Is it wonderful that seeing he sees not, and hearing he hears not; and that, lightly regarding all the gifts of Christ, he feels no reverence for the treasure house wherein they are stored?

But we, who trust that so far we are doing God's will, inasmuch as we are keeping to those ordinances and rules which His Son has left us, we may humbly rejoice in this day, with a joy the world cannot take away, any more than it can understand. Truly, in this time of rebuke and blasphemy, we cannot but be sober and subdued in our rejoicing; yet our peace and joy may be deeper and fuller even for that very seriousness. For nothing can harm those who bear Christ within them. Trial or temptation, time of tribulation, time of wealth, pain, bereavement, anxiety, sorrow, the insults of the enemy, the loss of worldly goods, nothing can "separate us from the love of God, which is in Christ Jesus our Lord."[63] This the Apostle told us long since; but we, in this age of the world, over and above his word, have the experience of many centuries for our comfort. We have his own history to show us how Christ within us is stronger than the world around us, and will prevail. We have the history of all his fellow sufferers, of all the Confessors and Martyrs of early times and since, to show us that Christ's arm "is not shortened, that it cannot save"; that faith and love have a real abiding place on earth; that, come what will, His grace is sufficient for His Church, and His strength made perfect in weakness; that, "even to old age, and to hoar hairs, He will carry and deliver" her; that, in whatever time the powers of evil give challenge, Martyrs and Saints will start forth again; and rise from the dead, as plentiful as though they had never been before, even "the souls of them that were beheaded for the witness of Jesus, and for the Word of God, and which had not worshiped the beast, neither his image, neither had received his mark upon their foreheads, or in their hands."[64]

Meantime, while Satan only threatens, let us possess our hearts in patience; try to keep quiet; aim at obeying God, in all things, little as well as great; do the duties of our calling which lie before us, day by day; and "take no thought for the morrow, for sufficient unto the day is the evil thereof."[65]

[II, 13]

Chapter II

SAVING KNOWLEDGE

(Monday in Easter Week)

Hereby do we know that we know Him if we keep His commandments.
— 1 John 2:3

To know God and Christ, in Scripture language, seems to mean to live under the conviction of His presence, who is to our bodily eyes unseen. It is, in fact, to have faith, according to St. Paul's account of faith, as the substance and evidence of what is invisible. It is faith, but not faith such as a heathen might have, but Gospel faith; for only in the Gospel has God so revealed Himself, as to allow of that kind of faith which may be called, in a special manner, knowledge. The faith of heathens was *blind;* it was more or less a moving forward in the darkness, with hand and foot; therefore the Apostle says, "if haply they might *feel* after Him."[66] But the Gospel is a *manifestation,* and therefore addressed to the eyes of our mind. Faith is the same principle as before, but with the opportunity of acting through a more certain and satisfactory sense. We recognize objects by the eye at once; but not by the touch. We know them when we see them, but scarcely till then. Hence it is, that the New Testament says so much on the subject of spiritual knowledge. For instance, St. Paul prays that the Ephesians may receive "the spirit of wisdom and revelation in the knowledge of Christ, the eyes of their understanding being enlightened"; and he says, that the Colossians had "put on the new man, which is renewed in knowledge, after the image of Him that created him." St. Peter, in like manner, addresses his brethren with the salutation of "Grace and peace, through the knowledge of God, and of Jesus our Lord"; according to the declaration of our Lord Himself, "This is life eternal, to know Thee, the only true God, and Jesus Christ whom Thou hast sent."[67] Not of course as if Christian faith had not still abundant exercise for the other senses (so to call them) of the soul; but that the eye is its

peculiar sense, by which it is distinguished from the faith of heathens, nay, I may add, of Jews.

It is plain what is the object of spiritual sight which is vouchsafed us in the Gospel—"God manifest in the flesh." He who was
before unseen has shown Himself in Christ; not merely displayed
His glory, as (for instance) in what is called a providence, or visitation, or in miracles, or in the actions and character of inspired
men, but really He Himself has come upon earth, and has been
seen of men in human form. In the same kind of sense, in which
we should say we saw a servant of His, Apostle or Prophet,
though we could not see his soul, so man has seen the Invisible
God; and we have the history of His sojourn among His creatures
in the Gospels.

To know God is life eternal, and to believe in the Gospel manifestation of Him is to know Him; but how are we to "know that
we know Him"? How are we to be sure that we are not mistaking
some dream of our own for the true and clear vision? How can
we tell we are not like gazers upon a distant prospect through a
misty atmosphere, who mistake one object for another? The text
answers us clearly and intelligibly; though some Christians have
recourse to other proofs of it, or will not have patience to ask
themselves the question. They say they are quite certain that they
have true faith; for faith carries with it its own evidence, and
admits of no mistaking the true spiritual conviction being unlike
all others. On the other hand, St. John says, "Hereby do we know
that we know Him, if we keep His commandments." Obedience
is the test of faith.

Thus the whole duty and work of a Christian is made up of
these two parts, faith and obedience; "looking unto Jesus," the
Divine Object as well as Author of our faith, and acting according
to His will. Not as if a certain frame of mind, certain notions,
affections, feelings, and tempers, were not a necessary condition
of a saving state, but, so it is, the Apostle does not insist upon it, as
if it were sure to follow, if our hearts do but grow into these two
chief objects, the view of God in Christ and the diligent aim to
obey Him in our conduct.

I conceive that we are in danger, in this day, of insisting on
neither of these as we ought; regarding all true and careful con-

sideration of the Object of faith, as barren orthodoxy, technical subtlety, and the like, and all due earnestness about good works as a mere cold and formal morality; and, instead, making religion, or rather (for this is the point) making the test of our being religious, to consist in our having what is called a spiritual state of heart, to the comparative neglect of the Object from which it must arise, and the works in which it should issue. At this season, when we are especially engaged in considering the full triumph and manifestation of our Lord and Savior, when He was "declared to be the Son of God with power, by the resurrection from the dead," it may be appropriate to make some remarks on an error which goes far to deprive us of the benefit of His condescension.

St. John speaks of knowing Christ and of keeping His commandments, as the two great departments of religious duty and blessedness. To know Christ is (as I have said) to discern the Father of all, as manifested through His Only-begotten Son Incarnate. In the natural world we have glimpses, frequent and startling, of His glorious Attributes; of His power, wisdom, and goodness; of His holiness, His fearful judgments, His long remembrance of evil, His long-suffering towards sinners, and His strange encompassing mercy at times when we least looked for it. But to us mortals, who live for a day, and see but an arm's length, such disclosures are like reflections of a prospect in a broken mirror; they do not enable us in any comfortable sense to know God. They are such as faith may use indeed, but hardly enjoy. This then was one among the benefits of Christ's coming, that the Invisible God was then revealed in the form and history of man, revealed in those respects in which sinners most required to know Him, and nature spoke least distinctly, as a holy yet merciful Governor of His creatures. And thus the Gospels which contain the memorials of this wonderful grace, are our principal treasures. They may be called the text of the Revelation, and the Epistles, especially St. Paul's, are as comments upon it, unfolding and illustrating it in its various parts, raising history into doctrine, ordinances into sacraments, detached words or actions into principles, and thus everywhere dutifully preaching His Person, work, and will. St. John is both Prophet and Evangelist, recording and commenting on the Ministry of his Lord. Still, in every

case, He is the chief Prophet of the Church, and His Apostles do
but explain His words and actions; according to His own account
of the guidance promised to them, that it should "glorify" Him.
The like service is ministered to Him by the Creeds and doctrinal
expositions of the early Church, which we retain in our Services.
They speak of no ideal being, such as the imagination alone contemplates, but of the very Son of God, whose life is recorded in
the Gospels. Thus every part of the Dispensation tends to the
manifestation of Him who is its center.

Turning from Him to ourselves, we find a short rule given us,
"if ye love Me, keep My commandments." "He that saith he
abideth in Him, ought himself also go to walk, even as He
walked." "If ye then be risen with Christ, seek those things which
are above, where Christ sitteth on the right hand of God."[68] This
is all that is put upon us, difficult indeed to perform, but easy to
understand; all that is put upon us—and for this plain reason,
because Christ has done everything else. He has freely chosen us,
died for us, regenerated us, and now ever liveth for us; what
remains? Simply that we should do as He has done to us, showing
forth His glory by good works. Thus a correct (or as we commonly call it) an orthodox faith and an obedient life, is the whole
duty of man. And so, most surely, it has ever been accounted.
Look into the records of the early Church or into the writings of
our own revered bishops and teachers, and see whether this is not
the sum total of religion, according to the symbols of it in which
children are catechized, the Creed, the Lord's Prayer, and the Ten
Commandments.

However, it is objected that such a view of religious duty
encourages self-deception; that a man who does no more than
believe aright, and keep God's commandments, is what is called a
formalist; that his heart is not interested in the matter, his affections remain unrenewed; and that, till a change takes place there,
all the faith and all the obedience which mind can conceive are
but external, and avail nothing; that to his heart therefore we
must make our appeal, that we must bid him search himself,
examine his motives, look narrowly lest he rest upon himself, and
be sure that his feelings and thoughts are spiritual before he takes
to himself any comfort. The merits of this view of religion shall be
considered hereafter; at present, let us take it merely in the light

of an objection to what has been already stated. I ask then in reply, how is a man to know that his motives and affections are right except by their fruits? Can they possibly be their own evidence? Are they like colors, which a man knows at once without test or calculation? Is not every feeling and opinion, of one color or another, fair or unpleasant, in each man's own judgment, according to the center light which is set up in his soul? Is not the light that is in a man sometimes even darkness, sometimes twilight, and sometimes of this hue or that, tingeing every part of himself with its own peculiarity? How then is it possible that a man can duly examine his feelings and affections by the light within him? how can he accurately decide upon their character, whether Christian or not? It is necessary then that he go out of himself in order to assay and ascertain the nature of the principles which govern him; that is, he must have recourse to his works, and compare them with Scripture, as the only evidence to himself, whether or not his heart is perfect with God. It seems, therefore, that the proposed inquiry into the workings of a man's mind means nothing at all, comes to no issue, leaves us where it found us, unless we adopt the notion (which is seldom however openly maintained) that religious faith is its own evidence.

On the other hand, deeds of obedience are an intelligible evidence, nay, the sole evidence possible, and, on the whole, a satisfactory evidence of the reality of our faith. I do not say that this or that good work tells anything; but a course of obedience says much. Various deeds, done in different departments of duty support and attest each other. Did a man act merely a bold and firm part, he would have cause to say to himself, "Perhaps all this is mere pride and obstinacy." Were he merely yielding and forgiving, he might be indulging a natural indolence of mind. Were he merely industrious, this might consist with ill-temper, or selfishness. Did he merely fulfill the duties of his temporal calling, he would have no proof that he had given his heart to God at all. Were he merely regular at Church and Holy Communion, many a man is such who has a lax conscience who is not scrupulously fair dealing, or is censorious, or niggardly. Is he what is called a domestic character, amiable, affectionate, fond of his family? let him beware lest he put wife and children in the place of God who gave them. Is he only temperate, sober, chaste, correct in his language? it may arise from mere dullness and insensibility, or may consist with spiritual pride. Is he cheerful and obliging? it may arise from youthful spirits and ignorance of the world. Does he choose his friends by a strictly orthodox rule? he may be harsh and uncharitable; or, is he zealous and serviceable in defending the Truth? still he may be unable to condescend to men of low estate, to rejoice with those who rejoice, and to weep with those who weep. No one is without some good quality or other: Balaam had a scruple about misrepresenting God's message, Saul was brave, Joab was loyal, the Bethel Prophet reverenced God's servants, the witch of Endor was hospitable; and therefore, of course, no one good deed or disposition is the criterion of a spiritual mind. Still, on the other hand, there is no one of its characteristics which has not its appropriate outward evidence; and in proportion as these external acts are multiplied and varied, so does the evidence of it become stronger and more consoling. General conscientiousness is the only assurance we can have of possessing it; and at this we must aim, determining to obey God consistently, with a jealous carefulness about all things, little and great. This is, in Scripture language, to "serve God with a perfect heart"; as you will see at once, if you compare the respective reformations of Jehu and Josiah. As far then as a man has reason to hope that he is *consistent,* so far may he humbly trust that he has true faith. To be consistent, to "walk in all the ordinances of the Lord blameless," is his one business; still, all along looking reverently towards the Great Object of faith, the Father, the Son, and the Holy Ghost, Three Persons, One God, and the Son Incarnate for our salvation. Certainly he will have enough to direct his course by, with God in his eye, and his work in his hand, though he forbear curious experiments about his sensations and emotions; and, if it be objected that an evidence from works is but a cold comfort, as being at best but faint and partial, I reply, that, after all, it is more than sinners have a right to ask—that if it be little at first, it grows with our growth in grace—and moreover, that such an evidence, more than any other, throws us in faith upon the loving-kindness and meritorious sufferings of our Savior. Surely, even our best doings have that taint of sinfulness pervading them, which will remind us ever, while we regard them, where our True Hope is lodged. Men are satisfied with themselves, not when they attempt, but when they neglect the details of duty. Disobedience blinds the conscience; obedience makes it keen-sighted and sensitive. The more we *do,* the more shall we trust in Christ; and that surely is no morose doctrine, which, after giving us whatever evidence of our safety can be given, leads us to soothe our selfish restlessness, and forget our fears, in the vision of the Incarnate Son of God.

Lastly, it may be objected, that, since many deeds of obedience are themselves acts of the mind, to do them well we must necessarily examine our feelings; that we cannot pray, for instance, without reflecting on ourselves as we use the words of prayer, and keeping our thoughts upon God; that we cannot repress anger or impatience, or cherish loving and forgiving thoughts, without searching and watching ourselves. But such an argument rests on a misconception of what I have been saying. All I would maintain is, that our duty lies in acts, acts of course of every kind, acts of the mind, as well as of the tongue, or of the hand; but anyhow, it lies mainly in acts; it does not directly lie in moods or feelings. He who aims at praying well, loving sincerely, disputing meekly, as the respective duties occur, is wise and religious; but he who aims vaguely and generally at being in a spiritual frame of mind, is entangled in a deceit of words, which gain a meaning only by being made mischievous. Let us do our duty as it presents itself; this is the secret of true faith and peace. We have power over our deeds, under God's grace; we have no direct power over our habits. Let us but secure our actions, as God would have them, and our habits will follow. Suppose a religious man, for instance, [be] in the society of strangers; he takes things as they come, discourses naturally, gives his opinion soberly, and does good according to each opportunity of good. His heart is in his work, and his thoughts rest without effort on his God and Savior. This is the way of a Christian; he leaves it to the ill-instructed to endeavor after a (so-called) spiritual frame of mind amid the bustle of life, which has no existence except in attempt and profession. True spiritual mindedness is unseen by man, like the soul itself, of which it is a quality; and as the soul is known by its operations, so it is known by its fruits.

I will add too, that the office of self-examination lies rather in detecting what is bad in us than in ascertaining what is good. No harm can follow from contemplating our sins, so that we keep Christ before us, and attempt to overcome them; such a review of self will but lead to repentance and faith. And, while it does this, it will undoubtedly be molding our hearts into a higher and more heavenly state—but still indirectly—just as the mean is attained in action or art, not by directly contemplating and aiming at it, but negatively, by avoiding extremes.

To conclude. The essence of faith is to look out of ourselves; now, consider what manner of a believer he is who imprisons himself in his own thoughts, and rests on the workings of his own mind, and thinks of his Savior as an idea of his imagination, instead of putting self aside, and living upon Him who speaks in the Gospels.

So much then, by way of suggestion, upon the view of religious faith, which has ever been received in the Church Catholic, and which, doubtless, is saving. Tomorrow I propose to speak more particularly of that other system, to which these latter times have given birth.

[II, 14]

Chapter 12

SELF-CONTEMPLATION

(TUESDAY IN EASTER WEEK)

Looking unto Jesus, the Author and Finisher of our faith.
—Heb. 12:2

Surely it is our duty ever to look off ourselves, and to look unto Jesus, that is, to shun the contemplation of our own feelings, emotions, frame and state of mind, as if that were the main business of religion, and to leave these mainly to be secured in their fruits. Some remarks were made yesterday upon this "more excellent" and Scriptural way of conducting ourselves, as it has ever been received in the Church; now let us consider the merits of the rule for holy living, which the fashion of this day would substitute for it.

Instead of looking off to Jesus, and thinking little of ourselves, it is at present thought necessary, among the mixed multitude of religionists, to examine the heart with a view of ascertaining whether it is in a spiritual state or no. A spiritual frame of mind is considered to be one in which the heinousness of sin is perceived, our utter worthlessness, the impossibility of our saving ourselves, the necessity of some savior, the sufficiency of our Lord Jesus Christ to be that Savior, the unbounded riches of His love, the excellence and glory of His work of Atonement, the freeness and fullness of His grace, the high privilege of communion with Him in prayer, and the desirableness of walking with Him in all holy and loving obedience; all of them solemn truths, too solemn to be lightly mentioned, but our hearty reception of which is scarcely ascertainable by a direct inspection of our feelings. Moreover, if one doctrine must be selected above the rest as containing the essence of the truths, which (according to this system) are thus vividly understood by the spiritual Christian, it is that of the necessity of renouncing our own righteousness for the righteousness provided by our Lord and Savior; which is considered, not as an elementary and simple principle (as it really is), but as rarely and hardly acknowledged by any man, especially repugnant to a certain (so-called) pride of heart, which is supposed to run through the whole race of Adam, and to lead every man instinctively to insist even before God on the proper merit of his good deeds; so that, to trust in Christ is not merely the work of the Holy Spirit (as all good in our souls is), but is the especial and critical event which marks a man, as issuing from darkness, and sealed unto the privileges and inheritance of the sons of God. In other words, the doctrine of Justification by Faith is accounted to be the one cardinal point of the Gospel; and it is in vain to admit it readily as a clear Scripture truth (which it is), and to attempt to go on unto perfection: the very wish to pass forward is interpreted into a wish to pass over it, and the test of believing it at all is in fact to insist upon no doctrine but it. And this peculiar mode of inculcating that great doctrine of the Gospel is a proof (if proof were wanting) that the persons who adopt it are not solicitous even about *it* on its own score merely, considered as (what is called) a dogma, but as ascertaining and securing (as they hope) a certain state of heart. For, not content with the simple admission of it on the part of another, they proceed to divide faith into its kinds, living and dead, and to urge against him, that the Truth may be held in a carnal and unrenewed mind, and that men may speak without real feelings and convictions. Thus it is clear they do not contend for the doctrine of Justification as a truth external to the mind, or article of faith, any more than for the doctrine of the Trinity. On the other hand, since they use the same language about dead and living faith, however exemplary the life and conduct be of the individual under their review, they as plainly show that neither are the fruits of righteousness in their system an evidence of spiritual mindedness, but that a something is to be sought for in the frame of mind itself. All this is not stated at present by way of objection, but in order to settle accurately what they mean to maintain. So now we have the two views of doctrine clearly before us: the ancient and universal teaching of the Church, which insists on the Objects and fruits of faith, and considers the spiritual character of that faith itself sufficiently secured, if these are as they should be; and the method, now in esteem, of attempting instead to secure directly and primarily that "mind of the Spirit," which may savingly receive the truths and fulfill the obedience of the Gospel. That such a spiritual temper is indispensable is agreed on all hands. The simple question is, whether it is formed by the Holy Spirit immediately acting upon our minds, or, on the other hand, by our own particular acts (whether of faith or obedience), prompted, guided, and prospered by Him; whether it is ascertainable otherwise than by its fruits; whether such frames of mind as *are* directly ascertainable and profess to be spiritual are not rather a delusion, a mere excitement, capricious feeling, fanatic fancy, and the like. So much then by way of explanation.

1. Now, in the first place, this modern system certainly does disparage the revealed doctrines of the Gospel, however its more moderate advocates may shrink from admitting it. Considering a certain state of heart to be the main thing to be aimed at, they avowedly make the "truth as it is in Jesus" the definite Creed of the Church, secondary in their teaching and profession. They will defend themselves indeed from the appearance of undervaluing it, by maintaining that the existence of right religious affections is a security for sound views of doctrine. And this is abstractedly true; but not true in the use they make of it: for they unhappily conceive that they can ascertain in each other the presence of these affections; and when they find men possessed of them (as they conceive), yet not altogether orthodox in their belief, then they relax a little, and argue that an admission of (what they call) the strict and technical niceties of doctrine, whether about the Consubstantiality of the Son or the Hypostatic Union, is scarcely part of the definition of a spiritual believer. In order to support this position, they lay it down as self-evident, that the main purpose of revealed doctrine is to affect the heart—that that which does not seem to affect it does not affect it, that what does affect it is unnecessary—and that the circumstance that this or that person's heart seems rightly affected is a sufficient warrant that such Articles as he may happen to reject may safely be universally rejected, or at least are only accidentally important. Such principles, when once become familiar to the mind, induce a certain disproportionate attention to the doctrines connected with the work of Christ, in comparison of those which relate to His Person, from their more immediately interesting and exciting character; and carry on the more speculative and philosophical class to view the doctrines of

Atonement and Sanctification as the essence of the Gospel, and to advocate them in the place of those "Heavenly Things" altogether, which, as theologically expressed, they have already assailed; and of which they now openly complain as mysteries for bondsmen, not Gospel consolations. The last and most miserable stage of this false wisdom is, to deny that in matters of doctrine there is any one sense of Scripture such that it is true and all others false; to make the Gospel of Truth (so far) a revelation of words and a dead letter; to consider that inspiration speaks merely of divine operations, not of Persons; and that that is truth to each, which each man thinks to be true, so that one man may say that Christ is God, another deny His preexistence, yet each have received the Truth according to the peculiar constitution of his own mind, the Scripture doctrine having no real independent substantive meaning. Thus the system under consideration tends legitimately to obliterate the great Objects brought to light in the Gospel, and to darken what I called yesterday the eye of faith, to throw us back into the vagueness of heathenism, when men only felt after the Divine Presence, and thus to frustrate the design of Christ's Incarnation so far as it is a manifestation of the Unseen Creator.

2. On the other hand, the necessity of obedience in order to salvation does not suffer less from the upholders of this modern system than the articles of the Creed. They argue, and truly, that if faith is living, works must follow; but mistaking a following *in order of conception* for a following *in order of time,* they conclude that faith ever comes first, and works afterwards; and therefore, that faith must first be secured, and that, by some means in which works have no share. Thus, instead of viewing works as the concomitant development and evidence, and instrumental cause, as well as the subsequent result of faith, they lay all the stress upon the direct creation, in their minds, of faith and spiritual mindedness, which they consider to consist in certain emotions and desires, because they can form abstractedly no better or truer notion of those qualities. Then, instead of being "careful to maintain good works," they proceed to take it for granted, that since they have attained faith (as they consider), works will follow without their trouble as a matter of course. Thus the wise are taken in their own craftiness; they attempt to reason, and are

overcome by sophisms. Had they kept to the Inspired Record, instead of reasoning, their way would have been clear; and, considering the serious exhortations to keeping God's commandments, with which all Scripture abounds, from Genesis to the Apocalypse, is it not a very grave question, which the most charitable among Churchmen must put to himself, whether these random expounders of the Blessed Gospel are not risking a participation in the woe denounced against those who preach any other doctrine besides that delivered unto us, or who "take away from the words of the Book" of revealed Truth?

3. But still more evidently do they fall into this last imputation, when we consider how they are obliged to treat the Sacred Volume altogether, in order to support the system they have adopted. Is it too much to say that, instead of attempting to harmonize Scripture with Scripture, much less referring to Antiquity to enable them to do so, they either drop altogether, or explain away, whole portions of the Bible, and those most sacred ones? How does the authority of the Psalms stand with their opinions, except at best by a forced figurative interpretation? And our Lord's discourses in the Gospels, especially the Sermon on the Mount, are they not virtually considered as chiefly important to the persons immediately addressed, and of inferior instructiveness to us now that the Spirit (as it is profanely said) is come? In short, is not the rich and varied Revelation of our merciful Lord practically reduced to a few chapters of St. Paul's Epistles whether rightly (as they maintain) or (as we should say) perversely understood? If then the Romanists have added to the Word of God, is it not undeniable that there is a school of religionists among us who have taken from it?

4. I would remark, that the immediate tendency of these opinions is to undervalue ordinances as well as doctrines. The same argument evidently applies; for, if the renewed state of heart is (as it is supposed) attained, what matter whether Sacraments have or have not been administered? The notion of invisible grace and invisible privileges is, on this supposition, altogether superseded; that of communion with Christ is limited to the mere exercise of the affections in prayer and meditation, to sensible effects; and he who considers he has already gained this one essential gift of grace (as he calls it), may plausibly inquire, after the fashion of the

day, why he need wait upon ordinances which he has anticipated in his religious attainments—which are but means to an end, which *he* has not to seek, even if they be not outward forms altogether—and whether Christ will not accept at the last day all who believe, without inquiring if they were members of the Church, or were confirmed, or were baptized or received the blessing of mere men who are "earthen vessels."

5. The foregoing remarks go to show the utterly unevangelic character of the system in question; unevangelic in the full sense of the word, whether by the Gospel be meant the inspired document of it, or the doctrines brought to light through it, or the Sacramental Institutions which are the gift of it, or the theology which interprets it, or the Covenant which is the basis of it. A few words shall now be added, to show the inherent mischief of the system as such; which I conceive to lie in its necessarily involving a continual self-contemplation and reference to self, in all departments of conduct. He who aims at attaining sound doctrine or right practice, more or less looks out of himself; whereas, in laboring after a certain frame of mind, there is a habitual reflex action of the mind upon itself. That this is really involved in the modern system is evident from the very doctrine principally insisted on by it; for as if it were not enough for a man to look up simply to Christ for salvation, it is declared to be necessary that he should be able to recognize this in himself, that he should define his own state of mind, confess he is justified by faith alone, and explain what is meant by that confession. Now, the truest obedience is indisputably that which is done from love of God, without narrowly measuring the magnitude or nature of the sacrifice involved in it. He who has learned to give names to his thoughts and deeds, to appraise them as if for the market, to attach to each its due measure of commendation or usefulness, will soon involuntarily corrupt his motives by pride or selfishness. A sort of self-approbation will insinuate itself into his mind: so subtle as not at once to be recognized by himself—a habitual quiet self-esteem, leading him to prefer his own views to those of others, and a secret, if not avowed persuasion, that he is in a different state from the generality of those around him. This is an incidental, though of course not a necessary evil of religious journals; nay, of such compositions as Ministerial duties involve. They lead those

who write them, in some respect or other, to a contemplation of self. Moreover, as to religious journals, useful as they often are, at the same time I believe persons find great difficulty, while recording their feelings, in banishing the thought that one day these good feelings will be known to the world, and are thus insensibly led to modify and prepare their language as if for a representation. Seldom indeed is anyone in the *practice* of contemplating his better thoughts or doings without proceeding to display them to others; and hence it is that it is so easy to discover a conceited man. When this is encouraged in the sacred province of religion, it produces a certain unnatural solemnity of manner, arising from a wish to be, nay, to appear spiritual, which is at once very painful to beholders, and surely quite at variance with our Savior's rule of anointing our head and washing our face, even when we are most self-abased in heart. Another mischief arising from this self-contemplation is the peculiar kind of selfishness (if I may use so harsh a term) which it will be found to foster. They who make self instead of their Maker the great object of their contemplation will naturally exalt themselves. Without denying that the glory of God is the great end to which all things are to be referred, they will be led to connect indissolubly His glory with their own certainty of salvation; and this partly accounts for its being so common to find rigid predestinarian views, and the exclusive maintenance of Justification by Faith in the same persons. And for the same reason, the Scripture doctrines relative to the Church and its offices will be unpalatable to such persons; no one thing being so irreconcilable with another, as the system which makes a man's thoughts center in himself with that which directs them to a fountain of grace and truth, on which God has made him dependent.

And as self-confidence and spiritual pride are the legitimate results of these opinions in one set of persons, so in another they lead to a feverish anxiety about their religious state and prospects, and fears lest they are under the reprobation of their All-merciful Savior. It need scarcely be said that a contemplation of self is a frequent attendant, and a frequent precursor of a deranged state of the mental powers.

To conclude. It must not be supposed from the foregoing remarks that I am imputing all the consequences enumerated to

everyone who holds the main doctrine from which they legitimately follow. Many men zealously maintain principles which
they never follow out in their own minds, or after a time silently
discard, except as far as words go, but which are sure to receive a
full development in the history of any school or party of men
which adopts them. Considered thus, as the characteristics of a
school, the principles in question are doubtless anti-Christian; for
they destroy all positive doctrine, all ordinances, all good works;
they foster pride, invite hypocrisy, discourage the weak, and
deceive most fatally, while they profess to be the especial antidotes
to self-deception. We have seen these effects of them two centuries since in the history of the English Branch of the Church; for
what we know, a more fearful triumph is still in store for them.
But, however that may be, let not the watchmen of Jerusalem fail
to give timely warning of the approaching enemy, or to acquit
themselves of all cowardice or compliance as regards it. Let them
prefer the Old Commandment, as it has been from the beginning,
to any novelties of man, recollecting Christ's words, "Blessed is he
that watcheth, and keepeth his garments, lest he walk naked, and
they see his shame."[69]

[II, 15]

Chapter 13

GUILELESSNESS

(Feast of St. Bartholomew the Apostle)

*Jesus saw Nathanael coming to Him, and saith of him, Behold an Israelite
indeed, in whom is no guile!*
—John 1:47

St. Bartholomew, whose Festival we celebrate today, has been
supposed to be the same as the Nathanael mentioned in the text.
Nathanael was one of Christ's first converts, yet his name does not
occur again till the last chapter of St. John's Gospel, where he is
mentioned in company with certain of the Apostles, to whom
Christ appeared after His Resurrection. Now why should the call
of Nathanael have been recorded in the opening of the Gospel,
among the acts of Christ in the beginning of His Ministry, unless
he was an Apostle? Philip, Peter, and Andrew, who are mentioned at the same time, were all Apostles and Nathanael's name
is introduced without preface, as if familiar to a Christian reader.
At the end of the Gospel it appears again, and there too among
Apostles. Besides, the Apostles were the special witnesses of
Christ, when He was risen. He manifested Himself, "not to all
the people," says Peter, "but unto witnesses chosen before of God,
even to us, who did eat and drink with Him after He rose from
the dead."[70] Now, the occasion on which Nathanael is mentioned,
was one of these manifestations. "This is now the third time," says
the Evangelist, "that Jesus was manifested to His disciples, after
that He was risen from the dead." It was in the presence of
Nathanael, that He gave St. Peter his commission, and foretold
his martyrdom, and the prolonged life of St. John. All this leads
us to conjecture that Nathanael is one of the Apostles under
another name. Now, he is not Andrew, Peter, or Philip, for they
are mentioned in connection with him in the first chapter of the
Gospel; nor Thomas, James, or John, in whose company he is
found in the last chapter; nor Jude (as it would seem), because the
name of Jude occurs in St. John's fourteenth chapter. Four Apos-

tles remain, who are not named in his Gospel—St. James the Less, St. Matthew, St. Simon, and St. Bartholomew; of whom St. Matthew's second name is known to have been Levi, while St. James, being related, was not at any time a stranger to our Lord, which Nathanael evidently was. If then Nathanael were an Apostle, he was either Simon or Bartholomew. Now it is observable, that, according to St. John, Philip brought Nathanael to Christ; therefore Nathanael and Philip were friends: while in the other Gospels, in the list of Apostles, Philip is associated with Bartholomew; "Simon and Andrew, James and John, Philip and Bartholomew."[71] This is some evidence that Bartholomew and not Simon is the Nathanael of St. John. On the other hand, Matthias has been suggested instead of either, his name meaning nearly the same as Nathanael in the original language. However, since writers of some date decide in favor of Bartholomew, I shall do the like in what follows.

What then do we learn from his recorded character and history? It affords us an instructive lesson.

When Philip told him that he had found the long-expected Messiah of whom Moses wrote, Nathanael (that is, Bartholomew) at first doubted. He was well read in the Scriptures, and knew the Christ was to be born in Bethlehem; whereas Jesus dwelt at Nazareth, which Nathanael supposed in consequence to be the place of His birth, and he knew of no particular promises attached to that city, which was a place of evil report, and he thought no good could come out of it. Philip told him to come and see; and he went to see, as a humble single-minded man, sincerely desirous to get at the truth. In consequence, he was vouchsafed an interview with our Savior, and was converted.

Now, from what occurred in this interview, we gain some insight into St. Bartholomew's character. Our Lord said of him "Behold an Israelite indeed, in whom is no guile!" and it appears moreover, as if, before Philip called him to come to Christ, he was engaged in meditation or prayer, in the privacy which a fig tree's shade afforded him. And this, it seems, was the life of one who was destined to act the busy part of an Apostle; quietness without, guilelessness within. This was the tranquil preparation for great dangers and sufferings! We see who make the most heroic Christians, and are the most honored by Christ!

An even, unvaried life is the lot of most men, in spite of occasional troubles or other accidents; and we are apt to despise it, and to get tired of it, and to long to see the world—or, at all events, we think such a life affords no great opportunity for religious obedience. To rise up, and go through the same duties, and then to rest again, day after day—to pass week after week, beginning with God's service on Sunday, and then to our worldly tasks, so to continue till year follows year, and we gradually get old—an unvaried life like this is apt to seem unprofitable to us when we dwell upon the thought of it. Many indeed there are, who do not think at all, but live in their round of employments, without care about God and religion, driven on by the natural course of things in a dull irrational way like the beasts that perish. But when a man begins to feel he has a soul, and a work to do, and a reward to be gained, greater or less, according as he improves the talents committed to him, then he is naturally tempted to be anxious from his very wish to be saved, and he says, "What must I *do* to please God?" And sometimes he is led to think he ought to be useful on a large scale, and goes out of his line of life, that he may be doing something worth doing, as he considers it. Here we have the history of St. Bartholomew and the other Apostles to recall us to ourselves, and to assure us that we need not give up our usual manner of life, in order to serve God; that the most humble and quietest station is acceptable to Him, if improved duly—nay, affords means for maturing the highest Christian character, even that of an Apostle. Bartholomew read the Scriptures and prayed to God; and thus was trained at length to give up his life for Christ, when He demanded it.

But, further, let us consider the particular praise which our Savior gives him. "Behold an Israelite indeed, in whom is no guile!" This is just the character which (through God's grace) they may attain most fully, who live out of the world in the private way I have been describing, which is made least account of by man, and thought to be in the way of success in life, though our Savior chose it to make head against all the power and wisdom of the world. Men of the world think an ignorance of its ways is a disadvantage or disgrace; as if it were somehow unmanly and weak to have abstained from all acquaintance with its impieties and lax practices. How often do we hear them say that a man must do so-and-so, unless he would be singular and absurd; that he must not be too strict, or indulge high-flown notions of virtue, which may be good to talk about, but are not fit for this world! When they hear of any young person resolving on being consistently religious, or being strictly honest in trade, or observing a noble purity in language and demeanor, they smile and think it very well, but that it will and must wear off in time. And they are ashamed of being innocent, and pretend to be worse than they really are. Then they have all sorts of little ways—are mean, jealous, suspicious, censorious, cunning, insincere, selfish; and think others as low-minded as themselves, only proud, or in some sense hypocritical, unwilling to confess their real motives and feelings.

To this base and irreligious multitude is opposed the Israelite indeed, in whom there is no guile. David describes his character in the Fifteenth Psalm; and, taken in all its parts, it is a rare one. He asks, "Lord, who shall abide in Thy tabernacle? who shall dwell in Thy holy hill? He that walketh uprightly, and worketh righteousness, and speaketh the truth in his heart. He that backbiteth not with his tongue, nor doeth evil to his neighbor, nor taketh up a reproach against his neighbor. In whose eyes a vile person is condemned; but he honoreth them that fear the Lord. He that sweareth to his own hurt, and changeth not."

I say, it is a difficult and rare virtue, to mean what we say, to love without dissimulation, to think no evil, to bear no grudge, to be free from selfishness, to be innocent and straightforward. This character of mind is something far above the generality of men; and when realized in due measure, one of the surest marks of Christ's elect. And the instances which we may every now and then discover of it among Christians, will be an evidence to us, if evidence be wanting, that, in spite of all that groveling minds may say about the necessity of acquaintance with the world and with sin, in order to get on well in life, yet after all, inexperienced guilelessness carries a man on as safely and more happily. For, first, it is in itself a great privilege to a rightly disposed mind, not to be sensible of the moral miseries of the world; and this is eminently the lot of the simple-hearted. They take everything in good part which happens to them, and make the best of everyone;

thus they have always something to be pleased with, not seeing the bad, and keenly sensible of the good. And communicating their own happy peace to those around them, they really diminish the evils of life in society at large, while they escape from the knowledge of them themselves. Such men are cheerful and contented; for they desire but little, and take pleasure in the least matters, having no wish for riches and distinction. And they are under the tyranny of no evil or base thoughts, having never encouraged what in the case of other men often spreads disorder and unholiness through their whole future life. They have no phantoms of former sins, such as remain even to the penitent, when he has subdued their realities, rising up in their minds, harassing them, for a time domineering, and leaving a sting behind them. Guileless persons are, most of all men, skillful in shaming and silencing the wicked; for they do not argue, but take things for granted in so natural a way, that they throw back the sinner upon the recollection of those times of his youth, when he was pure from sin, and thought as they do now; and none but very hardened men can resist this sort of appeal. Men of irreligious lives live in bondage and fear; even though they do not acknowledge it to themselves. Many a one, who would be ashamed to own it, is afraid of certain places or times, or of solitude, from a sort of instinct that he is no company for good spirits, and that devils may then assail him. But the guileless man has a simple boldness and a princely heart; he overcomes dangers which others shrink from, merely because they are no dangers to him, and thus he often gains even worldly advantages, by his straightforwardness, which the most crafty persons cannot gain, though they risk their souls for them. It is true such single-hearted men often get into difficulties, but they usually get out of them as easily; and are almost unconscious both of their danger and their escape. Perhaps they have not received a learned education, and cannot talk fluently; yet they are ever a match for those who try to shake their faith in Christ by profane argument or ridicule, for the weakness of God is stronger than men.

Nor is it only among the poor and lowly that this blessed character of mind is found to exist. Secular learning and dignity have doubtless in their respective ways a powerful tendency to rob the heart of its brightness and purity; yet even in kings' courts, and

the schools of philosophy, Nathanaels may be discovered. Nay,
like the Apostles, they have been subjected to the world's buffet-
ings, they have been thwarted in their day, lived in anxiety, and
seemingly lost by their honesty, yet without being foiled either of
its present comfort or its ultimate fruit. Such was our great Arch-
bishop and Martyr, to whom perchance we owe it, that we who
now live are still members of a branch of the Church Catholic;
one of whose "greatest unpopular infirmities," according to the
historian of his times, was "that he believed innocence of heart,
and integrity of manners, was a guard strong enough to secure
any man in his voyage through this world, in what company
soever he traveled and through what ways soever he was to pass.
And sure," he adds, "never any man was better supplied with that
provision."

I have in these remarks spoken of guileless men as members of
society, because I wished to show that, even in that respect in
which they seem deficient, they possess a hidden strength, an
unconscious wisdom, which makes them live above the world,
and sooner or later triumph over it. The weapons of their warfare
are not carnal; and they are fitted to be Apostles, though they
seem to be ordinary men. Such is the blessedness of the innocent,
that is, of those who have never given way to evil, or formed
themselves to habits of sin; who in consequence literally do not
know its power or its misery; who have thoughts of truth and
peace ever before them, and are able to discern at once the right
and wrong in conduct, as by some delicate instrument which tells
truly because it has never been ill-treated. Nay, such may be the
portion (through God's mercy) even of those who have at one
time departed from Him, and then repented; in proportion as
they have learned to love God, and have purified themselves, not
only from sin, but from the recollections of it.

Lastly, more is requisite for the Christian, even than guilelessness such as Bartholomew's. When Christ sent forth him and his
brethren into the world, He said, "Behold, I send you forth as
sheep in the midst of wolves; be ye therefore wise as serpents and
harmless as doves." Innocence must be joined to prudence, discre-
tion, self-command, gravity, patience, perseverance in well doing,
as Bartholomew doubtless learned in due season under his Lord's
teaching; but innocence is the beginning. Let us then pray God to

fulfill in us "all the good pleasure of His goodness, and the work of faith with power"; that if it should please Him suddenly to bring us forward to great trials, as He did His Apostles, we may not be taken by surprise, but be found to have made a private or domestic life a preparation for the achievements of Confessors and Martyrs.

[II, 27]

Chapter 14

FAITH AND OBEDIENCE

If thou wilt enter into life, keep the commandments.
—Matt. 19:17

Let a plain man read the Gospels with a serious and humble mind, and as in God's presence, and I suppose he would be in no perplexity at all about the meaning of these words. They are clear as the day at first reading, and the rest of our Savior's teaching does but corroborate their obvious meaning. I conceive that if such a man, after reading them and the other similar passages which occur in the Gospels, were told that he had not mastered the sense of them, and that in matter of fact to attempt to enter into life by keeping the commandments, to attempt to keep the commandments in order to enter into life, were suspicious and dangerous modes of expression, and that the use of them showed an ignorance of the real spirit of Christ's doctrine, he would in despair say, "Then truly Scripture is not a book for the multitude, but for those only who have educated and refined understandings, so as to see things in a sense different from their obvious meaning."

Or, again, supposing one, who disbelieved our Lord's Divinity, fell in with persons who did thus consider that to keep the commandments by way of entering into life was a sign of spiritual blindness in a man, not to say of pride and reprobation; do you suppose there would be any possibility of their silencing him as regards his own particular heresy, with Scripture proofs of the sacred truth which he denied? For can the doctrine that Christ is God be more clearly enunciated than the precept that, to enter into life, we must keep the commandments? and is it not the way to make men think that Scripture has no definite meaning at all, and that each man may fairly put his own sense upon it, when they see our Lord's plain directions thus explained away?

The occasion of this unreal interpretation of Scripture, which, in fact, does exist among us to a great extent, is that St. Paul, in some passages of his Epistles, teaches us that we are accepted and saved by faith; and it is argued that, since he wrote under the guidance of the promised Spirit, his is the true Gospel mode of Speech, and that the language of Christ, the Eternal Word of God, must be drawn aside, however violently, into that certain meaning which is assumed as the only true sense of St. Paul. *How* our Divine Master's words are explained away, what ingenious refinements are used to deprive us of the plain and solemn sense which they bear on their very front, it profits not here to inquire; still no one, it may be presumed, can deny, that, whether rightly or wrongly, they *are* turned aside in a very unexpected way, unless rather they are put out of sight altogether, and forgotten, as if superseded by the Apostolic Epistles. Doubtless those Epistles are inspired by the Holy Spirit: but He was sent from Christ to glorify and illuminate the words of Christ. The two heavenly witnesses cannot speak diversely; faith will listen to them both. Surely our duty is, neither to resist the One nor the Other; but humbly to consider whether there is not some one substantial doctrine which they teach in common; and that with God's blessing I will now attempt to do.

How are we sinners to be accepted by Almighty God? Doubtless the sacrifice of Christ on the cross is the *meritorious cause* of our justification, and His Church is the *ordained instrument* of conveying it to us. But our present question relates to another subject, to *our own part* in appropriating it; and here I say Scripture makes two answers, saying sometimes "Believe, and you shall be saved," and sometimes "Keep the commandments, and you shall be saved." Let us consider whether these two modes of speech are not reconcilable with each other.

What is meant by faith? It is to feel in good earnest that we are creatures of God; it is a practical perception of the unseen world; it is to understand that this world is not enough for our happiness, to look beyond it on towards God, to realize His presence, to wait upon Him, to endeavor to learn and to do His will, and to seek our good from Him. It is not a mere temporary strong act or impetuous feeling of the mind, an impression or a view coming upon it, but it is a *habit,* a state of mind lasting and consistent. To have faith in God is to surrender oneself to God, humbly to put one's interests, or to wish to be allowed to put them into His hands who is the Sovereign Giver of all good.

Now, again, let me ask, what is obedience? it is the obvious mode, suggested by nature, of a creature's conducting himself in God's sight, who fears Him as his Maker, and knows that, as a sinner, he has especial cause for fearing Him. Under such circumstances he "will do what he can" to please Him, as the woman whom our Lord commended. He will look every way to see how it is possible to approve himself to Him, and will rejoice to find any service which may stand as a sort of proof that He is in earnest. And he will find nothing better as an offering, or as an evidence, than obedience to that Holy Law, which conscience tells him has been given us by God Himself; that is, he will be diligent in doing all his duty as far as he knows it and can do it. Thus, as is evident, the two states of mind are altogether one and the same: it is quite indifferent whether we say a man seeks God in faith, or say he seeks Him by obedience; and whereas Almighty God has graciously declared He will receive and bless all that seek Him, it is quite indifferent whether we say, He accepts those who *believe,* or those who *obey.* To believe is to look beyond this world to God, and to obey is to look beyond this world to God; to believe is of the heart, and to obey is of the heart; to believe is not a solitary act, but a consistent habit of trust; and to obey is not a solitary act, but a consistent habit of doing our duty in all things. I do not say that faith and obedience do not stand for separate ideas in our minds, but they stand for nothing more; they are not divided one from the other in fact. They are but one thing viewed differently.

If it be said that a man may keep from sin and do good without thinking of God, and therefore without being religious or having faith; this is true, but nothing to the purpose. It is, alas! too true that men often do what is in itself right, not from the thought of God, but for some purpose of this world; and all of us have our best doings sullied by the intrusion of bad thoughts and motives. But all this, I say, is nothing to our present purpose; for if a man does right, *not* for religion's sake but the world's sake, though he happens to be doing right, that is, to perform outwardly good actions, this is in no sense *obedience,* which is of the *heart.* And it was obedience, not mere outward good conduct, which I said belonged to the same temper of mind as faith. And I repeat it, for by obedience is meant obedience, not to the world, but to God—and habitually to obey God is to be constant in looking on to God—and to look on to Almighty God is to have faith; so that to "live by faith," or "walk by faith" (according to the Scripture phrases), that is, to have a habit of faith, and to be obedient, are one and the same general character of mind; viewed as sitting at Jesus' feet, it is called *faith;* viewed as running to do His will, it is called *obedience.*

If, again, it be said that a man may be obedient and yet proud of being so, that is, obedient, without having faith, I would maintain, on the other hand, that in matter of fact a man is proud, or (what is sometimes called) self-righteous, not when obedient, but in proportion to his disobedience. To be proud is to rest on oneself, which they are most chargeable with who do least; but a really obedient mind is necessarily dissatisfied with itself, and looks out of itself for help, from understanding the greatness of its task; in other words, in proportion as a man obeys, is he driven to faith, in order to learn the remedy of the imperfections of his obedience.

All this is clear and obvious to every thinking man; and this view of the subject was surely present to the minds of the inspired writers of Scripture—for this reason, because they use the two words, faith and obedience, indiscriminately, sometimes declaring we shall be accepted, saved, by *believing,* sometimes by *doing our duty.* And they so interchange these two conditions of God's favor, so quickly pass to and fro from the one view to the other, as to show that in truth the two do not differ, except in idea. If these apparently *two* conditions were merely connected, not substantially one, surely the inspired writers would compare them one with the other—surely they would be consistent in appropriating distinct offices to each. But, in very truth, from the beginning to the end of Scripture, the one voice of inspiration consistently maintains, not a uniform contrast between faith and obedience, but this *one* doctrine, that the only way of salvation open to us is the *surrender* of ourselves to our Maker in all things—supreme devotion, resignation of our will, the turning with all our heart to God; and this state of mind is ascribed in Scripture sometimes to

the believing, sometimes to the obedient, according to the particular passage; and it is no matter to which it is ascribed.

Now, I will cite some passages from Scripture in proof of what
I have said. The Psalmist says, "Lord, who shall abide in Thy
tabernacle? who shall dwell in Thy holy hill? He that walketh
uprightly, and worketh righteousness, and speaketh the truth in
his heart." "He that hath clean hands and a pure heart, who hath
not lifted up his soul unto vanity nor sworn deceitfully."[72] Here
obedience is described as securing a man's salvation. But, in
another Psalm, we read, "How great is Thy goodness which
Thou hast laid up for them that fear Thee; which Thou hast
wrought for them that *trust in Thee!*"[73] Here trust or faith is the
condition of God's favor. Again, in other Psalms, first, "What
man is he that desireth life? Keep thy tongue from evil, and thy
lips from speaking guile. *Depart from evil and do good,* seek peace
and pursue it." . . . Next, it is said, "The Lord is nigh unto them
that are of a *broken heart,* and saveth such as be of a *contrite spirit.*"
Lastly, "None of them that *trust in* Him shall be desolate." Here,
obedience, repentance, and faith are successively mentioned as
the means of obtaining God's favor; and why all of them, but
because they are all names for one and the same substantial character, only viewed on different sides of it, that one character of
mind which is pleasing and acceptable to Almighty God? Again,
the Prophet Isaiah says, "Thou wilt keep him in perfect peace
whose mind is stayed on Thee, because he trusteth in Thee."[74] Yet
in the preceding verse he had proclaimed, "Open ye the gates (of
the heavenly city) that the righteous nation, which keepeth the
Truth, may enter in." In like manner Solomon says. "By *mercy
and truth* iniquity is purged"; Daniel, that *"mercy to the poor"* is a
"breaking off of sin," and "an healing of error"; Nehemiah prays
God to "remember him," and "not wipe out his *good deeds for the
House of his God*"; yet Habakkuk says, the "just shall live by his
faith."[75]

What honor our Savior put on faith I need hardly remind you.
He blessed Peter's confession, and, in prospect, those who, though
they saw Him not on earth, as Thomas, yet believe; and in His
miracles of mercy, *faith* was the condition He exacted for the
exertion of His powers of healing and restoration. On one occa-

sion He says, "*All things* are possible to him that *believeth.*"[76] Yet, afterwards, in His solemn account of the last Judgment, He tells us that it is *obedience to His will* which will then receive His blessing, "Inasmuch as ye have done it unto one of the least of these My brethren, ye have done it unto Me."[77] Again, the Angel said to Cornelius, "Thy prayers and thine alms are come up for a memorial before God"; and Cornelius is described as "a devout man, and one that feared God with all his house, which gave much alms to the people and prayed to God alway."[78] Yet it is in the very same Book of Acts that we read St. Paul's words, "*Believe,* and thou shalt be saved."[79] His Epistles afford us still more striking instances of the intimate association existing in the Apostle's thoughts between believing and obeying, as though exhibitions of one and the same spiritual character of mind. For instance, he says that Abraham was accepted (not by ceremonial observances, but) by *faith,* yet St. James says he was accepted by works of *obedience.* The meaning is clear, that Abraham found favor in God's sight, *because he gave himself* up to Him: this is faith or obedience, whichever we please to call it. No matter whether we say, Abraham was favored because his faith embraced God's *promises,* or because his obedience cherished God's *commands,* for God's commands are promises, and His promises commands to a heart devoted to Him; so that, as there is no substantial difference between command and promise, so there is likewise none between obedience and faith. Perhaps it is scarcely correct even to say that faith comes first and obedience follows as an inseparable second step, and that faith, as being the first step, is accepted. For not a single act of faith can be named but what has in it the nature of obedience, that is, implies the making an effort and a consequent victory. What is the faith which earns Baptism—the very faith which appropriates the free gift of grace—but an acquiescence of the reason in the Gospel Mysteries? Even the thief upon the Cross had (it would seem) to rule his reason, to struggle against sight, and to bring under pride and obstinacy, when he turned to Him as his Savior, who seemed to mortal eyes only his fellow sufferer. A mere confession or prayer, which might not be really an act of obedience in us, might be such in him. On the other hand, faith does not cease with the first act, but continues. It works with obedience. In proportion as a man believes, so he obeys; they come together, and grow together, and last through life. Neither is perfect; both are on the same level of imperfection; they keep pace with each other; in proportion to the imperfection of one, so is the imperfection of the other; and, as the one advances, so does the other also.

And now I have described the temper of mind which has, in every age, been acceptable to Almighty God, in its two aspects of faith and obedience. In every age "the righteous shall live by faith." And it is remarkable that these words of the prophet Habakkuk, which St. Paul quotes three several times, to show the identity of true religion under all dispensations, do also represent it under these very two characteristics, righteousness and faith.

Before closing the subject, however, it may be necessary, in a few words, to explain *why* it is that, in some parts of St. Paul's Epistles, a certain stress is laid upon faith over and above the other parts of a religious character, in our justification. The reason seems to be as follows: the Gospel being preeminently a covenant of grace, faith is so far of more excellence than other virtues, because it confesses this beyond all others. Works of obedience witness to God's just claims upon us, not to His mercy: but faith comes empty-handed, hides even its own worth, and does but point at that precious scheme of redemption which God's love has devised for sinners. Hence, it is the frame of mind especially suitable to us, and is said, in a special way, to justify us, because it glorifies God, witnessing that He accepts those and those only, who confess they are not worthy to be accepted.

On this account, faith has a certain prerogative of dignity under the Gospel. At the same time we must never forget that the more usual mode of doctrine both with Christ and His Apostles is to refer our acceptance to obedience to the commandments, not to faith; and this, as it would appear, from a merciful anxiety in their teaching, lest, in contemplating God's grace, we should forget our own duties.

To conclude. If, after all, to believe and to obey be but different characteristics of one and the same state of mind, in what a most serious error are whole masses of men involved at this day, who are commonly considered religious! It is undeniable that there are multitudes who would avow with confidence and exultation that they put obedience only in the second place in their religious scheme, as if it were rather a necessary consequence of faith than requiring a direct attention for its own sake; a something subordinate to it, rather than connatural and contemporaneous with it. It is certain, however startling it is to reflect upon it, that numbers do not in any true sense believe that they shall be judged; they believe in a coming judgment as regards the wicked, but they do not believe that all men, that they themselves personally, will undergo it. I wish from my heart that the persons in question could be persuaded to read Scripture with their own eyes, and take it in a plain and natural way, instead of perplexing themselves with their human systems, and measuring and arranging its inspired declarations by an artificial rule. Are they quite sure that in the next world they will be able to remember these strained interpretations in their greatest need? Then surely, while we wait for the Judgment, the luminous sentences of Divine Truth will come over us, first one and then another, and we shall wonder how we ever misunderstood them! Then will they confront us in their simplicity and entireness, and we shall understand that nothing can be added to them, nothing taken away. Then at length, if not before, we shall comprehend our Lord's assurance, that "He will reward every man according to his works"; St. Paul's, that "we must all appear before the judgment seat of Christ, that every one may receive the things done in his body, according to that he hath done, whether it be good or bad"; St. Peter's, that "He is ordained of God to be the Judge of quick and dead"; St. James's, that "a man is justified by works and not by faith only"; and St. John's, that "they are blessed that do His commandments, that they might have right to the tree of life, and may enter in through the gates into the city."[80] Whatever else may be true, these declarations, so solemnly, so repeatedly made, must hold good in their plain and obvious sense, and may not be infringed or superseded. So many testimonies combined are "an anchor of the soul, sure and steadfast," and if they mean something else than what they all say, what part of Scripture can we dare trust in future as a guide and consolation?

"O Lord, Thy Word endureth forever in heaven!" but the expositions of men are written on the seashore, and are blotted out before the evening.

[III, 6]

Chapter 15

CHRISTIAN REPENTANCE

Father, I have sinned against heaven and before thee, and am no more worthy to be called thy son; make me as one of thy hired servants.
—Luke 15:18, 19

The very best that can be said of the fallen and redeemed race of Adam is that they confess their fall, and condemn themselves for it, and try to recover themselves. And this state of mind, which is in fact the only possible religion left to sinners, is represented to us in the parable of the prodigal son, who is described as receiving, then abusing, and then losing God's blessings, suffering from their loss, and brought to himself by the experience of suffering. A poor service indeed to offer, but the best we can offer, to make obedience our second choice when the world deserts us, when that is dead and lost to us wherein we were held!

Let it not be supposed, because I say this, that I think that in the lifetime of each one of us there is some clearly marked date at which he began to seek God, and from which he has served him faithfully. This may be so in the case of this person or that, but it is far from being the rule. We may not so limit the mysterious work of the Holy Ghost. He condescends to plead with us continually, and what He cannot gain from us at one time, He gains at another. Repentance is a work carried on at diverse times, and but gradually and with many reverses perfected. Or rather, and without any change in the meaning of the word *repentance,* it is a work never complete, never entire—unfinished both in its inherent imperfection, and on account of the fresh and fresh occasions which arise for exercising it. We are ever sinning, we must ever be renewing our sorrow and our purpose of obedience, repeating our confessions and our prayers for pardon. No need to look back to the first beginnings of our repentance, should we be able to trace these, as something solitary and peculiar in our religious course; we are *ever* but beginning; the most perfect Christian is to himself but a beginner, a penitent prodigal, who has squandered

God's gifts, and comes to Him to be tried over again, not as a son, but as a hired servant.

In this parable, then, we need not understand the description of the returning prodigal to imply that there is a state of disobedience and subsequent state of conversion definitely marked in the life of Christians generally. It describes the state of all Christians at all times, and is fulfilled more or less, according to circumstances, in this case or that; fulfilled in one way and measure at the beginning of our Christian course, and in another at the end. So I shall now consider it, viz. as describing the *nature* of all true repentance.

1. First, observe, the prodigal son said, "I am no more worthy to be called thy son, make me as one of thy hired servants." We know that God's service is perfect freedom, not a servitude; but this it is in the case of those who have long served Him; at first it *is* a kind of servitude, it is a task till our likings and tastes come to be in unison with those which God has sanctioned. It is the happiness of Saints and Angels in heaven to take pleasure in their duty, and nothing but their duty; for their mind goes that one way, and pours itself out in obedience to God, spontaneously and without thought or deliberation, just as man *sins* naturally. This is the state to which we are tending if we give ourselves up to religion; but in its commencement, religion is necessarily almost a task and a formal service. When a man begins to see his wickedness, and resolves on leading a new life, he asks, *What must I do?* he has a wide field before him, and he does not know how to enter it. He must be bid to do some particular plain acts of obedience, to fix him. He must be told to go to Church regularly, to say his prayers morning and evening, and statedly to read the Scriptures. This will limit his efforts to a certain end, and relieve him of the perplexity and indecision which the greatness of his work at first causes. But who does not see that this going to Church, praying in private, and reading Scripture, must in his case be, in great measure, what is called a form and a task? Having been used to do as he would, and indulge himself, and having very little understanding or liking for religion, he cannot take pleasure in these religious duties; they will necessarily be a weariness to him; nay, he will not be able even to give his attention to them. Nor will he see the use of them; he will not be able to find they make him bet-

ter though he repeat them again and again. Thus his obedience at first is altogether that of a hired servant, "The servant knoweth not what his lord doeth."[81] This is Christ's account of him. The servant is not in his lord's confidence, does not understand what he is aiming at, or why he commands this and forbids that. He executes the commands given him, he goes hither and thither, punctually, but by the mere letter of the command. Such is the state of those who *begin* religious obedience. They do not see anything come of their devotional or penitential services, nor do they take pleasure in them: they are obliged to defer to God's word simply because it is His word; to do which implies faith indeed, but also shows they are in that condition of a servant which the prodigal felt himself to be in at best.

Now, I insist upon this, because the conscience of a repentant sinner is often uneasy at finding religion a task to him. He thinks he ought to rejoice in the Lord at once, and it is true he is often told to do so; he is often taught to begin by cultivating high affections. Perhaps he is even warned against offering to God what is termed a *formal service*. Now this is reversing the course of a Christian's life. The prodigal son judged better, when he begged to be made one of his father's servants—he knew his place. We *must begin* religion with what looks like a form. Our fault will be, not in beginning it as a form, but in continuing it as a form. For it is our duty to be ever striving and praying to *enter* into the real spirit of our services, and in proportion as we understand them and love them, they will cease to be a form and a task, and will be the real expressions of our minds. Thus shall we gradually be changed in heart from servants into sons of Almighty God. And though from the very first, we must be taught to look to Christ as the Savior of sinners, still His very love will frighten, while it encourages us, from the thought of our ingratitude. It will fill us with remorse and dread of judgment, for we are not as the heathen, we have received privileges, and have abused them.

2. So much, then, on the condition of the repentant sinner; next, let us consider the motives which actuate him in his endeavors to serve God. One of the most natural, and among the first that arise in the mind, is that of *propitiating* Him. When we are conscious to ourselves of having offended another, and wish to be forgiven, of course we look about for some *means* of setting our-

selves right with him. If it be a slight offense, our overtures are in themselves enough, the mere expression that we wish our fault forgotten. But if we have committed some serious injury, or behaved with any special ingratitude, we, for a time, keep at a distance, from a doubt how we shall be received. If we can get a common friend to mediate in our behalf, our purpose is best answered. But even in that case we are not satisfied with leaving our interests to another; we try to do something for ourselves; and on perceiving any signs of compassion or placability in the person offended, we attempt to approach him with propitiations of our own, either very humble confession, or some acceptable service. It was under this feeling that Jacob attempted to conciliate the governor of Egypt (whom he knew not to be his son Joseph), with a present of the best fruits of the land, "a little balm, and a little honey, spices, and myrrh, nuts, and almonds." And this holds good when applied to the case of sinners desiring forgiveness from God. The marks of His mercy all around us are strong enough to inspire us with some general hope. The very fact that He still continues our life, and has not at once cast us into hell, shows that He is waiting awhile before the wrath comes upon us to the uttermost. Under these circumstances it is *natural* that the conscience-stricken sinner should look around him for some atonement with which to meet his God. And this in fact has been the usual course of religion in all ages. Whether "with burnt offerings and calves of a year old, with thousands of rams, and ten thousands of rivers of oil, with the offering of a man's firstborn for his transgression, the fruit of his body for the sin of his soul"; or, in a higher way, "by doing justly, loving mercy, and walking humbly with our God";[82] by some means or other, repentant sinners have attempted to win God's attention and engage His favor. And this mode has, before now, been graciously accepted by God, though He generally chose the gift which He would accept. Thus Jacob was instructed to sacrifice on the altar at Bethel, after his return from Padan-aram. David, on the other hand, speaks of the more spiritual sacrifice in the Fifty-first Psalm: "The sacrifices of God are a broken spirit; a broken and a contrite heart, O God, Thou wilt not despise." Such are the services of the penitent, as suggested by nature, and approved by God Himself in the Old Testament.

But now, turning to the parable of the prodigal son, we find nothing of this kind in it. There is no mention made here of any offering on his part to his father, any propitiatory work. This should be well observed. The truth is, that our Savior has shown us in all things a more perfect way than was ever before shown to man. As He promises us a more exalted holiness, an exacter self-command, a more generous self-denial, and a fuller knowledge of truth, so He gives us a more true and noble repentance. The most noble repentance (if a fallen being can be noble in his fall), the most decorous conduct in a conscious sinner, is an *unconditional surrender* of himself to God—not a bargaining about terms, not a scheming (so to call it) to be received back again, but an instant *surrender* of himself in the first instance. Without knowing what will become of him, whether God will spare or not, merely with so much hope in his heart as not utterly to despair of pardon, still not looking merely to pardon as an *end,* but rather looking to the claims of the Benefactor whom he has offended, and smitten with shame, and the sense of his ingratitude, he must *surrender himself* to his lawful Sovereign. He is a runaway offender; he must come back, as a very first step, before anything can be determined about him, bad or good; he is a rebel, and must lay down his arms. Self-devised offerings might do in a less serious matter; as an atonement for sin, they imply a defective view of the evil and extent of sin in his own case. Such is that perfect way which nature shrinks from, but which our Lord enjoys in the parable—a surrender. The prodigal son waited not for his father to show signs of placability. He did not merely approach a space, and then stand as a coward, curiously inquiring, and dreading how his father felt towards him. He made up his mind at once to degradation at the best, perhaps to rejection. He arose and went straight on towards his father, with a collected mind; and though his relenting father saw him from a distance, and went out to meet him, still his purpose was that of an instant frank submission. Such must be Christian repentance: First we must put aside the idea of finding a remedy for our sin; then, though we feel the guilt of it, yet we must set out firmly towards God, not knowing for certain that we shall be forgiven. He, indeed, meets us on our way with the tokens of His favor, and so He bears up human faith, which else would sink under the apprehension of meeting the Most High

God; still, for our repentance to be Christian, there must be in it that generous temper of self-surrender, the acknowledgment that we are unworthy to be called anymore His sons, the abstinence from all ambitious hopes of sitting on His right hand or His left, and the willingness to bear the heavy yoke of bond servants, if He should put it upon us.

This, I say, is Christian repentance. Will it be said, "It is too hard for a beginner?" true: but I have not been describing the case of a beginner. The parable teaches us what the character of the true penitent is, not how men actually *at first* come to God. The longer we live, the more we may hope to *attain* this higher kind of repentance, viz., in proportion as we advance in the other graces of the perfect Christian character. The truest kind of repentance as little comes at first, as perfect conformity to any other part of God's Law. It is gained by long practice—it will come at length. The dying Christian will fulfill the part of the returning prodigal more exactly than he ever did in his former years. When first we turn to God in the actual history of our lives, our repentance is mixed with all kinds of imperfect views and feelings. Doubtless there is in it something of the true temper of simple submission; but the wish of appeasing God on the one hand, or a hard-hearted insensibility about our sins on the other, mere selfish dread of punishment, or the expectation of a sudden easy pardon, these, and suchlike principles, influence us, whatever we may say or may think we feel. It is, indeed, easy enough to have good words put into our mouths, and our feelings roused, and to profess the union of utter self-abandonment and enlightened sense of sin; but to claim is not really to possess these excellent tempers. Really to gain these is a work of time. It is when the Christian has long fought the good fight of faith, and by experience knows how few and how imperfect are his best services; then it is that he is able to acquiesce, and most gladly acquiesces in the statement, that we are accepted by faith only in the merits of our Lord and Savior. When he surveys his life at the close of it, what is there he can trust in? what act of it will stand the scrutiny of the Holy God? of course no part of it, so much is plain without saying a word. But further, what part of it even is a sufficient evidence to himself of his own sincerity and faithfulness? This is the point which I urge. How shall he know that he is still in a state of grace after all his sins? Doubtless he may have some humble hope of his acceptance. St. Paul speaks of the testimony of his conscience as consoling him; but his conscience also tells him of numberless actual sins, and numberless omissions of duty; and with the awful prospect of eternity before him, and in the weakness of declining health, how shall he collect himself to appear before God? Thus he is after all, in the very condition of the returning prodigal, and cannot go beyond him, though he has served God ever so long. He can but *surrender* himself to God, as after all, a worse than unprofitable servant, resigned to God's will, whatever it is, with more or less hope of pardon, as the case may be; doubting not that Christ is the sole meritorious Author of all grace, resting simply on Him who, "if He will, can make him clean," but not without fears about himself, because unable, as he well knows, to read his own heart in that clear unerring way in which God reads it. Under these circumstances, how vain it is to tell him of his own good deeds, and to bid him look back on his past consistent life! This reflection will rarely comfort him; and when it does, it will be the recollection of the instances of God's mercy towards him in former years which will be the chief ground of encouragement in it. No, his true stay is that Christ came "to call sinners to repentance," that "He died for the ungodly." He acknowledges and adopts, as far as he can, St. Paul's words, and nothing beyond them, "This is a faithful saying, and worthy of all acceptation, that Christ Jesus came into the world to save *sinners,* of whom I am chief."[83]

Who shall dare approach Christ at the dreadful Day of Judgment, who has rejected the calling of His Spirit here? Who shall then dare to surrender himself to the great God, when hell is opened ready to receive him? Alas! it is only because *some* hope is left to us that we dare give ourselves up to Him *here; despair* ever keeps away. But then, when He takes His seat as the severe Judge of sinners, who, among His slothful disobedient servants, will willingly present himself? Surely the time of *submission* will then be over; resignation has no place among fallen spirits; they are swept away by the uncontrollable power of God. "Bind him *hand and foot,* and take him away";[84] such will be the dreadful command. They *would* struggle if they *could.*

And in hell they will be still tormented by the worm of proud rebellious hatred of God! Not even ages will reconcile them to a hard endurance of their fate; not even the dry apathy in which unbelievers on earth take refuge will be allowed them. There is no fatalism in the place of torment. The devils see their doom was their own fault, yet they are unable to be sorry for it. It is their *will* that is in direct energetic variance with the will of God, and they know it.

Consider this, my brethren, and lay it to heart. Doubtless you must render yourselves to God's mercy here, or else be forced away before His anger hereafter.

"Today, while it is called today, harden not your hearts."[85]

[III, 7]

Chapter 16

A PARTICULAR PROVIDENCE AS REVEALED
IN THE GOSPEL

Thou God seest me.
—Gen. 16:13

When Hagar fled into the wilderness from the face of her mistress, she was visited by an Angel, who sent her back; but, together with this implied reproof of her impatience, he gave her a word of promise to encourage and console her. In the mixture of humbling and cheerful thoughts thus wrought in her, she recognized the presence of her Maker and Lord, who ever comes to His servants in a twofold aspect, severe because He is holy, yet soothing as abounding in mercy. In consequence, she called the name of the Lord that spake unto her, "Thou God seest me."

Such was the condition of man before Christ came, favored with some occasional notices of God's regard for individuals, but, for the most part, instructed merely in His general Providence, as seen in the course of human affairs. In this respect even the Law was deficient though it abounded in proofs that God was a living, all-seeing, all-recompensing God. It was deficient, in comparison of the Gospel, in evidence of the really existing relation between each soul of man and its Maker, independently of everything else in the world. Of Moses, indeed, it is said, that "the Lord spake unto him *face to face,* as a man speaketh unto his friend."[86] But this was an especial privilege vouchsafed to him only and some others, as to Hagar, who records it in the text, not to all the people. But, under the New Covenant, this distinct regard, vouchsafed by Almighty God to every one of us, is clearly revealed. It was foretold of the Christian Church, "*All* thy children shall be taught of the Lord; and great shall be the peace of thy children."[87] When the Eternal Son came on earth in our flesh, men saw their invisible Maker and Judge. He showed Himself no longer through the mere powers of nature, or the maze of human affairs, but in our own likeness to Him. "God, who commanded the light to shine out of darkness, hath shined in our hearts, to give the light of the knowledge of the glory of God in the face of Jesus Christ";[88] that is, in a sensible form, as a really existing individual being. And, at the same time, He forthwith began to speak to *us* as individuals. He, on the one hand, addressed each of us on the other. Thus it was in some sense a revelation face to face.

This is the subject on which I propose now to make a few remarks. And first, let me observe, it is very difficult, in spite of the revelation made us in the Gospel, to master the idea of this particular Providence of God. If we allow ourselves to float down the current of the world, living as other men, gathering up our notions of religion here and there, as it may be, we have little or no true comprehension of a particular Providence. We conceive that Almighty God works on a large plan; but we cannot realize the wonderful truth that He sees and thinks of individuals. We cannot believe He is really present everywhere, that He is wherever we are, though unseen. For instance, we can understand, or think we understand, that He was present on Mount Sinai, or within the Jewish Temple, or that He clave the ground under Dathan and Abiram. But we do not in any sufficient sense believe that He is in like manner "about *our* path, and about *our* bed, and spieth out all *our* ways."[89] We cannot bring ourselves to get fast hold of the solemn fact that He sees what is going on among ourselves at this moment; that this man falls and that man is exalted, at His silent, invisible appointment. We use, indeed, the prayers of the Church, and intercede, not only for all conditions of men, but for the King and the Nobility, and the Court of Parliament, and so on, down to individual sick people in our own parish; yet in spite of all this, we do not bring home to our minds the truth of His omniscience. We know He is in heaven, and forget that He is also on earth. This is the reason why the multitude of men are so profane. They use light words; they scoff at religion; they allow themselves to be lukewarm and indifferent; they take the part of wicked men; they push forward wicked measures; they defend injustice, or cruelty, or sacrilege, or infidelity; because they have no grasp of a truth, which nevertheless they have no intention to deny, that God sees them. There is, indeed, a self-will, and self-deceit, which would sin on even in God's visible presence. This was the sin of Balaam, who took part with the enemies of Israel

for reward; and of Zimri, the son of Salu, a prince of the Sime-
onites, on whom Phineas did judgment; and such the sin of Saul,
of Judas, of Ananias and Sapphira. Alas! doubtless such is the sin
of many a man now in England, unless human nature is other
than it was aforetime; alas! such a sin is in a measure our own
from time to time, as anyone may know for certain who is used to
self-examination. Yet, over and above this, certainly there is also a
great deal of profane sinning from our *forgetting,* not comprehending that we are in God's presence; not comprehending, or (in
other words) believing, that He sees and hears and notes down
everything we do.

   This, again, is often the state in which persons find themselves
on falling into trouble. The world fails them, and they despair,
because they do not realize to themselves the loving-kindness and
the presence of God. They find no comfort in a truth which to
them is not a substance but an opinion. Therefore it was that
Hagar, when visited in the wilderness by the Angel, called the
name of the Lord that spake unto her, "Thou God seest me!" It
came as a new truth to her that, amid her trouble and her waywardness, the eye of God was upon her. The case is the same now.
Men talk in a general way of the goodness of God, His benevolence, compassion, and long-suffering; but they think of it as of a
flood pouring itself out all through the world, as the light of the
sun, not as the continually repeated action of an intelligent and
living Mind, contemplating whom it visits and intending what it
effects. Accordingly, when they come into trouble, they can but
say, "It is all for the best—God is good," and the like; and this
does but fall as cold comfort upon them, and does not lessen their
sorrow, because they have not accustomed their minds to feel that
He is a merciful God, regarding them individually, and not a
mere universal Providence acting by general laws. And then, perhaps, all of a sudden the true notion breaks on them, as it did
upon Hagar. Some especial Providence, amid their infliction,
runs right into their heart, and brings it close home to them, in a
way they never experienced before, that God sees them. And
then, surprised at this, which is a something quite new to them,
they go into the other extreme, in proportion to their former apathy, and are led to think that they are especial objects of God's
love, more than all other men. Instead of taking what has hap-

pened to them as an evidence of His particular Providence over all, as revealed in Scripture, they still will not believe a jot or tittle more than they see; and, while discovering He loves them individually, they do not advance one step, on that account, to the general truth, that He loves other men individually also. Now, had they been all along in the practice of studying Scripture, they would have been saved from both errors—their first, which was blindness to a particular Providence altogether—their second, which was a narrow-minded limiting of it to themselves, as if the world at large were rejected and reprobate; for Scripture represents this privilege as the portion of all men one by one.

I suppose it is scarcely necessary to prove to those who have allowed their minds to dwell on the Gospels, that the peculiar character of our Lord's goodness, as displayed therein, is its tenderness and its considerateness. These qualities are the very perfection of kindness between man and man; but, from the very extent and complication of the world's system, and from its Maker's being invisible, our imagination scarcely succeeds in attributing them to Him, even when our reason is convinced, and we wish to believe accordingly. His Providence manifests itself in general laws, it moves forward upon the lines of truth and justice; it has no respect of persons, rewarding the good and punishing the bad, not as individuals, but according to their character. How shall He who is most holy direct His love to this man or that for the sake of each, contemplating us one by one, without infringing on His own perfections? Or even were the Supreme Being a God of unmixed benevolence, how, even then, shall the thought of Him come home to our minds with that constraining power which the kindness of a human friend exerts over us? The greatest acknowledgment we can make of the kindness of a superior, is to say that he acts as if he were personally interested in us. The mass of benevolent men are kind and generous, because it is their way to be so, irrespectively of the person whom they benefit. Natural temper, a flow of spirits, or a turn of good fortune, opens the heart, which pours itself out profusely on friend and enemy. They scatter benefits as they move along. Now, at first sight, it is difficult to see how our idea of Almighty God can be divested of these earthly notions, either that His goodness is imperfect, or that it is fated and necessary; and wonderful indeed, and adorable is the condescension by which He has met our infirmity. He has met and aided it in that same dispensation by which He redeemed our souls. In order that we may understand that in spite of His mysterious perfections He has a separate knowledge and regard for individuals, He has taken upon Him the thoughts and feelings of our own nature, which we all understand *is* capable of such personal attachments. By becoming man, He has cut short the perplexities and the discussions of our reason on the subject, as if He would grant our objections for argument's sake, and supersede them by taking our own ground.

The most winning property of our Savior's mercy (if it is right so to speak of it), is its dependence on time and place, person and circumstance; in other words, its tender discrimination. It regards and consults for each individual as he comes before it. It is called forth by some as it is not by others, it cannot (if I may say so) manifest itself to every object alike; it has its particular shade and mode of feeling for each; and on some men it so bestows itself, as if He depended for His own happiness on their well-being. This might be illustrated, as is often done, by our Lord's tender behavior towards Lazarus and his sisters, or His tears over Jerusalem; or by His conduct towards St. Peter, before and after his denial of Him, or towards St. Thomas when he doubted, or by His love of His Mother, or of St. John. But I will direct your attention rather to His treatment of the traitor Judas; both because it is not so commonly referred to, and, also, because if there was a being in the whole world whom one might suppose to be cast out of His presence as hateful and reprobate, it was he who He foresaw would betray Him. Yet we shall find that even this wretched man was followed and encompassed by His serene though grave regard till the very hour he betrayed Him.

Judas was in darkness and hated the light, and "went to his own place"; yet he found it, not by the mere force of certain natural principles working out their inevitable results—by some unfeeling fate, which sentences the wicked to hell—but by a Judge who surveys him from head to foot, who searches him through and through, to see if there is any ray of hope, any latent spark of faith; who pleads with him again and again, and, at length abandoning him, mourns over him the while with the wounded affection of a friend rather than the severity of the

Judge of the whole earth. For instance, first a startling warning a year before his trial: "Have not I chosen you twelve, and one of you is a devil?" Then, when the time was come, the lowest act of abasement towards one who was soon to betray Him, and to suffer the unquenchable fire. "He riseth from supper, and ... poureth water into a basin, and began to wash the disciples' feet,"[90] and Judas in the number. Then a second warning at the same time, or rather a sorrowful lament spoken as if to Himself, "Ye are not all clean." Then openly, "Verily, verily, I say unto you, that one of you shall betray Me." "The Son of Man goeth as it is written of Him; but woe unto that man by whom the Son of Man is betrayed! it had been good for that man if he had not been born. Then Judas, which betrayed Him, answered and said, Master, is it I? He said unto him, Thou hast said it." Lastly, when He was actually betrayed by him, "Friend, wherefore art thou come?" "Judas" (He addresses him by name), "betrayest thou the Son of Man with a kiss?"[91] I am not attempting to reconcile His divine foreknowledge with this special and prolonged anxiety, this personal feeling towards Judas; but wish you only to dwell upon the latter, in order to observe what is given us by the revelation of Almighty God in the Gospels, viz., an acquaintance with His providential regard for *individuals,* making His sun to rise on the evil as well as on the good. And, in like manner doubtless, at the last day, the wicked and impenitent shall be condemned, not in a mass, but one by one—one by one, appearing each in his own turn before the righteous Judge, standing under the full glory of His countenance, carefully weighed in the balance and found wanting, dealt with, not indeed with a weak and wavering purpose, where God's justice claims satisfaction, yet, at the same time, with all the circumstantial solicitude and awful care of one who would fain make, if He could, the fruit of His passion more numerous than it is.

This solemn reflection may be further enforced by considering our Lord's behavior towards strangers who came to Him. Judas was His friend; but *we* have never seen Him. How will He look, and how does He look upon us? Let His manner in the Gospels towards the multitude of men assure us. All-holy, Almighty as He is, and has shown Himself to be, yet in the midst of His Divine Majesty, He could display a tender interest in all who approached

Him; as if He could not cast His eyes on any of His creatures without the overflowing affection of a parent for his child, regarding it with a full satisfaction, and simply desiring its happiness and highest good. Thus, when the rich young man came to him, it is said, "And Jesus beholding him, *loved him,* and said unto him, One thing thou lackest." When the Pharisees asked a sign, "He sighed deeply in His Spirit." At another time, "He looked round about on them"—as if on every one, to see if here or there perchance there might be an exception to the general unbelief, and to condemn, one by one, those who were guilty[92]—"He looked round about on them with anger, being grieved for the hardness of their hearts." Again, when a leper came to Him, He did not simply heal him, but, "moved with compassion, He put forth His hand."[93]

How gracious is this revelation of God's particular Providence to those who seek Him! how gracious to those who have discovered that this world is but vanity, and who are solitary and isolated in themselves, whatever shadows of power and happiness surround them! The multitude, indeed, go on without these thoughts, either from insensibility, as not understanding their own wants, or changing from one idol to another, as each successively fails. But men of keener hearts would be overpowered by despondency, and would even loathe existence, did they suppose themselves under the mere operation of fixed laws, powerless to excite the pity or the attention of Him who has appointed them. What should they do especially, who are cast among persons unable to enter into their feelings, and thus strangers to them, though by long custom ever so much friends! or who have perplexities of mind they cannot explain to themselves, much less remove, and no one to help them; or who have affections and aspirations pent up within them, because they have not met with objects to which to devote them; or who are misunderstood by those around them, and find they have no words to set themselves right with them, or no principles in common by way of appeal; or who seem to themselves to be without place or purpose in the world, or to be in the way of others; or who have to follow their own sense of duty without advisers or supporters, nay, to resist the wishes and solicitations of superiors or relatives; or who have the burden of some painful secret, or of some incommunicable solitary grief! In all such cases the Gospel narrative supplies our very need, not simply presenting to us an unchangeable Creator to rely upon, but a compassionate Guardian, a discriminating Judge and Helper.

God beholds thee individually, whoever thou art. He "calls thee by thy name." He sees thee, and understands thee, as He made thee. He knows what is in thee, all thy own peculiar feelings and thoughts, thy dispositions and likings, thy strength and thy weakness. He views thee in thy day of rejoicing, and thy day of sorrow. He sympathizes in thy hopes and thy temptations. He interests Himself in all thy anxieties and remembrances, all the risings and fallings of thy spirit. He has numbered the very hairs of thy head and the cubits of thy stature. He compasses thee round and bears thee in His arms; He takes thee up and sets thee down. He notes thy very countenance, whether smiling or in tears, whether healthful or sickly. He looks tenderly upon thy hands and thy feet; He hears thy voice, the beating of thy heart, and thy very breathing. Thou dost not love thyself better than He loves thee. Thou canst not shrink from pain more than He dislikes thy bearing it; and if He puts it on thee, it is as thou wilt put it on thyself, if thou art wise, for a greater good afterwards. Thou art not only His creature (though for the very sparrows He has a care, and pitied the "much cattle" of Nineveh), thou art man redeemed and sanctified, His adopted son, favored with a portion of that glory and blessedness which flows from Him everlastingly unto the Only-begotten. Thou art chosen to be His, even above thy fellows who dwell in the East and South. Thou wast one of those for whom Christ offered up His last prayer, and sealed it with His precious Blood. What a thought is this, a thought almost too great for our faith! Scarce can we refrain from acting Sarah's part, when we bring it before us, so as to "laugh" from amazement and perplexity. What is man, what are we, what am I, that the Son of God should be so mindful of me? What am I, that He should have raised me from almost a devil's nature to that of an Angel's, that He should have changed my soul's original constitution, new-made me, who from my youth up have been a transgressor, and should Himself dwell personally in this very heart of mine, making me His temple? What am I, that God the Holy

Ghost should enter into me, and draw up my thoughts heavenward "with plaints unutterable"?

These are the meditations which come upon the Christian to
console him, while he is with Christ upon the holy mount. And,
when he descends to his daily duties, they are still his inward
strength, though he is not allowed to tell the vision to those
around him. They make his countenance to shine, make him
cheerful, collected, serene, and firm in the midst of all temptation,
persecution, or bereavement. And with such thoughts before us,
how base and miserable does the world appear in all its pursuits
and doctrines! How truly miserable does it seem to seek good
from the creature; to covet station, wealth, or credit; to choose for
ourselves, in fancy, this or that mode of life; to affect the manners
and fashions of the great; to spend our time in follies; to be discontented, quarrelsome, jealous or envious, censorious or resentful;
fond of unprofitable talk, and eager for the news of the day; busy
about public matters which concern us not; hot in the cause of this
or that interest or party; or set upon gain; or devoted to the
increase of barren knowledge! And at the end of our days, when
flesh and heart fail, what will be our consolation, though we have
made ourselves rich, or have served an office, or been the first
man among our equals, or have depressed a rival, or managed
things our own way, or have settled splendidly, or have been intimate with the great, or have fared sumptuously, or have gained a
name! Say, even if we obtain that which lasts longest, a place in
history, yet, after all, what ashes shall we have eaten for bread!
And, in that awful hour, when death is in sight, will He, whose
eye is now so loving towards us, and whose hand falls on us so
gently, will He acknowledge us anymore? or, if He still speaks,
will His voice have any power to stir us? rather will it not repel
us, as it did Judas, by the very tenderness with which it would
invite us to Him?

Let us then endeavor, by His grace, rightly to understand
where we stand, and what He is towards us; most tender and piti-
ful, yet, for all His pity, not passing by the breadth of a single hair
the eternal lines of truth, holiness, and justice; He who can condemn to the woe everlasting, though He weeps and laments
beforehand, and who, when once the sentence of condemnation

has gone forth, will wipe out altogether the remembrance of us, "and know us not." The tares were "bound in bundles" for the burning, indiscriminately, promiscuously, contemptuously. "Let us then fear, lest a promise being left us of entering into His rest, any of us should seem to come short of it."

[III, 9]

Chapter 17

THE STRICTNESS OF THE LAW OF CHRIST

Being then made free from sin, ye became the servants of righteousness.
—Rom. 6:18

In the passage of which these words form a part, St. Paul insists again and again on the great truth which they declare, that Christians are not their own, but bought with a price, and, as being so, are become the servants or rather the slaves of God and His righteousness; and this, upon their being rescued from the state of nature. The great Apostle is not content with speaking half the truth; he does not merely say that we are set free from guilt and misery, but he adds, that we have become the servants of Christ; nay, he uses a word which properly means *slaves*. Slaves are bought and sold; we were by nature slaves to sin and Satan; we are bought by the blood of Christ: we do not cease to be slaves. We no longer indeed belong to our old master; but a master we have, unless slaves on being bought become freemen. We are still slaves, but to a new master, and that master is Christ. He has not bought us, and then set us loose upon the world; but He has done for us what alone could complete His first benefit, bought us to be His servants or slaves. He has given us that only liberty which is really such, bond service to Himself; lest if left to ourselves, we should fall back again, as we certainly should, to the cruel bondage from which He redeemed us. But anyhow, whatever be the consequences it involves, whatever the advantage, whatever the trial, we did not cease to be slaves on being set free from Satan; but we became subject to a new Master, to Him who bought us.

This needs insisting on; for a number of persons who are not unwilling to confess that they are slaves by nature, from some cause or other have learned to think that they are not bound to any real service at all, now that Christ has set them free. Now if by the word *slavery,* some cruel and miserable state of suffering is meant, such as human masters often inflict on their slaves, in that sense indeed Christians are not slaves, and the word is improper to apply to them; but if by being slaves, is meant that we cannot throw up our service, change our place, and do as we will, in that sense it is literally true, that we are more than servants to Christ, we are, as the text really words it, slaves. Men often speak as if the perfection of human happiness lay in our being free to do or not to do, to choose and to reject. Now we are indeed thus free, as far as this—that if we do not choose to be Christ's servants, we can go back to that old bondage from which He rescued us, and be slaves again to the powers of evil. But though we are free to make our situation worse, we are not free to be without service or post of any kind. It is not in man's nature to be out of all service and to be self-dependent. We may choose our master, but God or mammon we must serve. We cannot possibly be in a neutral or intermediate state. Such a state does not exist. If we will not be Christ's servants, we are forthwith Satan's; and Christ set us free from Satan only by making us His servants. Satan's kingdom touches upon Christ's, the world touches on the Church; and we cease to be Satan's property by becoming Christ's. We cannot be without a master, such is the law of our nature; yet a number of persons, as I have said, overlook it, and think their Christian liberty lies in being free from all law, even from the law of God. Such an error seems to have obtained even in St. Paul's time, and is noticed in the chapter before us. Men seem to have thought that, since the law of sin was annulled, and the terrors of the law of nature removed, that therefore they were under no law at all; that their own will was their law, and that faith stood instead of obedience. In opposition to this great mistake, St. Paul reminds his brethren in the text, that when they were "made free from *sin*," they "became the servants of *righteousness*." And again, "Sin shall not have dominion over you; for ye are not under the law," that is, the law of nature, "but under grace," or (as he elsewhere expresses it), "the law of faith," or, "the law of the Spirit of life." They were not without a master, but they had a gracious and bountiful one.

He says the same in other Epistles. For instance, "He that is called, being free" (that is, free as regards this world), "is Christ's servant" or slave. "Ye are bought with a price: be not ye slaves of *men*," but, that is, be slaves of Christ. Again, after saying, "Slaves obey in all things your masters according to the flesh," he adds, "for ye are slaves to the Lord Christ." Elsewhere he speaks of himself as "Paul a servant," or slave, as the word really means, "of Jesus Christ"; and again, as "not without law to God, but under the law to Christ."[94]

Religion then is a necessary service; of course it is a privilege too, but it becomes more and more of a privilege, the more we exercise ourselves in it. The perfect Christian state is that in which our duty and our pleasure are the same, when what is right and true is natural to us, and in which God's "service is perfect freedom." And this is the state towards which all true Christians are tending; it is the state in which the Angels stand; entire subjection to God in thought and deed is their happiness; an utter and absolute captivity of their will to His will is their fullness of joy and everlasting life. But it is not so with the best of us, except in part. Upon our regeneration indeed, we have a seed of truth and holiness planted within us, a new law introduced into our nature; but still we have that old nature to subdue, "the old man, which is corrupt according to the deceitful lusts."[95] That is, we have a work, a conflict all through life. We have to master and bring under all we are, all we do, expelling all disorder and insubordination, and teaching and impressing on every part of us, of soul and body, its due place and duty, till we are wholly Christ's in will, affections, and reason, as we are by profession; in St. Paul's words, "casting down imaginations and every high thing that exalteth itself against the knowledge of God, and bringing into captivity every thought to the obedience of Christ."[96]

Now I may seem to have been saying what everyone will at once confess. And yet, after all, nothing perhaps is so rare among those who profess to be Christians, as an assent in practice to the doctrine that they are under a law; nothing so rare as strict obedience, unreserved submission to God's will, uniform conscientiousness in doing their duty, as a few instances will at once show.

Most Christians then will allow in general terms that they are under a law, but then they admit it with a reserve; they claim for themselves some dispensing power in their observance of the law. What I am saying is quite independent of the question, what is the *standard* of obedience which each man proposes to himself? One man puts the line of his duty higher than another; some men take a low view of it, confining it to mere personal morality; others confine it to their social obligations; others limit it by some conventional law, which is received in particular classes or circles; others include religious observances. But whether men view the law of conscience as high or low, as broad or narrow, few indeed there are who make it a rule to themselves; few there are who make their own notion of it, whatever that be, binding on themselves; few who even profess to act up to it uniformly and consistently. Inquire of the multitude of men, as you meet them in the world, and you will find that one and all think it allowable at times to put themselves above the law, even according to their own standard of it; to make exceptions and reserves, as if they were absolute sovereigns of their conscience, and had a dispensing power upon occasions.

What is the sort of man whom the world accounts respectable and religious, in a high rank or a lower? At best he is such as this. He has a number of good points in his character; but some of these he has by nature, and if others have been acquired by trouble, it is either because outward circumstances compelled him to acquire them, or that he has from nature some active principle within him, of one kind or another, which has exerted itself, and brought other principles under, and rules him. He has acquired a certain self-command, because no one is respected without it. He has been forced into habits of diligence, punctuality, precision, and honesty. He is courteous and obliging; and has learned not to say all he thinks and feels, or to do all he wishes to do, on all occasions. The great mass of men of course are far from having in them so much that is really praiseworthy as this; but I am supposing the best. I am supposing then, that a man's character and station are such, that only now and then he will feel his inclinations or his interest to run counter to his duty. Such times constitute his trial; there is nothing to hinder him serving God in the ordinary course, but the proof of his sincerity lies in his conduct on these extraordinary occasions. Now this is the point to which I wish to draw attention; for these very occasions, which alone are his times of trial, are just the times on which he is apt to consider that he has a leave to dispense with the law. He dispenses with it at those very times when it is simply the law of God, without being also the law of self, and of the world. He does what is right, while the road of religion runs along the road of the world; when they part company awhile, he chooses the world, and calls his choice an exception. He does right for ninety-nine days, but on the hundredth he knowingly and willfully does wrong; and if he does not justify, at least he absolves himself in doing it.

For instance; he *generally* comes to Church, it is his *practice*; but some urgent business at a certain time presses on him, or some scheme of pleasure tempts him: he omits his attendance; he knows this is wrong, and says so, but it is only once in a way.

Again: he is strictly honest in his dealings; he speaks the truth, that is, it is his rule to do so; but if hard-pressed, he allows himself now and then in a falsehood, particularly if it is a slight one. He knows he should not lie; he confesses it, but he thinks it cannot be helped; it is unavoidable from circumstances, as being his only way of escaping some great difficulty. In *such* a case it is, as he says, all fair, and so he gets over it; that is, in a case where he must either disobey God, or incur some temporal disadvantage.

Again: he has learned to curb his temper and his tongue; but on some unusual provocation they get the better of him. He becomes angry, says what he should not, perhaps curses and swears. Are not all men subject to be overtaken with anger or ill temper? that is not the point: the point is this—that he does not feel compunction afterwards, he does not feel he has done anything which needs forgiveness. On the contrary, he defends himself to himself, on the plea that such language is very *unusual* with him; he does not understand that he is under a law, which he may not put himself above, which he may not dispense with.

Once more: he is in general sober and temperate; but he joins a party of friends and makes merry; he is tempted to exceed. Next day he says that it is a long time since such a thing happened to him; it is not at all his way; he hardly touches wine or the like in common. He does not understand he has any sin to repent of, because it is but once in a way.

And now, I suppose, you quite understand what I mean, and I need not say more in explanation. Such men, being thus indulgent to themselves, are indulgent to each other; they make allowance for all around them, as taking what they give freely. This is the secret of being friends with the world, to have a sympathy and a share in its sins. They who are strict with themselves are strict with the world; but where men grant themselves a certain license of disobedience, they do not draw the line very rigidly

as regards others. Conscious of what might be said against themselves, they are cautious what they say against others; and they
meet them on the understanding of a mutual sufferance. They
learn to say, that the private habits of their neighbors are nothing
to them; and they hold intercourse with them only as public men,
or members of society, or in the way of business, not at all as with
responsible beings having immortal souls. They desire to see and
know nothing but what is on the surface; and they call a man's
personal history sacred, because it is sinful. In their eyes, their sole
duty to their neighbor is, not to offend him; whatever his morals,
whatever his creed, is nothing to them. Such are they in mature
and advanced life; in youth, they are pliable as well as indulgent,
they readily fall in with the ways of the world, as they come across
them. They are, and have the praise of being pleasant, good-
tempered, and companionable. They are not bad-principled, or
evilly disposed, or flagrantly irregular, but they are lax. They in
no sense live by rule. They have high spirits, and all the natural
amiableness which youth has to show, and they generally go
right; but, since they have no root in themselves, an accident from
within or without, the stirring of a passion, or the incitement of a
friend, makes them swerve at once. They swerve, and they have
little compunction afterwards; they forget it. They shrink from
the notion of being under a law, and think religion gloomy as
imposing it. They like their own way, and without any great
extreme of sin, or at least any habits of sin, follow it. They are
orderly and well-conducted, when among well-conducted people, at home, for instance; but they indulge themselves abroad,
when temptation comes in their way. They have the world at will;
they are free; alas! what a melancholy freedom! yet in one sense a
freedom it is. A religious man must withdraw his eyes from sights
which inflame his heart, recollecting our Savior's caution; but a
man of the world thinks it no harm to gaze where he should not,
because he goes no further. A religious man watches his words;
but the other utters whatever his heart prompts, and excuses himself for profane language, on the plea that he means nothing by it.
A religious man will scruple about his society; but the other takes
part in jests and excesses, though he condemns while he shares
them, but not himself for sharing, and despises those with whom
he shares them. He can see life, as it is called. He can go among all

sorts of people, for he has no troublesome ceremonial, no rule of religion to shackle him. Perhaps he goes abroad, and then for a time he considers himself to be in disguise, as an unknown person in unknown countries, permitted to fall in with all things bad and good, as they come. Or again, he may be so circumstanced, whatever his station, as to find himself engaged in what are called politics; and then he thinks that though truth and religion are certainly all-commanding and all-important, yet still the world could not go on, public business would be at a stand, political parties would be unable to act, all that he really loves and reveres would become but of secondary concern, if religion refused at all times to give way ever so little. Again: a religious man carries his religion into his conduct throughout the day; but lax persons will do many things in private, which they would not like to be known. They will overreach, if they can do it without noise. They will break promises when made to an inferior. Or, if they have time on their hands, they will be curious and meddlesome; they will speak against others and spread scandals. They will pry into things which do not concern them, according to their station in life. They will listen where they have no right to listen; they will read what they have no right to read. Or they will allow themselves in petty thefts, where they think they do no injury, excusing themselves on the plea that what they take will never be missed. Or in matters of trade, they think a certain sort and degree of double-dealing allowable, and no dishonesty. They argue with themselves as if it were not their business to be true and just, but of others to find them out; and as if fraud and cheating did not imply sin in the one party, but dullness in the other. If in humble life, they think it no harm to put on an appearance; to profess what is not strictly true, if they are to gain by it; to color a story; or to affect to be more religious than they are; or to pretend to agree in religion with persons from whom they hope something; or to take up a religion if it is their interest to do so; or to profess two or three religions at once, when any alms or other benefit is to be given away.

These are a few out of a multitude of traits which mark an easy religion, the religion of the world; which would cast in its lot with Christian truth, were not that truth so very strict, and quarrels with it and its upholders, not as if it were not good and right, but because it is so unbending, because it will not suit itself to times and emergencies, and to the private and occasional likings and tastes of individuals. This is the kind of religion which St. Paul virtually warns us against, as often as he speaks of the Gospel as really being a law and a servitude. He indeed glories in its being such; for, as the happiness of all creatures lies in their performing their parts well, where God has placed them, so man's greatest good lies in obedience to God's Law and in imitation of God's perfections. But the Apostle knew that the world would not think so, and therefore he insists on it. Therefore it is that he insists on the necessity of Christians "*fulfilling* the righteousness of the law"; fulfilling it, because till we aim at complete, unreserved obedience in all things, we are not really Christians at all. Hence St. James says, "Whosoever shall keep the whole law, and yet offend in one point, he is guilty of all." And our Savior assures us that "whosoever shall break one of these least commandments, and shall teach men so he shall be called least in the kingdom of heaven"; and that "except our righteousness shall exceed the righteousness of the Scribes and Pharisees," which was thus partial and circumscribed, "we shall in no case enter into the kingdom of heaven." And when the young man came to Him, saying that he had kept all the commandments, and asking what he lacked, He pointed out the "one thing" wanting in him; and when he would not complete his obedience by that one thing, but went away sorrowful, then, as if all his obedience in other points availed him nothing, Christ added, "Children, how hard is it for them that trust in riches to enter into the kingdom of God?"[97] Let us not then deceive ourselves; what God demands of us is to fulfill His Law, or at least to aim at fulfilling it; to be content with nothing short of perfect obedience, to attempt everything, to avail ourselves of the aids given us, and throw ourselves, not first, but afterwards on God's mercy for our shortcomings. This is, I know, at first hearing a startling doctrine; and so averse are our hearts to it, that some men even attempt to maintain that it is an unchristian doctrine. A forlorn expedient indeed, with the Bible to refer to, and its statements about the strait gate and the narrow way. Still men would fain avail themselves of it, if they could; they argue that all enforcement of religion as a service or duty is erroneous, or what they call legal, and that no observance is right but what proceeds from impulse, or what they call the heart. They would fain prove that the Law is not binding on us, because Christ has fulfilled it; or because, as is the case, faith would be accepted instead of obedience in those who had not yet had time to begin fulfilling it.

Such persons appeal to Scripture, and they must be refuted, as is not difficult, from Scripture; but the multitude of men do not take so much trouble about the matter. Instead of even professing to discover what God has said, they take what they call a commonsense view of it. They maintain it is impossible that religion should really be so strict according to God's design. They condemn the notion as overstrained and morose. They profess to admire and take pleasure in religion as a whole, but think that it should not be needlessly pressed in details, or, as they express it, carried too far. They complain only of its particularity, if I may use the term, or its want of indulgence and consideration in little things; that is, in other words, they like religion before they have experience of it—in prospect, at a distance, *till* they have to be religious. They like to talk of it, they like to see men religious; they think it commendable and highly important; but directly religion comes home to them in real particulars of whatever kind, they like it not. It suffices them to have seen and praised it; they feel it a burden whenever they feel it at all, whenever it calls upon them to do what otherwise they would not do. In a word, the state of the multitude of men is this—their hearts are going the wrong way; and their real quarrel with religion, if they know themselves, is not that it is strict, or engrossing, or imperative, not that it goes too far, but that it *is* religion. It is religion itself which we all by nature dislike, not the excess merely. Nature tends towards the earth, and God is in heaven. If I want to travel north, and all the roads are cut to the east, of course I shall complain of the roads. I shall find nothing but obstacles; I shall have to surmount walls, and cross rivers and go round about, and after all fail of my end. Such is the conduct of those who are not bold enough to give up a profession of religion, yet wish to serve the world. They try to reach Babylon by roads which run to Mount Zion. Do you not see that they necessarily must meet with thwartings, crossings, disappointments, and failure? They go mile after mile, watching in vain for the turrets of the city of Vanity, because they are on the wrong road; and, unwilling to own what they are really seeking, they find fault with the road as circuitous and wearisome. They accuse religion of interfering with what they consider their innocent pleasures and wishes. But religion is a bondage only to those who have not the heart to like it, who are not cast into its mold. Accordingly, in the verse before the text St. Paul thanks God that his brethren had "obeyed from the *heart* that *form* of teaching, into which they had been delivered." We Christians are cast into a certain mold. So far as we keep within it, we are not sensible that it is a mold, or has an outline. It is when our hearts would overflow in some evil direction, then we discover that we are confined, and consider ourselves in prison. It is the law in our members warring against the Law of the Spirit which brings us into a distressing bondage. Let us then see where we stand, and what we must do. Heaven cannot change; God is "without variableness or shadow of turning." His "word endureth forever in heaven." His Law is from everlasting to everlasting. *We* must change. We must go over to the side of heaven. Never had a soul true happiness but in conformity to God, in obedience to His will. We must become what we are not; we must learn to love what we do not love, and practice ourselves in what is difficult. We must have the Law of the Spirit of life written and set up in our hearts, "that the righteousness of the Law may be fulfilled in us," and that we may learn to please and to love God.

Lastly, as some men defend their want of strictness on what they consider the authority of Scripture, and others, that is, the majority, try to persuade themselves that religion cannot really be strict, whatever strong expressions or statements may be found in Scripture, others again there are, who take a more candid, but a more daring course. Instead of making excuses, such as I have been considering, they frankly admit the fact, and then go on to urge it as a valid argument against religion altogether. Instead of professing to like religion, *all but* its service, they boldly object that religion is altogether unnatural, and therefore cannot be incumbent on us. They say that it is very well for its ministers and teachers to set up a high doctrine, but that men are men, and the world is the world, and that life was not meant to be a burden, and that God sent us here for enjoyment, and that He will never punish us hereafter for following the law of our nature. I answer, doubtless this life was meant to be enjoyment; but why not a rejoicing in the Lord? We were meant to follow the law of our nature; but why of our old nature, why not of our new? Were we indeed in the state of our first nature, under the guilt and defilement of our birth sin, then this argument might be urged speciously, though not conclusively of course then; but how does it apply to Christians? Now that God has opened the doors of our prison house, and brought us into the kingdom of His Son, if men are still carnal men, and the world a sinful world, and the life of Angels a burden, and the law of our nature not the Law of God, whose fault is it?

We Christians are indeed under the law as other men, but, as I have already said, it is the new law, the Law of the Spirit of Christ. We are under grace. That Law, which to nature is a grievous bondage, is to those who live under the power of God's presence, what it was meant to be, a rejoicing. When then we feel reluctant to serve God, when thoughts rise within us as if He were a hard Master, and that His promises are not attractive enough to balance the strictness of His commandments, let us recollect that we, as being Christians, are not in the flesh, but in the Spirit, and let us act upon the conviction of it. Let us go to Him for grace. Let us seek His face. Let us come where He gives grace. Let us come to the ordinances of grace, in which Christ gives His Holy Spirit, to enable us to do that which by nature we cannot do, and to be "the servants of righteousness." They who pray for His saving help to change their likings and dislikings, their tastes, their views, their wills, their hearts, do not indeed all at once gain what they seek; they do not gain it at once asking; they do not *perceive* they gain it while they gain it, but if they come continually day by day to Him—if they come humbly, if they come in faith, if they come, not as a trial how they shall like God's service, but throwing (as far as may be) their whole hearts and souls into their duty as a sacrifice to Him, if they come, not seeking a sign, but determined to go on seeking Him, honoring Him, serving Him, trusting Him, whether they see light, or feel comfort, or discern their growth, or no—such men *will* gain, though they know it not; they will find, even while they are still seeking; before they call, He will answer them and they will in the end find themselves saved wondrously, to their surprise, how they know not, and when their crown seemed at a distance. "They that wait on the Lord," says the Prophet, "shall renew their strength; they shall mount up with wings as eagles; they shall run and not be weary, and they shall walk and not faint."[98]

[IV, 1]

Chapter 18

THE INDIVIDUALITY OF THE SOUL

The spirit shall return unto God, who gave it.
—Eccles. 12:7

Here we are told that upon death the spirit of man returns to God. The sacred writer is not speaking of good men only, or of God's chosen people, but of men generally. In the case of all men, the soul, when severed from the body, returns to God. God gave it: He made it, He sent it into the body, and He upholds it there; He upholds it in distinct existence, wherever it is. It animates the body while life lasts; it returns again, it relapses into the unseen state upon death. Let us steadily contemplate this truth, which at first sight we may fancy we altogether enter into. The point to be considered is this, that every soul of man which is or has been on earth, has a separate existence; and that, in eternity, not in time merely, in the unseen world, not merely in this, not only during its mortal life, but ever from the hour of its creation, whether joined to a body of flesh or not.

Nothing is more difficult than to realize that every man has a distinct soul, that every one of all the millions who live or have lived, is as whole and independent a being in himself, as if there were no one else in the whole world but he. To explain what I mean: do you think that a commander of an army realizes it, when he sends a body of men on some dangerous service? I am not speaking as if he were wrong in so sending them; I only ask in matter of fact, does he, think you, commonly understand that each of those poor men has a soul, a soul as dear to himself, as precious in its nature, as his own? Or does he not rather look on the body of men collectively, as one mass, as parts of a whole, as but the wheels or springs of some great machine, to which he assigns the individuality, not to each soul that goes to make it up?

This instance will show what I mean, and how open we all lie to the remark, that we do not understand the doctrine of the distinct individuality of the human soul. We class men in masses, as we might connect the stones of a building. Consider our common way of regarding history, politics, commerce, and the like, and you will own that I speak truly. We generalize, and lay down laws, and then contemplate these creations of our own minds, and act upon and towards them, as if they were the real things, dropping what are more truly such. Take another instance: when we talk of national greatness, what does it mean? Why, it really means that a certain distinct, definite number of immortal individual beings happen for a few years to be in circumstances to act together and one upon another, in such a way as to be able to act upon the world at large, to gain an ascendancy over the world, to gain power and wealth, and to look like one, and to be talked of and to be looked up to as one. They seem for a short time to be some one thing: and we, from our habit of living by sight, regard them as one, and drop the notion of their being anything else. And when this one dies and that one dies, we forget that it is the passage of separate immortal beings into an unseen state, that the whole which appears is but appearance, and that the component parts are the realities. No, we think nothing of this; but though fresh and fresh men die, and fresh and fresh men are born, so that the whole is ever shifting, yet we forget all that drop away, and are insensible to all that are added; and we still think that this whole which we call the nation is one and the same, and that the individuals who come and go exist only in it and for it, and are but as the grains of a heap or the leaves of a tree.

Or again, survey some populous town: crowds are pouring through the streets; some on foot, some in carriages; while the shops are full, and the houses too, could we see into them. Every part of it is full of life. Hence we gain a general idea of splendor, magnificence, opulence, and energy. But what is the truth? why, that every being in that great concourse is his own center, and all things about him are but shades, but a "vain shadow," in which he "walketh and disquieteth himself in vain." He has his own hopes and fears, desires, judgments, and aims; he is everything to himself, and no one else is really anything. No one outside of him can really touch him, can touch his soul, his immortality; he must live with himself forever. He has a depth within him unfathomable, an infinite abyss of existence; and the scene in which he bears part for the moment is but like a gleam of sunshine upon its surface.

Again: when we read history, we meet with accounts of great slaughters and massacres, great pestilences, famines, conflagrations, and so on; and here again we are accustomed in an especial way to regard collections of people as if individual units. We cannot understand that a multitude is a collection of immortal souls.

I say immortal souls: each of those multitudes, not only *had* while he was upon earth, but *has* a soul, which did in its own time but return to God who gave it, and not perish, and which now lives unto Him. All those millions upon millions of human beings who ever trod the earth and saw the sun successively, are at this very moment in existence all together. This, I think, you will grant we do not duly realize. All those Canaanites, whom the children of Israel slew, every one of them is somewhere in the universe, now at this moment, where God has assigned him a place. We read, "They utterly destroyed all that was in" Jericho, "young and old." Again, as to Ai, "So it was that all that fell that day, both of men and women, were twelve thousand." Again, "Joshua took Makkedah, Libnah, Lachish, Eglon, Hebron, Debir, and smote them with the edge of the sword, and utterly destroyed all the souls that were therein."[99] Every one of those souls still lives. They had their separate thoughts and feelings when on earth, they have them now. They had their likings and pursuits; they gained what they thought good and enjoyed it; and they still somewhere or other live, and what they then did in the flesh surely has its influence upon their present destiny. They live, reserved for a day which is to come, when all nations shall stand before God.

But why should I speak of the devoted nations of Canaan, when Scripture speaks of a wider, more comprehensive judgment, and in one place appears to hint at the present state of awful waiting in which they are who were involved in it? What an overwhelming judgment was the Flood! all human beings on the earth but eight were cut off by it. That old world of souls still lives, though its material tabernacle was drowned. Scripture, I say, signifies this; obscurely indeed, yet still, as it appears, certainly. St. Peter speaks of "the spirits in prison," that is, *then* in prison, who had been "disobedient," "when once the long-suffering of God waited in the days of Noah."[100] Those many, many souls, who were violently expelled from their bodies by the waters of the deluge, were alive two thousand years afterwards, when St. Peter wrote. Surely they are alive still.

And so of all the other multitudes we anywhere read of: All the Jews who perished in the siege of Jerusalem still live; Sennacherib's army still lives; Sennacherib himself still lives; all the persecutors of the Church that ever were are still alive. The kings of Babylon are still alive; they are still, as they are described by the Prophet, weak indeed now, and in "hell beneath," but having an account to give, and waiting for the day of summons. All who have ever gained a name in the world, all the mighty men of war that ever were, all the great statesmen, all the crafty counselors, all the scheming aspirants, all the reckless adventurers, all the covetous traders, all the proud voluptuaries, are still in being, though helpless and unprofitable. Balaam, Saul, Joab, Ahithophel, good and bad, wise and ignorant, rich and poor, each has his separate place, each dwells by himself in that sphere of light or darkness, which he has provided for himself here. What a view this sheds upon history! We are accustomed to read it as a tale or a fiction, and we forget that it concerns immortal beings, who cannot be swept away, who are what they were, however this earth may change.

And so again all the names we see written on monuments in churches or churchyards, all the writers whose names and works we see in libraries, all the workmen who raised the great buildings, far and near, which are the wonder of the world, they are all in God's remembrance, they all live.

It is the same with those whom we ourselves have seen, who now are departed. I do not now speak of those whom we have known and loved. These we cannot forget; we cannot rid our memory of them: but I speak of all whom we have *ever* seen; it is also true that they live. Where we know not, but live they do. We may recollect when children, perhaps, once seeing a certain person; and it is almost like a dream to us now, that we did. It seems like an accident which goes and is all over, like some creature of the moment, which has no existence beyond it. The rain falls, and the wind blows; and showers and storms have no existence beyond the time when we felt them; they are nothing in themselves. But if we have but once seen any child of Adam, we have seen an immortal soul. It has not passed away as a breeze or sunshine, but it lives; it lives at this moment in one of those many places, whether of bliss or misery, in which all souls are reserved until the end.

Or again, let us call to mind those whom we knew a little better, though not intimately: all who died suddenly or before their time, all whom we have seen in high health and spirits, all whom we have seen in circumstances which in any way brought out their characters, and gave them some place in our memories. They are gone from our sight, but they all live still, each with his own thoughts; they are waiting for the Judgment.

I think we shall see that these thoughts concerning others are not familiar to us; yet no one can say they are not just. And I think too that the thoughts concerning others, which *are* familiar to us, are not those which become believers in the Gospel; whereas these which I have been tracing, do become us, as tending to make us think less of this world, with its hopes and fears, its plans, successes, and enjoyments.

Moreover, every one of all the souls which have ever been on earth is, as I have already implied, in one of two spiritual states, so distinct from one another, that the one is the subject of God's favor, and the other under His wrath; the one on the way to eternal happiness, the other to eternal misery. This is true of the dead, and is true of the living also. All are tending one way or the other; there is no middle or neutral state for anyone; though as far as the sight of the external world goes, all men seem to be in a middle state common to one and all. Yet, much as men look the same, and impossible as it is for us to say where each man stands in God's sight, there are two, and but two classes of men, and these have characters and destinies as far apart in their tendencies as light and darkness: this is the case even of those who are in the body, and it is much more true of those who have passed into the unseen state.

No thought of course is more overpowering than that everyone who lives or has lived is destined for endless bliss or torment. It is far too vast for us to realize. But what especially increases the mind's confusion when it attempts to do so is just this very thing which I have been mentioning, that there are but these two states, that every individual among us is either in one or the other, that the states in which we individually are placed are so unspeakably contrary to each other, while we look so like each other. It is certainly quite beyond our understandings, that all we should now be living together as relatives, friends, associates, neighbors; that we should be familiar or intimate with each other, that there should be among us a general intercourse, circulation of thought, interchange of good offices, the action of mind upon mind, and will upon will, and conduct upon conduct, and yet after all that there should be a bottomless gulf between us, running among us invisibly, and cutting us off into two parties—not indeed a gulf impassable here, God be praised! not impassable till we pass into the next world, still really existing, so that every person we meet is in God's unerring eye either on the one side or the other, and, did He please to take him hence at once, would find himself either in paradise or in the place of torment. Our Lord observes this concerning the Day of Judgment, "Two women shall be grinding at the mill; the one shall be taken, and the other left. Two men shall be in the field; the one shall be taken, and the other left."

What makes this thought still more solemn, is that we have reason to suppose that souls on the wrong side of the line are far more numerous than those on the right. It is wrong to speculate; but it is safe to be alarmed. This much we know, that Christ says expressly, "Many are called, few are chosen"; "Broad is the way that leadeth to destruction, and many there be who go in thereat"; whereas "narrow is the way that leadeth to life, and few there be who find it."

If then it is difficult, as I have said it is, to realize that all who ever lived still live, it is as difficult at least to believe that they are in a state either of eternal rest or eternal woe; that all whom we have known and who are gone, are, and that we who still live, were we now to die, should then at once be, either in the one state or the other. Nay, I will say more: when we think seriously on the subject, it is almost impossible to comprehend, I do not say that a great number, but that any person whom we see before us, however unsatisfactory appearances may be, is really under God's displeasure, and in a state of reprobation. So hard is it to live by faith! People feel it to be a difficulty to have to admit certain other doctrines of the Church, which are more or less contrary to sight. For instance, they say as an argument against regeneration in Baptism, "Is it possible that all who have been baptized can have been born again, considering what lives they lead?" They make the evidence of sight tell against a doctrine which demands their faith. Yet, after all, is there anything more startling, more difficult to believe, than that any one person, whom we see, however sinful his life, is at present under God's eternal wrath, and would incur it if he were to die at once, and will incur it unless he repents? This is what we cannot bring ourselves to believe. All we commonly allow is, that certain persons are what we call "in *danger* of hell." Now, if by using this cautious phrase we mean merely to express that irreligious men may repent before death, or that men may seem to be irreligious to us who are not so, and therefore that it is safer to speak of men being in danger of God's wrath than actually under it; so far is well. But we are in error if we mean, as is often the case, to deny thereby that irreligious men, as such, whether man can ascertain them or not, are at this very time not only in danger, but actually under the power of God's wrath. Healthy men in a sickly country may be said to be in danger of sickness; soldiers in a battle are in danger of wounds; but irreligious men not only hazard, but do lie under God's eternal curse; and when we see an irreligious man, we see one who is under it, only we speak guardedly, both as hoping that he may repent, and as feeling that we may be mistaken. But whether or not men may be what they seem, or whether or not they are to change, certain it is that everyone who dies, passes at once into one or other of two states; and if he dies unsanctified and unreconciled to God, into a state of eternal misery.

How little the world at large realizes this, is shown by the conduct of surviving friends after a loss. Let a person who is taken away have been ever so notorious a sinner, ever so confirmed a drunkard, ever so neglectful of Christian ordinances, and though they have no reason for supposing anything hopeful was going on in his mind, yet they will generally be found to believe that he has gone to heaven; they will confidently talk of his being at peace, of his pains being at an end, of his happy release, and the like. They enlarge on these subjects; whereas their duty lies in keeping silence, waiting in trembling hope, and being resigned. Now, why is it they speak and think in this manner? Apparently because they cannot conceive it possible that he or that they should be lost. Even the worst men have qualities which endear them to those who come near them. They have human affections in some shape or other. Even the witch of Endor showed a sympathy and kindness towards her guest, which move us. Human feelings cannot exist in hell, and we cannot bring ourselves to think that they are subjects of hell who have them. And for this reason men cannot admit the bare possibility of another being lost; they reject the idea, and therefore, when a man dies, they conclude, as the only alternative, that he must be in Abraham's bosom; and they boldly say so, and they catch at some half sentence which he said during his illness, when he was calmer or weaker, or at the ease with which he died, in confirmation of their belief.

And if it is difficult to believe that there are any persons among us at this moment in a state of spiritual death, how shall we understand, what perchance is the case, that there are many such, perhaps multitudes? how shall we persuade ourselves of the great truth that, in spite of outward appearances, human society, as we find it, is but a part of an invisible world, and is really divided into but two companies, the sons of God, and the children of the wicked one; that some souls are ministered unto by Angels, others led captive by devils; that some are "fellow citizens of the saints," and of the invisible "household of God," and others companions of those His enemies in time past, who now are waiting in prison for the Judgment.

How blessed would it be, if we really understood this! What a change it would produce in our thoughts, unless we were utterly reprobate, to understand what and where we are, accountable beings on their trial, with God for their friend and the devil for their enemy, and advanced a certain way on their road either to heaven or to hell. No truths indeed, ever so awful, ever so fully brought home to the mind, will change it, if the love of God and of holiness be not there; but none among us, as we may humbly trust, is in this reprobate state. One wishes to think that no one has so done despite to the Spirit of grace, and so sinned against the Blood of the Covenant, as to have nothing of his regenerate nature left to him; no one among us, but, if he shut his eyes to the external world, and opened them to the world within him, contemplated his real state and prospects, and called to mind his past life, would be brought to repentance and amendment. Endeavor then, my brethren, to realize that you have souls, and pray God to enable you to do so. Endeavor to disengage your thoughts and opinions from the things that are seen; look at things as God looks at them, and judge of them as He judges. Pass a very few years, and you will actually experience what as yet you are called on to believe. There will be no need of the effort of mind to which I invite you, when you have passed into the unseen state. There will be no need of shutting your eyes to this world, when this world has vanished from you, and you have nothing before you but the throne of God, and the slow but continual movements about it in preparation of the Judgment. In that interval, when you are in that vast receptacle of disembodied souls, what will be your thoughts about the world which you have left! how poor will then seem to you its highest aims, how faint its keenest pleasures, compared with the eternal aims, the infinite pleasures, of which you will at length feel your souls to be capable! O, my brethren, let this thought be upon you day by day, especially when you are tempted to sin. Avoid sin as a serpent; it looks and promises well; it bites afterwards. It is dreadful in memory, dreadful even on earth; but in that awful period, when the fever of life is over, and you are waiting in silence for the Judgment, with nothing to distract your thoughts, who can say how dreadful may be the memory of sins done in the body? Then the very apprehension of their punishment, when Christ shall suddenly visit, will doubtless outweigh a thousandfold the gratification, such as it was, which you felt in committing them; and if so, what will be the proportion between it and that punishment, if after all it be actually inflicted? Let us lay to heart our Savior's own most merciful words, "Be not afraid," He says, "of them that kill the body, and after that have no more that they can do. But I will forewarn you, whom ye shall fear. Fear Him, which, after He hath killed, hath power to cast into hell. Yea, I say unto you, Fear Him."

[IV, 6]

Chapter 19

THE COMMUNION OF SAINTS

All Thy works praise Thee, O Lord, and Thy saints give thanks unto Thee:
they show the glory of Thy kingdom, and talk of Thy power.
—Ps. 145:10, 11

It was the great promise of the Gospel, that the Lord of all, who had hitherto manifested Himself externally to His servants, should take up His abode in their hearts. This, as you must recollect, is frequently the language of the Prophets; and it was the language of our Savior when He came on earth: "I will love him," He says, speaking of those who love and obey Him, "and will manifest Myself to him. . . . We will come unto him, and make our abode with him."[101] Though He had come in our flesh, so as to be seen and handled, even this was not enough. Still He was external and separate; but after His ascension He descended again by and in His Spirit, and then at length the promise was fulfilled.

There must indeed be a union between all creatures and their Almighty Creator even for their very existence; for it is said, "In Him we live, and move, and have our being"; and in one of the Psalms, "When Thou lettest Thy breath go forth, they shall be made."[102] But far higher, more intimate, and more sacred is the indwelling of God in the hearts of His elect people—so intimate, that compared with it, He may well be said not to inhabit other men at all; His presence being specified as the characteristic privilege of His own redeemed servants.

From the day of Pentecost, to the present time, it has been their privilege, according to the promise, "I will pray the Father, and He shall give You another Comforter, that He may abide with you *forever*"—forever: not like the Son of Man, who having finished His gracious work went away. Then it is added, "even the *Spirit* of Truth": that is, He who came forever, came as a Spirit, and, so coming, did for His own that which the visible flesh and blood of the Son of Man, from its very nature, could not do, viz.,

He came into the souls of all who believe, and taking possession of them, He, being One, knit them all together into one. Christ, by coming in the flesh, provided an external or apparent unity, such as had been under the Law. He formed His Apostles into a visible society; but when He came again in the Person of His Spirit, He made them all in a real sense one, not in name only. For they were no longer arranged merely in the form of unity, as the limbs of the dead may be, but they were parts and organs of one unseen power; they really depended upon, and were offshoots of that which was One; their separate persons were taken into a mysterious union with things unseen, were grafted upon and assimilated to the spiritual body of Christ, which is One, even by the Holy Ghost, in whom Christ has come again to us. Thus Christ came, not to make us one, but to die for us: the Spirit came to make us one in Him who had died and was alive, that is, to form the Church.

This then is the special glory of the Christian Church, that its members do not depend merely on what is visible, they are not mere stones of a building, piled one on another, and bound together from without, but they are one and all the births and manifestations of one and the same unseen spiritual principle or power, "*living* stones," internally connected, as branches from a tree, not as the parts of a heap. They are members of the Body of Christ. That divine and adorable Form, which the Apostles saw and handled, after ascending into heaven become a principle of life, a secret origin of existence to all who believe, through the gracious ministration of the Holy Ghost. This is the fruitful Vine, and the rich Olive tree upon and out of which all Saints, though wild and barren by nature, grow, that they may bring forth fruit unto God. So that in a true sense it may be said, that from the day of Pentecost to this hour there has been in the Church but One Holy One, the King of kings, and Lord of lords Himself, who is in all believers, and through whom they are what they are; their separate persons being but as separate developments, vessels, instruments, and works of Him who is invisible. Such is the difference between the Church before the Spirit of Christ came, and after. Before, God's servants were as the dry bones of the Prophet's vision, connected by profession, not by an inward principle; but since, they are all the organs as if of one invisible, governing Soul, the hands, or the tongues, or the feet, or the eyes of one and the same directing Mind, the types, tokens, beginnings, and glimpses of the Eternal Son of God. Hence the text, in speaking of the kingdom of Christ, enlarges upon the special office of His Saints—"All Thy works praise Thee, O Lord, and Thy Saints give thanks unto Thee: they show the glory of Thy kingdom, and talk of Thy power, that Thy power, Thy glory, and mightiness of Thy kingdom might be known unto men."

Such is the Christian Church, a *living* body, and *one*; not a mere framework artificially arranged to *look* like one. Its being alive is what makes it one; were it dead, it would consist of as many parts as it has members; but the Living *Spirit* of God came down upon it at Pentecost, and made it *one,* by giving it *life*.

On this great day then,[103] when we commemorate the quickening or vivifying of the Church, the birth of the spiritual and new creature out of an old world "as good as dead," it will be seasonable to consider the nature and attributes of this Church, as manifested in the elect, as invisible, one, living, and spiritual; or what is otherwise called the doctrine of the Communion of Saints with each other, and in the Holy Trinity, in whom their communion with each other consists. And this I the rather do, because the Communion of Saints is an article of the Creed, and therefore is not a matter of secondary importance, of doubt or speculation.

The Church then, properly considered, is that great company of the elect, which has been separated by God's free grace, and His Spirit working in due season, from this sinful world, regenerated, and vouchsafed perseverance unto life eternal. Viewed so far as it merely consists of persons *now* living in this world, it is of course a visible company; but in its nobler and truer character it is a body invisible, or nearly so, as being made up, not merely of the few who happen still to be on their trial, but of the many who sleep in the Lord. At first, indeed, in the lifetime of the Apostles, a great proportion of the whole body was in this world: that is, not taking into account those Saints who had lived in Jewish times, and whom Christ, on His departure, made partakers of the privileges then purchased by His death for *all* believers. St. Stephen and St. James the Greater were the first distinguished Saints of the New Covenant, who were gathered in to enrich the elder company of Moses, Elias, and their brethren. But from that time they have flowed in space; and as years passed away, greater and greater has become the proportion which the assembly of spirits made perfect bears to that body militant which is its complement in God's new creation. At present, we who live are but one generation out of fifty, which since its formation have been newborn into it, and endowed with spiritual life and the hope of glory. Fifty times as many Saints are in the invisible world sealed for immortality as are now struggling on upon earth towards it; unless indeed the later generations have a greater measure of Saints than the former ones. Well then may the Church be called invisible, not only as regards her vital principle, but in respect to her members. "That which is born of the Spirit is spirit"; and, since God the Holy Ghost is invisible, so is His work. The Church is invisible, because the greater number of her true children have been perfected and removed, and because those who are still on earth cannot be ascertained by mortal eye; and had God so willed, she might have had no visible tokens at all of her existence, and been as entirely and absolutely hidden from us as the Holy Ghost is, her Lord and Governor. But seeing that the Holy Ghost is our life, so that to gain life we must approach Him, in mercy to us, His place of abode, the Church of the Living God, is not so utterly veiled from our eyes as He is; but He has given us certain outward signs, as tokens for knowing, and means for entering that living Shrine in which He dwells. He dwells in the hearts of His Saints, in that temple of living stones, on earth and in heaven, which is ever showing the glory of His kingdom, and talking of His power; but since faith and love and joy and peace cannot be seen, since the company of His people are His secret ones, He has given us something outward as a guide to what is inward, something visible as a guide to what is spiritual.

Now, what is that outward visible guide, having the dispensation of what is unseen, but the Christian Ministry, which directs and leads us to the very Holy of Holies, in which Christ dwells by His Spirit? As landmarks or buoys inform the steersman, as the shadow on the dial is an index of the sun's course; so, if we would cross the path of Christ, if we would arrest His eye and engage His attention, if we would interest ourselves in the special virtue and fullness of His grace, we must join ourselves to that Ministry which, when He ascended up on high, He gave us as a relic, and let drop from Him as the mantle of Elijah, the pledge and token of his never-failing grace from age to age. "Tell me, O Thou whom my soul loveth, where Thou feedest, where Thou makest Thy flock to rest at noon; for why should I be as one that turneth aside by the flocks of Thy companions?"[104] Such is the petition, as it were, of the soul that seeks for Christ. His answer is as precise as the question: "If thou know not, O thou fairest among women, go thy way forth by the *footsteps* of the flock, and feed thy kids beside the *shepherds' tents*." Out of the Church is no salvation; I mean to say out of that great invisible company, who are one and all incorporate in the one mystical Body of Christ, and quickened by one Spirit: now, by adhering to the visible Ministry which the Apostles left behind them, we approach unto what we see not, to Mount Zion, to the heavenly Jerusalem, to the spirits of the just, to the firstborn elected to salvation, to Angels innumerable, to Jesus the One Mediator, and to God. This heavenly Jerusalem is the true Spouse of Christ and virgin Mother of Saints; and the visible ministry on earth, the Bishops and Pastors, together with Christians depending on them, at this or that day is *called* the Church, though really but a fragment of it, as being that part of it which is seen and can he pointed out, and as resembling it in type, and witnessing it, and leading towards it. This *invisible* body is the *true* Church, because it changes not, though it is ever increasing. What it has, it keeps and never loses; but what is visible is fleeting and transitory, and continually passes off into the invisible. The visible is ever dying for the increase of the invisible company, and is ever reproduced from out the mass of human corruption, by the virtue of the Spirit lodged in the invisible, and acting upon the world. Generation after generation is born, tried, sifted, strengthened, and perfected. Again and again the Apostles live in their successors, and their successors in turn are gathered unto the Apostles. Such is the efficacy of that inexhaustible grace which Christ has lodged in His Church, as a principle of life and increase, till He comes again. The expiring breath of His Saints is but the quickening of dead souls.

And now we may form a clearer notion than is commonly taken of the one Church Catholic which is in all lands. Properly it is not on earth, except so far as heaven can be said to be on earth, or as the dead are still with us. It is not on earth, except in such

sense as Christ or His Spirit are on earth. I mean it is not locally or
visibly on earth. The Church is not in time or place, but in the
region of spirits; it is in the Holy Ghost; and as the soul of man is
in every part of his body, yet in no part, not here nor there, yet
everywhere; not so in any one part, head or heart, hands or feet,
as not to be in every other; so also the heavenly Jerusalem, the
mother of our new birth, is in all lands at once, fully and entirely
as a spirit; in the East and in the West, in the North and in the
South, that is, wherever her outward instruments are to be found.
The Ministry and Sacraments, the bodily presence of Bishop and
people, are given us as keys and spells, by which we bring ourselves into the presence of the great company of Saints; they are as
much as this, but they are no more; they are not identical with
that company; they are but the outskirts of it; they are but porches
to the pool of Bethesda, entrances into that which is indivisible
and one. Baptism admits, not into a mere visible society, varying
with the country in which it is administered, Roman here, and
Greek there, and English there, but *through* the English, *or* the
Greek, *or* the Roman porch into the one invisible company of
elect souls, which is independent of time and place, and untinc-
tured with the imperfections or errors of that visible porch by
which entrance is made. And its efficacy lies in the inflowing
upon the soul of the grace of God lodged in that unseen body into
which it opens, not, in any respect, in the personal character of
those who administer or assist in it. When a child is brought for
Baptism, the Church invisible claims it, begs it of God, receives it,
and extends to it, as God's instrument, her own sanctity. When
we praise God in Holy Communion, we praise Him with the
Angels and Archangels, who are the guards, and with the Saints,
who are the citizens of the City of God. When we offer our Sacrifice of praise and thanksgiving, or partake of the sacred elements
so offered, we solemnly eat and drink of the powers of the world
to come. When we read the Psalms, we use before many witnesses
the very words on which those witnesses themselves—I mean, all
successive generations of that holy company—have sustained
themselves in their own day, for thousands of years past, during
their pilgrimage heavenward. When we profess the Creed, it is no
self-willed, arbitrary sense, but in the presence of those innumerable Saints who well remember what its words mean, and are

witnesses of it before God, in spite of the heresy or indifference of this or that day. When we stand over their graves, we are in the very vestibule of that dwelling which is "all-glorious within," full of light and purity, and of voices crying, "Lord, how long?" When we pray in private, we are not solitary; others "are gathered together" with us "in Christ's Name," though we see them not, with Christ in the midst of them. When we approach the Ministry which He has ordained, we approach the steps of His throne. When we approach the Bishops, who are the centers of that Ministry, what have we before us but the Twelve Apostles, present but invisible? When we use the sacred Name of Jesus, or the Sign given us in Baptism, what do we but bid defiance to devils and evil men, and gain strength to resist them? When we protest, or confess, or suffer in the Name of Christ, what are we but ourselves types and symbols of the Cross of Christ, and of the strength of Him who died on it? When we are called to battle for the Lord, what are we who are seen, but mere outposts, the advanced guard of a mighty host, ourselves few in number and despicable, but bold beyond our numbers, because supported by chariots and fire and horses of fire round about the Mountain of the Lord of Hosts under which we stand?

Such is the City of God, the Holy Church Catholic throughout the world, manifested in and acting through what is called in each country the Church visible; which visible Church really depends solely on it, on the invisible—not on civil power, not on princes or any child of man, not on its endowments, not on its numbers, not on anything that is seen, unless indeed heaven can depend on earth, eternity on time, Angels on men, the dead on the living. The unseen world through God's secret power and mercy encroaches upon this world; and the Church that is seen is just that portion of it by which it encroaches; and thus though the visible Churches of the Saints in this world seem rare, and scattered to and fro, like islands in the sea, they are in truth but the tops of the everlasting hills, high and vast and deeply rooted, which a deluge covers.

Now these thoughts are so very foreign from the world's ordinary view of things, which walks by sight, not by faith, and never allows anything to exist in what comes before it, but what it can touch and handle, that it is necessary to insist and enlarge upon them. The world then makes *itself* the standard of perfection and the center of all good; and when the souls of Christians pass from it into the place of spirits, it fancies that this is *their* loss, not its own; it pities them in its way of speaking of them, and calls them by names half compassionate, half contemptuous, as if its own presence and society were some great thing. It pities them too as thinking that they do not witness the termination of what they began or saw beginning, that they are ignorant of the fortunes of their friends or of the Church, are powerless over their own schemes, or rather careless about them, as being insensible, and but shadows, and ghosts not substances; as if we who live were the real agents in the course of events, and they were attached to us only as a churchyard to a church, which it is decent to respect, unsuitable to linger in. Such is its opinion of the departed; as though *we* were in light and *they* in darkness, we in power and influence, they in weakness, we the living, and they the dead; yet with the views opened on us in the Gospel, with the knowledge that the One Spirit of Christ ever abides, and that those who are made one with Him are never parted from Him, and that those who die in Him are irrevocably knit into Him and one with Him, shall we dare to think slightly of these indefectible members of Christ and vessels of future glory? Shall we presume to compare that great assemblage of the elect, perfected and at rest, shall we weigh in the balance that glorious Church invisible, so populous in souls, so pure from sin, so rid of probation, with ourselves, poor strugglers with the flesh and the devil, who have but the earnest not the crown of victory, whose names are not so written in the heavens, but they may be blotted out again? Shall we doubt for a moment, though St. Paul was martyred centuries upon centuries since, that he, who even while in the body was present in spirit at Corinth when he was at Ephesus, is present in the Church still, more truly alive than those who are called living, more truly and awfully an Apostle now upon a throne, than when he had fightings without and fears within, a thorn in his flesh, and a martyrdom in prospect? Shall we be as infidels to suppose that the Church is only what she seems to be, a poor, helpless, despised, and human institution, scorned by the wealthy, plundered by the violent, outreasoned by the sophist, and patronized by the great, and not rather believe that she is serving in presence of the Eternal Throne, round which are the "four and twenty seats, and upon the seats" are "four and twenty elders sitting, clothed in white raiment," and "on their heads crowns of gold"?[105] Nay shall we not dimly recognize amid the aisles of our churches and along our cloisters, about our ancient tombs, and in ruined and desolate places, which once were held sacred, not in cold poetical fancy, but by the eye of faith, the spirits of our fathers and brethren of every time, past and present, whose works have long been "known" to God, and whose former dwelling places remain among us, pledges (as we trust) that He will not utterly forsake us, and make an end? Can aught mortal and earthly, force without, or treachery within, the popular voice, or any will of man, aught in the whole universe, height or depth, or any other creature, aught save the decree of God, issued for our sins, chase away our holy unseen companions from us, and level us with the grass of the field? Can all the efforts of the children of men, their accurate delineations of our outward form, their measurement of our visible territory, their summing up of our substance, their impairing of our civil rights, their numbering of our supporters, circumscribe the City of the Living God, or localize the site of Eden, and the Mountain of the Saints?

But here it may be asked, whether such a belief in the ever-abiding presence among us of the Church invisible, in that Spirit whom all believe to be ever present with us to the end, does not interfere with our comfortable assurance that it is at rest. "Christ (it may be said) worketh hitherto as His Father worketh; and the Angels excel in strength; but human nature, even in its purest and more heavenly specimens, is unequal to this incessant watchfulness, and when it dies is said to fall asleep—why should we not leave to it so comfortable and gracious a portion?" Now, however we answer this question, so far is certain, for we have St. Paul's authority for saying it, that in coming to the Church, we approach not God alone, nor Jesus the Mediator of the New Covenant, nor Angels innumerable, but also, as he says expressly, "the spirits of the just made perfect." And in thus speaking, he is evidently speaking neither of saints on earth nor saints after the resurrection, were it only that he designates especially "the *spirits* of the *just*." Certainly, then, the Church, in St. Paul's judgment, is made up of the dead as well as of the living; and though this be so, though the dead be present, it does not follow they are not at rest also. Such presence in the Church does not involve any labor or toil, any active interference, on the part of those who (we are told) "rest from their labors." For it is plain, though they "live unto God," and have power with Him, this does not imply that they *act,* or that they are *conscious* of their power. This holds good, through God's mercy, in the case of those who labor in the flesh, who pray and preach, work righteousness, and glorify God. They too see none of those fruits which notwithstanding do follow them. Had Noah, Daniel, and Job been in any evil city, and saved it by their righteousness from destruction, would they have known what they were enabled to do? We have no reason to say they would; for it is one thing to do good, another to see we do it.

But again it may be quite true that in one sense they are at rest, and yet in another active promoters of the Church's welfare, as by prayer; though we know not *how* they are active, or *how* they are at rest, or *how* they can be both at once. It is said that God "rested on the seventh day from all the work which He had made," yet nevertheless that He "worketh hitherto." Surely, in Him who is eternal and all-sufficient, is found absolutely and perfectly that incomprehensible union of Almighty power with everlasting repose; and what He is in fullness, He may graciously impart in its degree, and according to their capacity to His chosen. If it is no contradiction in terms that God should rest and yet work, that the Son of God should die and yet have an eternal essence, that the Son of Man should be in heaven while He spoke to Nicodemus, it may be no contradiction that the soul of man should sleep in the intermediate state, and yet be awake. I say, what God has infinitely and by nature, He may bestow in part to us; and thus it may be true that though the Saints are "joyful with glory," and "rejoice in their beds," and "the praises of God" are "in their mouths," yet at the same time "a two-edged sword" is "in their hands, to be avenged of the heathen, and to rebuke the people; to bind their kings in chains and their nobles with links of iron; that they may be avenged of them, as it is written: Such honor have all His Saints."[106]

Lastly, while we thus think of the invisible Church, we are restrained by many reasons from such invocations of her separate members as are unhappily so common in other Christian countries. First, because the practice was not primitive, but an addition when the world had poured into the Church; next, because we are told to pray to God only, and invocation may easily be corrupted into prayer, and then becomes idolatrous. And further, it must be considered that though the Church is represented in Scripture as a channel of God's gifts to us, yet it is only as a body and sacramentally, not as an agent, nor in her members one by one. St. Paul does not say that we are brought near to this saint or that saint, but to all together, "to the spirits of just men made perfect"; one by one they have to undergo the Day of Judgment, but as a body they are the City of God, the immaculate Spouse of the Lamb.

Let us then stand in that lot in which God has placed us, and thank Him for what He has so mercifully, so providentially done for us. He has done all things well, neither too much nor too little. He has neither told us to neglect the faithful servants of Christ departed, nor to pay them undue honor; but to think of them, yet not speak to them; to make much of them, but to trust solely in Him. Let us follow His rule, neither exceeding nor wanting in our duty; but according to St. Paul's injunction, "using" His gifts "without abusing" them; not ceasing to use, lest we *should* abuse, but abstaining from the abuse, while we adhere thankfully to the use.

These are inspiring thoughts for the solitary, the dejected, the harassed, the defamed, or the despised Christian; and they belong to him, if by act and deed he unites in that Communion which he professes. He joins the Church of God, not merely who speaks about it, or who defends it, or who contemplates it, but who loves it. He loves the unseen company of believers, who loves those who are seen. The test of our being joined to Christ is love; the test of love towards Christ and His Church, is loving those whom we actually see. "He that loveth not his brother whom he hath seen, how can he love God, whom he hath not seen?"[107] As then we would be worthy to hold communion with believers of every time and place, let us hold communion duly with those of our own day and our own neighborhood. Let us pray God, to teach us what we are so deficient in, and save us from using words and cherishing thoughts which our actions put to shame. It is a very easy thing to say fine things, which we have no right to say. Let us feel tenderly affectioned towards all whom Christ has made His own by Baptism. Let us sympathize with them, and have kind thoughts towards them, and be warmhearted, and loving, and simple-minded, and gentle-tempered towards them, and consult for their good, and pray for their growth in faith and holiness. "Let us not love in word, neither in tongue, but in deed and in truth." For "God is love"; and if we love one another, "God dwelleth in us, and His love is perfected in us."

[IV, 11]

Chapter 20

MORAL EFFECTS OF COMMUNION WITH GOD

One thing have I desired of the Lord, which I will require; even that I may
dwell in the house of the Lord all the days of my life, to behold the fair
beauty of the Lord, and to visit His Temple.
—Ps. 27:4

What the Psalmist desired, we Christians enjoy to the full—
the liberty of holding communion with God in His Temple all
through our life. Under the Law, the presence of God was but in
one place; and therefore could be approached and enjoyed only at
set times. For far the greater part of their lives, the chosen people
were in one sense "cast out of the sight of His eyes";[108] and the
periodical return to it which they were allowed was a privilege
highly coveted and earnestly expected. Much more precious was
the privilege of continually dwelling in His sight which is spoken
of in the text. "One thing," says the Psalmist, "have I desired of
the Lord . . . that I may dwell in the house of the Lord all the days
of my life, to behold the fair beauty of the Lord, and to visit His
Temple." He desired to have continually that communion with
God in prayer, praise, and meditation, to which His presence
admits the soul; and this, I say, is the portion of Christians. Faith
opens upon us Christians the Temple of God wherever we are; for
that Temple is a spiritual one, and so is everywhere present. "We
have access," says the Apostle, that is, we have admission or introduction, "by faith into this grace wherein we stand, and rejoice in
hope of the glory of God." And hence he says elsewhere, "Rejoice
in the Lord alway, and again I say, Rejoice." "Rejoice evermore,
pray without ceasing; in everything give thanks." And St. James,
"Is any afflicted? let him pray: is any merry? let him sing
Psalms."[109] Prayer, praise, thanksgiving, contemplation, are the
peculiar privilege and duty of a Christian, and that for their own
sakes, from the exceeding comfort and satisfaction they afford
him, and without reference to any definite results to which prayer
tends, without reference to the answers which are promised to it,

from a general sense of the blessedness of being under the shadow of God's throne.

I propose, then, in what follows, to make some remarks on communion with God, or prayer in a large sense of the word; not as regards its external consequences, but as it may be considered to affect our own minds and hearts.

What, then, is prayer? It is (if it may be said reverently) *conversing* with God. We converse with our fellow men, and then we use familiar language, because they *are* our fellows. We converse with God, and then we use the lowliest, awfulest, calmest, concisest language we can, because He *is* God. Prayer, then, is *divine* converse, differing from human as God differs from man. Thus St. Paul says, "Our conversation is in heaven"[110]—not indeed thereby meaning converse of words only, but intercourse and manner of living generally; yet still in an especial way converse of words or prayer, because language is the special means of all intercourse. Our intercourse with our fellow men goes on, not by sight, but by sound, not by eyes, but by ears. Hearing is the social sense, and language is the social bond. In like manner, as the Christian's conversation is in heaven, as it is his duty, with Enoch and other Saints, *to walk with God,* so his voice is in heaven, his heart "inditing of a good matter," of prayers and praises. Prayers and praises are the mode of his intercourse with the next world, as the converse of business or recreation is the mode in which this world is carried on in all its separate courses. He who does not pray, does not claim his citizenship with heaven, but lives, though an heir of the kingdom, as if he were a child of earth.

Now, it is not surprising if that duty or privilege, which is the characteristic token of our heavenly inheritance, should also have an especial influence upon our fitness for claiming it. He who does not use a gift, loses it; the man who does not use his voice or limbs, loses power over them, and becomes disqualified for the state of life to which he is called. In like manner, he who neglects to pray, not only suspends the enjoyment, but is in a way to lose the possession, of his divine citizenship. We are members of another world; we have been severed from the companionship of devils, and brought into that invisible kingdom of Christ which faith alone discerns, that mysterious Presence of God which encompasses us, which is in us, and around us, which is in our heart, which enfolds us as though with a robe of light, hiding our scarred and discolored souls from the sight of Divine Purity, and, making them shining as the Angels; and which flows in upon us too by means of all forms of beauty and grace which this visible world contains, in a starry host or (if I may so say) a milky way of divine companions, the inhabitants of Mount Zion, where we dwell. Faith, I say, alone apprehends all this; but yet there *is* something which is not left to faith—our own tastes, likings, motives, and habits. Of these we are conscious in our degree, and we can make ourselves more and more conscious; and as consciousness tells us what they are, reason tells us whether they are such as become, as correspond with, that heavenly world into which we have been translated.

I say then, it is plain to common sense that the man who has not accustomed himself to the language of heaven will be no fit inhabitant of it when, in the last day, it is perceptibly revealed. The case is like that of a language or style of speaking of this world; we know well a foreigner from a native. Again, we know those who have been used to kings' courts or educated society from others. By their voice, accent, and language, and not only so, by their gestures and gait, by their usages, by their mode of conducting themselves and their principles of conduct, we know well what a vast difference there is between those who have lived in good society and those who have not. What indeed is called *good society* is often very worthless society. I am not speaking of it to praise it; I only mean, that, as the manners which men call refined or courtly are gained only by intercourse with courts and polished circles, and as the influence of the words there used (that is, of the ideas which those words, striking again and again on the ear, convey to the mind) extends in a most subtle way over all that men do, over the turn of their sentences, and the tone of their questions and replies, and their general bearing, and the spontaneous flow of their thoughts, and their mode of viewing things, and the general maxims or heads to which they refer them, and the motives which determine them, and their likings and dislikings, hopes and fears, and their relative estimate of persons, and the intensity of their perceptions towards particular objects; so a habit of prayer, the practice of turning to God and the unseen world, in every season, in every place, in every emergency (let alone its supernatural effect of prevailing with God)—prayer, I say, has what may be called a *natural* effect, in spiritualizing and elevating the soul. A man is no longer what he was before; gradually, imperceptibly to himself, he has imbibed a new set of ideas, and become imbued with fresh principles. He is as one coming from kings' courts, with a grace, a delicacy, a dignity, a propriety, a justness of thought and taste, a clearness and firmness of principle, all his own. Such is the power of God's secret grace acting through those ordinances which He has enjoined us, such the evident fitness of those ordinances to produce the results which they set before us. As speech is the organ of human society, and the means of human civilization, so is prayer the instrument of divine fellowship and divine training.

I will give, for the sake of illustration, some instances in detail of one particular fault of mind, which among others a habit of prayer is calculated to cure.

For instance, many a man seems to have no grasp at all of doctrinal truth. He cannot get himself to think it of importance what a man believes, and what not. He tries to do so; for a time he does; he does for a time think that a certain faith is necessary for salvation, that certain doctrines are to be put forth and maintained in charity to the souls of men. Yet though he thinks so one day, he changes the next; he holds the truth, and then lets it go again. He is filled with doubts; suddenly the question crosses him, "Is it possible that such and such a doctrine *is* necessary?" and he relapses into an uncomfortable skeptical state, out of which there is no outlet. Reasonings do not convince him; he *cannot* be convinced; he has no grasp of truth. Why? Because the next world is not a reality to him; it only exists in his mind in the form of certain conclusions from certain reasonings. It is but an inference; and never can be more, never can be present to his mind, until he acts, instead of arguing. Let him but act as if the next world were before him; let him but give himself to such devotional exercises as we ought to observe in the presence of an Almighty, All-holy, and All-merciful God, and it will be a rare case indeed if his difficulties do not vanish.

Or again: a man may have a natural disposition towards caprice and change; he may be apt to take up first one fancy, then another, from novelty or other reason; he may take sudden likings or dislikings, or be tempted to form a scheme of religion for himself, of what he thinks best or most beautiful out of all the systems which divide the world.

Again: he is troubled perhaps with a variety of unbecoming thoughts, which he would fain keep out of his mind if he could. He finds himself unsettled and uneasy, dissatisfied with his condition, easily excited, sorry at sin one moment, forgetting it the next, feebleminded, unable to rule himself, tempted to dote upon trifles, apt to be caught and influenced by vanities, and to abandon himself to languor or indolence.

Once more: he has not a clear perception of the path of truth and duty. This is an especial fault among us nowadays: men are actuated perhaps by the best feelings and the most amiable motives, and are not fairly chargeable with insincerity; and yet there is a want of straightforwardness in their conduct. They allow themselves to be guided by expediency, and defend themselves, and perhaps so plausibly, that though you are not convinced, you are silenced. They attend to what others think, more than to what God says; they look at Scripture more as a gift to man than as a gift from God; they consider themselves at liberty to modify its plain precepts by a certain discretionary rule; they listen to the voice of great men, and allow themselves to be swayed by them; they make comparisons and strike the balance between the impracticability of the whole that God commands, and the practicability of effecting a part, and think they may consent to give up something, if they can secure the rest. They shift about in opinion, going first a little this way, then a little that, according to the loudness and positiveness with which others speak; they are at the mercy of the last speaker, and they think they observe a safe, judicious, and middle course, by always keeping a certain distance behind those who go furthest. Or they are rash in their religious projects and undertakings, and forget that they may be violating the lines and fences of God's Law, while they move about freely at their pleasure. Now, I will not judge another; I will not say that in this or that given case the fault of mind in question (for anyhow it is a fault), does certainly arise from some certain cause which I choose to guess at: but at least there are cases where this wavering of mind *does* arise from scantiness of prayer; and if so, it is worth a man's considering, who is thus unsteady, timid, and dim-sighted, whether this scantiness be not perchance the true reason of such infirmities in his own case, and whether a "continuing instant in prayer"—by which I mean, not merely prayer morning and evening, but something suitable to his disease, something extraordinary, as medicine is extraordinary, a "redeeming of time" from society and recreation in order to pray more—whether such a change in his habits would not remove them?

For what is the very promise of the New Covenant but stability? what is it, but a clear insight into the truth, such as will enable us to know how to walk, how to profess, how to meet the circumstances of life, how to withstand gainsayers? Are we built upon a rock or upon the sand? are we after all tossed about on the sea of opinion, when Christ has stretched out His hand to us, to help and encourage us? "Thou wilt keep him in perfect peace whose mind is stayed on Thee, because he trusteth in Thee."[111] Such is the word of promise. Can we possibly have apprehensions about what man will do to us or say of us, can we flatter the great ones of earth, or timidly yield to the many, or be dazzled by talent, or drawn aside by interest, who are in the habit of divine conversations? "Ye have an unction from the Holy One," says St. John, "and ye know all things. I have not written unto you because ye know not the truth, but because ye know it, and that no lie is of the truth. . . . The anointing which ye have received of Him abideth in you, and ye need not that any man teach you. . . . Whosoever is born of God, doth not commit sin, for his seed remaineth in him; and he cannot sin, because he is born of God."[112] This is that birth, by which the baptized soul not only enters, but actually embraces and realizes the kingdom of God. This is the true and effectual regeneration, when the seed of life takes root in man and thrives. Such men have accustomed themselves to speak to God, and God has ever spoken to them; and they feel "the powers of the world to come" as truly as they feel the presence of this world, because they have been accustomed to speak and act as if it were real. All of us must rely on something; all must look up to, admire, court, make themselves one with something. Most men cast in their lot with the visible world; but true Christians with Saints and Angels.

Such men are little understood by the world because they are not of the world; and hence it sometimes happens that even the better sort of men are often disconcerted and vexed by them. It cannot be otherwise; they move forward on principles so different from what are commonly assumed as true. They take for granted, as first principles, what the world wishes to have proved in detail. They have become familiar with the sights of the next world, till they talk of them as if all men admitted them. The immortality of truth, its oneness, the impossibility of falsehood coalescing with it, what truth is, what it should lead one to do in particular cases, how it lies in the details of life—all these points are mere matters of debate in the world, and men go through long processes of argument, and pride themselves on their subtleness in defending or attacking, in making probable or improbable, ideas which are assumed without a word by those who have lived in heaven, as the very ground to start from. In consequence, such men are called bad disputants, inconsecutive reasoners, strange, eccentric, or perverse thinkers, merely because they do not take for granted, nor go to prove, what others do, because they do not go about to define and determine the sights (as it were), the mountains and rivers and plains, and sun, moon, and stars, of the next world. And hence in turn they are commonly unable to enter into the ways of thought or feelings of other men, having been engrossed with God's thoughts and God's ways. Hence, perhaps, they seem abrupt in what they say and do; nay, even make others feel constrained and uneasy in their presence. Perhaps they appear reserved too, because they take so much for granted which might be drawn out, and because they cannot bring themselves to tell all their thoughts from their sacredness, and because they are drawn off from free conversation to the thought of heaven, on which their minds rest. Nay, perchance, they appear severe, because their motives are not understood, nor their sensitive jealousy for the honor of God and their charitable concern for the good of their fellow Christians duly appreciated. In short, to the world they seem like *foreigners*. We know how foreigners strike us; they are often to *our* notions strange and unpleasing in their manners; why is this? merely *because* they are of a different country. Each country has its own manners—one may not be better than other; but we naturally like our own ways, and we do not understand other. We do not use their meaning. We misconstrue them; we think they mean something unpleasant, something rude, or over-free, or haughty, or unrefined, when they do not. And in like manner, the world at large, not only is not Christian, but cannot discern or understand the Christian. Thus our Blessed Lord Himself was not recognized or honored by His relatives, and (as is plain to every reader of Scripture) He often seems to speak abruptly and severely. So too St. Paul was considered by the Corinthians as contemptible in speech. And hence St. John, speaking of "what manner of love the Father hath bestowed upon us that we should be called the sons of God," adds, "therefore the world *knoweth* us not, because it knew Him not."[113] Such is the effect of divine meditations: admitting us into the next world, and withdrawing us from this; making us children of God, by withal "strangers unto our brethren, even aliens unto our mother's children."[114] Yea, though the true servants of God increase in meekness and love day by day, and to those who know them will seem what they really are; and though their good works are evident to all men, and cannot be denied, yet such is the eternal law which goes between the Church and the world—we cannot be friends of both; and they who take their portion with the Church, will seem, except in some remarkable cases, unamiable to the world, for the "world knoweth them not," and does not like them though it can hardly tell why; yet (as St. John proceeds) they have this blessing, that "when He shall appear, they shall be like Him, for they shall see Him as He is."[115]

And if, as it would seem, we must choose between the two, surely the world's friendship may be better parted with than our fellowship with our Lord and Savior. What indeed have we to do with courting men, whose faces are turned towards God? We know how men feel and act when they come to die; they discharge their worldly affairs from their minds, and try to realize the unseen state. Then this world is nothing to them. It may praise, it may blame; but they feel it not. They are leaving their goods, their deeds, their sayings, their writings, their names, behind them; and they care not for it, for they wait for Christ. To one thing alone they are alive, His coming; they watch against it, if so be they may then be found without shame. Such is the conduct of dying men; and what all but the very hardened do at the last, if their senses fail not and their powers hold, that does the true Christian all life long. He is ever dying while he lives; he is on his bier, and the prayers for the sick are saying over him. He has no work but that of making his peace with God, and preparing for the Judgment. He has no aim but that of being found worthy to escape the things that shall come to pass and to stand before the Son of Man. And therefore day by day he unlearns the love of this world, and the desire of its praise; he can bear to belong to the nameless family of God, and to seem to the world strange in it and out of place, for so he is.

And when Christ comes at last, blessed indeed will be his lot. He has joined himself from the first to the conquering side; he has risked the present against the future, preferring the chance of eternity to the certainty of time; and then his reward will be but beginning, when that of the children of this world is come to an end. In the words of the wise man, "Then shall the righteous man stand in great boldness before the face of such as have afflicted him, and made no account of his labors. When they see it they shall be troubled with terrible fear, and shall be amazed at the strangeness of His salvation, so far beyond all that they looked for. And they, repenting and groaning for anguish of spirit, shall say within themselves, This is he whom we had sometimes in derision and a proverb of reproach; we fools counted his life madness, and his end to be without honor. How is he numbered among the children of God, and his lot is among the saints!"[116]

[IV, 15]

Chapter 21

WATCHING

Take ye heed, watch and pray; for ye know not when the time is.
—Mark 13:33

Our Savior gave this warning when He was leaving this world, leaving it, that is, as far as His visible presence is concerned. He looked forward to the many hundred years which were to pass before He came again. He knew His own purpose and His Father's purpose gradually to leave the world to itself, gradually to withdraw from it the tokens of His gracious presence. He contemplated, as contemplating all things, the neglect of Him which would spread even among his professed followers; the daring disobedience, and the loud words, which would be ventured against Him and His Father by many whom He had regenerated: and the coldness, cowardice, and tolerance of error which would be displayed by others, who did not go so far as to speak or to act against Him. He foresaw the state of the world and the Church, as we see it this day, when His prolonged absence has made it practically thought, that He never will come back in visible presence: and in the text, He mercifully whispers into our ears, not to trust in what we see, not to share in that general unbelief, not to be carried away by the world, but to "take heed, watch,[117] pray," and look out for His coming.

Surely this gracious warning should be ever in our thoughts, being so precise, so solemn, so earnest. He foretold His first coming, yet He took His Church by surprise when He came; much more will He come suddenly the second time, and overtake men, now that He has not measured out the interval before it, as then He did, but left our watchfulness to the keeping of faith and love.

Let us then consider this most serious question, which concerns every one of us so nearly: What it is to *watch* for Christ? He says, "*Watch* ye therefore, for ye know not when the Master of the house cometh; at even, or at midnight, or at the cock crowing, or in the morning; lest coming suddenly He find you sleeping. And what I say unto you, I say unto all, *Watch.*"[118] And again, "If the goodman of the house had known what hour the thief would come, he would have *watched,* and not have suffered his house to be broken through."[119] A like warning is given elsewhere both by our Lord and by His Apostles. For instance, we have the parable of the ten virgins, five of whom were wise and five foolish; on whom the bridegroom, after tarrying came suddenly, and five were found without oil. On which our Lord says, "*Watch* therefore, for ye know neither the day nor the hour wherein the Son of Man cometh."[120] Again He says, "Take heed to yourselves, lest at any time your hearts be overcharged with surfeiting and drunkenness, and cares of this life, and so that day come upon you unawares; for as a snare shall it come on all them that dwell on the face of the whole earth. *Watch* ye therefore, and pray always, that ye may be accounted worthy to escape all these things that shall come to pass, and to stand before the Son of Man."[121] In like manner He upbraided Peter thus: "Simon, sleepest thou? couldest not thou *watch* one hour?"[122]

In like manner St. Paul in his Epistle to the Romans: "Now it is high time to awake out of sleep. . . . The night is far spent, the day is at hand."[123] Again, "*Watch* ye, stand fast in the faith, quit you like men, be strong."[124] "Be strong in the Lord, and in the power of His might; put on the whole armor of God, that ye may be able to stand against the wiles of the devil; . . . that ye may be able to withstand in the evil day, and having done all to stand."[125] "Let us not sleep as do others, but let us *watch* and be sober."[126] In like manner St. Peter, "The end of all things is at hand; be ye therefore sober, and *watch* unto prayer." "Be sober, be *vigilant,* because your adversary the devil, as a roaring lion, walketh about seeking whom he may devour."[127] And St. John, "Behold I come as a thief; blessed is he that *watcheth* and keepeth his garments."[128]

Now I consider this word *watching,* first used by our Lord, then by the favored Disciple, then by the two great Apostles, Peter and Paul, is a remarkable word; remarkable because the idea is not so obvious as might appear at first sight, and next because they all inculcate it. We are not simply to believe, but to watch; not simply to love, but to watch; not simply to obey, but to watch; to watch for what? for that great event, Christ's coming. Whether then we consider what is the obvious meaning of the word, or the Object towards which it directs us, we seem to see a special duty enjoined on us, such as does not naturally come into our minds. Most of us have a general idea what is meant by believing, fearing, loving, and obeying; but perhaps we do not contemplate or apprehend what is meant by watching.

And I conceive it is one of the main points, which, in a practical way, will be found to separate the true and perfect servants of God from the multitude called Christians; from those who are, I do not say false and reprobate, but who are such that we cannot speak much about them, nor can form any notion what will become of them. And in saying this, do not understand me as saying, which I do not, that we can tell for certain who are the perfect, and who the double-minded or incomplete Christians; or that those who discourse and insist upon these subjects are necessarily on the right side of the line. I am but speaking of two *characters,* the true and consistent character, and the inconsistent; and these I say will be found in no slight degree discriminated and distinguished by this one mark—true Christians, whoever they are, watch, and inconsistent Christians do not. Now what is watching?

I conceive it may be explained as follows: Do you know the feeling in matters of this life, of expecting a friend, expecting him to come, and he delays? Do you know what it is to be in unpleasant company, and to wish for the time to pass away, and the hour strike when you may be at liberty? Do you know what it is to be in anxiety lest something should happen which may happen or may not, or to be in suspense about some important event, which makes your heart beat when you are reminded of it, and of which you think the first thing in the morning? Do you know what it is to have a friend in a distant country, to expect news of him, and to wonder from day to day what he is now doing, and whether he is well? Do you know what it is so to live upon a person who is present with you, that your eyes follow his, that you read his soul, that you see all its changes in his countenance, that you anticipate his wishes, that you smile in his smile, and are sad in his sadness, and are downcast when he is vexed, and rejoice in his successes? To watch for Christ is a feeling such as all these; as far as feelings of this world are fit to shadow out those of another.

He watches for Christ who has a sensitive, eager, apprehensive mind; who is awake, alive, quick-sighted, zealous in seeking and honoring Him; who looks out for Him in all that happens, and who would not be surprised, who would not be overagitated or overwhelmed, if he found that He was coming at once.

And he watches *with* Christ, who, while he looks on to the future, looks back on the past, and does not so contemplate what his Savior has purchased for him, as to forget what He has suffered for him. He watches with Christ, who ever commemorates and renews in his own person Christ's Cross and Agony, and gladly takes up that mantle of affliction which Christ wore here, and left behind Him when he ascended. And hence in the Epistles, often as the inspired writers show their desire for His second coming, as often do they show their memory of His first, and never lose sight of His Crucifixion in His Resurrection. Thus if St. Paul reminds the Romans that they "wait for the redemption of the body" at the last day, he also says, "If so be that we *suffer with Him,* that we may be also glorified together." If he speaks to the Corinthians of "waiting for the coming of our Lord Jesus Christ," he also speaks of "always bearing about in the body the *dying* of the Lord Jesus, *that* the life also of Jesus might be made manifest in our body." If to the Philippians of "the power of His resurrection," he adds at once *"and the fellowship of His sufferings,* being made conformable unto His death." If he consoles the Colossians with the hope "when Christ shall appear," of their "appearing with Him in glory," he has already declared that he *"fills up that which remains of the afflictions of Christ* in his flesh for His body's sake, which is the Church."[129] Thus the thought of what Christ is must not obliterate from the mind the thought of what He was; and faith is always sorrowing with Him while it rejoices. And the same union of opposite thoughts is impressed on us in Holy Communion, in which we see Christ's death and Resurrection together, at one and the same time; we commemorate the one, we rejoice in the other; we make an offering, and we gain a blessing.

This then is to watch; to be detached from what is present, and to live in what is unseen; to live in the thought of Christ as He came once, and as He will come again; to desire His second coming, from our affectionate and grateful remembrance of His first. And this it is, in which we shall find that men in general are

wanting. They are indeed without faith and love also; but at least
they profess to have these graces, nor is it easy to convince them
that they have not. For they consider they have faith, if they do
but own that the Bible came from God, or that they trust wholly
in Christ for salvation; and they consider they have love if they
obey some of the most obvious of God's commandments. Love
and faith they think they have; but surely they do not even fancy
that they watch. What is meant by watching, and how it is a duty,
they have no definite idea; and thus it accidentally happens that
watching is a suitable test of a Christian, in that it is that particular property of faith and love, which, essential as it is, men of this
world do not even profess; that particular property, which is the
life or energy of faith and love, the way in which faith and love, if
genuine, show themselves.

It is easy to exemplify what I mean: from the experience which
we all have of life. Many men indeed are open revilers of religion,
or at least openly disobey its laws; but let us consider those who
are of a more sober and conscientious cast of mind. They have a
number of good qualities, and are in a certain sense and up to a
certain point religious but they do not watch. Their notion of religion is briefly this: loving God indeed, but loving this world too;
not only doing their *duty,* but finding their chief and highest *good,*
in that state of life to which it has pleased God to call them, resting in it, taking it as their portion. They serve God, and they seek
Him; but they look on the present world as if it were the eternal,
not a mere temporary, scene of their duties and privileges, and
never contemplate the prospect of being separated from it. It is
not that they forget God, or do not live by principle, or forget that
the goods of this world are His gift; but they love them for their
own sake more than for the sake of the Giver, and reckon on their
remaining, as if they had that permanence which their duties and
religious privileges have. They do not understand that they are
called to be strangers and pilgrims upon the earth, and that their
worldly lot and worldly goods are a sort of accident of their existence, and that they really have no property, though human law
guarantees property to them. Accordingly, they set their heart
upon their goods, be they great or little, not without a sense of
religion the while, but still idolatrously. *This* is their fault—
an identifying God with this world, and therefore an idolatry

towards this world; and so they are rid of the trouble of looking out for their God, for they think they have found Him in the goods of this world. While, then, they are really praiseworthy in many parts of their conduct, benevolent, charitable, kind, neighborly, and useful in their generation, nay, constant perhaps in the ordinary religious duties which custom has established, and while they display much right and amiable feeling, and much correctness in opinion, and are even in the way to improve in character and conduct as time goes on, correct much that is amiss, gain greater command over themselves, mature in judgment, and are much looked up to in consequence; yet still it is plain that they love this world, would be loath to leave it, and wish to have more of its good things. They like wealth and distinction, and credit, and influence. They may improve in conduct, but not in aims; they advance, but they do not mount; they are moving on a low level, and were they to move on for centuries, would never rise above the atmosphere of this world. "I will stand upon my watch, and set me upon the tower, and will watch to see what He will say unto me, and what I shall answer when I am reproved."[130] This is the temper of mind which they have not; and when we reflect how rarely it *is* found among professing Christians, we shall see why our Lord is so urgent in enforcing it, as if He said, "I am not warning you, My followers, against open apostasy; that will not be; but I foresee that very few will keep awake and watch while I am away. Blessed are the servants who do so; few will open to me *immediately,* when I knock. They will have something to do first; they will have to get ready. They will have to recover from the surprise and confusion which overtake them on the first news of My coming, and will need time to collect themselves, and summon about them their better thoughts and affections. They feel themselves very well off as they are; and wish to serve God as they are. They are satisfied to remain on earth; they do not wish to move; they do not wish to change."

Without denying, then, to these persons the praise of many religious habits and practices, I would say that they want the tender and sensitive heart which hangs on the thought of Christ, and lives in His love. The breath of the world has a peculiar power in what may be called rusting the soul. The mirror within them, instead of reflecting back the Son of God their Savior, has become dim and discolored; and hence, though (to use a common expression) they have a good deal of good *in* them, it is only *in* them, it is not through them, around them, and upon them. An evil crust is *on* them: they think with the world; they are full of the world's notions and modes of speaking; they appeal to the world, and have a sort of reverence for what the world will say. There is a want of naturalness, simplicity, and childlike teachableness in them. It is difficult to touch them, or (what may be called) get at them, and to persuade them to a straightforward course in religion. They start off when you least expect it: they have reservations, make distinctions, take exceptions, indulge in refinements, in questions where there are really but two sides, a right and a wrong. Their religious feelings do not flow forth easily, at times when they ought to flow; either they are diffident, and can say nothing, or else they are affected and strained in their mode of conversing. And as a rust preys upon metal and eats into it, so does this worldly spirit penetrate more and more deeply into the soul which once admits it. And this is one great end, as it would appear, of afflictions, viz., to rub away and clear off these outward defilements, and to keep the soul in a measure of its baptismal purity and brightness.

Now, it cannot surely be doubted that multitudes in the Church are such as I have been describing, and that they would not, could not, at once welcome our Lord on His coming. We cannot, indeed, apply what has been said to this or that individual; but on the whole, viewing the multitude, one cannot be mistaken. There may be exceptions; but after all conceivable deductions, a large body must remain thus double-minded, thus attempting to unite things incompatible. This we might be sure of, though Christ had said nothing on the subject; but it is a most affecting and solemn thought, that He has actually called our attention to this very danger, the danger of a worldly religiousness, for so it may be called, though it *is* religiousness; this mixture of religion and unbelief, which serves God indeed, but loves the fashions, the distinctions, the pleasures, the comforts of this life—which feels a satisfaction in being prosperous in circumstances, likes pomps and vanities, is particular about food, raiment, house, furniture, and domestic matters, courts great people, and aims at having a position in society. He warns His disciples of the danger of having their minds drawn off from the thought of Him, by whatever cause; He warns them against *all* excitements, *all* allurements of this world; He solemnly warns them that the world will not be prepared for His coming, and tenderly entreats of them not to take their portion with the world. He warns them by the instance of the rich man whose soul was required, of the servant who ate and drank, and of the foolish virgins. When He comes, they will one and all want time; their heads will be confused, their eyes will swim, their tongues falter, their limbs totter, as men who are suddenly awakened. They will not all at once collect their senses and faculties. Oh fearful thought! the bridal train is sweeping by— Angels are there—the just made perfect are there—little children, and holy teachers, and white-robed saints, and Martyrs washed in blood; the marriage of the Lamb is come, and His wife hath made herself ready. She has already attired herself: while we have been sleeping, she has been robing; she has been adding jewel to jewel, and grace to grace; she has been gathering in her chosen ones, one by one, and has been exercising them in holiness, and purifying them for her Lord; and now her marriage hour is come. The holy Jerusalem is descending, and a loud voice proclaims, "Behold, the bridegroom cometh; go ye out to meet Him!" but we, alas! are but dazzled with the blaze of light, and neither welcome the sound nor obey it—and all for what? what shall we have gained then? what will this world have then done for us? wretched, deceiving world! which will then be burned up, unable not only to profit us, but to save itself. Miserable hour, indeed, will that be, when the full consciousness breaks on us of what we will not believe now, viz., that we *are* at present serving the world. We trifle with our conscience now; we deceive our better judgment; we repel the hints of those who tell us that we are joining ourselves to this perishing world. We *will* taste a little of its pleasures, and follow its ways, and think it no harm, so that we do not altogether neglect religion. I mean, we allow ourselves to covet what we have not, to boast in what we have, to look down on those who have less; or we allow ourselves to profess what we do not try to practice, to argue for the sake of victory, and to debate when we should be obeying; and we pride ourselves on our reasoning powers, and think ourselves enlightened, and despise those who had less to say for themselves, and set forth and defend our own theories; or we are overanxious, fretful, and careworn about worldly matters, spiteful, envious, jealous, discontented, and evil-natured: in one or other way we take our portion with this world, and we will not believe that we do. We obstinately refuse to believe it; we know we are not altogether irreligious, and we persuade ourselves that we are religious. We learn to think it is possible to be too religious; we have taught ourselves that there is nothing high or deep in religion, no great exercise of our affections, no great food for our thoughts, no great work for our exertions. We go on in a self-satisfied or a self-conceited way, not looking out of ourselves, not standing like soldiers on the watch in the dark night; but we kindle our own fire, and delight ourselves in the sparks of it. This is our state, or something like this, and the Day will declare it; the Day is at hand, and the Day will search our hearts, and bring it home even to ourselves, that we have been cheating ourselves with words, and have not served Christ, as the Redeemer of the soul claims, but with a meager, partial, worldly service, and without really contemplating Him who is above and apart from this world.

Year passes after year silently; Christ's coming is ever nearer than it was. Oh that, as He comes nearer earth, we may approach nearer heaven! O, my brethren, pray Him to give you the heart to seek Him in sincerity. Pray Him to make you in earnest. You have one work only, to bear your cross after Him. Resolve in His strength to do so. Resolve to be no longer beguiled by "shadows of religion," by words, or by disputings, or by notions, or by high professions, or by excuses, or by the world's promises or threats. Pray Him to give you what Scripture calls "an honest and good heart," or "a perfect heart," and, without waiting, begin at once to obey Him with the best heart you have. Any obedience is better than none, any profession which is disjoined from obedience is a mere pretense and deceit. Any religion which does not bring you nearer to God is of the world. You have to seek His face; obedience is the only way of seeking Him. All your duties are obediences. If you are to believe the truths He has revealed, to regulate yourselves by His precepts, to be frequent in His ordinances, to adhere to His Church and people, why is it, except because *He* has bid you? and to do what He bids is to obey Him, and to obey Him is to approach Him. Every act of obedience is an approach; an approach to Him who is not far off, though He seems so, but close behind this visible screen of things which hides Him for us. He is behind this material framework; earth and sky are but a veil going between Him and us; the day will come when He will rend that veil, and show Himself to us. And then, according as we have waited for Him, will He recompense us. If we have forgotten Him, He will not know us; but "blessed are those servants whom the Lord, when He cometh shall find watching. . . . He shall gird Himself, and make them sit down to meat, and will come forth and serve them. And if He shall come in the second watch, or come in the third watch, and find them so, blessed are those servants."[131] May this be the portion of every one of us! It is hard to attain it; but it is woeful to fail. Life is short; death is certain; and the world to come is everlasting.

[IV, 22]

Chapter 22

WORSHIP, A PREPARATION FOR
CHRIST'S COMING
(ADVENT)

*Thine eyes shall see the King in His beauty: they shall behold the
land that is very far off.*
—Isa. 33:17

Year after year, as it passes, brings us the same warnings again
and again, and none perhaps more impressive than those with
which it comes to us at this season. The very frost and cold, rain
and gloom, which now befall us, forebode the last dreary days of
the world, and in religious hearts raise the thought of them. The
year is worn out; spring, summer, autumn, each in turn, have
brought their gifts and done their utmost; but they are over, and
the end is come. All is past and gone, all has failed, all has sated;
we are tired of the past; we would not have the seasons longer;
and the austere weather which succeeds, though ungrateful to the
body, is in tone with our feelings, and acceptable. Such is the
frame of mind which befits the end of the year; and such the
frame of mind which comes alike on good and bad at the end of
life. The days have come in which they have no pleasure; yet they
would hardly be young again, could they be so by wishing it. Life
is well enough in its way; but it does not satisfy. Thus the soul is
cast forward upon the future, and in proportion as its conscience
is clear and its perception keen and true, does it rejoice solemnly
that "the night is far spent, the day is at hand," that there are "new
heavens and a new earth" to come, though the former are failing;
nay, rather that, because they are failing, it will "soon see the King
in His beauty," and "behold the land which is very far off." These
are feelings for holy men in winter and in age, waiting, in some
dejection perhaps, but with comfort on the whole, and calmly
though earnestly, for the Advent of Christ.

And such, too, are the feelings with which we now come before
Him in prayer day by day. The season is chill and dark, and the

breath of the morning is damp, and worshipers are few, but all this befits those who are by profession penitents and mourners, watchers and pilgrims. More dear to them that loneliness, more cheerful that severity, and more bright that gloom, than all those aids and appliances of luxury by which men nowadays attempt to make prayer less disagreeable to them. True faith does not covet comforts. It only complains when it is forbidden to kneel, when it reclines upon cushions, is protected by curtains, and encompassed by warmth. Its only hardship is to be hindered, or to be ridiculed, when it would place itself as a sinner before its Judge. They who realize that awful Day when they shall see Him face to face, whose eyes are as a flame of fire, will as little bargain to pray pleasantly now, as they will think of doing so then.

One year goes and then another, but the same warnings recur. The frost or the rain comes again; the earth is stripped of its brightness; there is nothing to rejoice in. And then, amid this unprofitableness of earth and sky, the well-known words return; the Prophet Isaiah is read; the same Epistle and Gospel, bidding us "awake out of sleep," and welcome Him "that cometh in the Name of the Lord"; the same Collects, beseeching Him to prepare us for judgment. Oh blessed they who obey these warning voices, and look out for Him whom they have not seen, because they "love His appearing"!

We cannot have fitter reflections at this Season than those which I have entered upon. What may be the destiny of other orders of beings we know not; but this we know to be our own fearful lot, that before us lies a time when we must have the sight of our Maker and Lord face to face. We know not what is reserved for other beings; there may be some, which, knowing nothing of their Maker, are never to be brought before Him. For what we can tell, this may be the case with the brute creation. It may be the law of their nature that they should live and die, or live on an indefinite period, upon the very outskirts of His government, sustained by Him, but never permitted to know or approach Him. But this is not our case. We are destined to come before Him; nay, and to come before Him in judgment; and that on our first meeting; and that suddenly. We are not merely to be rewarded or punished, we are to be judged. Recompense is to come upon our actions, not by a mere general provision or course of nature, as it does at present, but from the Lawgiver Himself in person. We have to stand before His righteous presence, and that one by one. One by one we shall have to endure His holy and searching eye. At present we are in a world of shadows. What we see is not substantial. Suddenly it will be rent in twain and vanish away, and our Maker will appear. And then, I say, that first appearance will be nothing less than a personal intercourse between the Creator and every creature. He will look on us, while we look on Him.

I need hardly quote any of the numerous passages of Scripture which tell us this, by way of proof; but it may impress the truth of it upon our hearts to do so. We are told then expressly, that good and bad shall see God. On the one hand holy Job says, "Though after my skin worms destroy this body, yet in my flesh shall I see God: whom I shall see for myself, and mine eyes shall behold, and not another." On the other hand unrighteous Balaam says, "I shall see Him, but not now; I shall behold Him, but not nigh; there shall come a Star out of Jacob, and a Scepter shall rise out of Israel." Christ says to His disciples, "Look up, and lift up your heads, for your redemption draweth nigh"; and to His enemies, "Hereafter ye shall see the Son of Man sitting on the right hand of power, and coming in the clouds of heaven." And it is said generally of all men, on the one hand, "Behold He cometh with clouds; and every eye shall see Him, and they also which pierced Him; and all kindreds of the earth shall wail because of Him." And on the other, "When He shall appear, we shall be like Him; for we shall see Him as He is." Again, "Now we see through a glass, darkly; but then face to face"; and again, "They shall see His face; and His Name shall be in their foreheads."[132]

And, as they see Him, so will He see them, for His coming will be to judge them. "We must all appear before the judgment seat of Christ," says St. Paul. Again, "We shall all stand before the judgment seat of Christ. For it is written, As I live, saith the Lord, every knee shall bow to Me, and every tongue shall confess to God. So then every one of us shall give account of himself to God." And again, "When the Son of Man shall come in His glory, and all the holy Angels with Him, then shall He sit upon the throne of His glory. And before Him shall be gathered all nations; and He shall separate them one from another, as a shepherd divideth his sheep from the goats."[133]

Such is our first meeting with our God; and, I say, it will be as sudden as it is intimate. "Yourselves know perfectly," says St. Paul, "that the day of the Lord so cometh as a thief in the night. For when they shall say, Peace and safety, then sudden destruction cometh upon them." This is said of the wicked, elsewhere He is said to surprise good as well as bad. "While the bridegroom tarried," the wise and foolish virgins "all slumbered and slept. And at midnight there was a cry made, Behold, the bridegroom cometh; go ye out to meet Him."[134]

Now, when this state of the case, the prospect which lies before us, is brought home to our thoughts, surely it is one which will lead us anxiously to ask, Is this all that we are told, all that is allowed to us, or done for us? Do we know only this, that all is dark now, and all will be light then; that now God is hidden, and one day will be revealed? that we are in a world of sense, and are to be in a world of spirits? For surely it is our plain wisdom, our bounden duty, to prepare for this great change; and if so, are any directions, hints, or rules given us *how* we are to prepare? "Prepare to meet thy God," "Go ye out to meet Him," is the dictate of natural reason, as well as of inspiration. But *how* is this to be?

Now observe, that it is scarcely a sufficient answer to this question to say that we must strive to obey Him, and so to approve ourselves to Him. This indeed might be enough, were reward and punishment to follow in the mere way of nature, as they do in this world. But, when we come steadily to consider the matter, appearing before God, and dwelling in His presence, is a very different thing from being merely subjected to a system of moral laws, and would seem to require another preparation, a special preparation of thought and affection, such as will enable us to endure His countenance, and to hold communion with Him as we ought. Nay, and, it may be, a preparation of the soul itself for His presence, just as the bodily eye must be exercised in order to bear the full light of day, or the bodily frame in order to bear exposure to the air.

But, whether or not this be safe reasoning, Scripture precludes the necessity of it, by telling us that the Gospel Covenant is intended, among its other purposes, to prepare us for this future glorious and wonderful destiny, the sight of God—a destiny which, if not most glorious, will be most terrible. And in the worship and service of Almighty God, which Christ and His Apostles have left to us, we are vouchsafed means, both moral and mystical, of approaching God, and gradually learning to bear the sight of Him.

This indeed is the most momentous reason for religious worship, as far as we have grounds for considering it a true one. Men sometimes ask, Why need they *profess* religion? Why need they go to church? Why need they observe certain rites and ceremonies? Why need they watch, pray, fast, and meditate? Why is it not enough to be just, honest, sober, benevolent, and otherwise virtuous? Is not this the true and real worship of God? Is not activity in mind and conduct the most acceptable way of approaching Him? How can they please Him by submitting to certain religious forms, and taking part in certain religious acts? Or if they must do so, why may they not choose their own? Why must they come to church for them? Why must they be partakers in what the Church calls Sacraments? I answer, they must do so, first of all and especially, because God tells them so to do. But besides this, I observe that we see this plain reason why, that they are one day to change their state of being. They are not to be here forever. Direct intercourse with God on their part now, prayer and the like, may be necessary to their meeting Him suitably hereafter: and direct intercourse on His part with them, or what we call sacramental communion, may be necessary in some incomprehensible way, even for preparing their very nature to bear the sight of Him.

Let us then take this view of religious service; it is "going out to meet the bridegroom," who, if not seen "in His beauty," will appear in consuming fire. Besides its other momentous reasons, it is a preparation for an awful event, which shall one day be. What it would be to meet Christ at once without preparation, we may learn from what happened even to the Apostles when His glory was suddenly manifested to them. St. Peter said, "Depart from me, for I am a sinful man, O Lord." And St. John, "when he saw Him, fell at His feet as dead."[135]

This being the case, it is certainly most merciful in God to vouchsafe to us the means of preparation, and such means as He has actually appointed. When Moses came down from the Mount, and the people were dazzled at his countenance, he put a veil over it. That veil is so far removed in the Gospel, that we are in a state of preparation for its being altogether removed. We are with Moses in the Mount so far, that we have a sight of God; we are with the people beneath it so far, that Christ does not visibly show Himself. He has put a veil on, and He sits among us silently and secretly. When we approach Him, we know it only by faith; and when He manifests Himself to us, it is without our being able to realize to ourselves that manifestation.

Such then is the spirit in which we should come to all His ordinances, considering them as anticipations and first fruits of that sight of Him which one day must be. When we kneel down in prayer in private, let us think to ourselves, Thus shall I one day kneel down before His very footstool, in this flesh and this blood of mine; and He will be seated over against me, in flesh and blood also, though divine. I come, with the thought of that awful hour before me, I come to confess my sin to Him now, that He may pardon it then, and I say, "O Lord, Holy God, Holy and Strong, Holy and Immortal, in the hour of death and in the day of judgment, deliver us, O Lord!"

Again, when we come to church, then let us say: The day will be when I shall see Christ surrounded by His Holy Angels. I shall be brought into that blessed company, in which all will be pure, all bright. I come then to learn to endure the sight of the Holy One and His Servants; to nerve myself for a vision which is fearful before it is ecstatic, and which they only enjoy whom it does not consume. When men in this world have to undergo any great thing, they prepare themselves beforehand, by thinking often of it, and they call this making up their mind. Any unusual trial they thus make familiar to them. Courage is a necessary step in gaining certain goods, and courage is gained by steady thought. Children are scared, and close their eyes, at the vision of some mighty warrior or glorious king. And when Daniel saw the Angel, like St. John, "his comeliness was turned in him into corruption, and he retained no strength."[136] I come then to the Church, because I am an heir of heaven. It is my desire and hope one day to take possession of my inheritance: and I come to make myself ready for it, and I would not see heaven yet, for I could not bear to see it. I am allowed to be in it without seeing it, that I may learn to see it. And by psalm and sacred song, by confession and by praise, I learn my part.

And what is true of the ordinary services of religion, public and private, holds in a still higher or rather in a special way, as regards the sacramental ordinances of the Church. In these is manifested in greater or less degree, according to the measure of each, that Incarnate Savior, who is one day to be our Judge, and who is enabling us to bear His presence then, by imparting it to us in measure now. A thick black veil is spread between this world and the next. We mortal men range up and down it, to and fro, and see nothing. There is no access through it into the next world. In the Gospel this veil is not removed; it remains, but every now and then marvelous disclosures are made to us of what is behind it. At times we seem to catch a glimpse of a Form which we shall here-after see face to face. We approach, and in spite of the darkness, our hands, or our head, or our brow, or our lips become, as it were, sensible of the contact of something more than earthly. We know not where we are, but we have been bathing in water, and a voice tells us that it is blood. Or we have a mark signed upon our foreheads, and it spake of Calvary. Or we recollect a hand laid upon our heads, and surely it had the print of nails in it, and resembled His who with a touch gave sight to the blind and raised the dead. Or we have been eating and drinking; and it was not a dream surely, that One fed us from His wounded side, and renewed our nature by the heavenly meat He gave. Thus in many ways He, who is Judge to us, prepares us to be judged, He, who is to glorify us, prepares us to be glorified, that He may not take us unawares; but that when the voice of the Archangel sounds, and we are called to meet the Bridegroom, we may be ready.

Now consider what light these reflections throw upon some remarkable texts in the Epistle to the Hebrews. If we have in the Gospel this supernatural approach to God and to the next world, no wonder that St. Paul calls it an "enlightening," "a tasting of the heavenly gift," a being "made partaker of the Holy Ghost," a "tasting of the good word of God, and the powers of the world to come." No wonder, too, that utter apostasy after receiving it should be so utterly hopeless; and that in consequence, any profanation of it, any sinning against it, should be so perilous in proportion to its degree. If He, who is to be our Judge, condescend here to manifest Himself to us, surely if that privilege does not fit us for His future glory, it does but prepare us for His wrath.

And what I have said concerning ordinances, applies still more fully to Holy Seasons, which include in them the celebration of many ordinances. They are times when we may humbly expect a larger grace, because they invite us especially to the means of grace. This in particular is a time for purification of every kind. When Almighty God was to descend upon Mount Sinai, Moses was told to "sanctify the people," and bid them "wash their clothes," and to "set bounds to them round about": much more is this a season for "cleansing ourselves from all defilement of the flesh and spirit, perfecting holiness in the fear of God";[137] a season for chastened hearts and religious eyes; for severe thoughts, and austere resolves, and charitable deeds; a season for remembering what we are and what we shall be. Let us go out to meet Him with contrite and expectant hearts; and though He delays His coming, let us watch for Him in the cold and dreariness which must one day have an end. Attend His summons we must, at any rate, when He strips us of the body; let us anticipate, by a voluntary act, what will one day come on us of necessity. Let us wait for Him solemnly, fearfully, hopefully, patiently, obediently; let us be resigned to His will, while active in good works. Let us pray Him ever, to "remember us when He cometh in His kingdom"; to remember all our friends; to remember our enemies; and to visit us according to His mercy here, that He may reward us according to His righteousness hereafter.

[V, 1]

Chapter 23

REMEMBRANCE OF PAST MERCIES

(CHRISTMAS)

I am not worthy of the least of all the mercies, and of all the truth, which
Thou hast showed unto Thy servant.
—Gen. 32:10

The spirit of humble thankfulness for past mercies which these words imply is a grace to which we are especially called in the Gospel. Jacob, who spoke them, knew not of those great and wonderful acts of love with which God has since visited the race of man. But though he might not know the depths of God's counsels, he knew himself so far as to know that he was worthy of no good thing at all, and he knew also that Almighty God had shown him great mercies and great truth: mercies, in that He had done for him good things, whereas he had deserved evil; and truth, in that He had made him promises, and had been faithful to them. In consequence, he overflowed with gratitude when he looked back upon the past; marveling at the contrast between what he was in himself and what God had been to him.

Such thankfulness, I say, is eminently a Christian grace, and is enjoined on us in the New Testament. For instance, we are exhorted to be "thankful," and to let "the Word of Christ dwell in us richly in all wisdom; teaching and admonishing one another in psalms and hymns and spiritual songs, singing with grace in our hearts to the Lord."

Elsewhere, we are told to "speak to ourselves in psalms and hymns and spiritual songs, singing and making melody in our heart to the Lord: giving thanks always for all things unto God and the Father, in the Name of our Lord Jesus Christ."

Again: "Be careful for nothing: but in everything by prayer and supplication, with thanksgiving, let your requests be made known unto God."

Again: "In everything give thanks: for this is the will of God in Christ Jesus concerning you."[138]

The Apostle, who writes all this, was himself an especial pattern of a thankful spirit: "Rejoice in the Lord alway," he says: "and again I say, Rejoice." "I have learned, in whatsoever state I am; therewith to be content. I have all and abound; I am full." Again: "I thank Christ Jesus our Lord, who hath enabled me, for that He counted me faithful, putting me into the ministry; who was before a blasphemer and a persecutor, and injurious. But I obtained mercy, because I did it ignorantly in unbelief. And the grace of our Lord was exceeding abundant, with faith and love which is in Christ Jesus."[139] O great Apostle! how could it be otherwise, considering what he had been and what he was—transformed from an enemy to a friend, from a blind Pharisee to an inspired preacher? And yet there is another Saint, besides the Patriarch Jacob, who is his fellow in this excellent grace—like them, distinguished by great vicissitudes of life, and by the adoring love and the tenderness of heart with which he looked back upon the past—I mean, "David, the son of Jesse, the man who was raised up on high, the anointed of the God of Jacob, and the sweet Psalmist of Israel."[140]

The Book of Psalms is full of instances of David's thankful spirit, which I need not cite here, as we are all so well acquainted with them. I will but refer to his thanksgiving, when he set apart the precious materials for the building of the Temple, as it occurs at the end of the First Book of Chronicles; when he rejoiced so greatly, because he and his people had the heart to offer freely to God, and thanked God for his very thankfulness. "David, the king . . . rejoiced with great joy; wherefore David blessed the Lord before all the congregation; and David said, Blessed be Thou, Lord God of Israel, our Father, forever and ever. . . . Both riches and honor come of Thee, and Thou reignest over all; and in Thine hand is power and might, and in Thine hand it is to make great, and to give strength unto all. Now, therefore, our God, we thank Thee, and praise Thy glorious Name. But who am I, and what is my people, that we should be able to offer so willingly after this sort? for all things come of Thee, and of Thine own have we given Thee."[141]

Such was the thankful spirit of David, looking back upon the past, wondering and rejoicing at the way in which his Almighty Protector had led him on, and at the works He had enabled him to do; and praising and glorifying Him for His mercy and truth. David, then, Jacob, and St. Paul, may be considered the three great patterns of thankfulness, which are set before us in Scripture—Saints, all of whom were peculiarly the creation of God's grace, and whose very life and breath it was humbly and adoringly to meditate upon the contrast between what, in different ways, they had been, and what they were. A perishing wanderer had unexpectedly become a patriarch; a shepherd, a king; and a persecutor, an Apostle: each had been chosen, at God's inscrutable pleasure, to fulfill a great purpose, and each, while he did his utmost to fulfill it, kept praising God that he was made His instrument. Of the first, it was said, "Jacob have I loved, but Esau have I hated"; of the second, that "he refused the tabernacle of Joseph, and chose not the tribe of Ephraim, but chose the tribe of Judah, even the hill of Zion, which He loved: He chose David also His servant, and took him away from the sheepfolds." And St. Paul says of himself, "Last of all, He was seen of me also, as of one born out of due time."[142]

These thoughts naturally come over the mind at this season, when we are engaged in celebrating God's grace in making us His children, by the incarnation of His Only-begotten Son, the greatest and most wonderful of all His mercies. And to the Patriarch Jacob our minds are now particularly turned, by the First Lessons for this day,[143] taken from the Prophet Isaiah, in which the Church is addressed and comforted under the name of Jacob. Let us then, in this season of thankfulness, and at the beginning of a new year, take a brief view of the character of this Patriarch; and though David and Isaiah be the prophets of grace, and St. Paul its special herald and chief pattern, yet, if we wish to see an actual specimen of a habit of thankfulness occupied in the remembrance of God's mercies, I think we shall not be wrong in betaking ourselves to Jacob.

Jacob's distinguishing grace then, as I think it may be called, was a habit of affectionate musing upon God's providences towards him in times past, and of overflowing thankfulness for them. Not that he had not other graces also, but this seems to have been his distinguishing grace. All good men have in their measure all graces; for He, by whom they have any, does not give one apart from the whole: He gives the root, and the root puts forth branches. But since time, and circumstances, and their own use of the gift, and their own disposition and character, have much influence on the mode of its manifestation, so it happens, that each good man has his own distinguishing grace, apart from the rest, his own particular hue and fragrance and fashion, as a flower may have. As, then, there are numberless flowers on the earth, all of them flowers, and so far like each other; and all springing from the same earth, and nourished by the same air and dew, and none without beauty; and yet some are more beautiful than others; and of those which are beautiful, some excel in color, and others in sweetness, and others in form; and then, again, those which are sweet have such perfect sweetness, yet so distinct, that we do not know how to compare them together, or to say which is the sweeter: so is it with souls filled and nurtured by God's secret grace. Abraham, for instance, Jacob's forefather, was the pattern of faith. This is insisted on in Scripture, and it is not here necessary to show that he was so. It will be sufficient to say, that he left his country at God's word; and, at the same word, took up the knife to slay his own son. Abraham seems to have had something very noble and magnanimous about him. He could realize and make present to him things unseen. He followed God in the dark as promptly, as firmly, with as cheerful a heart, and bold a stepping, as if he were in broad daylight. There is something very great in this; and, therefore, St. Paul calls Abraham *our* father, the father of Christians as well as of Jews. For we are especially bound to walk by faith, not by sight; and are blessed in faith, and justified by faith, as was faithful Abraham. Now (if I may say it, with due reverence to the memory of that favored servant of God, in whose praise I am now speaking) that faith in which Abraham excelled was not Jacob's characteristic excellence. Not that he had not faith, and great faith, else he would not have been so dear to God. His buying the birthright and gaining the blessing from Esau were proofs of faith. Esau saw nothing or little precious in them—he was profane; easily parted with the one, and had no high ideas of the other. However, Jacob's faith, earnest and vigorous as it was, was not like Abraham's. Abraham kept his affections loose from everything earthly, and was ready, at God's word, to slay his only son. Jacob had many sons, and may we not even say that he indulged them overmuch? Even as regards Joseph, whom he so deservedly loved, beautiful and touching as his love of him is, yet there is a great contrast between his feelings towards the "son of his old age" and those of Abraham towards Isaac, the unexpected offspring of his hundredth year—nor only such, but his long-promised only son, with whom were the promises. Again: Abraham left his country, so did Jacob; but Abraham, at God's word, Jacob, from necessity on the threat of Esau. Abraham, from the first, felt that God was his portion and his inheritance, and, in a great and generous spirit, he freely gave up all he had, being sure that he should find what was more excellent in doing so. But Jacob, in spite of his really living by faith, wished (if we may so say), as one passage of his history shows, to see before he fully believed. When he was escaping from Esau and came to Bethel, and God appeared to him in a dream and gave him promises, but not yet the performance of them, what did he do? Did he simply accept them? He says, "*If* God will be with me, and will keep me in this way that I go, and will give me bread to eat, and raiment to put on, so that I come again to my father's house in peace, *then* shall the Lord be my God."[144] He makes his obedience, in some sense, depend on a condition; and although we must not, and need not, take the words as if he meant that he would not serve God *till* and *unless* He did for him what He had promised, yet they seem to show a fear and anxiety, gentle indeed, and subdued, and very human (and therefore the more interesting and winning in the eyes of us common men, who read his words), yet an anxiety which Abraham had not. We feel Jacob to be more like ourselves than Abraham was.

What, then, was Jacob's distinguishing grace, as faith was Abraham's? I have already said it: I suppose, thankfulness. Abraham appears ever to have been looking forward in *hope,* Jacob looking back in *memory:* the one rejoicing in the future, the other in the past; the one setting his affections on the future, the other on the past; the one making his way towards the promises, the other musing over their fulfillment. Not that Abraham did not look back also, and Jacob, as he says on his deathbed, did not "wait for the salvation" of God; but this was the difference between them, Abraham was a hero, Jacob "a plain man, dwelling in tents."

Jacob seems to have had a gentle, tender, affectionate, timid mind—easily frightened, easily agitated, loving God so much that he feared to lose Him, and, like St. Thomas perhaps, anxious for sight and possession from earnest and longing desire of them. Were it not for faith, love would become impatient, and thus Jacob desired to possess, not from cold incredulity or hardness of heart, but from such a loving impatience. Such men are easily downcast, and must be treated kindly; they soon despond, they shrink from the world, for they feel its rudeness, which bolder natures do not. Neither Abraham nor Jacob loved the world. But Abraham did not fear, did not feel it. Jacob felt and winced, as being wounded by it. You recollect his touching complaints, "All these things are against me!" "Then shall ye bring down my gray hairs with sorrow to the grave." "If I am bereaved of my children, I am bereaved." Again, elsewhere we are told, "All his sons and all his daughters rose up to comfort him, but he refused to be comforted." At another time, "Jacob's heart fainted, for he believed them not." Again, "The spirit of Jacob their father revived."[145] You see what a childlike, sensitive, sweet mind he had. Accordingly, as I have said, his happiness lay, not in looking forward to the hope, but backwards upon the experience, of God's mercies towards him. He delighted lovingly to trace, and gratefully to acknowledge, what had been given, leaving the future to itself.

For instance, when coming to meet Esau, he brings before God in prayer, in words of which the text is part, what He had already done for him, recounting His past favors with great and humble joy in the midst of his present anxiety. "O God of my father Abraham," he says, "and God of my father Isaac, the Lord which saidst unto me, Return unto thy country, and to thy kindred, and I will deal well with thee: I am not worthy of the least of all the mercies, and of all the truth, *which Thou hast showed unto Thy servant; for with my staff I passed over this Jordan, and now I am become two bands.*" Again, after he had returned to his own land, he proceeded to fulfill the promise he had made to consecrate Bethel as a house of God, "Let us arise, and go up to Bethel; and I will make there an altar unto God, *who answered me in the day of my distress, and was with me in the way which I went.*" Again, to Pharaoh, still dwelling on the past: "The days of the years of my pilgrimage are a hundred and thirty years; few and evil have the days of the years of my life been," he means, in themselves, and as separate from God's favor, "and have not attained unto the days of the years of the life of my fathers, in the days of their pilgrimage." Again, when he was approaching his end, he says to Joseph, "God Almighty *appeared unto me* at Luz," that is, Bethel, "in the land of Canaan, and blessed me." Again, still looking back, "As for me, when I came from Padan, Rachel died by me in the land of Canaan, in the way, when yet there was but a little way to come to Ephrath; and I buried her there in the way of Ephrath." Again, his blessing upon Ephraim and Manasseh: "God, before whom my fathers Abraham and Isaac did walk, *the God which fed me all my life long unto this day,* the Angel which redeemed me from all evil, bless the lads." Again he looks back on the land of promise, though in the plentifulness of Egypt: "Behold, I die, but God shall be with you, and bring you again unto the land of your fathers." And when he gives command about his burial, he says: "I am to be gathered unto my people; bury me with my fathers in the cave that is in the field of Ephron the Hittite." He gives orders to be buried with his fathers; this was natural, but observe, he goes on to *enlarge* on the subject, after his special manner: "There they buried Abraham and Sarah his wife; there they buried Isaac and Rebekah his wife; and *there I buried Leah.*" And further on, when he speaks of waiting for God's salvation, which is an act of hope, he so words it as at the same time to dwell upon the past: "I *have* waited," he says, that is, all my life long, "I have waited for Thy salvation, O Lord."[146] Such was Jacob, living in memory rather than in hope, counting times, recording seasons, keeping days; having his history by heart, and his past life in his hand; and as if to carry on his mind into that of his descendants, it was enjoined upon them, that once a year every Israelite should appear before God with a basket of fruit of the earth, and call to mind what God had done for him and his father Jacob, and express his thankfulness for it. "A Syrian ready to perish was my father," he had to say, meaning Jacob; "and he went down into Egypt, and sojourned there, and became a nation, great, mighty, and populous. . . . And the Lord brought us forth out of Egypt with an outstretched arm, and with great terribleness, and with signs, and with wonders; and hath brought us into this land . . . that floweth with milk and honey. And now, behold, I have brought the first fruits of the land, which Thou, O Lord, hast given me."[147]

Well were it for us, if we had the character of mind instanced in Jacob, and enjoined on his descendants; the temper of dependence upon God's Providence, and thankfulness under it, and careful memory of all He has done for us. It would be well if we were in the habit of looking at all we have as God's gift, undeservedly given, and day by day continued to us solely by His mercy. He gave; He may take away. He gave us all we have, life, health, strength, reason, enjoyment, the light of conscience; whatever we have good and holy within us; whatever faith we have; whatever of a renewed will; whatever love towards Him; whatever power over ourselves; whatever prospect of heaven. He gave us relatives, friends, education, training, knowledge, the Bible, the Church. All comes from Him. He gave; He may take away. Did He take away, we should be called on to follow Job's pattern, and be resigned: "The Lord gave, and the Lord hath taken away. Blessed be the Name of the Lord."[148] While He continues His blessings, we should follow David and Jacob, by living in constant praise and thanksgiving, and in offering up to Him of His own.

We are not our own, any more than what we possess is our own. We did not make ourselves; we cannot be supreme over ourselves. We cannot be our own masters. We are God's property by creation, by redemption, by regeneration. He has a triple claim upon us. Is it not our happiness thus to view the matter? Is it any happiness, or any comfort, to consider that we *are* our own? It may be thought so by the young and prosperous. These may think it a great thing to have everything, as they suppose, their own way, to depend on no one, to have to think of nothing out of sight, to be without the irksomeness of continual acknowledgment, continual prayer, continual reference of what they do to the will of another. But as time goes on, they, as all men, will find that independence was not made for man—that it is an unnatural state—may do for a while, but will not carry us on safely to the end. No, we are creatures; and, as being such, we have two duties, to be resigned and to be thankful.

Let us then view God's providences towards us more religiously than we have hitherto done. Let us try to gain a truer view of what we are, and where we are, in His kingdom. Let us humbly and reverently attempt to trace His guiding hand in the years which we have hitherto lived. Let us thankfully commemorate the many mercies He has vouchsafed to us in time past, the many sins He has not remembered, the many dangers He has averted, the many prayers He has answered, the many mistakes He has corrected, the many warnings, the many lessons, the much light, the abounding comfort which He has from time to time given. Let us dwell upon times and seasons, times of trouble, times of joy, times of trial, times of refreshment. How did He cherish us as children! How did He guide us in that dangerous time when the mind began to think for itself, and the heart to open to the world! How did He with His sweet discipline restrain our passions, mortify our hopes, calm our fears, enliven our heavinesses, sweeten our desolateness, and strengthen our infirmities! How did He gently guide us towards the strait gate! How did He allure us along His everlasting way, in spite of its strictness, in spite of its loneliness, in spite of the dim twilight in which it lay! He has been all things to us. He has been, as He was to Abraham, Isaac, and Jacob, our God, our shield, and great reward, promising and performing, day by day. "Hitherto hath He helped us." "He hath been mindful of us, and He will bless us." He has not made us for naught; He has brought us thus far, in order to bring us further, in order to bring us on to the end. He will never leave us nor forsake us; so that we may boldly say, "The Lord is my Helper; I will not fear what flesh can do unto me." We may "cast all our care upon Him, who careth for us." What is it to us how our future path lies, if it be but His path? What is it to us whither it leads us, so that in the end it leads to Him? What is it to us what He puts upon us, so that He enables us to undergo it with a pure conscience, a true heart, not desiring anything of this world in comparison of Him? What is it to us what terror befalls us, if He be but at hand to protect and strengthen us? "Thou, Israel," He says, "art My servant Jacob, whom I have chosen, the seed of Abraham My friend." "Fear not, thou worm Jacob, and ye men of Israel; I will help thee, saith the Lord, and thy Redeemer, the Holy One of Israel." "Thus saith the Lord that created thee, O Jacob, and He that formed thee, O Israel, Fear not; for I have redeemed thee, I have called thee by thy name; thou art Mine.

When thou passest through the waters, I will be with thee; and through the rivers, they shall not overflow thee; when thou walkest through the fire, thou shalt not be burned; neither shall the flame kindle upon thee. For I am the Lord thy God, the Holy One of Israel, thy Savior."[149]

[V, 6]

Chapter 24

THE LAW OF THE SPIRIT

(Epiphany)

Christ is the end of the Law for righteousness to everyone that believeth.
—Rom. 10:4

In the Epistle to the Romans, St. Paul argues against Jews who rejected the Gospel; in his Epistles to the Corinthians, he rebukes Christians who had abused it. The sin of the fickle and vainglorious Corinthians was very different from that of the hard-hearted Jews; and yet in either case it rose from one and the same root, pride. Both Jews and Greeks prided themselves on what they were, on what Moses had left them, or what Christ's Apostles had brought them; both forgot that whatever they had was God's gift, and that it was their duty to be dependent and watchful. But in appearance they differed: the Jews insisted on God's former mercies unseasonably; and the Greeks of Corinth thought even of His last and best, lightly and unthankfully.

Sinful feelings and passions generally take upon themselves the semblance of reason, and affect to argue. It was in this way that the Jews, whom St. Paul is opposing in the text, disguised from themselves their own unbelief; and this has turned out a benefit to the Church ever since, as having led St. Paul, in consequence, to set forth views of the Gospel which otherwise might not have come to us with the authority of inspiration. The text contains such a view, expressed very concisely, which I now propose to explain; and after doing so, I will add a few words on the feelings of the Jews, in contrast with the doctrine it contains.

St. Paul tells us, that "Christ is the end of the Law for righteousness to everyone that believeth." Here are three subjects which call for remark: the Law, righteousness, and faith. I will speak of them in succession.

1. In the first place, of "the Law." By the Law is meant the eternal, unchangeable Law of God, which is the revelation of His will, the standard of perfection, and the mold and fashion to

which all creatures must conform, as they would be happy. God is holy, and His Law is holy. His Law is the image of Himself; it is the word of Life and Truth commanding that, of which He is the perfect pattern. "Be ye holy," He says, "for I am holy." "Be ye perfect, even as your Father which is in heaven is perfect."[150] His Law is the declaration of His infinite and glorious attributes, and thereby becomes the rule by which all beings imitate, approach, and resemble Him. And when He created them, He provided that it should be to them what it ought to be. God loves holiness, and therefore, as became a good and kind Father, He created all His children holy. He created them to be His children, not His enemies; beings in whom He might take pleasure; who might be near Him, not far off from Him; whom He might love and reward. He formed them upon the pattern of the Law; He molded them into symmetry by means of it. He created man "in His own image, and after His likeness"; that is, upon the type of the Law. He put His Spirit within him and set up the Law in his heart; so that, what He is in His infinite nature, such was man, such was Adam in a finite nature—perfect after his kind.

And in this sense, the Law given to the Israelites from Mount Sinai is called in Scripture, and may be considered, the holy and eternal Law of God. Not that any number of commandments, uttered in man's language and written upon tables, could be commensurate with what is of an infinite and of a spiritual nature; not that a code of precepts, addressed to one portion of a fallen race, in one country, and in one particular state of moral and social existence, could rise to the majesty and beauty of what is perfect—but that the Law of Moses represented the Law of God in its place and age; was the fullest revelation of it, and the nearest approximation to it, then vouchsafed; and was that Law, as far as it went. As Adam, a child of the dust, was also an "image of God," so the Jewish Law, though earthly and temporary, had at the same time a divine character. It was the light of God shining in a gross medium, in order that it might be "comprehended"; and if it did not teach the chosen people all, it taught them much, and in the only way in which they could be taught it. And hence, as in the text, St. Paul, when on the subject of the Jews, speaks of their Law as if it were the eternal Law of God; and so it was, but only as brought down to its hearers, and condescending to their infirmity.

2. Such is "the Law," as spoken of in the text; and by "righteousness" is meant conformity to the Law, that one state of soul which is pleasing to God. It is a relative word, having reference to a standard set up, and expressing the fulfillment of its requirements. To be righteous is to act up to the Law, whatever the Law be, and thereby to be acceptable to Him who gave it. Such Adam was in paradise; the Law was his inward life, and Almighty God dealt with him accordingly—He called, accounted, dealt with him as righteous, because he was righteous.

It was far otherwise with him when he had fallen. He then forfeited the presence of the Holy Spirit; he no longer fulfilled the Law; he lost his righteousness, and he knew he had lost it. He knew it before God told him; he condemned himself, he pronounced himself unrighteous, before God formally rejected him from his state of justification. And in this unrighteous state he has remained, viewed in himself, ever since; knowing the Law, but not doing it; admiring, not loving; assenting, not following; not utterly without the Law, yet not with it; with the Law not within him, but before him, not any longer in his heart, as the pillar of a cloud, which was a gracious token and a guide to the Israelites, but departing from him, and moving away, and taking up its place, as it were over against him, and confronting him as an enemy, accuser, and avenger. It was a cloud of thick darkness, instead of a pillar of light; and from it the Lord looked out upon him, and troubled him. Or in St. Paul's words, "the commandment, which was ordained to life, he found to be unto death."[151] What had been a law of innocence, became a law of conscience; what was freedom, became bondage; what was peace, became dread and misery.

Let us thank God that dread and misery are left us. Better is it that the Law remain to us externally, and in the way of an upbraiding conscience, than that it should be utterly removed. While, and so far as it so remains, our own judgment upon ourselves is a warning to us, what the judgment of God will be hereafter, what His view of us is at present. For is not the pain of a bad conscience different from any other pain that we know? I do not ask whether it is greater or less than other pain, but whether it is not unlike any other, peculiar and individual. Can that pain be compensated and overcome by the wages of sin, whatever they be—or rather, does it not, while it lasts, remain distinctly perceptible and entire in the midst of them? In conscience, then, we have the figure of the wrath of God upon transgressors of the Law; the pain which it inflicts on us at times, or in certain cases, is a sort of indication how God regards, and will one day visit, all sins, according to the sure word of Scripture. Take an instance, which, though extreme, will serve to explain what I would say. What accounts do we read of the frightful sleepless remorse which murderers have before now shown! so much so that, though no one knew their crime, yet they could not help confessing it, as if death were a lighter suffering than a bad conscience. Here you see the misery of being unjustified. Or, again, consider the peculiar piercing distress which follows upon the commission of sins of impurity; here you have a corroboration in a particular instance of what Scripture affirms generally, concerning the misery of sinning. Or, think of those indescribable feelings in our nature, to which our first parent alludes, when he says, "I heard Thy voice in the garden, and I was afraid, because I was naked; and I hid myself."[152] Are not these feelings a type of the horror with which Angels now look, with which we shall look hereafter, upon all transgression of the Law, or unrighteousness?

Unrighteousness then is a state of misery, frightful as the murderer's, acute as theirs who follow Belial, and overpowering as Adam's when he fled from God. And from this state Christ came to save us, by bringing us back again to righteousness. Man was righteous at the first, because the Law of God ruled him; he became unrighteous when this Law ceased to rule him; and he becomes righteous again by the Law of God once more ruling him. He was righteous at the first by the presence of the Holy Spirit, which enabled him to obey the Law; and such too is his second righteousness. And thus the words of the text are fulfilled; "Christ is the end of the Law for" or unto "righteousness." He effects what the Law contemplates and enjoins, but cannot accomplish, our righteousness. And how? St. Paul does not mention it in the text, but in many other places in his Epistles; viz. by that great gift of His passion, the abiding influence of the Holy Ghost, which enables us to offer to God an acceptable obedience, such as by nature we cannot offer.

Now let me show from Scripture some of these points on which I have been insisting.

First, not much need be said to make it plain that by nature we cannot please God, or, in other words, have no principle of righteousness in us. St. Paul says in so many words, "They that are in the flesh cannot please God"; and just before, "The carnal mind is in enmity against God; for it is not subject to the Law of God, neither indeed can be." In the foregoing chapter he says, "We know that the Law is spiritual; but I am carnal, sold under sin. For that which I do, I allow not; for what I would, that do I not: but what I hate, that do I. I know that in me (that is, in my flesh) dwelleth no good thing." Again, "By the deeds of the Law there shall no flesh be justified in His sight for by the Law is the knowledge of sin." In like manner the prophet Isaiah says, "We are all as an unclean thing; and all our righteousnesses are as filthy rags."[153] Such is our state by nature: the best things we do are displeasing to God in themselves, as savoring of the Old Adam, and being works of the flesh and not spiritual.

And as this is our natural state, so the desire of religious men, and the one promise of a merciful God has ever been, that we should be made obedient to the Law, or righteous. Thus David says, "Thou requirest truth *in the inward parts*; and shalt make me to understand wisdom secretly. Thou shalt purge me with hyssop, and I shall be clean; Thou shalt wash me, and I shall be *whiter than snow.* Make me a *clean heart,* O God, and renew a right spirit within me. Oh give me the comfort of Thy help again; and stablish me with Thy free Spirit." Again, "I will wash my hands in *innocency,* O Lord, and so will I go to Thine altar." Again, "Give me understanding, and I shall keep Thy Law, yea, *I shall keep it* with my *whole heart.* . . . Behold, my delight is in Thy commandments. Oh quicken me in Thy righteousness." "Teach me to do the thing that pleaseth Thee; for Thou art my God: let Thy loving Spirit lead me forth into the land of *righteousness.*"[154]

And what Psalmists ask, Prophets promise. They make it the one great distinction of Gospel times, that that original righteousness which is so necessary for us and from which we are so far gone, should be vouchsafed again to us, and that through the Spirit. Daniel states the object of Christ's coming to be the "making reconciliation for iniquity, *and* bringing in everlasting *righteousness*." Malachi says that Christ should "purify the sons of Levi," that they may "offer unto the Lord and an offering in *righteousness*." In Isaiah, Almighty God speaks to them "that know *righteousness*," viz. "the people in whose heart is My *law*"; and he also speaks of "the *Spirit* being poured upon us from on high," and in consequence of "*righteousness* remaining in the fruitful field, and the work of righteousness being *peace*, and the effect of righteousness, *quietness and assurance* forever." Still more clear is the Prophet Jeremiah in declaring what the Gospel gift consists in: "Behold, the days come, saith the Lord, that I will make a new covenant with the house of Israel and with the house of Judah: I will *put My law in their inward parts*, and write it in their hearts." In similar terms does the Prophet Ezekiel describe the great gift of the Gospel, "*A new heart* also will I give you, and a *new spirit* will I put within you; and I will put *My Spirit* within you, and *cause you* to walk in My statutes, and ye shall keep My judgments and do them." Again elsewhere the Prophet Isaiah calls this new nature, or righteousness, or gift of the Spirit, which the Gospel furnishes, a sort of garment or robe of the soul, being that glory which Adam had before sin stripped him of it: "He hath clothed me with the garment of salvation, He hath covered me with *the robe of righteousness*, as a bridegroom decketh himself with ornaments, and as a bride adorneth herself with her jewels." With this passage must be compared St. John's words in the Revelation, "The marriage of the Lamb is come, and His wife hath made herself ready. And to her was granted that she should be arrayed in fine linen, clean and white; *for the fine linen is the righteousness of saints*." Our Lord also speaks of the great gift of the Gospel under the same figure, when he tells us of the man who came to the marriage feast without a wedding garment, that is, without righteousness or holiness.[155]

Thus, if we listen to the voices of the Prophets, we must believe that the righteousness of the Law really *is* fulfilled in us under the Gospel through the Spirit; but as this is a truth in this day denied by some persons, it may be well to insist upon it.

Now that it is a plain truth of Scripture is proved, in addition to what has been said, by those numerous passages which speak of holy men as "righteous *before God*." This is an expression to which we shall do well to attend, as being an additional explanation of the word *righteousness*; for if holy men are righteous *before God,* they come up to God's *standard* of perfection. The phrase "in the sight of" or "before" often occurs in Scripture, and it means "in the *judgment,*" "with the *witness*" of him or them to whom it is applied. Thus in the last chapter of St. Luke, where it is said, "Their words seemed to them as idle tales," this stands in the original Greek, "Their words seemed *in their sight*" or "*before them,*" that is, "*in their judgment.*" And hence when St. Paul speaks with an oath, he uses these words, "Now the things which I write unto you, behold, *before God,* I lie not," that is, "with the *witness* of God." And so Peter and John answer the council, "Whether it be right *in the sight of God* to hearken unto you more than unto God, judge ye," *i.e.,* "in the *presence,*" and "with the *witness* of God." And hence the Angels are said "to stand in the *presence* of God," or to be "before His throne," for they can bear it. And on the other hand, the prodigal son says, "Father, I have sinned *before Thee,*" that is, I know that Thou art conscious of my sin. When then it is said, as it so often is said in Scripture, that the righteous are righteous "before God," this means that their righteousness is not merely the name or semblance of righteousness, nor righteousness up to an earthly standard, but a real and true righteousness which approves itself to God. They are able to stand before God and yet not be condemned. They are not sinners before God, but they are righteous before God, and bear His scrutiny. By nature no one can stand in His presence. "All the world becomes guilty *before God.*" "By the deeds of the law no flesh shall be justified in *His sight.*" *How* then are we able to come before Him? How shall we stand in His sight? The answer is given us in the Old Testament, in the words of Balaam to Balak. Balak asked, "Wherewith shall I *come before the Lord,* and bow myself before the High God?" and the answer was, "He hath showed thee, O man, what is good; and what doth the Lord require of thee, but to do justly, and to love mercy, and to walk humbly with thy God?" Or again, the answer may be given in the words of Zacharias, who blesses the Lord God of Israel for fulfilling His promise, and enabling us to come into His presence to "serve Him, *without fear,* in holiness and righteousness *before Him.*" And accordingly, to come to the case of individuals, Noah, even before the Gospel times, is said to have "found grace in the eyes of the Lord." Why? Because, in the words of Almighty God to him, "*Thee* have I seen righteous *before Me,*" or, in My sight, "in this generation"; and Daniel escaped the lions, "forasmuch as *before God* innocency was found in him." In like manner Zacharias and Elizabeth "were both righteous *before* God," or in the judgment of God. It was told to Cornelius that "his prayers and alms had come up for a memorial *in the sight,*" or judgment, of God. And St. Paul speaks of intercession for governors being "good and acceptable *in the sight* of God our Savior." And he prays for his brethren that God would "work *in* them that which is well pleasing in *His sight,*" or judgment. St. Peter too speaks of a "meek and quiet spirit," being, "in the *sight of God,* of great price." And St. John, that "we receive what we ask of Him, because we do those things that are pleasing *in His sight.*" And Christ warns the Church of Sardis to "be watchful, and strengthen the things which remain, which are ready to die"; for He says, "I have not found thy works perfect *before God,*" or in the witness of God. And accordingly the word *witness* is itself used elsewhere to express the same thing, as in the instance of Abel, who, St. Paul says, by his "more excellent sacrifice," "*obtained witness* that he was righteous; God testifying of his gifts."[156] If then it is plain from Scripture, as it is, that by nature we are unrighteous in God's sight, and cannot stand before God, the same Scripture also proves that by the gift of grace we *are* righteous, and can stand before Him; and it is as easy, by some evasion, to explain away the Scripture proofs for the doctrine of original sin, as to get rid of those which Scripture furnishes us for the doctrine of implanted righteousness, and that through the Spirit.

St. Paul has a number of other passages concerning the office of the Holy Spirit, which are equally apposite to show that He it is who vouchsafes to give us inward righteousness under the Gospel, or to justify, or make us acceptable to God. For instance, he says, "Ye are washed, ye are sanctified, ye are *justified* in the Name of the Lord Jesus, and by the *Spirit* of our God." Elsewhere he first calls the Gospel "the ministration of the *Spirit,*" and in the next verse, "the ministration of righteousness." Elsewhere he speaks of the Holy Ghost as "the Spirit of *adoption.*" And he intimates that "the *righteousness* of the law" is "*fulfilled*" in those "who walk after the *Spirit.*" Again he says that the presence of the Spirit in us pleads, as it were, for us with the Father, "making intercession for us with plaints unutterable"; and that God, "who searcheth the hearts," "*knoweth* what is the mind of the Spirit, because He maketh intercession for the saints, according," or, in a way acceptable, "to God." And elsewhere he contrasts the state of nature and the state of grace in this plain way, clearly implying that that inward gift of righteousness which we lost in Adam we have recovered in Christ; "As by the offense of one, judgment came upon all men to condemnation, even so by the righteousness of One the free gift came upon all men unto justification *of life.* For *as* by one man's disobedience many were made sinners, *so* by the obedience of One shall many be *made righteous* . . . that, as sin hath reigned unto death, even so might grace reign through righteousness unto eternal life by Jesus Christ our Lord."[157] Sin, which we derive through Adam, is not a name merely, but a dreadful reality; and so our new righteousness also is a real and not a merely imputed righteousness. It is real righteousness, because it comes from the Holy and Divine Spirit, who vouchsafes, in our Church's language, to pour His gift into our hearts, and who thus makes us acceptable to God, whereas by nature, on account of original sin, we are displeasing to Him. We are "not in the flesh, but in the Spirit," and therefore in a state of *grace.* Again, St. Paul speaks of the "offering of the Gentiles being *acceptable.*" How acceptable? He proceeds, "being sanctified by the Holy Ghost." He speaks of presenting our "bodies as a living sacrifice, holy, *acceptable* unto God." He says that Christ has "saved us, according to His mercy, by the washing of regeneration, and the renewing of the Holy Ghost," and that we are able thereby to "walk worthy of the Lord unto all *pleasing.*"[158]

Such then is the meaning of the words of the text, "Christ is the end of the Law for righteousness." As if the Apostle said, Would you fulfill the righteousness of the Law? You cannot in your own strength. You cannot without that divine gift which His passion has purchased, the gift of the Spirit; with it "the righteousness of the Law *may* be fulfilled in you." Christ then is the end of the Law for righteousness, because He effects the purpose of the Law. He brings that about which "the Law cannot do, because it is weak through the flesh," through our unregenerate, unrenewed, carnal nature.

3. But here this question may be asked, "How can we be said to *fulfill* the Law, and to offer an *acceptable* obedience, since we do not obey *perfectly?* At best we only obey in part; the best obedience of ours is sullied with imperfection. Even with the gift of the Spirit, we do nothing which will bear the strict inspection of a holy and just Judge. Adam, on the other hand, had no sinful nature at all, before his fall; there was nothing in him to counteract or to defile the influences of grace. He then might be justified by his inward righteousness, but we cannot."

I answer as follows: We can only be justified, certainly, by what is perfect; no work of ours, as far as it is ours, is perfect: and therefore by no work of ours, viewed in its human imperfections, are we justified. But when I speak of our righteousness I speak of the work of the Spirit, and this work, though imperfect, considered as ours, is perfect as far as it comes from Him. Our works, done in the Spirit of Christ, have a justifying *principle* in them, and that is the presence of the All-holy Spirit. His influences are infinitely pleasing to God, and able to overcome in His sight all our own infirmities and demerits. This we are expressly told by St. Paul in reference to one work of the Holy Ghost, the exercise of prayer, as I just now quoted his words. "He that searcheth the hearts, knoweth what is the mind of the Spirit, because He maketh intercession for the saints," that is, in their hearts, "according to God."[159] Not then for anything of our own are we acceptable to God, but for the work of grace in us; and as having this work of grace in us we *are* acceptable. And this Divine Presence in us, makes us altogether pleasing to God. It makes those works pleasing to God, which it produces, though human infirmity be mixed with them: it hallows those acts, that life, that obedience of which it is the original cause, and which it orders and fashions; so that our new obedience or righteousness is justifying, though imperfect, not for its own sake, but for this new and heavenly principle of grace infused into it.

But again, there is another reason why, for Christ's sake, we are dealt with as perfectly righteous, though we be not so. Not only for the Spirit's presence in us, but for what is ours—not indeed what is now ours, but for what we shall be. We are not unreprovable, and unblemished in holiness yet, but we shall be at length through God's mercy. They who persevere to the end, will be perfect in soul and body, when they stand before God in heaven; and now that perfection is beginning in them, now they have a gift in them which will in due time, through God's mercy, leaven the whole mass within them. They will one day be presented blameless before the throne, and they are now to labor towards, and begin that perfect state. And in consideration that it is begun in them, God of His great mercy imputes it to them as if it were already completed. He anticipates what will be, and treats them as that which they are laboring to become. This is what is meant by faith being imputed for righteousness, which St. Paul often insists on, and which is implied in the last words of the text, which I have not yet explained. "Christ is the end of the Law for righteousness *to everyone that believeth.*" Faith is the element of all perfection; he who begins with faith, will end in unspotted and entire holiness. It is the earnest of a great deal more than itself, and therefore is allowed, in God's consideration, to stand for, to be a pledge of, to be taken in advance for that, which it for certain will end in. He who believes has not yet perfect righteousness and unblamableness, but he has the first fruits of it. And all through a man's life, whether his righteous deeds be more or less, or his righteousness of heart more or less, his faith is something quite distinct from anything he had in a state of nature, and though it does not satisfy the requirements of God's Law, yet since it tends to perfection, it is mercifully taken as perfection. "Abraham believed God, and it was counted to him for righteousness," because God, who sees the end from the beginning, knew it would end in perfect and unblemished righteousness. And in like manner to us "it shall be imputed, if we believe on Him that raised up Jesus our Lord from the dead, who was delivered for our offenses, and raised again for our justification."[160]

4. Lastly, such being the Law, such our righteousness, such the work of Christ in us through the Spirit, and such the office of faith, we see what the mistake of the Jews was, of which so much is said in St. Paul's Epistle to the Romans, and which seems to be

the reason why the text itself was written. They were in a path which never would lead to holiness and heaven. They were in a state which was destitute of grace and help. They were under the threatening and condemning Law. Many good men doubtless there had been and were under the Law, but their spiritual excellence was not from the Law, but from the Gospel, the blessings of which were anticipated under it, and which the Apostle was at that time preaching throughout the world. But the Pharisees and others, not understanding the real nature and office of their Law, and the reason why God had given it through Moses, thought to be saved by it, thought it led to heaven. Whereupon St. Paul attempted to show them that they were, as I may say, in the wrong road. They aimed at eternal life; that was the object towards which they professed to be traveling. Now St. Paul told them that the Jewish Law did not lead to it. He said that if they desired to reach the eternal rest of heaven, they must betake themselves to another road. And that they could not as it were, cross over into it, but that they must go back and enter in at the gate, and that this gate was faith. He said that the further they went on in their present course, the less they would really advance, towards their object; and, though it seemed lost time to go back, it was not so. They might do as many works and services as they would in their present state, but these would not advance them at all, and why?—not that works were not necessary, God forbid! but that such works were not good works; that no works were good works but those done in the Spirit, and that nothing could gain them the gift of the Spirit but faith in Christ. They desired to be righteous; it was well; but Christ alone was "the end of the Law for righteousness to everyone that believed." They desired to fulfill the Law; well then, let them seek "the Law of the Spirit of life," whereby "the righteousness of the Law might be fulfilled in them." They desired the reward of righteousness: be it so; let them then "wait through the Spirit for the hope of righteousness by faith."[161] But they were too proud to confess that they had anything to learn, that they had to begin again, to submit to be taught, to believe in Him they had crucified, to come suppliantly for the gift of the Spirit. They refused the true righteousness which God had provided, thinking they were righteous as they were, and that they could be saved in the flesh. Hence St. Paul says, "They, being ignorant of God's righteousness, and going about to establish their own righteousness, have not submitted themselves unto the righteousness of God."[162] They thought that faith was something mean and weak—so it was; and, therefore, that it was unable to do great things—so it was not; for Christ's strength is made perfect in weakness, and He has chosen the despicable things of this world to put to shame such as are highly esteemed. They considered that they were God's people by a sort of right, that they did not need grace, and that their outward ceremonies and their dead works would profit them. Therefore the Apostle warned them, that Abraham himself was justified, not by circumcision, but by faith; that circumcision was not taken for righteousness in his case, for it never would arrive at righteousness, but that faith would arrive, and therefore it was taken; that "to him that worketh not, but believeth on him that justifieth the ungodly, his faith is counted for righteousness";[163] that "by grace are we saved through faith, not of works, for we are *God's* workmanship, *created in* Christ Jesus *unto* good works";[164] that "if by grace, then is it no more of works, otherwise grace is no more grace; but if it be of works, then is it no more grace, otherwise work is no more work."[165] However, the Jews still preferred their old works to good works; they refused to go the way by which alone their persons, thoughts, words, actions, services could be made acceptable to God; they would not exercise that loving faith which alone could gain for them the gift of the Spirit, and was fruitful in true righteousness; they refused to be justified in God's way, and determined to use the Law of Moses for a purpose for which it was never given, for their justification in His sight, and for attaining eternal life.

And in consequence God turned from them, and gave to others what was first offered to them. He manifested Himself to the Gentiles. Those who had hitherto been without any tokens of God's favor outstripped in the race those who had long enjoyed it. The first became last, and the last first. "The Gentiles, which followed not after righteousness, have attained to righteousness, even the righteousness which is of faith; but Israel, which followed after the law of righteousness, hath not attained to the law of righteousness. Wherefore? Because they sought it, not by faith, but, as it were, by the works of the Law; for they stumbled at that stumbling stone."166

Let us see to it, lest in any way we too stumble at God's commands or promises; let us beg of Him to lead us on in His perfect and narrow way, and to be "a lantern to our feet, and a light to our path," while we walk in it.

[V, 11]

Chapter 25

SINS OF INFIRMITY

The flesh lusteth against the Spirit, and the Spirit against the flesh;
and these are contrary the one to the other, so that ye cannot
do the things that ye would.
—Gal. 5:16

It is not uncommonly said of the Church Catholic, and we may humbly and thankfully receive it, that though there is error, variance, and sin in an extreme degree in its separate members, yet what they do all in common, what they do in combination, what they do gathered together in one, or what they universally receive or allow, is divine and holy; that the sins of individuals are overruled, and their wanderings guided and brought around, so that they end in truth, in spite, or even in one sense, by means of error. Not as if error had any power of arriving at truth, or were a necessary previous condition of it, but that it pleases Almighty God to work out His great purposes in and through human infirmity and sin. Thus Balaam had a word put in his mouth in the midst of his enchantments, and Caiaphas prophesied in the act of persuading our Lord's death.

What is true of the Church as a body is true also of each member of it who fulfills his calling: the continual results, as I may call them, of his faith, are righteous and holy, but the process through which they are obtained is one of imperfection; so that could we see his soul as Angels see it, he would, when seen at a distance, appear youthful in countenance, and bright in apparel; but approach him, and his face has lines of care upon it, and his dress is tattered. His righteousness then seems, I do not mean superficial, this would be to give a very wrong idea of it, but though reaching deep within him, yet not whole and entire in the depth of it; but, as it were, wrought out of sin, the result of a continual struggle—not spontaneous nature, but habitual self-command.

True faith is not shown here below in peace, but rather in conflict; and it is no proof that a man is not in a state of grace that he continually sins, provided such sins do not remain on him as what I may call ultimate results, but are ever passing on into something beyond and unlike themselves, into truth and righteousness. As we gain happiness through suffering, so do we arrive at holiness through infirmity, because man's very condition is a fallen one, and in passing out of the country of sin, he necessarily passes through it. And hence it is that holy men are kept from regarding themselves with satisfaction, or resting in anything short of our Lord's death, as their ground of confidence; for, though that death has already in a measure wrought life in them, and effected the purpose for which it took place, yet to themselves they seem but sinners, their renewal being hidden from them by the circumstances attending it. The utmost they can say of themselves is, that they are not in the commission of any such sins as would plainly exclude them from grace; but how little of firm hope can be placed on such negative evidence is plain from St. Paul's own words on the subject, who, speaking of the censures passed upon him by the Corinthians, says, "I know nothing by myself," that is, I am conscious of nothing, "yet am I not hereby justified; but He that judgeth me is the Lord." As men in a battle cannot see how it is going, so Christians have no certain signs of God's presence in their hearts, and can but look up towards their Lord and Savior, and timidly hope. Hence they will readily adopt the well-known words, not as expressing a matter of doctrine, but as their own experience about themselves: "The little fruit which we have in holiness, it is, God knoweth, corrupt and unsound; we put no confidence at all in it; . . . our continual suit to Him is, and must be, to bear with our infirmities and pardon our offenses."[167]

Let us then now enumerate some of the infirmities which I speak of; infirmities which, while they certainly beset those who are outcasts from God's grace, and that with grievous additions and fatal aggravations, yet are also possible in a state of acceptance, and do not in themselves imply the absence of true and lively faith. The review will serve to humble all of us, and perhaps may encourage those who are depressed by a sense of their high calling, by reminding them that they are not reprobate, though they be not all they should be.

1. Now of the sins which stain us, though without such a consent of the will as to forfeit grace, I must mention first original sin.

How it is that we are born under a curse which we did not bring upon us, we do not know; it is a mystery; but when we become Christians, that curse is removed. We are no longer under God's wrath; our guilt is forgiven us, but still the infection of it remains. I mean, we still have an evil principle within us, dishonoring our best services. How far, by God's grace, we are able in time to chastise, restrain, and destroy this infection, is another question; but still it is not removed at once by Baptism, and if not, surely it is a most grievous humiliation to those who are striving to "walk worthy of the Lord unto all pleasing."[168] It is involuntary, and therefore does not cast us out of grace; yet in itself it is very miserable and very humbling: and everyone will discover it in himself, if he watches himself narrowly. I mean, what is called the old Adam, pride, profaneness, deceit, unbelief, selfishness, greediness, the inheritance of the Tree of the knowledge of good and evil; sins which the words of the serpent sowed in the hearts of our first parents, which sprang up and bore fruit, some thirtyfold, some sixty, some a hundred, and which have been by carnal descent transmitted to us.

2. Another class of involuntary sins, which often are not such as to throw us out of grace, any more than the infection of nature, but are still more humbling and distressing, consists of those which arise from our former habits of sin, though now long abandoned. We cannot rid ourselves of sin when we would; though we repent, though God forgives us, yet it remains in its power over our souls, in our habits, and in our memories. It has given a color to our thoughts, words, and works; and though, with many efforts, we would wash it out from us, yet this is not possible except gradually. Men have been slothful, or self-conceited, or self-willed, or impure, or worldly-minded in their youth, and afterwards they turn to God, and would fain to be other than they have been, but their former self clings to them, as a poisoned garment, and eats into them. They cannot do the things that they would, and from time to time they seem almost reduced back again to that heathen state, which the Apostle describes, when he cries out, "Oh wretched man that I am! who shall deliver me from the body of this death?"[169]

3. Another class of involuntary sins are such as arise from want of self-command; that is, from the mind being possessed of more

light than strength, the conscience being informed, but the governing principal weak. The soul of man is intended to be a well-ordered polity, in which there are many powers and faculties, and each has its due place; and for these to exceed their limits is sin; yet they cannot be kept within those limits except by being governed, and we are unequal to this task of governing ourselves except after long habit. While we are learning to govern ourselves, we are constantly exposed to the risk, or rather to the occurrence, of numberless failures. We have failures by the way, though we triumph in the end; and thus, as I just now implied, the process of learning to obey God is, in one sense, a process of sinning, from the nature of the case. We have much to be forgiven; nay, we have the more to be forgiven the more we attempt. The higher our aims, the greater our risks. They who venture much with their talents, gain much, and in the end they hear the words, "Well done, good and faithful servant"; but they have so many losses in trading by the way, that to themselves they seem to do nothing but fail. They cannot believe that they are making any progress; and though they do, yet surely they have much to be forgiven in all their services. They are like David, men of blood; they fight the good fight of faith, but they are polluted with the contest.

I am not speaking of cases of extraordinary devotion, but of what everyone must know in his own case, how difficult it is to command himself, and do that he wishes to do; how weak the governing principle of his mind is, and how poorly and imperfectly he comes up to his own notions of right and truth; how difficult it is to command his feelings, grief, anger, impatience, joy, fear; how difficult to govern his tongue, to say just what he would; how difficult to rouse himself to do what he would, at this time or that; how difficult to rise in the morning; how difficult to go about his duties and not be idle; how difficult to eat and drink just what he should, how difficult to fix his mind on his prayers; how difficult to regulate his thoughts through the day; how difficult to keep out of his mind what should be kept out of it.

We are feebleminded, excitable, effeminate, wayward, irritable, changeable, miserable. We have no lord over us, because we are but partially subject to the dominion of the true King of Saints. Let us try to do right as much as we will, let us pray as earnestly, yet we do not, in a time of trial, come up even to our own notions of perfection, or rather we fall quite short of them, and do perhaps just the reverse of what we had hoped to do. While there is no external temptation present, our passions sleep, as we think all is well. Then we think, and reflect, and resolve what we will do; and we anticipate no difficulty in doing it. But when the temptation is come, where are we then? We are like Daniel in the lions' den; and our passions are the lions; except that we have not Daniel's grace to prevail with God for the shutting of the lions' mouths lest they devour us. Then our reason is but like the miserable keeper of wild beasts, who in ordinary seasons is equal to them, but not when they are excited. Alas! Whatever the affection of mind may be, how miserable it is! It may be a dull, heavy sloth, or cowardice, which throws its huge limbs around us, binds us close, oppresses our breath, and makes us despise ourselves, while we are impotent to resist it; or it may be anger, or other baser passion, which, for the moment, escapes from our control after its prey, to our horror and our disgrace; but anyhow, what a miserable den of brute creatures does the soul then become, and we at the moment (I say) literally unable to help it! I am not, of course, speaking of *deeds* of evil, the fruits of willfulness—malice, or revenge, or uncleanness, or intemperance, or violence, or robbery, or fraud—alas the sinful heart often goes on to commit sins which hide from it at once the light of God's countenance; but I am supposing what was Eve's case, when she looked at the tree and saw that the fruit was good, but before she plucked it, when lust had conceived and was bringing forth sin, but ere sin was finished and had brought forth death. I am supposing that we do not exceed so far as to estrange God from us, that He mercifully chains the lions at our cry, before they do more than frighten us by their moanings or their roar, before they fall on us to destroy us: yet, at best, what misery, what pollution, what sacrilege, what a chaos is there then in that consecrated spot, which is the temple of the Holy Ghost! How is it that the lamp of God does not go out in it at once, when the whole soul seems tending to hell, and hope is almost gone? Wonderful mercy indeed it is, which bears so much! Incomprehensible patience in the Holy One, so to dwell, in such a wilderness, with the wild beasts! Exceeding and divine virtue in the grace given us, that it is not stifled! Yet such is the promise, not to those who sin contentedly after they have received grace; there is no hope while they so sin; but where sin is not part of a course, though it is still sin, whether sin of our birth, or of habits formed long ago, or of want of self-command which we are trying to gain, God mercifully allows and pardons it, and "the blood of Jesus Christ cleanseth us from" it all.

4. Further, I might dwell upon sins which we fall into from being taken unawares—when the temptation is sudden—as St. Peter, when he first denied Christ; though whether it became of a different character, when he denied twice and thrice, is a further question.

5. And again, those sins which rise from the devil's temptations; inflaming the wounds and scars of past sins healed, or nearly so; exciting the memory, and hurrying us away; and thus making use of our former selves against our present selves contrary to our will.

6. And again, I might speak of those which rise from a deficiency of practical experience, or from ignorance how to perform duties which we set about. Men attempt to be munificent, and their acts are prodigal; they wish to be firm and zealous, and their acts are cruel; they wish to be benevolent, and they are indulgent and weak; they do harm when they mean to do good; they engage in undertakings, or they promote designs, or they put forth opinions, or they set a pattern, of which evil comes; they countenance evil; they mistake falsehood for truth; they are zealous for false doctrines; they oppose the cause of God. One can hardly say all this is without sin, and yet in them it may be involuntary sin and pardonable on the prayer of faith.

7. Or I might speak of those unworthy motives, low views, mistakes in principle, false maxims, which abound on all sides of us, and which we catch (as it were) from each other—that spirit of the world which we breathe, and which defiles all we do, yet which can hardly be said to be a willful pollution; but rather it is such sin as is consistent with the presence of the grace of God in us, which that grace will blot out and put away.

8. And, lastly, much might be said on the subject of what the Litany calls "negligences and ignorances," on forgetfulnesses, heedlessnesses, want of seriousness, frivolities, and a variety of

weaknesses, which [we] may be conscious of in ourselves, or see in others.

Such are some of the classes of sins which may be found, if it so happen, where the will is right, and faith lively; and which in such cases are not inconsistent with the state of grace, or may be called infirmities. Of course it must be ever recollected, that infirmities are not always to be regarded *as* infirmities; they attach also to those who live in the commission of willful sins, and who have no warrant whatever for considering themselves in a saving state. Men do not cease to be under the influence of original sin or sins of past years, they do not gain self-command, or unlearn negligences and ignorances, by adding to these offenses others of a more grievous character. Those who are out of grace, have infirmities and much more. And there will always be a tendency in such persons to explain away their willful sins into infirmities. This is ever to be borne in mind. I am not attempting to draw the line between infirmities and transgressions; I only say, that to whomsoever besides such infirmities do attach, they may happen to attach to those who are free from transgressions, and who need to despond, or be miserable on account of failings which in them are not destructive of faith or incompatible with grace. Who these are He only knows for certain, who "tries the reins and the heart," who "knoweth the mind of the Spirit," and "discerns between the righteous and the wicked." He is able, amid the maze of contending motives and principles within us, to trace out the perfect work of righteousness steadily going on there, and the rudiments of a new world rising from out the chaos. He can discriminate between what is habitual and what is accidental; what is on the growth and what is on the decay; what is a result and what is indeterminate; what is of us and what is in us. He estimates the difference between a will that is honestly devoted to Him, and one that is insincere. And where there is a willing mind, He accepts it "according to that a man hath, and not according to that he hath not."[170] In those whose wills are holy, He is present for sanctification and acceptance; and, like the sun's beams in some cave of the earth, His grace sheds light on every side, and consumes all mists and vapors as they rise.

We indeed have not knowledge such as His; were we ever so

high in God's favor, a certainty of our justification would not belong to us. Yet, even to know only thus much, that infirmities are no necessary mark of reprobation, that God's elect have infirmities, and that our own sins may possibly be no more than infirmities, this surely, by itself, is a consolation. And to reflect that at least God continues us visibly in His Church; that He does not withdraw from us the ordinances of grace; that He gives us means of instruction, patterns of holiness, religious guidance, good books; that He allows us to frequent His house, and to present ourselves before Him in prayer and Holy Communion; that He gives us opportunities of private prayer; that He has given us a care for our souls; an anxiety to secure our salvation; a desire to be more strict and conscientious, more simple in faith, more full of love than we are; all this will tend to soothe and encourage us, when the sense of our infirmities makes us afraid. And if further, God seems to be making us His instruments for any purpose of His, for teaching, warning, guiding, or comforting others, resisting error, spreading the knowledge of the truth, or edifying His Church, this too will create in us the belief, not that God is certainly pleased with us, for knowledge of mysteries may be separated from love, but that He has not utterly forsaken us in spite of our sins, that He still remembers us, and knows us by name, and desires our salvation. And further, if, for all our infirmities, we can point to some occasions on which we have sacrificed anything for God's service, or to any habit of sin or evil tendency of nature which we have more or less overcome, or to any habitual self-denial which we practice, or to any work which we have accomplished to God's honor and glory; this perchance may fill us with the humble hope that God is working in us, and therefore is at peace with us. And, lastly, if we have, through God's mercy, an inward sense of our own sincerity and integrity, if we feel that we can appeal to God with St. Peter, that we love Him only, and desire to please Him in all things—in proportion as we feel this, or at such times as we feel it, we have an assurance shed abroad on our hearts, that we are at present in His favor, and are in training for the inheritance of His eternal kingdom.

[V, 15]

Chapter 26

SINCERITY AND HYPOCRISY

If there be first a willing mind, it is accepted according to that a man hath,
and not according to that he hath not.
— 2 Cor. 8:12

Men may be divided into two great classes, those who profess religious obedience, and those who do not; and of those who do profess to be religious, there are again those who perform as well as profess, and those who do not. And thus on the whole there are three classes of men in the world, open sinners, consistent Christians, and between the two (as speaking with the one, and more or less acting with the other) professing Christians, or, as they are sometimes called, nominal Christians. Now the distinction between open and consistent Christians is so clear, that there is no mistaking it; for they agree in nothing; they neither profess the same things nor practice the same. But the difference between professing Christians and true Christians is not so clear, for this reason, that true Christians, however consistent they are, yet do sin, as being not yet perfect; and so far as they sin, are inconsistent, and this is all that professing Christians are. What then, it may be asked, is the real difference between true and professing Christians, since both the one and the other profess more than they practice? Again, if you put the question to one of the latter class, however inconsistent his life may be, yet he will be sure to say that he wishes he was better; that he is sorry for his sins; that the flesh is weak; that he cannot overcome it; that God alone can overcome it; that he trusts God will, and that he prays to Him to enable him to do it. There is no form of words conceivable which a mere professing Christian cannot use—nay, more, there appears to be no sentiment which he cannot feel—as well as the true Christian, and at first sight apparently with the same justice. He *seems* just in the very position of the true Christian, only perhaps behind him; not *so* consistent, not advanced so much; still, on the same line.

Both confess to a struggle within them; both sin, both are sorry; what then is the difference between them?

There are many differences; but, before going on to mention that one to which I shall confine my attention, I would have you observe that I am speaking of differences in God's sight. Of course, we men may after all be unable altogether, and often are unable, to see differences between those who, nevertheless, are on different sides of the line of life. Nor may we judge anything absolutely before the time, whereas God "searcheth the hearts." He alone, "who searcheth the hearts," "knoweth what is the mind of the Spirit." We do not even know ourselves absolutely. "Yea, I judge not mine own self," says St. Paul, "but He that judgeth me is the Lord." God alone can unerringly discern between sincerity and insincerity, between the hypocrite and the man of perfect heart. I do not, of course, mean what we can form no judgment at all upon ourselves, or that it is not useful to do so; but here I will chiefly insist upon the point of *doctrine,* viz. how does the true Christian differ in God's sight from the insincere and double-minded?—leaving any practical application which it admits, to be incidentally brought out in the course of my remarks.

Now the real difference between the true and the professing Christian seems to be given us in the text, "If there be a willing mind, it is accepted." St. Paul is speaking of almsgiving; but what he says seems to apply generally. He is laying down a principle, which applies of course in many distinct cases, though he uses it with reference to one in particular. An honest, unaffected *desire* of doing right is the test of God's true servants. On the other hand, a double mind, a pursuing other ends besides the truth, and in consequence an inconsistency in conduct, and a half-consciousness (to say the least) of inconsistency, and a feeling of the necessity of defending oneself to oneself, and to God, and to the world; in a word, hypocrisy; these are the signs of the merely professed Christian. Now I am going to give some instances of this distinction, in Scripture and in fact.

For instance: The two great Christian graces are faith and love. Now, how are these characterized in Scripture? By their being honest or single-minded. Thus St. Paul, in one place, speaks of "the end of the commandment being love"; what love? "love *out of pure heart,*" he proceeds, "and of a *good conscience*"; and still further, "and of faith:—what kind of faith?—faith *unfeigned*"; or, as it may be more literally translated, "unhypocritical faith; for so the word means in Greek. Again, elsewhere he speaks of his "calling to remembrance the *unfeigned* faith" which dwelt in Timothy, and in his mother and grandmother before him; that is, literally, "unhypocritical faith." Again, he speaks of the Apostles approving themselves as the ministers of God, "by kindness, by the Holy Ghost, by love *unfeigned,*" or more literally, "unhypocritical love." Again, as to love towards man, "Let love be *without dissimulation,*" or, more literally, as in other cases, "let love be unhypocritical." In like manner, St. Peter speaks of Christians "having purified their souls in obeying the truth through the Spirit unto unhypocritical love of the brethren." And in like manner, St. James speaks of "the wisdom that is from above, being first *pure . . .*" and, presently, "without partiality, and *without hypocrisy.*"[171] Surely it is very remarkable that three Apostles, writing on different subjects and occasions, should each of them thus speak about whether faith or love is without hypocrisy.

A true Christian, then, may almost be defined as one who has a ruling sense of God's presence within him. As none but justified persons have that privilege, so none but the justified have that practical perception of it. A true Christian, or one who is in a state of acceptance with God, is he, who, in such sense, has faith in Him, as to live in the thought that He is present with him—present not externally, not in nature merely, or in providence, but in his innermost heart, or in his *conscience.* A man is justified whose conscience is illuminated by God, so that he habitually realizes that all his thoughts, all the first springs of his moral life, all his motives and his wishes, are open to Almighty God. Not as if he was not aware that there is very much in him impure and corrupt, but he wishes that all that is in him should be bare to God. He believes that it is so, and he even joys to think that it is so, in spite of his fear and shame at its being so. He alone admits Christ into the shrine of his heart; whereas others wish in some way or other, to be by themselves, to have a home, a chamber, a tribunal, a throne, a self where God is not—a home within them which is not a temple, a chamber which is not a confessional, a tribunal without a judge, a throne without a king—that self may be king and judge; and that the Creator may rather be dealt with and approached as though a second party, instead of His being that true and better self, of which self itself should be but an instrument and minister.

Scripture tells us that God the Word, who died for us and rose again, and now lives for us, and saves us, is "quick and powerful, and sharper than any two-edged sword, piercing even to the dividing asunder of soul and spirit, and of the joints and marrow, and a discerner of the thoughts and intents of the heart. Neither is there any creature that is not manifest in His sight; but all things are naked and opened unto the eyes of Him with whom we have to do."[172] Now the true Christian realizes this; and what is the consequence? Why, that he enthrones the Son of God in his conscience, refers to Him as a sovereign authority, and uses no reasoning with Him. He does not reason, but he says, "Thou, God, seest me." He feels that God is too near him to allow of argument, self-defense, excuse, or objection. He appeals in matters of duty, not to his own reason, but to God Himself, whom with the eyes of faith he sees, and whom he makes the Judge; not to any fancied fitness, or any preconceived notion, or any abstract principle, or any tangible experience.

The Book of Psalms continually instances this temper of profound, simple, openhearted confidence in God. "O Lord, Thou hast searched me out and known me. Thou knowest my downsitting and mine uprising. Thou understandest my thoughts long before. . . . There is not a word in my tongue but Thou knowest it altogether." "My soul hangeth upon Thee. Thy right hand hath upholden me." "When I wake up, I am present with Thee." "Into Thy hands I commend my spirit, for Thou hast redeemed me, O Lord, Thou God of Truth." "Commit thy way unto the Lord, and put thy trust in Him, and He shall bring it to pass. He shall make thy righteousness as clear as the light, and thy just dealing as the noonday." "Against Thee only have I sinned, and done this evil in Thy sight." "Hear the right, O Lord, consider my complaint, and hearken unto my prayer that goeth not out of feigned lips. Let my sentence come forth from Thy presence, and let Thine eyes look upon the thing that is equal. Thou hast proved and visited mine heart in the night season. Thou hast tried me, and shalt find no wickedness in me; for I am utterly purposed that my mouth shall not offend." Once more, "Thou shalt guide me with Thy counsel, and after that receive me with glory. Whom have I in heaven but Thee? and there is none upon earth that I desire in comparison of Thee. My flesh and my heart faileth, but God is the strength of mine heart and my portion forever."[173]

Or, again, consider the following passage in St. John's First Epistle: "If our heart condemn us, God is greater than our heart and knoweth all things. Beloved, if our heart condemn us not, then have we confidence towards God." And in connection with this, the following from the same Epistle: "God is Light, and in Him is no darkness at all. If we say that we have fellowship with Him, and walk in darkness, we lie, and do not the truth. . . . If we confess our sins, He is faithful and just to forgive us our sins, and to cleanse us from all unrighteousness." Again, "the darkness is past, and the true light now shineth." Again, "Hereby we know that He abideth in us, by the Spirit which He hath given us." And again, "He that believeth on the Son of God, hath the witness in himself." And, in the same connection, consider St. Paul's statement, that "the Spirit itself beareth witness with our spirit, that we are the children of God."[174]

And, now, on the other hand, let us contrast such a temper of mind, which loves to walk in the light, with that of the merely professing Christian, or, in Scripture language, of the *hypocrite*. Such are they who have two ends which they pursue, religion *and* the world; and hence St. James calls them "double-minded." Hence, too, our Lord, speaking of the Pharisees who were hypocrites, says, "Ye cannot serve God *and* mammon."[175] A double-minded man, then, as having two ends in view, dare not come to God, lest he should be discovered; for "all things that are reproved are made manifest by the light."[176] Thus, whereas the prodigal son "rose and came to his father," on the contrary, Adam hid himself among the trees of the garden. It was not simple dread of God, but dread joined to an unwillingness to be restored to God. He had a secret in his heart which he kept from God. He felt towards God—as it would seem, or at least his descendants so feel—as one man often feels towards another in the intercourse of life. You sometimes say of a man, "he is friendly, or courteous, or respectful, or considerate, or communicative; but, after all, there is something, perhaps without his knowing it, in the background. He professes to be agreed with me; he almost displays his agreement; he says he pursues the same objects as I; but still I do not know him, I do not make progress with him, I have no confidence in him, I do not know him better than the first time I saw him." Such is the way in which the double-minded approach the Most High—they have a something private, a hidden self at bottom. They look on themselves, as it were, as independent parties, treating with Almighty God as one of their fellows. Hence, so far from seeking God, they hardly like to be sought by Him. They would rather keep their position and stand where they are, on earth, and so make terms with God in heaven; whereas, "he that doeth truth, cometh to the light, that his deeds may be made manifest that they are wrought in God."[177]

This being the case, there being in the estimation of the double-minded man two parties, God and self, it follows (as I have said) that reasoning and argument is the mode in which he approaches his Savior and Judge; and that for two reasons—first, because he will not *give* himself up to God, but stands upon his rights and appeals to his notions of fitness: and next, because he has some secret misgiving after all that he is dishonest, or some consciousness that he may appear so to others; and therefore, he goes about to fortify his position, to explain his conduct, or to excuse himself.

Some such argument or excuse had the unprofitable servant, when called before his Lord. The other servants said, "Lord, Thy pound hath gained ten," or "five pounds." They said no more; nothing more was necessary; the case spoke for itself. But the unprofitable servant did not dare leave his conduct to tell its own tale at God's judgment seat; he said not merely, "Lord, I have kept Thy pound laid up in a napkin": he appealed, as it were, to the reasonableness of his conduct against his Maker: he felt he must make out a case, and he went on to attempt it. He trusted not his interests to the Eternal and All-perfect Reason of God, before whom he stood, but entrenched himself in his own.

Again: When our Lord said to the scribe, who had answered Him that eternal life was to be gained by loving God and his neighbor, "Thou hast answered right," this ought to have been enough. But his object was not to please God, but to exalt himself. And, therefore, he went on to make an objection. "But he, willing to *justify himself,* said unto Jesus, And who is my neighbor?" whereas they only are justified in God's judgment, who give up the notion of justifying themselves by word or deed, who start with the confession that they are unjust, and who come to God, not upon their own merits, but for His mercy.

Again: we have the same arguing and insincere spirit exposed in the conduct of the Pharisees, when they asked Christ for the authority on which He acted. They said, "By what authority doest thou these things?" This might be the question of sincere inquirers or mere objectors, of faith or of hypocrisy. Observe how our Lord detects it. He asked them about St. John's baptism; meaning to say, that if they acknowledged St. John, they must acknowledge Himself, of whom St. John spake. They, unwilling to submit to Christ as a teacher and Lord, preferred to deny John to going on to acknowledge Him. Yet, on the other hand, they dare not openly deny the Baptist, because of the people; so, between hatred of our Lord and dread of the people, they would give no answer at all. "They *reasoned* among themselves," we are told. In consequence, our Lord left them to their reasonings; He refused to tell them what, had they reasoned sincerely, they might learn for themselves.

What is seen in the Gospels, had taken place from the beginning. Our first parents were as ready with excuses, as their posterity when Christ came. First, Adam says, "I hid myself, for I was afraid"; though fear and shame were not the sole or chief reasons why he fled, but an incipient hatred, if it may be said, of his Maker. Again, he says, "The woman, whom Thou gavest me . . . she gave me of the tree." And the woman says, "The serpent beguiled me." They did not honestly surrender themselves to their offended God, but had something to say in their behalf. Again, Cain says, when asked where his brother was, whom he had murdered, "Am I my brother's keeper?"

Balaam, again, is a most conspicuous instance of a double mind, or of hypocrisy. He has a plausible reason for whatever he does; he can so skillfully defend himself, that to this day he looks like a good man, and his conduct and fortunes are a perplexity to many minds. But it is one thing to have good excuses, another to have good motives. He had not the love of the truth, the love of God, in his heart; he was covetous of worldly goods; and, therefore, all his excuses only avail to mark him as double-minded.

Again: Saul is another very remarkable instance of a man acting for his own ends, and yet having plausible *reasons* for what he did. He offered sacrifice on one occasion, not having a commission; this was a sin; yet what was his excuse?—a very fair one. Samuel had promised to come to offer the sacrifice, and did not. Saul waited some days, the people grew discouraged, his army fell off, and the enemy was at hand, so, as he says, he "*forced* himself."[178]

Such is the conduct of insincere men in difficulty. Perhaps their difficulty may be a real one; but in this they differ from the sincere: the latter seek God *in* their difficulty, feeling that He only who imposes it can remove it; but insincere men do not like to go to God; and to them the difficulty is only so much gain, for it gives them an apparent reason, a sort of excuse, for not going by God's rule, but for deciding in their own way. Thus Saul took his own course; thus Jeroboam, when in a difficulty, put up calves of gold and instituted a new worship without Divine command. Whereas, when Hezekiah was in trouble, he took the letter of Sennacherib, "and went up into the house of the Lord, and spread it before the Lord,"[179] And when St. Peter was sinking in the water, he cried out to Christ, "Lord, save me."[180] And in like manner holy David, after he had sinned in numbering the people, and was told to choose between three punishments offered him, showed the same honest and simple-hearted devotion in choosing that of the three which might be the most exactly called falling into the Lord's hands. If he must suffer, let the Lord chastise him. "I am in a great strait," he says; "let us fall now into the hands of the Lord; for His mercies are great; and let me not fall into the hand of man."[181]

Great, then, is the difference between sincere and insincere Christians, however like their words may be to each other; and it is needless to say, that what I have shown in a few examples, might be instanced again and again, from every part of Scripture, particularly from the history of the Jews, as contained in the Prophets. All men, even after the gift of God's grace, sin: God's true servants profess and sin—sin, and are sorry; and hypocrites profess and sin—sin and are sorry. Thus the two parties look like each other. But the word of God discriminates one from the other by this test, that Christ dwells in the conscience of one not of the other; that the one opens his heart to God, the other does not; the one views Almighty God only as an accidental guest, the other as

Lord and owner of all that he is; the one admits Him as if for a night, or some stated season, the other gives himself over to God, and considers himself God's servant and instrument now and forever. Not more different in the intimacy of friends from mere acquaintance; not more different is it to know a person in society, to be courteous and obliging to him, to interchange civilities, from opening one's heart to another, admitting him into it, seeing into his, loving him, and living in him; than the external worship of the hypocrite, from the inward devotion of true faith; approaching God with the lips, from believing on Him with the heart; so opening to the Spirit that He opens to us, from so living to self as to exclude the light of heaven.

Now, as to applying what I have been showing from Scripture to ourselves, this shall here be left, my brethren, to the consciences of each of us, and a few words will suffice to do this. Do you, then, habitually thus unlock your hearts and subject your thoughts to Almighty God? Are you living in this conviction of His Presence, and have you this special witness that that Presence is really set up within you unto your salvation, viz. that you live in the sense of it? Do you believe, and act on the belief, that His light penetrates and shines through your heart, as the sun's beams through a room? You know how things look when the sun's beams are on it—the very air then appears full of impurities, which, before it came out, were not seen. So is it with our souls. We are full of stains and corruptions, we see them not, they are like the air before the sun shines; but though we see them not, God sees them: He pervades us as the sunbeam. Our souls, in His view, are full of things which offend, things which must be repented of, forgiven, and put away. He, in the words of the Psalmist, "has set our misdeeds before Him, our secret sins in the light of His countenance."[182] This is most true, though it be not at all welcome doctrine to many. We cannot hide ourselves from Him; and our wisdom, as our duty, lies in embracing this truth, acquiescing in it, and acting upon it. Let us then beg Him to teach us the Mystery of His Presence in us, that, by acknowledging it, we may thereby possess it fruitfully. Let us confess it in faith, that we may possess it unto justification. Let us so own it, as to set Him before us in everything. "I have set God always before me," says the Psalmist, "for He is on my right hand, therefore I shall not fall."[183] Let us, in all circumstances, thus regard Him. Whether we have sinned, let us not dare keep from Him, but with the prodigal son, rise and go to Him. Or, if we are conscious of nothing, still let us not boast in ourselves or justify ourselves, but feel that "He who judgeth us is the Lord." In all circumstances, of joy or sorrow, hope or fear, let us aim at having Him in our inmost heart; let us have no secret apart from Him. Let us acknowledge Him as enthroned within us at the very springs of thought and affection. Let us submit ourselves to His guidance and sovereign direction; let us come to Him that He may forgive us, cleanse us, change us, guide us, and save us.

This is the true life of Saints. This is to have the Spirit witnessing with our spirits that we are sons of God. Such a faith alone will sustain the terrors of the last day; such a faith alone will be proof against those fierce flames which are to surround the Judge, when He comes with His Holy Angels to separate between "those who serve God, and those who serve Him not."[184]

[V 16]

Chapter 27

THE CROSS OF CHRIST THE MEASURE
OF THE WORLD

(Sixth Sunday in Lent)

And I, if I be lifted up from the earth, will draw all men unto Me.
—John 12:32

A great number of men live and die without reflecting at all upon the state of things in which they find themselves. They take things as they come, and follow their inclinations as far as they have the opportunity. They are guided mainly by pleasure and pain, not by reason, principle, or conscience; and they do not attempt to *interpret* this world, to determine what it means, or to reduce what they see and feel to system. But when persons, either from thoughtfulness of mind, or from intellectual activity, begin to contemplate the visible state of things into which they are born, then forthwith they find it a maze and a perplexity. It is a riddle which they cannot solve. It seems full of contradictions and without a drift. Why it is, and what it is to issue in, and how it is what it is, and how we come to be introduced into it, and what is our destiny, are all mysteries.

In this difficulty, some have formed one philosophy of life, and others another. Men have thought they have found the key, by means of which they might read what is so obscure. Ten thousand things come before us one after another in the course of life, and what are we to think of them? what color are we to give them? Are we to look at all things in a gay and mirthful way? or in a melancholy way? in a desponding or a hopeful way? Are we to make light of life altogether, or to treat the whole subject seriously? Are we to make greatest things of little consequence, or least things of great consequence? Are we to keep in mind what is past and gone, or are we look on to the future, or are we to be absorbed in what is present? *How* are we to look at things? this is the question which all persons of observation ask themselves, and answer each in his own way. They wish to think by rule; by something within them, which may harmonize and adjust what is without them. Such is the need felt by reflective minds. Now, let me ask, what *is* the real key, what is the Christian interpretation of this world? What is given us by revelation to estimate and measure this world by? The event of this season, the Crucifixion of the Son of God.

It is the death of the Eternal Word of God made flesh, which is our great lesson how to think and how to speak of this world. His Cross has put its due value upon everything which we see, upon all fortunes, all advantages, all ranks, all dignities, all pleasures; upon the lust of the flesh, and the lust of the eyes, and the pride of life. It has set a price upon the excitements, the rivalries, the hopes, the fears, the desires, the efforts, the triumphs of mortal man. It has given a meaning to the various, shifting course, the trials, the temptations, the sufferings, of his earthly state. It has brought together and made consistent all that seemed discordant and aimless. It has taught us how to live, how to use this world, what to expect, and what to desire, what to hope. It is the tone into which all the strains of this world's music are ultimately to be resolved.

Look around, and see what the world presents of high and low. Go to the court of princes. See the treasure and skill of all nations brought together to honor a child of man. Observe the prostration of the many before the few. Consider the form and ceremonial, the pomp, the state, the circumstance; and the vainglory. Do you wish to know the worth of it all? look at the Cross of Christ.

Go to the political world: see nation jealous of nation, trade rivaling trade, armies and fleets matched against each other. Survey the various ranks of the community, its parties and their contests, the strivings of the ambitious, the intrigues of the crafty. What is the end of all this turmoil? the grave. What is the measure? the Cross.

Go, again, to the world of intellect and science: consider the wonderful discoveries which the human mind is making, the variety of arts to which its discoveries give rise, the all but miracles by which it shows its power; and next, the pride and confidence of reason, and the absorbing devotion of thought to transitory objects, which is the consequence. Would you form a right judgment of all this? look at the Cross.

Again: look at misery, look at poverty and destitution, look at oppression and captivity; go where food is scanty, and lodging unhealthy. Consider pain and suffering, diseases long or violent, all that is frightful and revolting. Would you know how to rate all these? gaze upon the Cross.

Thus in the Cross, and Him who hung upon it, all things meet; all things subserve it, all things need it. It is their center and their interpretation. For He was lifted up upon it, that He might draw all men and all things unto Him.

But it will be said, that the view which the Cross of Christ imparts to us of human life and of the world is not that which we should take, if left to ourselves; that is not an obvious view; that if we look at things on their surface, they are far more bright and sunny than they appear when viewed in the light which this season casts upon them. The world seems made for the enjoyment of just such a being as man, and man is put into it. He has the *capacity* of enjoyment, and the world supplies the *means*. How natural this, what a simple as well as pleasant philosophy, yet how different from that of the Cross! The doctrine of the Cross, it may be said, disarranges two parts of a system which seem made for each other; it severs the fruit from the eater, the enjoyment from the enjoyer. How does this solve a problem? does it not rather itself create one?

I answer, first, that whatever force this objection may have, surely it is merely a repetition of that which Eve felt and Satan urged in Eden; for did not the woman see that the forbidden tree was "good for food," and "a tree to be *desired*"? Well, then, is it wonderful that we too, the descendants of this first pair, should still be in a world where there is a forbidden fruit, and that our trials should lie in being within reach of it, and our happiness in abstaining from it? The world, at first sight, appears *made* for pleasure, and the vision of Christ's Cross is a solemn and sorrowful sight interfering with this appearance. Be it so; but why may it not be our duty to abstain from enjoyment and notwithstanding, if it was a duty even in Eden?

But again: it is but a superficial view of things to say that this life is made for pleasure and happiness. To those who look under the surface, it tells a very different tale. The doctrine of the Cross does but teach, though infinitely more forcibly, still after all it does but teach the very same lesson which this world teaches to those who live long in it, who have much experience in it, who know it. The world is sweet to the lips, but bitter to the taste. It pleases at first, but not at last. It looks gay on the outside, but evil and misery lie concealed within. When a man has passed a certain number of years in it, he cries out with the Preacher, "Vanity of vanities, all is vanity." Nay, if he has not religion for his guide, he will be forced to go further, and say, "All is vanity and vexation of spirit"; all is disappointment; all is sorrow; all is pain. The sore judgments of God upon sin are concealed within it, and force a man to grieve whether he will or no. Therefore the doctrine of the Cross of Christ does but anticipate for us our experience of the world. It is true, it bids us grieve for our sins in the midst of all that smiles and glitters around us; but if we will not heed it, we shall at length be forced to grieve for them from undergoing their fearful punishment. If we will not acknowledge that this world has been made miserable by sin, from the sight of Him on whom our sins were laid, we shall experience it to be miserable by the recoil of those sins upon ourselves.

It may be granted, then, that the doctrine of the Cross is not on the surface of the world. The surface of things is bright only, and the Cross is sorrowful; it is a hidden doctrine; it lies under a veil; it at first sight startles us, and we are tempted to revolt from it. Like St. Peter, we cry out, "Be it far from Thee, Lord; this shall not be unto Thee."[185] And yet it is a true doctrine; for truth is not on the surface of things, but in the depths.

And as the doctrine of the Cross, though it be the true interpretation of this world, is not prominently manifested in it, upon its surface, but is concealed; so again, when received into the faithful heart, there it abides as a living principle, but deep, and hidden from observation. Religious men, in the words of Scripture, "live by the faith of the Son of God, who loved them and gave Himself for them":[186] but they do not tell this to all men; they leave others to find it out as they may. Our Lord's own command to His disciples was, that when they fast, they should "anoint their head and wash their face."[187] Thus they are bound not to make a display, but ever to be content to look outwardly different from what they are really inwardly. They are to carry a cheerful countenance with them, and to control and regulate their feelings, that those feelings, by not being expended on the surface, may retire deep into their hearts and there live. And thus "Jesus Christ and He crucified" is, as the Apostle tells us, "a hidden wisdom"—hidden in the world, which seems at first sight to speak a far other doctrine, and hidden in the faithful soul, which to persons at a distance, or to chance beholders, seems to be living but an ordinary life, while really it is in secret holding communion with Him who was "manifested in the flesh," "crucified through weakness," "justified in the Spirit, seen of Angels, and received up into glory."

This being the case, the great and awful doctrine of the Cross of Christ, which we now commemorate, may fitly be called, in the language of figure, the *heart* of religion. The heart may be considered as the seat of life; it is the principle of motion, heat, and activity; from it the blood goes to and fro to the extreme parts of the body. It sustains the man in his powers and faculties; it enables the brain to think; and when it is touched, man dies. And in like manner the sacred doctrine of Christ's Atoning Sacrifice is the vital principle on which the Christian lives, and without which Christianity is not. Without it no other doctrine is held profitably; to believe in Christ's Divinity, or in His manhood, or in the Holy Trinity, or in a judgment to come, or in the resurrection of the dead, is an untrue belief, not Christian faith, unless we receive also the doctrine of Christ's sacrifice. On the other hand, to receive it presupposes the reception of other high truths of the Gospel besides; it involves the belief in Christ's true Divinity, in His true incarnation, and in man's sinful state by nature; and it prepares the way to belief in the sacred Eucharistic feast, in which He who was once crucified is ever given to our souls and bodies, verily and indeed, in His Body and in His Blood. But again, the heart is hidden from view: it is carefully and securely guarded; it is not like the eye set in the forehead, commanding all, and seen of all: and so in like manner the sacred doctrine of the Atoning Sacrifice is not one to be talked of, but to be lived upon; not to be put forth irreverently, but to be adored secretly; not to be used as a necessary instrument in the conversion of the ungodly, or for the satisfaction of reasoners of this world, but to be unfolded to the docile and obedient; to young children, whom the world has not corrupted; to the sorrowful, who need comfort; to the sincere and earnest, who need a rule of life; to the innocent, who need warning; and to the established, who have earned the knowledge of it.

One more remark I shall make, and then conclude. It must not be supposed because the doctrine of the Cross makes us sad, that therefore the Gospel is a sad religion. The Psalmist says. "They that sow in tears shall reap in joy"; and our Lord says, "They that mourn shall be comforted." Let no one go away with the impression that the Gospel makes us take a gloomy view of the world and of life. It hinders us indeed from taking a superficial view, and finding a vain transitory joy in what we see; but it forbids our immediate enjoyment, only to grant enjoyment in truth and fullness afterwards. It only forbids us to *begin* with enjoyment. It only says, If you begin with pleasure, you will end with pain. It bids us begin with the Cross of Christ, and in that Cross we shall at first find sorrow, but in a while peace and comfort will rise out of that sorrow. That Cross will lead us to mourning, repentance, humiliation, prayer, fasting; we shall sorrow for our sins, we shall sorrow with Christ's sufferings; but all this sorrow will only issue, nay, will be undergone in a happiness far greater than the enjoyment which the world gives—though careless worldly minds indeed will not believe this, ridicule the notion of it, because they never have tasted it, and consider it a mere matter of words, which religious persons think it decent and proper to use, and try to believe themselves, and to get others to believe, but which no one really feels. This is what they think; but our Savior said to His disciples, "Ye now therefore have sorrow, but I will see you again, and your heart shall rejoice, and your joy no man taketh from you." . . . "Peace I leave with you; My peace I give unto you; not as the world giveth, give I unto you." And St. Paul says, "The natural man receiveth not the things of the Spirit of God; for they are foolishness unto him; neither can he know them, because they are spiritually discerned." "Eye hath not seen, nor ear heard, neither have entered into the heart of man, the things which God hath prepared for them that love Him."[188] And thus the Cross of Christ, as telling us of our redemption as well as of His sufferings, wounds us indeed, but so wounds as to heal also.

And thus, too, all that is bright and beautiful, even on the surface of this world, though it has no substance, and may not suitably be enjoyed for its own sake, yet is a figure and promise of that true joy which issues out of the Atonement. It is a promise before-hand of what is to be: it is a shadow, raising hope because the sub-stance is to follow, but not to be rashly taken instead of the substance. And it is God's usual mode of dealing with us, in mercy to send the shadow before the substance, that we may take comfort in what is to be, before it comes. Thus our Lord before His Passion rode into Jerusalem in triumph, with the multitudes crying Hosanna, and strewing His road with palm branches and their garments. This was but a vain and hollow pageant, nor did our Lord take pleasure in it. It was a shadow which stayed not, but flitted away. It could not be more than a shadow, for the Pas-sion had not been undergone by which His true triumph was wrought out. He could not enter into His glory before He had first suffered. He could not take pleasure in this semblance of it, knowing that it was unreal. Yet that first shadowy triumph was the omen and presage of the true victory to come, when He had overcome the sharpness of death. And we commemorate this fig-urative triumph on the last Sunday in Lent, to cheer us in the sor-row of the week that follows, and to remind us of the true joy which comes with Easter Day.

And so, too, as regards this world, with all its enjoyments, yet disappointments. Let us not trust it; let us not give our hearts to it; let us not begin with it. Let us begin with faith; let us begin with Christ; let us begin with His Cross and the humiliation to which it leads. Let us first be drawn to Him who is lifted up, that so He may, with Himself, freely give us all things. Let us "seek first the kingdom of God and His righteousness," and then all those things of this world "will be added to us." They alone are able truly to enjoy this world, who begin with the world unseen. They alone enjoy it, who have first abstained from it. They alone can truly feast, who have first fasted; they alone are able to use the world, who have learned not to abuse it; they alone inherit it, who take it as a shadow of the world to come, and who for that world to come relinquish it.

[VI, 7]

Chapter 28

THE SPIRITUAL PRESENCE OF CHRIST
IN THE CHURCH
(EASTER)

*A little while, and ye shall not see Me: and again, a little while,
and ye shall see Me, because I go to the Father.*
—John 16:16

Very opposite lessons are drawn in different parts of Scripture
from the doctrine of Christ's leaving the world and returning to
His Father; lessons so opposite the one to the other, that at first
sight a reader might even find a difficulty in reconciling them
together. In an earlier season of His ministry, our Lord intimates
that when He was removed, His disciples should sorrow—that
then was to be the special time for humiliation. "Can the children
of the Bride chamber mourn," He asks, "as long as the Bridegroom is with them? but the days will come, when the Bridegroom shall be taken from them, and *then* shall they fast."[189] Yet
in the words following the text, spoken by Him when He was
going away, He says, "I will see you again, and your heart shall
rejoice, and your joy no man taketh from you." And He says
shortly before it, "It is expedient for you that I go away." And
again: "I will leave you comfortless, I will come to you. Yet a little
while, and the world seeth Me no more: but ye see Me." Thus
Christ's going to the Father is at once a source of sorrow, because
it involves His absence; and of joy, because it involves His presence. And out of the doctrine of His Resurrection and Ascension,
spring those Christian paradoxes, often spoken of in Scripture,
that we are sorrowing, yet always rejoicing; as having nothing,
yet possessing all things.

This, indeed, is our state at present; we have lost Christ and we
have found Him; we see Him not, yet we discern Him. We
embrace His feet, yet He says, "Touch Me not." How is this? it is
thus: we have lost the sensible and conscious perception of Him;
we cannot look on Him, hear Him, converse with Him, follow

Him from place to place; but we enjoy the spiritual, immaterial, inward, mental, real sight and possession of Him; a possession more real and more present than that which the Apostles had in the days of His flesh, *because* it is spiritual, *because* it is invisible. We know that the closer any object of this world comes to us, the less we can contemplate it and comprehend it. Christ has come so close to us in the Christian Church (if I may so speak), that we cannot gaze on Him or discern Him. He enters into us, He claims and takes possession of His purchased inheritance; He does not present Himself to us, but He takes us to Him. He makes us His members. Our faces are, as it were, turned from Him; we see Him not, and know not of His presence, except by faith, because He is over us and within us. And thus we may at the same time lament because we are not conscious of His presence, as the Apostles enjoyed it before His death; and may rejoice because we know we do possess it even more than they, according to the text, "whom having not seen (that is, with the bodily eyes) ye love; in whom, though now ye see Him not, yet believing, ye rejoice with joy unspeakable and full of glory; receiving the end of your faith, even the salvation of your souls."[190]

Concerning this great and mysterious gift, the presence of Christ, invisible to sense, apprehended by faith, which seems to be spoken of in the text, and is suggested by this season of the year, I purpose now to say some few words.

Now observe what the promise is, in the text and the verses following—a new era was to commence, or what is called in Scripture "a day of the Lord." We know how much is said in Scripture about the awfulness and graciousness of a *day* of the Lord, which seems to be some special time of visitation, grace, judgment, restoration, righteousness, and glory. Much is said concerning days of the Lord in the Old Testament. In the beginning we read of those august days, seven in number, each perfect, perfect all together, in which all things were created, finished, blessed, acknowledged, approved by Almighty God. And all things will end with a day greater still, which will open with the coming of Christ from heaven, and the Judgment; this is especially the day of the Lord, and will introduce an eternity of blessedness in God's presence for all believers. And another special day predicted and fulfilled, is that long season which precedes and prepares for the day of heaven, viz. the day of the Christian Church, the day of the Gospel, the day of grace. This is a day much spoken of in the Prophets, and it is the day of which our Savior speaks in the passage before us. Observe how solemn, how high a day it is: this is His account of it, "I will see you again, and your heart shall rejoice; your joy no man taketh from you. And in that day ye shall ask Me nothing. Verily, verily, I say unto you, Whatsoever ye shall ask the Father in My Name, He will give it you. Hitherto have ye asked nothing in My name; ask, and ye shall receive, that your joy may be full. . . . At that day ye shall ask in my Name, and I say not unto you, that I will pray the Father for you, for the Father Himself loveth you, because ye have loved Me, and have believed that I came out from God. I came forth from the Father, and am come into the world; again I leave the world, and go to the Father." The day, then, that dawned upon the Church at the Resurrection and beamed forth in full splendor at the Ascension, that day which has no setting, which will be, not ended, but absorbed in Christ's glorious appearance from heaven to destroy sin and death; that day in which we now are, is described in these words of Christ as a state of special Divine manifestation, of special introduction into the presence of God. By Christ, says the Apostle, "we have the access by faith into this grace wherein we stand." He "hath raised us up together, and made us sit together in heavenly places in Christ Jesus." "Your life is hid with Christ in God." "Our conversation is in heaven, from whence also we look for the Savior, the Lord Jesus Christ." "God, who commanded the light to shine out of darkness, hath shined in our hearts, to give the light of the knowledge of the glory of God in the face of Jesus Christ." "As many as have been baptized into Christ have put on Christ." And our Lord says, "I will love him, and will manifest Myself to him. . . . We will come unto him, and make Our abode with him." Thus we Christians stand in the courts of God Most High, and, in one sense, see His face; for He who once was on earth, has now departed from this visible scene of things in a mysterious, twofold way, both to His Father and into our hearts, thus making the Creator and His creatures one; according to His own words, "I will not leave you comfortless: I will come to you. Yet a little while, and the world seeth Me no more; but ye see Me: because I live, ye shall live also. At that day ye shall know that I am in the Father, and ye in Me, and I in you."[191]

Now, in behalf of this mystery, I observed:

First, that Christ really is with us now, whatever be the mode of it. This He says expressly Himself; "Lo, I *am with you* alway, even unto the end of the world." He even says, "Where two or three are gathered together in My Name, there am I in the midst of them."[192] And in a passage already quoted more than once, "I will not leave you comfortless: I will come to you." Christ's presence, then, is promised to us still, though He is on the right hand of the Father. You will say. "Yes; He is present as God." Nay, I answer; more than this, He is the Christ, and the Christ is promised, and Christ is man as well as God. This surely is plain even from the words of the text. He said He was going away. Did He go away as God or as man? "A little while, and ye shall not see Me"; this was on His death. He went away as man. He died as man; if, then, He promises to come again, surely He must mean that He would return as man, in the only sense, that is, in which He could return. As God He is ever present, never was otherwise than present, never went away; when His body died on the Cross and was buried, when His soul departed to the place of spirits, still He was with His disciples in His Divine ubiquity. The separation of soul and body could not touch His impassible, everlasting Godhead. When then He says He should go away, and come again and abide forever, He is speaking, not merely of His omnipresent Divine Nature, but of His human nature. As being Christ, He says that He, the Incarnate Mediator, shall be with His Church forever.

But again: you may be led to explain His declaration thus: "He *has* come again, but in His Spirit; that is, His Spirit has come instead of Him; and when it is said that He is with us, this only means that His Spirit is with us." No one, doubtless, can deny this most gracious and consolatory truth, that the Holy Ghost is come; but why has He come? to supply Christ's absence, or to accomplish His presence? Surely to make Him present. Let us not for a moment suppose that God the Holy Ghost comes in such sense that God the Son remains away. No; He has not so come that Christ does not come, but rather He comes that Christ may come in His coming. Through the Holy Ghost we have communion with Father and Son. "In Christ we are builded together," says St. Paul, "for an habitation of God through the Spirit." "Ye are the temple of God, and the Spirit of God dwelleth in you." "Strengthened with might by His Spirit in the inner man, that Christ may dwell in your hearts by faith." The Holy Spirit causes, faith welcomes, the indwelling of Christ in the heart. Thus the Spirit does not take the place of Christ in the soul, but secures that place to Christ. St. Paul insists much on this presence of Christ in those who have His Spirit. "Know ye not," he says, "that your bodies are the members of Christ?" "By one Spirit are we all baptized into one Body . . . ye are the body of Christ, and members in particular." "Know ye not your own selves, how that Jesus Christ is in you, except ye be reprobates?" "Christ in you, the hope of glory." And St. John: "He that hath the Son, hath Life; and he that hath not the Son of God, hath not Life." And our Lord Himself, "Abide in Me and I in you: I am the Vine, ye are the branches. He that abideth in Me, and I in Him, the same bringeth forth much fruit." The Holy Spirit, then, vouchsafes to come to us, that by His coming Christ may come to us, not carnally or visibly, but may enter into us. And thus He is both present and absent; absent in that He has left the earth, present in that He has not left the faithful soul; or, as He says Himself, "The *world* seeth Me no more, but *ye* see Me."[193]

You will say, How can He be present to the Christian and in the Church, yet not be on earth; but on the right hand of God? I answer, that the Christian Church is made up of faithful *souls,* and how can any of us say where the soul is, simply and really? The soul indeed acts through the body, and perceives through the body; but where is it? or what has it to do with place? or why should it be a thing incredible that the power of the Spirit should so visit the soul as to open upon it a Divine manifestation, which yet it perceives not, because its present perceptions are only through the body? Who shall limit the power of the gracious Spirit of God? How know we, for instance, but that He makes Christ present with us, by making us present with Christ? As the earth goes round the sun, yet the sun is said to move, so our souls, in fact, may be taken up to Christ, when He is said to come to us. But no need to insist on one mode in which the mystery may be conceived, when ten thousand ways are possible with God, of which we know nothing. Scripture says enough to show us that influences may be exerted upon the soul so marvelous, that we cannot decide whether the soul remains in the body or not, while subjected to them. St. Paul, speaking of himself, says, "Whether in the body, I cannot tell, or whether out of the body, I cannot tell; God knoweth: . . . caught up to the third heaven." And he repeats his statement: "I knew such a man," meaning himself, "whether in the body I cannot tell, or out of the body I cannot tell, God knoweth: how that he was caught up into paradise, and heard unspeakable words which it is not lawful for a man to utter." St. Paul was brought into paradise, yet his body remained where it was; and whether his soul was separated from it, was a question which he could not decide. How can we pretend to decide what the Holy Spirit may or may not do towards faithful souls now, and whether He does not manifest Christ to and in them, by bringing them to Christ? Again; consider Satan's power in show- ing our Lord all the kingdoms of the world "in *a moment of time*"; may not the Almighty Spirit much more do with us, what the evil one did with our Lord? May He not in less than a moment bring our souls into God's presence, while our bodies are on earth?

And again: while we know so little about our own souls, on the other hand, we are utterly ignorant of the state in which our Blessed Lord exists at present, and the relation of this visible world to Him; or whether it may not be possible for Him, in some mysterious way, to come to us, though He is set down on the right hand of God. Did He not, after His Resurrection, come into a room, of which the doors were shut, yet suffer Himself to be han- dled, to prove that He was not a spirit? Certainly then, though He is clothed in our nature, and is perfect man, yet His glorified body is not confined by those under which our mortal bodies lie.

But further, whether it is difficult to conceive or no, Scripture actually gives us at least one instance of His appearing after His Ascension, as if to satisfy us that His presence is possible, though it be mysterious. We all know that He has often vouchsafed to appear to His saints in *visions*. Thus He appeared to St. John, as related in the Book of Revelation; and to St. Paul, when he was at Corinth, at Jerusalem several times, and in the ship. *These* appear- ances were not an actual presence of Christ, as we may conjecture, but impressions divinely made, and shadows cast upon the mind. And in the same way we may explain His appearing to St. Stephen. When that blessed Martyr said, "Behold I see the heavens open, and the Son of Man standing on the right hand of God," we may suppose he did not see this great sight really, but only had a vision of it. These, I repeat, may be *visions*; but what shall we say to Christ's appearance to St. Paul on his conversion, while he was on the way to Damascus? For then the Lord Jesus plainly was seen and heard by him close at hand. "He fell to the earth, and heard a voice saying unto him, Saul, Saul, why persecutest thou Me? And he said, Who art Thou, Lord? And the Lord said, I am Jesus, whom thou persecutest."[194] How was this? We do not know. Can a body be in two places at once? I do not say so; I only say, Here is a mystery. By way of contrast with this *real sight* of the Lord, we are presently told that to Ananias the Lord appeared "in *a vision*." And hence, moreover, when Ananias came to Saul, he said that God had chosen him that *he* should "*see* that Just One, and *hear* the voice of His mouth."[195] And hence, too, he says himself in his Epistle to the Corinthians, "Am I not an Apostle? am I not free? have I not *seen* Jesus Christ our Lord?"[196] Would he have said this, if he had had but a vision of Him? Had he not many more visions of Him, not one only? And again, after mentioning our Lord's appearance to St. Peter, the Eleven, and five hundred brethren at once, and St. James, he adds, "last of all, He was seen of me also, as of one born out of due time."[197] That is, he speaks of his having been favored with a sight of Christ in as real, true, and literal a sense, as that in which the other Apostles had seen Him. St. Paul then saw Him, and heard Him speak, who was on the right hand of God. And this literal sight seems to have been, for some unknown reason, necessary for the office of an Apostle; for, in accordance with St. Paul's words, just now cited, St. Peter says, when an Apostle was to be chosen in the place of Judas, "Of these men which have companied with us . . . from the baptism of John unto the same day when He was taken up from us, must one be ordained to be a witness with us of his Resurrection." And again, to Cornelius, "Him God raised up the third day, and showed Him openly, not to all the people, but unto witnesses chosen before of God, even to us."[198] If St. Paul saw only a vision of Christ, and not Christ "verily and indeed," in that case he was not a witness of His Resurrection. But if he *did* see Him, it is possible for Christ to be present with *us* also, as with him.

Once more: it may be said that "St. Paul was *conscious* of the presence of Christ on his conversion, and that he actually *saw* the sights and *heard* the sounds of paradise, but that we see and hear nothing. We, then, are not in Christ's presence, else we should be conscious of it." Now, with a view of meeting this objection, let us turn to the account of His appearances to His disciples after the Resurrection, which are most important, first, as showing that such an unconscious communion with Christ is possible; next, that it is likely to be the sort of communion now granted to us, from the circumstance that in that period of forty days after the Resurrection, He began to be in that relation towards His Church, in which He is still, and probably intended to intimate to us thereby what His presence with us is now.

Now observe what was the nature of His presence in the Church after His Resurrection. It was this, that He came and went as He pleased; that material substances, such as the fastened doors, were no impediments to His coming; and that when He was present His disciples did not, as a matter of course, know Him. St. Mark says He appeared to the two disciples who were going into the country, to Emmaus, "*in another form*. St. Luke, who gives the account more at length, says, that while He talked with them their hearts burned within them. And it is worth remarking, that the two disciples do not seem to have been conscious of this at the time, but on looking back, they recollected that as *having* been, which did not strike them while it *was*. "*Did* not," they say, "*did* not our hearts burn within us, while He talked with us by the way, and while He opened to us the Scriptures?" But at the time, their hearts seem to have been holden (if we may use the expression) as well as their eyes. They were receiving impressions, but could not *realize* to themselves that they were receiving them; afterwards, however, they became aware of what had been. Let us observe, too, *when* it was that their eyes were opened; here we are suddenly introduced to the highest and most solemn ordinance of the Gospel, for it was when He consecrated and brake the Bread that their eyes were opened. There is evidently a stress laid on this, for presently St. Luke sums up his account of the gracious occurrence with an allusion to it in particular: "They told what things were done in the way, and how He was known of them in breaking of bread." For so it was ordained, that Christ should not be both seen and known at once; first He was seen, then He was known. Only by faith is He known to be present; He is not recognized by sight. When He opened His disciples' eyes, He at once vanished. He removed His visible presence, and left but a memorial of Himself. He vanished from sight that He might be present in a sacrament; and in order to connect His visible presence with His presence invisible, He for one instant manifested Himself to their open eyes; manifested Himself, if I may so speak, while He passed from His hiding place of sight without knowledge, to that of knowledge without sight.

Or again: consider the account of His appearing to St. Mary Magdalene. While she stood at the Sepulchre weeping He appeared, but she knew Him not. When he revealed Himself, He did not, at once vanish away, but He would not let her touch Him; as if, in another way, to show that His presence in His new kingdom was not to be one of sense. The two disciples were not allowed to *see* Him after recognizing Him, St. Mary Magdalene was not allowed to *touch* Him. But afterwards, St. Thomas *was* allowed both to see and touch; he had the full evidence of sense: but observe what our Lord says to him, "Thomas, because thou hast seen Me, thou hast believed; blessed are they that have not seen, and yet have believed." Faith is better than sight or touch.

Let so much suffice, by way of suggesting thoughts upon this most solemn and elevating subject. Christ has promised He will be with us to the end, be with us, not only as He is in the unity of the Father and the Son, not in the Omnipresence of the Divine Nature, but personally, as the Christ, as God and man; not present with us locally and sensibly, but still really, in our hearts and to our faith. And it is by the Holy Ghost that this gracious communion is effected. How He effects it we know not; in what precisely it consists we know not. We see Him not; but we are to believe that we possess Him, that we have been brought under the virtue of His healing hand, of His life-giving breath, of the manna flowing from His lips, and of the blood issuing from His side. And hereafter, on looking back, we shall be conscious that we have been thus favored. Such is the day of the Lord in which we find ourselves, as if in fulfillment of the words of the prophet, "The

Lord my God shall come, and all the saints with Thee. And it shall come to pass in that day, that the light shall not be clear, nor dark: but it shall be one day which shall be known to the Lord, not day, nor night: but it shall come to pass, that at evening time it shall be light.[199] Nay, even before the end comes, Christians, on looking back on years past, will feel, at least in degree, that Christ has been with them, though they knew it not, only believed it, at the time. They will even recollect then the burning of their hearts. Nay, though they seemed not even to believe anything at the time, yet afterwards, if they have come to Him in sincerity, they will experience a sort of heavenly fragrance and savor of immortality, when they least expect it, rising upon their minds, as if in token that God has been with them, and investing all that has taken place, which before seemed to them but earthly, with beams of glory. And this is true, in one sense, of all the rites and ordinances of the Church, of all providences that happen to us; that, on look-ing back on them, though they seemed without meaning at the time, elicited no strong feeling, or were even painful and distaste-ful, yet if we come to them and submit to them in faith, they are afterwards transfigured, and we feel that it has been good for us to be there; and we have a testimony, as a reward of our obedi-ence, that Christ has fulfilled His promise, and, as He said, is here through the Spirit, though He be with the Father.

May He enable us to make full trial of His bounty, and to obtain a full measure of blessing. "There is a river, the streams whereof shall make glad the city of God, the holy place of the tabernacles of the Most High. God is in the midst of her; she shall not be moved: God shall help her and that right early. . . . Be still, and know that I am God; I will be exalted among the heathen, I will be exalted in the earth. The Lord of hosts is with us; the God of Jacob is our refuge."[200]

[VI,10]

Chapter 29

THE EUCHARISTIC PRESENCE

(Easter)

This is the Bread which cometh down from heaven,
that a man may eat thereof and not die.
—John 6:50

The quarter of the year from Ash Wednesday to Trinity Sunday may fittingly be called the Sacramental Season, as the Season preceding it is the Season of grace; and as we are specially called in the Christmas Season to sincerity of purpose, so now we are called to faith. God does good to those who are good and true of heart; and He reveals His mysteries to the believing. The earnest heart is the good ground in which faith takes root, and the truths of the Gospel are like the dew, the sunshine, and the soft rain, which make that heavenly seed to grow.

The text speaks of the greatest and highest of all the Sacramental mysteries, which faith has been vouchsafed, that of Holy Communion. Christ, who died and rose again for us, is in it spiritually present, in the fullness of His death and of His Resurrection. We call His presence in this Holy Sacrament a spiritual presence, not as if "spiritual" were but a name or mode of speech, and He were really absent, but by way of expressing that He who is present there can neither be seen nor heard; that He cannot be approached or ascertained by any of the senses; that He is not present in place, that He is not present carnally, though He is really present. And how this is, of course is a mystery. All that we know or need know is that He *is* given to us, and that in the Sacrament of Holy Communion.

Now, with reference to the text and the chapter from which it is taken, I begin by observing, what at first sight one would think no one could doubt, that this chapter of St. John does treat of the Lord's Supper, and is, in fact, a comment upon the account of it, given by the other three Evangelists. We know it is St. John's way to supply what his brethren omit, and that especially in matters of doctrine; and in like manner to omit what they record. Hence, while all three give an account of the institution of Holy Communion at the Last Supper, St. John omits it; and, because they omit to enlarge upon the great gift contained in it, he enters upon it. This, I say, is his rule: thus, for instance, St. Matthew and St. Mark give an account of the accusation brought against our Lord at His trial, that He had said He could destroy and build again the Temple of God in three days. They do not inform us when He so said; accordingly, St. John supplies the omission; and, while he passes over the charge at the time of His trial, he relates in his second chapter the circumstances some years before out of which it was framed. The Jews had come to Him and asked Him for a sign; then said He, referring in His mind to His resurrection which was to be, "Destroy this Temple, and in three days I will raise it up"; meaning by Temple His own body, and by His raising it up His Resurrection, after He had been put to death.

Again: St. Matthew and St. Mark also give an account of His instituting the Sacrament of Baptism. Christ instituted it on His ascending on high, but He did not explain the meaning and value of Baptism, at least there is no record of His doing so in St. Matthew and St. Mark. But St. John, while He omits mention of the institution of that Sacrament after the Resurrection, does teach us its doctrinal meaning, by means of a previous discourse of our Lord's with Nicodemus on the subject, a discourse which he alone of the Evangelists introduces. And in like manner, I say, in the chapter before us he explains as a doctrine what the other Evangelists deliver as an ordinance. And, further, it is remarkable that in our Lord's discourse with Nicodemus, no express mention is made of Baptism, though Baptism is evidently the subject of that discourse. Our Lord speaks of being born "of *water* and the Spirit"; He does not say, "of Baptism and the Spirit," yet none of us can doubt that Baptism is meant. In like manner, in the passage before us, He does not say definitely that bread and wine are His Body and Blood; but He speaks only of bread, and, again, of His flesh and blood; words, however, which as evidently refer to the Sacrament of His Supper, as His discourse to Nicodemus refers to Baptism, in spite of His not naming Baptism in express words. Of course it would be very unreasonable to say that when He spoke of "water and the Spirit," He did not allude to Baptism; and it is as unreasonable, surely, to say that in the chapter before us He does not refer to His Holy Supper.

The bearing, then, of our Lord's sacred words would seem to be as follows, if one may venture to investigate it. At Capernaum, in the chapter now before us, He solemnly declares to His Apostles that none shall live forever, but such as eat and drink His flesh and blood; and then afterwards, just before He was crucified, as related in the other three Gospels, He points out to them the way in which this mystery of grace was to be fulfilled in them. He assigns the consecrated Bread as that Body of which He had spoken, and the consecrated Wine as His Blood; and in partaking of the Bread and the Cup, they were partakers of His Body and Blood.

It is remarkable, too, considering that our Lord's institution of His Supper took place just before His betrayal of Judas, and that Judas had just partaken of it, that in the discourse before us He alludes to Judas. "Have I not chosen you twelve, and one of you is a devil?" as if He had before His mind, in His divine prescience, what was to take place when He instituted the Sacrament formally. Observe, too, at the time of that Last Supper, He recurs to the idea of *choosing* them: "I speak not of you all; I know whom I have chosen."[201]

When, then, Christ used the words of the text and of other parts of the chapter containing it, He was describing prospectively that gift, which, in due season, the consecrated Bread and Wine were to convey to His Church forever. Speaking with reference to what was to be, He says, "I am the Bread of Life. Your fathers did eat manna in the wilderness, and are dead. This is the Bread which cometh down from heaven, that a man may eat thereof and not die. I am the Living Bread which came down from heaven: if any man eat of this Bread he shall live forever, and the Bread that I will give is My flesh, which I will give for the life of the world."

In corroboration I would observe, that our Lord had been just then working the miracle of the loaves, in which He had actually blessed and broken the Bread; *upon this,* He goes on to say as follows, "I have wrought a miracle on the bread and fed you, but the time shall come when I will give you the true Eucharistic Bread, which is not like these perishable barley loaves, but such, that by it you shall live forever, for it is My flesh." When, then, before He was taken away, He *did* take bread, and blessed, and brake, using just the same action as He had used in the instance of the miracle of the loaves, and even *called it* His body, how could the Apostles doubt that by that significant action He intended to recall to their minds His discourse recorded in the sixth chapter of St. John, and that they were to recognize in that action the interpretation of His discourse? He had said He would give them a bread which should be His flesh and should have life, and surely they recollected this well. Who among us, had he been present, would not under such circumstances have recognized in His institution of His Supper the fulfillment of that previous promise? Surely, then, we cannot doubt that this announcement in St. John does look on towards, and is accomplished in, the consecrated Bread and Wine of Holy Communion.

If this be so, it requires no proof at all how great is the gift in that Sacrament. If this chapter does allude to it, then the very words "Flesh and Blood" show it. Nor do they show it at all the less, if we do not know what they precisely mean; for on the face of the matter they evidently mean something very high, so high that *therefore* we cannot comprehend it.

Nothing can show more clearly how high the blessing is, than to observe that the Church's tendency has been, not to detract from its marvelousness, but to increase it. The Church has never thought little of the gift; so far from it, we know that one very large portion of Christendom holds more than we hold. That belief, which goes beyond ours, shows how great the gift is really. I allude to the doctrine of what is called Transubstantiation, which we do not admit; or that the Bread and Wine cease to be, and that Christ's sacred Body and Blood are directly seen, touched, and handled, under the *appearances* of Bread and Wine. This our Church considers there is no ground for saying, and our Lord's own words contain marvel enough, even without adding anything to them by way of explanation. Let us, then, now consider them in themselves, apart from additions which came afterwards.

He says, then, "Except ye eat the flesh of the Son of Man and drink His blood, ye have no life in you. Whoso eateth My Flesh and drinketh My Blood, hath eternal life, and I will raise him up at the last day. For My Flesh is meat indeed, and My Blood is drink indeed."

1. About these words I observe, first, that they evidently declare on the face of them some very great mystery. How can they be otherwise taken? If they do not, they must be a figurative way of declaring something which is not mysterious, but plain and intelligible. But is it conceivable that He who is the Truth and Love itself should have used difficult words when plain words would do? Why should He have used words, the sole effect of which, in that case, would be to perplex, to startle us needlessly? Does His mercy delight in creating difficulties? Does He put stumbling blocks in our way without cause? Does He excite hopes, and then disappoint them? It is possible; He may have some deep purpose in so doing: but which is more likely, that His meaning is beyond us, or His words beyond His meaning? All who read such awful words as those in question will be led by the first impression of them, either with the disciples to go back, as at a hard saying, or with St. Peter to welcome what is promised: they will be excited in one way or the other, with incredulous surprise or with believing hope? And are the feelings of these opposite witnesses, discordant indeed, yet all of them deep, after all unfounded? Are they to go for nothing? Are they no token of our Savior's real meaning? This desire, and again this aversion, so naturally raised, are they without a real object, and the mere consequence of a general mistake on all hands, of what Christ meant as imagery, for literal truth? Surely this is very improbable.

2. Next, consider our Lord's allusion to the manna. Persons there are who explain our eating Christ's flesh and blood, as merely meaning our receiving a *pledge* of the *effects* of the *passion* of His Body and Blood; that is, in other words, of the *favor* of Almighty God: but how can Christ's giving us His Body and Blood mean merely His giving us a pledge of His favor? Surely these awful words are far too clear and precise to be thus carelessly treated. Christ, as I have said, surely would not use such definite terms did He intend to convey an idea so far removed from their meaning and so easy of expression in simple language. Now it increases the force of this consideration to observe that the manna, to which He compares His gift, was not a figure of speech, but a something definite and particular, really given,

really received. The manna was not simply health, or life, or God's favor, but a certain something which caused health, continued life, and betokened God's favor. The manna was a gift external to the Israelites, and external also to God's own judgment of them and resolve concerning them, a gift created by Him and partaken by His people. And Christ, in like manner, says, that He Himself is to us the *true* Manna, the *true* Bread that came down from heaven; not like that manna which could not save its partakers from death, but a life-imparting manna. What therefore the manna was in the wilderness, that surely is the spiritual manna in the Christian Church; the manna in the wilderness was a real gift, taken and eaten; so is the manna in the Church. It is not God's mercy, or favor, or imputation; it is not a state of grace, or the promise of eternal life, or the privileges of the Gospel, or the new covenant; it is not, much less, the doctrine of the Gospel, or faith in that doctrine; but it is what our Lord says it is, the gift of His own precious Body and Blood, really given, taken, and eaten as the manna might be (though in a way unknown), at a certain particular time, and a certain particular spot; namely, as I have already made it evident, at the time and spot when and where the Holy Communion is celebrated.

3. Next, I observe, that our Lord reproves the multitude, for not dwelling on the miracle of the loaves *as* a miracle, but only as a means of gaining food for the body. Now observe, this is *contrary* to what He elsewhere says, with a view of discountenancing the Jews' desire after signs and wonders. It would seem then as if there must be something peculiar and singular in what He is here setting before them. He generally represses their desire for signs, but here He stimulates it. He finds fault here, because they did not dwell upon the *miracle.*" "Ye seek Me," He says, "not because ye saw the miracles, but because ye did eat of the loaves and were filled." Now supposing the Eucharistic Gift is a special sign, the sign which He meant to give them forever of His Divine Power, this will account for the difference between His conduct on this occasion and on others, it being as unbelieving to overlook signs when given, as to ask for them when withheld. It will account for His bidding them marvel, when about to promise them Bread from heaven. They were but imitating their ancestors in the wilderness. Their ancestors, on the seventh day, went out to

gather manna in spite of Moses' telling them they would not find it. What was this but to look for mere food, and to forget that it was miraculously given, and as such immediately dependent on the Giver? Let me ask, is their conduct in this age very different, who come to the Lord's Table without awe, admiration, hope; without that assemblage of feelings which the expectation of so transcendent a marvel should raise in us? Let us fear, lest a real, though invisible work of power being vouchsafed to us, greater far than that of the loaves, which related only to this life's sustenance, we lose the benefit of it by disbelieving it. This reflection is strengthened by finding that St. Paul expressly warns the Corinthians of the great peril of "not *discerning* the Lord's Body."

4. In what has been said, it has been implied that the miracle of the loaves was a type of Holy Communion; this it is all but declared to be in the chapter before us, and much follows from it. For let it be considered, if the type be a miracle, which it is, how great must the fulfillment be, unless the shadow be greater than the reality? unless indeed we are willing to argue in the spirit of those who deny the Atonement, on the ground that though the Jewish priests were types of Christ, the antitype need not be a Priest Himself. Moreover, the incomprehensible nature of the miracle of the loaves is a kind of protection of the mystery of the Eucharist against objections with which men are wont to assail it; as, for instance, that it is impossible. For to speak of five thousand persons being fed with five loaves, may be speciously represented to be almost a contradiction in terms. How could it be? did the substance of the bread grow? or was it the same bread here and there and everywhere, for this man and for that, at one and the same time? Or was it created in the shape of bread, in that ultimate condition into which the grain is reduced by the labor of man, and this created again and again out of nothing, till the whole five thousand were satisfied. What, in short, is *meant* by multiplying the loaves? As to Christ's other miracles, they are, it may be said, intelligible though supernatural. We do not know *how* a blind man's eyes are opened, or the dead raised; but we know what *is meant* by saying that the blind saw, or the dead arose: but what *is meant* by saying that the loaves fed five thousand persons? Such then is the objection which may be brought against the miracle of the loaves; and let it be observed, it is just

such as this which is urged against the mystery of Christ's presence in Holy Communion. If the marvelousness of the miracle of the loaves is no real objection to its truth, neither is the marvelousness of the Eucharistic presence any real difficulty in our believing that gift.

And as if still more closely to connect this Holy Sacrament with the miracle of the loaves, and to make the latter interpret the former, our Lord, as I have observed, wrought the miracle of the loaves by means of the same outward acts, which he observed in the mystery of His Supper, and which His Apostles have carefully recorded as the appointed means of consecrating it. St. John says, He *took* the loaves, and when He *had given thanks,* He *distributed* to the disciples." Compare this with St. Luke's account of the institution of the Lord's Supper. "He *took* bread, and *gave thanks,* and brake it, and *gave* unto them." Again, a fuller account of the consecration of the loaves is given by the other Evangelists thus: "He . . . *took* the five loaves and the two fishes," says St. Matthew, "and looking up to heaven, He *blessed,* and *brake,* and *gave* the loaves to His disciples." And what, on the other hand, is told us by the same Evangelist, in his account of the institution of the Holy Communion? "Jesus *took* bread and *blessed* it, and *brake* it, and *gave* it to the disciples." Again, in the second miracle of the seven loaves, He observed the same form: "He *took* the seven loaves and the fishes, and *gave thanks,* and *brake* them, and *gave* to His disciples." And the form is the same in the account of our Lord's celebration of the Sacrament after His Resurrection: "As He sat at meat with them, He *took* bread and *blessed* it, and *brake,* and *gave* to them." And of St. Paul we read, "he *took* bread and *gave thanks* to God in the presence of them all, and when he had *broken* it, he began to eat."[202]

One cannot doubt, then, that the taking bread, blessing or giving thanks, and breaking is a necessary form in the Lord's Supper, since it is so much insisted on in these narratives; and it evidently betokens something extraordinary—else why *should* it be insisted on?— and what that is, the miracle of the loaves tells us. For there the same form is observed, and there it was Christ's outward instrument in working a great "work of God." The feeding then of the multitude with the loaves interprets the Lord's Supper; and as the one is a supernatural work, so is the other also.

5. One more observation I will make besides. At first sight, an objection may be brought against what has been said from a circumstance which, when examined, will be found rather to tell the other way. The Jews objected to our Lord, that He had said what was incredible, when He spoke of giving us His flesh. They "strove among themselves, saying, How can this man give us His flesh to eat?" Our Savior in answer, instead of retracting what He had said, spoke still more strongly—"Except ye eat the flesh of the Son of Man, and drink His blood, ye have no life in you." But when they still murmured at it, and said, "This is a hard saying, who can hear it?"—then He did in appearance withdraw His words. He said, "It is the Spirit that quickeneth, the flesh profiteth nothing." It would take us too long to enter now into the meaning of this declaration; but let us, for argument's sake, allow that He seems in them to qualify the wonderful words He had used at first; what follows from such an admission? This: that our Lord acted according to His usual course on other occasions, when persons refused His gracious announcements, not urging and insisting on them, but as if withdrawing them, and thus in one sense aiding those persons even in rejecting what they ought to have accepted without hesitation. This rule of God's dealings with unbelief we find most fully exemplified in the instance of Pharaoh, whose heart God hardened because he himself hardened it. And so in this very chapter, as if in allusion to some such great law, He says, "Murmur not among yourselves; No man can come to Me, except the Father which hath sent Me draw him"; as if He said, "It is by a Divine gift that ye believe; beware, lest by objections you provoke God to take from you His aid, His preventing and enlightening grace." And then, after they *had* complained, He did in consequence withdraw from them that gracious light which He had given, and spoke the words in question about the flesh and spirit, which would seem to carnal minds to unsay, or explain away, what He had said. But observe, He adds, "There are some of you that believe not. . . . *Therefore* said I unto you, that no man can come unto Me, except it were given unto Him of My Father."

All this is parallel, let it be observed, to His dealings with the Jews in the tenth chapter of the same Gospel. He there declares, "I and My Father are One." The Jews, instead of embracing, stumble at the truth, and accuse Him of blasphemy, as if He being a man made Himself God. This was their inference from His words, and a correct inference, just as in the other case they rightly understood Him to promise that He would give us His flesh to eat. But when they, instead of embracing the truth which they had correctly inferred, instead of humbling themselves before the Mystery, repel it from them, He does not force it upon them. He does not tell them, that it *is* a correct conclusion which they had drawn, but He recedes (as it were) and explains away His words. He asks them whether the rulers and prophets spoken of in the Old Testament were not called gods figuratively; if so, much more might He call Himself God, and the Son of God, being the Christ. He does not tell them that He *is* God, though He is; but He argues with them as if He admitted as true the ground of their objection. In judgment, He reduces His creed to names and figures. As then He is really God, though He seemed on one occasion to say that He was but called so figuratively, so He gives us verily and indeed His Body and Blood in Holy Communion, though, on another occasion, after saying so, He seemingly went on to explain those words merely into a strong saying; and as none but heretics take advantage of His apparent denial that He is God, so none but they ought to make use of His apparent denial that He vouchsafes to us His flesh, and that the Holy Communion is a high and heavenly means of giving it.

Such reflections as the foregoing lead us to this conclusion, to understand that it is our duty to make much of Christ's miracles of love; and instead of denying or feeling cold towards them, to desire to possess our hearts with them. There is indeed a mere carnal curiosity, a high-minded, irreverent prying into things sacred; but there is also a holy and devout curiosity which all who love God will in their measure feel. The former is exemplified in the instance of the men of Bethshemesh, when they looked into the ark; the latter in the case of the Holy Angels, who (as St. Peter tells us) "desire to look into" the grace of God in the Gospel. Under the Gospel surely there are wonders performed, such as "eye hath not seen, nor ear heard, neither have entered into the heart of man." Let us feel interest and awful expectation at the news of them; let us put ourselves in the way of them; let us wait upon God day by day for the treasures of grace, which are hid in Christ, which are great beyond words or thought.

Above all, let us pray Him to draw us to Him, and to give us faith. When we feel that His mysteries are too severe for us, and occasion us to doubt, let us earnestly wait on Him for the gift of humility and love. Those who love and who are humble will apprehend them—carnal minds do not seek them, and proud minds are offended at them—but while love desires them, humility sustains them. Let us pray Him then to give us such a real and living insight into the blessed doctrine of the Incarnation of the Son of God, of His birth of a Virgin, His atoning death, and Resurrection, that we may desire that the Holy Communion may be the effectual type of that gracious Economy. No one realizes the Mystery of the Incarnation but must feel disposed towards that of Holy Communion. Let us pray Him to give us an earnest longing after Him—a thirst for His presence—an anxiety to find Him—a joy on hearing that He is to be found, even now, under the veil of sensible things—and a good hope that *we* shall find Him there. Blessed indeed are they who have not seen, and yet have believed. They have their reward *in* believing; they enjoy the contemplation of a mysterious blessing, which does not even enter into the thoughts of other men; and while they are more blessed than others, in the gift vouchsafed to them, they have the additional privilege of knowing that they are vouchsafed it.

[VI,11]

Chapter 30

THE GOSPEL FEAST

When Jesus then lifted up His eyes, and saw a great company come unto Him, He saith unto Philip, Whence shall we buy bread that these may eat?
—John 6:5

After these words the Evangelist adds, "And this He said to prove him, for He Himself knew what He would do." Thus, you see, our Lord had secret meanings when He spoke, and did not bring forth openly all His Divine sense at once. He knew what He was about to do from the first, but He wished to lead forward His disciples, and to arrest and open their minds, before He instructed them: for all cannot receive His words, and on the blind and deaf the most sacred truths fall without profit.

And thus, throughout the course of his gracious dispensations from the beginning, it may be said that the Author and Finisher of our faith has hid things from us in mercy, and listened to our questionings, while He Himself knew what He was about to do. He has hid, in order afterwards to reveal, that then, on looking back on what He said and did before, we may see in it what at the time we did not see, and thereby see it to more profit. Thus He hid Himself from the disciples as He walked with them to Emmaus: thus Joseph, too, under different and yet similar circumstances, hid himself from his brethren.

With this thought in our minds, surely we seem to see a new and further meaning still, in the narrative before us. Christ spoke of buying bread, when He intended to create or make bread; but did He not, in that bread which He made, intend further that heavenly bread which is the salvation of our souls?—for He goes on to say, "Labor not for the meat" or food "which perisheth, but for that food which endureth unto everlasting life, which the Son of Man shall give unto you." Yes, surely the wilderness is the world, and the Apostles are His priests, and the multitudes are His people; and that feast, so suddenly, so unexpectedly provided, is the Holy Communion. He alone is the same, He the provider of

[267]

the loaves then, of the heavenly manna now. All other things change, but He remaineth.

And what is that Heavenly Feast which we now are vouchsafed, but in its own turn the earnest and pledge of that future feast in His Father's kingdom, when "the marriage of the Lamb shall come, and His wife hath made herself ready," and "holy Jerusalem cometh down from God out of heaven," and "blessed shall they be who shall eat bread in the kingdom of God"?

And further, since to that Feast above we do lift up our eyes, though it will not come till the end; and as we do not make remembrance of it once only, but continually, in the sacred rite which foreshadows it; therefore, in like manner, not in the miracle of the loaves only, though in that especially, but in all parts of Scripture, in history, and in percept, and in promise, and in prophecy, is it given us to see the Gospel Feast typified and prefigured, and that immortal and never-failing supper in the visible presence of the Lamb which will follow upon it at the end. And if they are blessed who shall eat and drink of that table in the kingdom, so too blessed are they who meditate upon it, and hope for it now, who read Scripture with it in their thoughts, and endeavor to look beneath the veil of the literal text, and to catch a sight of the gleams of heavenly light which are behind it. "Blessed are your eyes, for they see; and your ears, for they hear, for verily I say unto you, that many prophets and righteous men have desired to see those things which ye see, but have not seen them; and to hear those things which ye hear, and have not heard them." "Blessed are they which have not seen, and yet have believed." Blessed they who see in and by believing, and who have, because they doubt not.

Let us, then, at this time of year,[203] as is fitting, follow the train of thought thus opened upon us, and, looking back into the Sacred Volume, trace the intimations and promises there given of that sacred and blessed Feast of Christ's Body and Blood which it is our privilege now to enjoy till the end come.

Now the Old Testament, as we know, is full of figures and types of the Gospel; types various, and, in their literal wording, contrary to each other, but all meeting and harmoniously fulfilled in Christ and His Church. Thus the histories of the Israelites in the wilderness, and the Israelites when settled in Canaan, alike are ours, representing our present state as Christians. Our Christian life is a state of faith and trial; it is also a state of enjoyment. It has the richness of the promised land; it has the marvelousness of the desert. It is "good land, a land of brooks of water, of fountains and depths that spring out of valleys and hills; a land of wheat and barley, and vines, and fig trees, and pomegranates; a land of oil olive, and honey; a land wherein thou shalt eat bread without scarceness; thou shalt not lack anything in it; a land whose stones are iron, and out of whose hills thou mayest dig brass." And, on the other hand, it is still a land which to the natural man seems a wilderness, a "great and terrible wilderness, wherein are fiery serpents, and scorpions, and drought, where there is no water"; where faith is still necessary, and where, still more forcibly than in the case of Israel, the maxim holds, that "man doth not live by bread only, but by every word that proceedeth out of the mouth of the Lord doth man live."

This is the state in which we are—a state of faith and of possession. In the desert the Israelites lived by the signs of things, without the realities: manna was to stand for the corn, oil, and honey of the good land promised; water, for the wine and milk. It was a time for faith to exercise itself; and when they came into the promised land, then was the time of possession. That was the land of milk and honey; they needed not any divinely provided compensations or expedients. Manna was not needed, nor the pillar of the cloud, nor the water from the rock. But we Christians, on the contrary, are at once in the wilderness and in the promised land. In the wilderness, because we live amid wonders; in the promised land, because we are in a state of enjoyment. That we are in the state of enjoyment is surely certain, unless all the prophecies have failed; and that we are in a state in which faith alone has that enjoyment, is plain from the fact that God's great blessings are not seen, and in that the Apostle says, "We walk by faith, not by sight." In a word, we are in a supernatural state—a word which implies both its greatness and its secretness; for what is above nature, is at once not seen, and is more precious than what is seen; "the things which are seen are temporal, the things which are not seen are eternal."

And if our state altogether is parallel to that of the Israelites, as an antitype to its type, it is natural to think that so great a gift as

Holy Communion would not be without its appropriate figures and symbols in the Old Testament. All that our Savior has done is again and again shadowed out in the Old Testament; and this, therefore, it is natural to think, as well as other things: His miraculous birth, His life, His teaching, His death, His priesthood, His sacrifice, His resurrection, His glorification, His kingdom, are again and again prefigured: it is not reasonable to suppose that if this so great gift is really given us, it should be omitted. He who died for us is He who feeds us; and as His death is mentioned, so we may beforehand expect will be mentioned the feast He gives us. Not openly indeed, for neither is His death nor His priesthood taught openly, but covertly, under the types of David or Aaron, or other favored servants of God; and in like manner we might expect, and we shall find, the like reverent allusions to His most gracious Feast—allusions which we should not know to be allusions but for the event; just as we should not know that Solomon, Aaron, or Samuel stood for Christ at all, except that the event explains the figure. When Abraham said to Isaac, "God will provide Himself a lamb for a burnt offering," who can doubt this is a prophecy concerning Christ?—yet we are nowhere told it in Scripture. The case is the same as regards the Sacrament of Baptism. Now that it is given, we cannot doubt that the purifications of the Jews, Naaman's bathing, and the prophecy of a fountain being opened for sin and all uncleanness have reference to it, as being the visible fulfillment of the great spiritual cleansing: and St. Peter expressly affirms this of the Deluge, and St. Paul of the passage of the Red Sea. And in like manner passages in the Bible, which speak prophetically of the Gospel Feast, cannot but refer (if I may so speak) to the Holy Sacrament of the Lord's Supper, as being, in fact, the Feast given us under the Gospel.

And let it be observed, directly we know that we have this great gift, and that the Old Testament history prefigures it, we have a light thrown upon what otherwise is a difficulty; for, it may be asked with some speciousness whether the Jews were not in a higher state of privilege than we Christians, until we take this gift into account. It may be objected that our blessings are all future or distant—the hope of eternal life, which is to be fulfilled hereafter, God's forgiveness, who is in heaven: what do we gain now and here above the Jews? God loved the Jews, and He *gave* them something; He gave them present gifts; the Old Testament is full of the description of them; He gave them "the precious things of heaven, and the dew, and the deep that coucheth beneath, and precious things brought forth by the sun, and by the moon, and the chief things of the ancient mountains, and the precious things of the lasting hills, and the precious things of the earth, and the fullness thereof," "honey out of the rock, and oil out of the flinty rock, butter of kine, and milk of sheep, with fat of lambs, and rams of the breed of Bashan, and goats, with the fat of kidneys of wheat, and the pure blood of the grape."[204] These were present real blessings. What has He given *us?*—*nothing* in possession? *all* in promise? This, I say, is in itself not likely; it is not likely that He should so reverse His system, and make the Gospel inferior to the Law. But the knowledge of the great gift under consideration clears up this perplexity; for every passage in the Old Testament which speaks of the temporal blessings given by God to His ancient people, instead of conveying to us a painful sense of destitution, and exciting our jealousy, reminds us of our greater blessedness; for every passage which belongs to them is fulfilled now in a higher sense to us. We have no need to envy them. God did not take away their blessings, without giving us greater. The Law was not so much taken away, as the Gospel given. The Gospel supplanted the Law. The Law went out by the Gospel's coming in. Only our blessings are not seen; *therefore* they are higher, *because* they are unseen. Higher blessings could not be visible. How could spiritual blessings be visible ones? If Christ now feeds us, not with milk and honey, but "with the spiritual food of His most precious Body and Blood"; if "our sinful bodies are made clean by His Body, and our souls washed through His most precious Blood," truly we are not without our precious things, any more than Israel was: but they are unseen, because so much greater, so spiritual; they are given only under the veil of what is seen: then thus we Christians are both with the Church in the wilderness as regards faith, and in the Church in Canaan as regards enjoyment; having the fulfillment of the words spoken by Moses, repeated by our Lord, to which I just now referred, "Man shall not live by bread only, but by every word which proceedeth out of the mouth of God."

Now then, I will refer to some passages of both the Old Testament and the New, which both illustrate and are illustrated by this great doctrine of the Gospel.

1. And, first, let it be observed, from the beginning, the greatest rite of religion has been a feast; the partaking of God's bounties, in the way of nature, has been consecrated to a more immediate communion with God Himself. For instance, when Isaac was weaned, Abraham "made a great feast,"[205] and then it was that Sarah prophesied, "Cast out this bondwoman and her son," she said, prophesying the introduction of the spirit, grace, and truth, which the Gospel contains, instead of the bondage of the outward forms of the Law. Again, it was at a feast of savory meat that the spirit of prophecy came upon Isaac, and he blessed Jacob. In like manner the first beginning of our Lord's miracles was at a marriage feast, when He changed water into wine; and when St. Matthew was converted he entertained our Lord at a feast. At a feast, too, our Lord allowed the penitent woman to wash with tears and anoint His feet, and pronounced her forgiveness; and at a feast, before His passion, He allowed Mary to anoint them with costly ointment, and to wipe them with her hair. Thus with our Lord, and with the Patriarchs, a feast was a time of grace; so much so, that He was said by the Pharisees to come eating and drinking, to be "a winebibber and gluttonous, a friend of publicans and sinners."[206]

2. And next, in order to make this feasting still more solemn, it had been usual at all times to precede it by a direct act of religion—by a prayer, or blessing, or sacrifice, or by the presence of a priest, which implied it. Thus, when Melchizedek came out to meet Abraham, and *bless* him, "he brought forth bread and wine";[207] to which it is added, "and he was the priest of the Most High God." Such, too, was the lamb of the Passover, which was eaten roast with fire, and with unleavened bread, and bitter herbs, with girded loins and shoes on, and staff in hand; as the Lord's Passover, being a solemn religious feast, even if not a sacrifice. And such seems to have been the common notion of communion with God all the world over, however it was gained; viz. that we arrived at the possession of His invisible gifts by participation in His visible; that there was some mysterious connection between the seen and the unseen; and that, by setting aside the choicest of His earthly bounties, as a specimen and representative of the

whole, presenting it to Him for His blessing, and then taking, eating, and appropriating it, we had the best hope of gaining those unknown and indefinite gifts which human nature needs. This the heathen practiced towards their idols also; and St. Paul seems to acknowledge that in that way they did communicate, though most miserably and fearfully, with those idols, and with the evil spirits which they represented. "The thing which the Gentiles sacrifice, they sacrifice to devils, and not to God; and I would not that ye should hold communion with devils."[208] Here, as before, a feast is spoken of as the means of communicating with the unseen world, though, when the feast was idolatrous, it was the fellowship of evil spirits.

3. And next let this be observed, that the descriptions in the Old Testament of the perfect state of religious privilege, viz. that under the Gospel which was then to come, are continually made under the image of a feast, a feast of some special and choice goods of this world, corn, wine, and the like; goods of this world chosen from the mass as a specimen of all, as types and means of seeking, and means of obtaining, the unknown spiritual blessings, which "eye hath not seen nor ear heard." And these special goods of nature, so set apart, are more frequently than anything else, corn or bread, and wine, as the figures of what was greater, though others are mentioned also. Now the first of these of which we read is the fruit of the tree of life, the leaves of which are also mentioned in the Prophets. The tree of life was that tree in the garden of Eden, the eating of which would have made Adam immortal; a divine gift lay hid in an outward form. The Prophet Ezekiel speaks of it afterwards in the following words, showing that a similar blessing was in store for the redeemed: "By the river, upon the bank thereof, on this side, and on that side, shall grow all trees for meat, whose leaf shall not fade, neither shall the fruit thereof be consumed. It shall bring forth new fruits according to his months, because their waters they issued out of the sanctuary; and the fruit thereof shall be for meat, and the leaf thereof for medicine."[209] Like to which is St. John's account of the tree of life, "which bare twelve manner of fruits, and yielded her fruit every month; and the leaves of the tree were for the healing of the nations."[210] And hence we read in the Canticles of the apple tree, and of sitting down under its shadow, and its fruit being sweet to

the taste. Here then in type is signified the sacred gift of which I am speaking; and yet it has not seemed good to the gracious Giver literally to select fruit or leaves as the means of His invisible blessings. He might have spiritually fed us with such, had He pleased—for man liveth not by bread only, but by the word of His mouth. His Word might have made the fruit of the tree His Sacrament, but He was willed otherwise.

The next selection of gifts of the earth which we find in Scripture is the very one which He at length fixed on, bread and wine, as in the history of Melchizedek; and there the record stands as a prophecy of what was to be: for who is Melchizedek but our Lord and Savior, and what is the bread and wine but the very feast which He has ordained?

Next the great gift was shadowed out in the description of the promised land, which was said to flow with milk and honey, and in all other precious things of nature which I have already recounted as belonging to the promised land, oil, butter, corn, wine, and the like. These all may be considered to refer to the Gospel Feast typically, because they were the rarest and most exquisite of the blessings given to the Jews, as the Gospel Feast is the most choice and most sacred of all the blessings given to us Christians; and what is most precious under the one Dispensation is signified by what is most precious under the other.

Now let us proceed to the Prophets, and we shall find the like anticipation of the Gospel Feast.

For instance, you recollect, the prophet Hosea says: "It shall come to pass in that day, I will hear, saith the Lord, I will hear the heavens, and they shall hear the earth, and the earth shall hear the corn, and the wine, and the oil, and they shall hear Jezreel. And I will sow her unto Me in the earth."[211] By Jezreel is meant the Christian Church; and the Prophet declares in God's name, that the time was to come when the Church would call upon the corn, wine, and oil, and they call on the earth, and the earth on the heavens, and the heavens on God; and God should answer the heavens, and the heavens should answer the earth, and the earth should answer the corn, wine, and oil, and they should answer to the wants of the Church. Now, doubtless, this may be fulfilled only in a general way; but considering Almighty God has appointed corn or bread, and wine, to be the special instruments of His ineffable grace—He, who sees the end from the beginning, and who views all things in all their relations at once—He, when He spoke of corn and wine, knew that the word would be fulfilled, not generally only, but even literally in the Gospel.

Again: the prophet Joel says, "It shall come to pass in that day that the mountains shall drop down new wine, and the hills shall flow with milk, and all the rivers of Judah shall flow with waters, and a fountain shall come forth of the house of the Lord, and shall water the valley of Shittim."[212] How strikingly is this fulfilled, if we take it to apply to what God has given us in the Gospel, in the feast of the Holy Communion!

Again: the prophet Amos says: "Behold, the days come, saith the Lord, when the plowman shall overtake the reaper, and the treader of grapes him that soweth seed; and the mountains shall drop sweet wine, and all the hills shall melt";[213] that is, with God's marvelous grace, whereby He gives us gifts new and wonderful.

And the Prophet Isaiah: "In this mountain shall the Lord of Hosts make unto all people a feast of fat things, a feast of wines on the lees; of fat things full of marrow, of wines on the lees well refined." And again: "Surely I will no more give thy corn to be meat for thine enemies, and the sons of the stranger shall not drink thy wine, for the which thou hast labored; but they that have gathered it shall eat it, and praise the Lord, and they that have brought it together shall drink it in the courts of My holiness." And again: "Behold My servants shall eat, but ye shall be hungry; behold My servants shall drink, but ye shall be thirsty."[214]

Again: the Prophet Jeremiah says: "They shall come and sing in the height of Zion, and shall flow together to the goodness of the Lord, for wheat, and for wine, and for oil, and for the young of the flock and of the herd; and their soul shall be as a watered garden, and they shall not sorrow anymore at all. . . . And I will satiate the soul of the priests with fatness, and My people shall be satisfied with My goodness, saith the Lord."[215]

And the Prophet Zechariah: "How great is His goodness, and how great is His beauty! corn shall make the young men cheerful, and new wine the maids."[216]

And under a different image, but with the same general sense, the Prophet Malachi: "From the rising of the sun even unto the going down of the same, My Name shall be great among the Gentiles; and in every place incense shall be offered unto My Name, and a pure offering, for My Name shall be great among the heathen, saith the Lord of Hosts."[217]

Further, if the Psalms are intended for Christian worship, as surely they are, the Prophetic Spirit, who inspired them, saw that they too would in various places describe that sacred Christian feast, which we feel they do describe; and surely we may rightly call this coincidence between the ordinance in the Christian Church and the form of words in the Psalms a mark of design. For instance: "Thou shalt prepare a Table before me against them that trouble me. Thou hast anointed my head with oil, and my Cup shall be full." "I will wash my hands in innocency, O Lord, and so will I go to Thine Altar." "Oh send out Thy light and Thy truth, that they may lead me, and bring me unto Thy holy hill, and to Thy dwelling; and that I may go unto the Altar of God, even unto the God of my joy and gladness." "The children of men shall put their trust under the shadow of Thy wings. They shall be satisfied with the plenteousness of Thy house, and Thou shalt give them drink of Thy pleasures as out of the river. For with Thee is the well of life, and in Thy light shall we see light." "Blessed is the man whom Thou choosest and receivest unto Thee; he shall dwell in Thy court, and shall be satisfied with the pleasures of Thy house, even of Thy Holy Temple." "My soul shall be satisfied, even as it were with marrow and fatness, when my mouth praiseth Thee with joyful lips ... because Thou hast been my helper, therefore under the shadow of Thy wings will I rejoice."[218]

The same wonderful feast is put before us in the Book of Proverbs, where Wisdom stands for Christ. "Wisdom hath builded her house," that is, Christ has built His Church; "she hath hewn out her seven pillars, she hath killed her beasts, she hath mingled her wine (that is, Christ has prepared His Supper), she hath also furnished her table (that is, the Lord's Table), she hath sent forth her maidens (that is, the priests of the Lord), she crieth upon the highest places of the city, Whoso is simple, let him turn in hither; as for him that wanteth understanding, she saith to him, Come, eat of My Bread and drink of the Wine which I have mingled"[219]—which is like saying, "Come unto Me all ye that labor and are heavy laden and I will refresh you." Like which are the Prophet Isaiah's words: "Ho, every one that thirsteth, come ye to the waters, and he that hath no money, come ye buy and eat; yea, come, buy wine and milk without money and without price."[220] And such too is the description in the Book of Canticles: "The fig tree putteth forth her green figs, and the vines with the tender grapes give a good smell." "Until the day break and the shadows flee away, I will get me to the mountain of myrrh, and to the hill of frankincense." "I have gathered My myrrh with My spice, I have eaten My honeycomb with My honey, I have drunk My wine with My milk; eat, O friends, drink, yea drink abundantly, O beloved!"[221] In connection with such passages as these should be observed St. Paul's words, which seem from the antithesis to be an allusion to the same most sacred ordinance: "Be not drunk with wine, wherein is excess, but be filled with the Spirit," with that new wine which God the Holy Spirit ministers in the Supper of the Great King.

God grant that we may be able ever to come to this Blessed Sacrament with feelings suitable to the passages which I have read concerning it! May we not regard it in a cold, heartless way, and keep at a distance from fear, when we should rejoice! May the spirit of the unprofitable servant never be ours, who looked at his lord as a hard master instead of a gracious benefactor! May we not be in the number of those who go on year after year, and never approach Him at all! May we not be of those who went, one to his farm, another to his merchandise, when they were called to the wedding! Nor let us be of those who come in a formal, mechanical way, as a mere matter of obligation, without reverence, without awe, without wonder, without love. Nor let us fall into the sin of those who complained that they have nothing to gather but the manna, wearying of God's gifts.

But let us come in faith and hope, and let us say to ourselves, May this be the beginning in us of everlasting bliss! May these be the first fruits of that banquet which is to last forever and ever; ever new, ever transporting, inexhaustible, in the city of our God!

[VII,12]

Chapter 31

RELIGION PLEASANT TO THE RELIGIOUS

*O taste and see how gracious the Lord is: blessed is the man
that trusteth in Him.*
—Ps. 34:8

You see by these words that love Almighty God has towards us,
and what claims He has upon our love. He is the Most High, and
All-holy. He inhabiteth eternity: we are but worms compared
with Him. He would not be less happy though He had never created us; He would not be less happy though we were all blotted
out again from creation. But He is the God of love; He brought us
all into existence, because He found satisfaction in surrounding
Himself with happy creatures: He made us innocent, holy,
upright, and happy. And when Adam fell into sin and his descendants after him, then ever since He has been imploring us to
return to Him, the Source of all good, by true repentance. "Turn
ye, turn ye," He says, "why will ye die? As I live I have no pleasure in the death of the wicked." "What could have been done
more to My vineyard that I have not done to it?"[222] And in the
text He condescends to invite us to Him: "O taste and see how
gracious the Lord is: blessed is the man that trusteth in Him." As
if He said, "If you would but make trial, one trial, if you would
but be persuaded to taste and judge for yourself, so excellent is
His graciousness, that you would never cease to desire, never
cease to approach Him": according to the saying of the wise man,
"They that eat Me shall yet be hungry, and they that drink Me
shall yet be thirsty."[223]

This excellence and desirableness of God's gifts is a subject
again and again set before us in Holy Scripture. Thus the Prophet
Isaiah speaks of the "feast of fat things, a feast of wines on the lees;
of fat things full of marrow, of wines on the lees well refined."[224]
And again, under images of another kind: "He hath sent Me . . .
to give . . . beauty for ashes, the oil of joy for mourning, the garment of praise for the spirit of heaviness, that they may be called

Trees of Righteousness."[225] Or again, the Prophet Hosea: "I will be as the dew unto Israel: he shall grow as the lily, and cast forth his roots as Lebanon. His branches shall spread, and his beauty shall be as the olive tree, and his smell as Lebanon. They that dwell under his shadow shall return; they shall revive as the corn, and grow as the vine: the scent thereof shall be as the wine of Lebanon."[226] And the Psalmist: "Oh that My people would have hearkened unto Me. . . . the haters of the Lord should have been found liars, but their time should have endured forever. He should have fed them also with the finest wheat flour, and with honey out of the stony rock should I have satisfied thee."[227] You see all images of what is pleasant and sweet in nature are brought together to describe the pleasantness and sweetness of the gifts which God gives us in grace. As wine enlivens, and bread strengthens, and oil is rich, and honey is sweet, and flowers are fragrant, and dew is refreshing, and foliage is beautiful; so, and much more, are God's gifts in the Gospel enlivening, and strengthening, and rich, and sweet, and fragrant, and refreshing, and excellent. And as it is natural to feel satisfaction and comfort in these gifts of the visible world, so it is but natural and necessary to be delighted and transported with the gifts of the world invisible; and as the visible gifts are objects of desire and search, so much more is it, I do not merely say a duty, but a privilege and blessedness to "taste and see how gracious the Lord is."

Other passages in the Psalms speak of this blessedness, besides the text. "Thou hast put gladness in my heart," says the Psalmist, "since the time that their corn and wine and oil increased."[228] "The lot is fallen unto me in a fair ground, yea, I have a goodly heritage."[229] Again, "The statutes of the Lord are right, and rejoice the heart, . . . more to be desired are they than gold, yea, than much fine gold, sweeter also than honey and the honeycomb."[230] "My heart trusted in Him, and I am helped; therefore my heart danceth for joy, and in my song will I praise Him."[231] Once more: "Blessed is the man whom Thou choosest and receivest unto Thee: he shall dwell in Thy courts, and shall be satisfied with the pleasures of Thy house, even of Thy holy temple."[232]

I wish it were possible, my brethren, to lead men to greater holiness and more faithful obedience by setting before them the high and abundant joys which they have who serve God: "In His presence is fullness of joy," "the well of life"; and they are satisfied with "the plenteousness of His house," and "drink of His pleasures as out of a river"; but this is, I know, just what most persons will not believe. They think that it is very right and proper to be religious; they think that it would be better for themselves in the world to come if they were religious now. They do not at all deny either the duty or the expedience of leading a new and holy life; but they cannot understand how it can be pleasant: they cannot believe or admit that it is more pleasant than a life of liberty, laxity, and enjoyment. They, as it were, say, "Keep within bounds, speak within probability, and we will believe you; but do not shock our reason. We will admit that we *ought* to be religious, and that, when we come to die, we shall be very glad to have led religious lives: but to tell us that it is a *pleasant* thing to be religious, this is too much: it is not true; we feel that it is not true; all the world knows and feels it is not true; religion is something unpleasant, gloomy, sad, and troublesome. It imposes a number of restraints on us; it keeps us from doing what we would; it will not let us have our own way; it abridges our liberty; it interferes with our enjoyments; it has fewer, far fewer, joys at present than a worldly life, though it gains for us more joys hereafter." This is what men say, or would say, if they understood what they feel, and spoke their minds freely.

Alas! I cannot deny that this *is* true in the case of most men. Most men do not like the service of God, though it be perfect freedom; they like to follow their own ways, and they are only religious so far as their conscience obliges them; they are like Balaam, desirous of "the death of the righteous," not of his life. Indeed, this is the very thing I am lamenting and deploring. I lament, my brethren, that so many men, nay, I may say, that so many of you, do *not* like religious service. I do not deny it; but I lament it. I do not deny it: far from it. I know quite well how many there are who do not like coming to Church, and who make excuses for keeping away at times when they might come. I know how many there are who do not come to the Most Holy Sacrament. I know that there are numbers who do not say their prayers in private morning and evening. I know how many there are who are ashamed to be thought religious, who take God's name in vain, and live like the world. Alas! this is the very thing I lament—that God's service is not pleasant to you. It is not pleasant to those who do not like it: true; but it *is* pleasant to those who *do*. Observe, this is what I say; not that it is pleasant to those who like it not, but that it is pleasant to those who like it. Nay, what I say is that it is much *more* pleasant to those who like it than anything of this world is pleasant to those who do not like it. This is the point. I do not say that it is pleasant to most men; but I say that it is in itself the most pleasant thing in the world. Nothing is so pleasant as God's service to those *to whom* it is pleasant. The pleasures of sin are not to be compared in fullness and intensity to the pleasures of holy living. The pleasures of holiness are far more pleasant to the holy than the pleasures of sin to the sinner. Oh that I could get you to believe this! Oh that you had a heart to feel it and know it! Oh that you had a heart to taste God's pleasures and to make proof of them; to taste and see how gracious the Lord is!

None can know, however, the joys of being holy and pure but the holy. If an Angel were to come down from heaven, even he could not explain them to you; nor could he in turn understand what the pleasures of sin are. Do you think that an Angel could be made to understand what are the pleasures of sin? I trow not. You might as well attempt to persuade him that there was pleasure in feasting on dust and ashes. There are brute animals who wallow in the mire and eat corruption. This seems strange to us: much stranger to an Angel is it how anyone can take pleasure in anything so filthy, so odious, so loathsome as sin. Many men, as I have been saying, wonder what possible pleasure there can be in anything so melancholy as religion. Well: be sure of this—it is *more* wonderful to an Angel, what possible pleasure there can be in sinning. It is *more* wonderful, I say. He would turn away with horror and disgust, both because sin is so base a thing in itself, and because it is so hateful in God's sight.

Let no persons then be surprised that religious obedience should really be so pleasant in itself, when it seems to them so distasteful. Let them not be surprised that *what* the pleasure is cannot be explained to *them*. It is a secret till they try to be religious. Men know what sin is, by experience. They do not know what holiness is; and they cannot obtain the knowledge of its secret pleasure, till they join themselves truly and heartily to Christ, and devote themselves to His service, till they "taste," and thereby try. This pleasure is as hidden from them, as the pleasures of sin are hidden from the Angels. The Angels have never eaten the forbidden fruit, and their eyes are not open to know good and evil. And we *have* eaten the forbidden fruit—at least Adam did, and we are his descendants—and our eyes *are* open to know evil. And, alas! on the other hand, they have become blinded to good; they require opening to see, to know, to understand good. And till our eyes *are* opened spiritually, we *shall* ever think religion distasteful and unpleasant, and shall wonder how anyone can like it. Such is our miserable state—we are blind to the highest and truest glories, and dead to the most lively and wonderful of all pleasures; and no one can describe them to us. None other than God the Holy Spirit can help us in this matter, by enlightening and changing our hearts. So it is; and yet I will say one thing, by way of suggesting to you how great and piercing the joys of religion are. Think of this. Is there anyone who does not know how very painful the feeling of a bad conscience is? Do not you recollect, my brethren, sometime or other, having done something you knew to be wrong? and do you not remember afterwards what a piercing bitter feeling came on you? Is not the feeling of a bad conscience different from any other feeling, and more distressing than any other, till we have accustomed ourselves to it? Persons do accustom themselves and lose this feeling; but till we blunt our conscience, it is very painful. And why? It is the feeling of God's displeasure, and therefore it is so painful. Consider then: if God's displeasure is so distressing to us, must not God's approval and favor be just the reverse; like life from the dead, most exceedingly joyful and transporting? And this is what it is to be holy and religious. It is to have God's favor. And, as it is a great misery to be under God's wrath, so it is a great and wonderful joy to be under God's favor; and those who know what a misery the former is may fancy, though they do not know, how high a blessing the latter is. From what you know, then, judge of what you do not know. From the miseries of guilt, which, alas! you have experienced, conjecture the blessedness of holiness and purity which you have not experienced. From the pain of a bad conscience, believe in the unspeakable joy and gladness of a good conscience.

I have been addressing those who do not know what religious

peace and Divine pleasures are; but there are those present, I hope, who in a measure are not strangers to them. I know that none of us gain all the pleasure from God's service which it might afford us; still some of us, I hope, gain some pleasure. I hope there are some of those who hear me, who take a pleasure in coming to Church, in saying their prayers, in thinking of God, in singing Psalms, in blessing Him for the mercies of the Gospel, and in celebrating Christ's death and resurrection, as at this season of the year.[233] These persons have "tasted' and tried. I trust they find the taste so heavenly, that *they* will not need any proof that religion is a pleasant thing; nay, more pleasant than anything else, worth the following above all other things, and unpleasant only to those who are not religious.

Let such persons then think of this, that if a religious life is pleasant here, in spite of the old Adam interrupting the pleasure and defiling them, what a glorious day it will be, if it is granted to us hereafter to enter into the kingdom of heaven! None of us, even the holiest, can guess *how* happy we shall be; for St. John says, "We know not what we shall be";[234] and St. Paul, "Now we see in a glass darkly, but then face to face." Yet in proportion to our present holiness and virtue, we have some faint ideas of what will then be our blessedness. And in Scripture various descriptions of heaven are given us, in order to arrest, encourage, and humble us. We are told that the Angels of God are very bright, and clad in white robes. The Saints and Martyrs too are clad in white robes, with palms in their hands; and they sing praises unto Him that sitteth upon the Throne, and to the Lamb. When our Lord was transfigured, He showed us what heaven is. His raiment became white as snow, white and glistening. Again, at one time He appeared to St. John, and then, "His head and His hairs were white like wool, as white as snow; and His eyes were as a flame of fire; and His feet like unto fine brass; as if they burned in a furnace; and His countenance was as the sun shineth in his strength."[235] And what Christ is, such do His Saints become hereafter. Here below they are clad in a garment of sinful flesh; but when the end comes, and they rise from the grave, they shall inherit glory, and shall be ever young and ever shining. In that day, all men will see and be convinced, even bad men, that God's servants are really happy, and only they. In that day, even lost souls, though they will not be able to understand the blessedness of religion, will have no doubt at all of what they now doubt, or pretend to doubt, that religion *is* blessed. They laugh at religion, think of strictness to be narrowness of mind, and regularity to be dullness; and give bad names to religious men. They will not be able to do so then. They think themselves the great men of the earth now, and look down upon the religious; but then, who would not have been a religious man, to have so great a reward? who will then have any heart to speak against religion, even though he has not "a heart to fear God and keep all His commandments always"? In that day, they will look upon the righteous man, and "be amazed at the strangeness of his salvation, so far beyond all that they looked for. And they, repenting and groaning for anguish of spirit, shall say within themselves, "This was he, whom we had sometimes in derision, and a proverb of reproach. We fools accounted his life madness, and his end to be without honor; how is he numbered among the children of God, and his lot is among the saints!"[236]

Think of all this, my brethren, and rouse yourselves, and run forward with a good courage on your way towards heaven. Be not weary in well-doing, for in due season we shall reap, if we faint not. Strive to enter in at the strait gate. Strive to get holier and holier every day, that you may be worthy to stand before the Son of Man. Pray God to teach you His will, and to lead you forth in the right way, because of your enemies. Submit yourselves to His guidance, and you will have comfort given you, according to your day, and peace at the last.

[VII, 14]

Chapter 32

REVERENCE IN WORSHIP

Samuel ministered before the Lord, being a child,
girded with a linen ephod.
—1 Sam. 2:18

Samuel, viewed in his place in sacred history, that is, in the course of events which connect Moses with Christ, appears as a great ruler and teacher of his people; this is his prominent character. He was the first of the Prophets; yet, when we read the sacred narrative itself, in which his life is set before us, I suppose those passages are the more striking and impressive which represent him in the office which belonged to him by birth, as a Levite, or minister of God. He was taken into God's special service from the first; he lived in His Temple; nay, while yet a child, he was honored with the apparel of a sacred function, as the text tells us, "he ministered before the Lord, being a child, girded with a linen ephod."

His mother had "given him unto the Lord all the days of his life,"[237] by a solemn vow before his birth; and in him, if in anyone, were fulfilled the words of the Psalmist, "Blessed are they that dwell in Thy house, they will be always praising Thee."[238]

Such a constant abode in God's house would make common minds only familiar with holy things, and irreverent; but where God's grace is present in the heart, the effect is the reverse; which we might be sure would happen in the case of Samuel. "The Lord was with him," we are told; and therefore the more the outward signs of that Lord met his eye, the more reverent he became, not the more presuming. The more he acquainted himself with God, the greater would be his awe and holy fear.

Thus the first notice we have of his ministering before the Lord reminds us of the decency and gravity necessary at all times, and in all persons, in approaching Him. "He ministered before the Lord, being a child, girded with a linen ephod." His mother had made him yearly a little coat for his common use, but in Divine

Service he wore, not this, but a garment which would both express, and impress upon him, reverence.

And, in like manner, in his old age, when Saul sent to seek David at Naioth, where Samuel was, his messengers found Samuel and the prophets under him all in decent order. "They saw the company of prophets prophesying, and Samuel over them." And this was so impressive a sight, that it became an instrument of God's supernatural power towards them, and they prophesied also.

On the other hand, if we would have an example of the want of this reverence, we have it in Saul himself, the reprobate king, who, when he was on his way to Naioth, and was visited by God's Holy Spirit, did not thereupon receive the garment of salvation, nor was clothed in righteousness, but behaved himself in an unseemly wild way, as one whose destitution and shame were but detected by the visitation. He stripped off his clothes and prophesied before Samuel, and lay down in that state all that day and all that night.

This difference we see even at this day: of persons professing religion, some are like Samuel, some like Saul; some (as it were) cast off their garments and prophesy in disorder and extravagance; others minister before the Lord, "girded with a linen ephod," with "their loins girt and their lamps burning," like men awfully expecting the coming of their great and glorious Judge. By the latter, I mean the true children of the Holy Catholic Church; by the former, I mean heretics and schismatics.

There have ever been from the first these two kinds of Christians—those who belonged to the Church, and those who did not. There never was a time since the Apostles' day, when the Church was not; and there never was a time but men were to be found who preferred some other way of worship to the Church's way. These two kinds of professed Christians ever have been—Church Christians, and Christians not of the Church; and it is remarkable, I say, that while, on the one hand, reverence for sacred things has been a characteristic of Church Christians on the whole, so want of reverence has been the characteristic on the whole of Christians not of the Church. The one have prophesied after the figure of Samuel, the other after the figure of Saul.

Of course there are many exceptions to this remark in the case of individuals. Of course I am not speaking of inconsistent persons and exceptional cases, in the Church, or out of it; but of those who act up to what they profess. I mean that zealous, earnest, and faithful members of the Church have generally been reverent; and zealous, earnest, and faithful members of other religious bodies have generally been irreverent. Again, after all, there will be real exceptions in the case of individuals which we cannot account for; but I mean that, *on the whole*, it will be found that reverence is one of the marks or notes of the Church; true though it may be that some particular individuals, who have kept apart from it, have not been without a reverential spirit notwithstanding.

Indeed so natural is the connection between a reverential spirit in worshiping God, and faith in God, that the wonder only is, how anyone can for a moment imagine he has faith in God, and yet allow himself to be irreverent towards Him. To believe in God is to believe the being and presence of One who is All-holy, and All-powerful, and All-gracious; how can a man really believe thus of Him, and yet make free with Him? it is almost a contradiction in terms. Hence even heathen religions have ever considered faith and reverence identical. To believe, and not to revere, to worship familiarly, and at one's ease, is an anomaly and a prodigy unknown even to false religions, to say nothing of the true one. Not only the Jewish and Christian religions, which are directly from God, inculcate the spirit of "reverence and godly fear," but those other religions which have existed, or exist, whether in the East or the South, inculcate the same. Worship, forms of worship—such as bowing the knee, taking off the shoes, keeping silence, a prescribed dress, and the like—are considered as necessary for a due approach to God. The whole world, differing about so many things, differing in creed and rule of life, yet agree in this—that God being our Creator, a certain self-abasement of the whole man is the duty of the creature; that He is in heaven, we upon earth; that He is All-glorious, and we worms of the earth and insects of a day.

But those who have separated from the Church of Christ have in this respect fallen into greater than pagan error. They may be said to form an exception to the concordant voice of a whole world, always and everywhere; they break in upon the unanimous suffrage of mankind, and determine, at least by their conduct, that reverence and awe are not primary religious duties. They have considered that in some way or other, either by God's favor or by their own illumination, they are brought so near to God that they have no need to fear at all, or to put any restraint upon their words or thoughts when addressing Him. They have considered awe to be superstition, and reverence to be slavery. They have learned to be familiar and free with sacred things, as it were, on principle. I think this is really borne out by facts, and will approve itself to inquirers as true in substance, however one man will differ from another in the words in which he would express the fact itself.

Samuel was a little child who had never fallen away from God, but by His grace had ever served Him. Let us take a very different instance, the instance of a penitent sinner as set before us in the parable of the publican and Pharisee. I need hardly say which of the two was the most pleasing to God—the publican; whereas the Pharisee was not accepted by Him. Now what did the Pharisee do? He did not even go so far as to behave in an unseemly, extravagant way: he was grave and solemn, and yet what he did was enough to displease God, because he took too much upon himself, and made too much of himself. Though grave and solemn, he was not reverent; he spoke in a haughty, proud way, and made a long sentence, thanking God that he was not as other men are, and despising the publican. Such was the behavior of the Pharisee; but the publican behaved very differently. Observe how he came to worship God; "he stood afar off; he lift not up so much as his eyes unto heaven, but smote upon his breast, saying, God be merciful to me a sinner."[239] You see his words were few, and almost broken, and his whole conduct humble and reverent; he felt that God was in heaven, he upon earth, God All-holy and Almighty, and he a poor sinner.

Now all of us are sinners, all of us have need to come to God as the publican did; everyone, if he does but search his heart, and watch his conduct, and try to do his duty, will find himself to be full of sins which provoke God's wrath. I do not mean to say that all men are equally sinners; some are willful sinners, and of them there is no hope, till they repent; others sin, but they try to avoid sinning, pray to God to make them better, and come to Church to be made better; but all men are quite sinners enough to make it their duty to behave as the publican. Everyone ought to come into Church as the publican did, to say in his heart, "Lord, I am not worthy to enter this sacred place; my only plea for coming is the merits of Jesus Christ my Savior." When, then, a man enters Church, as many do, carelessly and familiarly, thinking of himself, not of God, sits down coldly and at his ease, either does not say a prayer at all, or merely hides his face for form's sake, sitting all the while, not standing or kneeling; then looks about to see who is in the Church, and who is not, and makes himself easy and comfortable in his seat, and uses the kneeler for no other purpose than to put his feet upon; in short, comes to Church as a place, not of meeting God and His Holy Angels, but of seeing what is to be seen with the bodily eyes, and hearing what is to be heard with the bodily ears, and then goes and gives his judgment about the sermon freely, and says, "I do not like this or that," or "This is a good argument, but that is a bad one," or "I do not like this person so much as that," and so on; I mean when a man acts in all respects as if he was at home, and not in God's House—all I can say is, that he ventures to do in God's presence what neither Cherubim nor Seraphim venture to do, for they veil their faces, and, as if not daring to address God, praise Him to each other, in few words, and those continually repeated, saying, Holy, holy, holy, Lord God of Sabaoth.

What I have said has been enough to suggest what it is to serve God acceptably, viz. "with reverence and godly fear," as St. Paul says. We must not aim at forms for their own sake, but we must keep in mind where we are, and then forms will come into our service naturally. We must in all respects act as if we saw God; that is, if we believe that God is here, we shall keep silence; we shall not laugh, or talk, or whisper during the Service, as many young persons do; we shall not gaze about us. We shall follow the example set us by the Church itself. I mean, as the words in which we pray in Church are not our own, neither will our looks, or our postures, or our thoughts, be our own. We shall, in the Prophet's words, not "do our own ways" there, nor "find our own pleasure," nor "speak our own words"; in imitation of all Saints before us, including the Holy Apostles, who never spoke their own words in solemn worship, but either those which Christ taught them, or which the Holy Ghost taught them, or which the

Old Testament taught them. This is the reason why we always pray from a book in Church; the Apostles said to Christ, "Lord, teach us to pray," and our Lord graciously gave them the prayer called the Lord's Prayer. For the same reason we too use the Lord's Prayer, and we use the Psalms of David and of other holy men, and hymns which are given us in Scripture, thinking it better to use the words of inspired Prophets than our own. And for the same reason we use a number of short petitions, such as "Lord, have mercy upon us," "O Lord, save the Queen," "O Lord, open Thou our lips," and the like, not using many words, or rounding our sentences, or allowing ourselves to enlarge in prayer.

Thus all we do in Church is done on a principle of *reverence*; it is done with the thought that we are in God's presence. But irreverent persons, not understanding this, when they come into Church, and find nothing there of a striking kind, when they find everything is read from a book, and in a calm, quiet way, and still more, when they come a second and a third time, and find everything just the same, over and over again, they are offended and tired. "There is nothing," they say, "to rouse or interest them." They think God's Service dull and tiresome, if I may use such words; for they do not come to Church to honor God, but to please themselves. They want something new. They think the prayers are long, and wish that there was more preaching, and that in a striking oratorical way, with loud voice and florid style. And when they observe that the worshipers in Church are serious and subdued in their manner, and will not look, and speak, and move as much at their ease as out of doors, or in their own houses, then (if they are very profane) they ridicule them, as weak and superstitious. Now is it not plain that those who are thus tired, and wearied, and made impatient by our sacred Services below, would most certainly get tired and wearied with heaven above? because there the Cherubim and Seraphim "rest not day and night," saying, "Holy, holy, holy, Lord God Almighty." Such as this, too, will be the way of the Saints in glory, for we are told that there will be a great voice of much people saying, Alleluia; and again they said Alleluia; and the four-and-twenty elders said Alleluia; and a voice of many waters and of mighty thunderings said Alleluia. Such, too was our Lord's way, when in His agony

He three times repeated the same words, "Thy will, not Mine, be done." It is the delight of all holy beings, who stand around the Throne, to use one and the same form of worship; they are not tired, it is ever new pleasure to them to say the words anew. They are never tired; but surely all those persons would be soon tired of hearing them, instead of taking part in their glorious chant, who are wearied of Church now, and seek for something more attractive and rousing.

Let all persons, then, now for certain, and be assured beforehand, that if they come to Church to have their hearts put into strange and new forms, and their feelings moved and agitated, they come for what they will not find. We wish them to join Saints and Angels in worshiping God; to say with the Seraphim, "Holy Lord God of Sabaoth"; to say with the Angels, "Glory to God in the highest, and in earth peace, goodwill towards men"; to say after our Lord and Savior, "Our Father, which art in heaven," and what follows; to say with St. Mary, "My soul doth magnify the Lord"; with St. Simeon, "Lord, now lettest Thou Thy servant depart in peace"; with the Three Children who were cast into the fiery furnace, "O all ye works of the Lord, bless ye the Lord, praise Him, and magnify Him forever"; with the Apostles, "I believe in God the Father Almighty, Maker of heaven and earth; and in Jesus Christ His only Son our Lord; and in the Holy Ghost." We wish to read to them words of inspired Scripture, and to explain its doctrine to them soberly after its pattern. This is what we wish them to say, again and again: "Lord, have mercy"; "We beseech Thee to hear us, O Lord"; "Good Lord, deliver us"; "Glory be to the Father, and to the Son, and to the Holy Ghost." All holy creatures are praising God continually—we hear them not, still they are praising Him and praying to Him. All the Angels, the glorious company of the Apostles, the goodly fellowship of the Prophets, the noble army of Martyrs, the Holy Church universal, all good men all over the earth, all the spirits and souls of the righteous, all our friends who have died in God's faith and fear, all are praising and praying to God: we come to Church to join them; our voices are very feeble, our hearts are very earthly, our faith is very weak. We do not deserve to come, surely not—consider what a great favor it is to be allowed to join in the praises and prayers of the City of the Living God, we being such sinners—we should not be allowed to come at all but for the merits of our Lord and Savior. Let us firmly look at the Cross, that is the token of our salvation. Let us ever remember the sacred Name of Jesus, in which devils were cast out of old time. These are the thoughts with which we should come to Church; and if we come a little before the Service begins, and want something to think about, we may look, not at who are coming in and when, but at the building itself, which will remind us of many good things; or we may look into the Prayer Book for such passages as the Eighty-fourth Psalm, which runs thus: "Oh how amiable are Thy dwellings, Thou Lord of hosts! my soul hath a desire and longing to enter into the Courts of the Lord: my heart and my flesh rejoice in the Living God."

Such will be our conduct and our thoughts in Church, if we be true Christians; and I have been giving this description of them, not only for the sake of those who are not reverent, but for the sake of those who try to be so, for the sake of all of us who try to come to Church soberly and quietly, that we may know why we do so, and may have an answer if anyone asks us. Such will be our conduct even when we are out of Church. I mean, those who come to Church again and again, in this humble and heavenly way, will find the effect of it, through God's mercy, in their daily walk. When Moses came down from Mount Sinai, where he had been forty days and forty nights, his face quite shone and dazzled the people, so that he was obliged to put a veil over it. Such is the effect of God's grace on those who come to Church in faith and love; their mode of acting and talking, their very manner and behavior, show they have been in God's presence. They are ever sober, cheerful, modest, serious, and earnest. They do not disgrace their profession, they do not take God's Name in vain, they do not use passionate language, they do not lie, they do not jest in an unseemly way, they do not use shameful words, they keep their mouth; they have kept their mouth in Church, and avoided rashness, so they are enabled to keep it at home. They have bright, smiling, pleasant faces. They do not wear a mock gravity, and, like the hypocrites whom Christ speaks of, make themselves sad countenances, but they are easy and natural, and without meaning it cannot help showing in their look, and voice, and manner, that they are God's dear children, and have His grace within them. They are civil and obliging, kind and friendly; not envious or jealous, not quarelsome, not spiteful or resentful, not selfish, not covetous, not niggardly, not lovers of the world, not afraid of the world, not afraid of what man can do against them.

Such are they who worship God in spirit and in truth in Church; they love Him and they fear Him. And, besides those who profess to love without fearing, there are two sorts of persons who fall short; first, and worst, those who neither fear nor love God; and, secondly, those who fear Him, but do not love Him. There are, everywhere, alas! some bold, proud, discontented persons, who, as far as they dare, speak against religion altogether; they do not come to Church, or if they come, come to see about what is going on, not to worship. These are those who neither love nor fear; but the more common sort of persons are they who have a sort of fear of God without the love of Him, who feel and know that some things are right, and others wrong, yet do not adhere to the right; who are conscious they sin from time to time, and that willfully, who have an uneasy conscience, who fear to die; who have, indeed a sort of serious feeling about sacred things, who reverence the Church and its ordinances, who would be shocked at open impiety, who do not make a mock at Baptism, much less at the Holy Communion, but, still, who have not the heart to love and obey God. This, I fear, my brethren, may be the state of some of you. See to it, that you are clear from the sin of knowing and confessing what is your duty, and yet not doing it. If you be such, and make no effort to become better; if you do not come to Church honestly, for God's grace to make you better, and seriously strive to be better and to do your duty more thoroughly, it will profit you nothing to be ever so reverent in your manner, and ever so regular in coming to Church. God hates the worship of the mere lips; He requires the worship of the heart. A person may bow, and kneel, and look religious, but he is not at all the nearer heaven, unless he tries to obey God in all things, and to do his duty. But if he does honestly strive to obey God, then his outward manner will be reverent also; decent forms will become natural to him; holy ordinances, though coming to him from the Church, will at the same time come (as it were) from his heart; they will be part of himself, and he will as little think of dispensing with them as he would dispense with his ordinary apparel, nay, as he could dispense with tongue or hand in speaking or doing. This is the true way of doing devotional service; not to have feelings without acts, or acts without feelings; but both to do and to feel; to see that our hearts and bodies are both sanctified together, and become one; the heart ruling our limbs, and making the whole man serve Him, who has redeemed the whole man, body as well as soul.

[VIII, 1]

Chapter 33

DIVINE CALLS

And the Lord came, and stood, and called as at other times, Samuel,
Samuel. Then Samuel answered, Speak; for Thy servant heareth.
— 1 Sam. 3:10

In the narrative of which these words form part, we have a
remarkable instance of a Divine call, and the manner in which it
is our duty to meet it. Samuel was from a child brought to the
house of the Lord; and in due time he was called to a sacred office,
and made a Prophet. He was called, and he forthwith answered
the call. God said, "Samuel, Samuel." He did not understand at
first who called, and what was meant; but on going to Eli he
learned who spoke, and what his answer should be. So when God
called again, he said, "Speak, Lord, for Thy servant heareth."
Here is prompt obedience.

Very different in its circumstances was St. Paul's call, but
resembling Samuel's in this respect, that, when God called, he,
too, promptly obeyed. When St. Paul heard the voice from
heaven, he said at once, trembling and astonished, "Lord, what
wilt Thou have me to do?"[240] This same obedient temper of his is
stated or implied in the two accounts which he himself gives of
his miraculous conversion. In the twenty-second chapter he says,
"And I said, What shall I do, Lord?" And in the twenty-sixth,
after telling King Agrippa what the Divine Speaker said to him,
he adds what comes to the same thing. "Whereupon, O King
Agrippa, *I was not disobedient* unto the heavenly vision." Such is
the account given us in St. Paul's case of that first step in God's
gracious dealings with him, which ended in his eternal salvation.
"Whom He did foreknow, He also did predestinate";[241]—"whom
He did predestinate, them he also called"—here was the first act
which took place in time—"and whom He called, them He also
justified; and whom He justified, them He also glorified." Such is
the Divine series of mercies; and you see that it was prompt obedi-

ence on St. Paul's part which carried on the first act of Divine grace into the second, which knit together the first mercy to the second. "Whom He called, them He also justified." St. Paul was called when Christ appeared to him in the way; he was justified when Ananias came to baptize him: and it was prompt obedience which led him from his call to his baptism. "Lord, what wilt Thou have me to do?"[242] The answer was, "Arise, and go into Damascus; and there it shall be told thee of all things which are appointed for thee to do." And when he came to Damascus, Ananias was sent to him by the same Lord who had appeared to him; and he reminded St. Paul of this when he came to him. The Lord had appeared for his call; the Lord appeared for his justification.

This, then, is the lesson taught us by St. Paul's conversion, promptly to obey the call. If we do obey it, to God be the glory, for He it is works in us. If we do not obey, to ourselves be all the shame, for sin and unbelief work in us. Such being the state of the case, let us take care to act accordingly, being exceedingly alarmed lest we should *not* obey God's voice when He calls us, yet not taking praise or credit to ourselves if we *do* obey it. This has been the temper of all saints from the beginning—working out their salvation with fear and trembling, yet ascribing the work to Him who wrought in them to will and do of His good pleasure; obeying the call, and giving thanks to Him who calls, to Him who fulfills in them their calling. So much on the pattern afforded us by St. Paul.

Very different in its circumstances was Samuel's call, when a child in the Temple, yet resembling St. Paul's in this particular, that for our instruction the circumstance of his obedience to it is brought out prominently even in the words put into his mouth by Eli in the text. Eli taught him what to say, when called by the Divine voice. Accordingly, when "the Lord came, and stood, and called as at other times, Samuel, Samuel. Then Samuel answered, Speak, Lord, for Thy servant heareth."

Such, again, is the temper of mind expressed by holy David in the Twenty-seventh Psalm, "When Thou saidst, Seek ye My face, my heart said unto Thee, Thy face, Lord, will I seek."

And this temper, which in the above instances is illustrated in words spoken, is in the case of many other Saints in Scripture shown in word and deed; and, on the other hand, is illustrated negatively by being neglected in the case of others therein mentioned, who might have entered into life, and did not.

For instance, we read of the Apostles, that "Jesus, walking by the sea of Galilee, saw two brethren, Simon called Peter, and Andrew his brother, casting a net into the sea; for they were fishers. And He saith unto them, Follow Me, and I will make you fishers of men. *And* they *straightway* left their nets and followed Him."[243] Again; when He saw James and John with their father Zebedee, "He *called* them; and they *immediately left the ship, and their father,* and *followed* Him." And so of St. Matthew at the receipt of custom, "He said unto him, Follow Me; and he left all, rose up, and followed Him."

Again, we are told in St. John's Gospel, "Jesus would go forth into Galilee, and findeth Philip, and saith unto Him, *Follow* Me." Again, "Philip findeth Nathanael," and in like manner says to him, "Come and see." "Jesus saw Nathanael coming unto Him, and saith of him, Behold an Israelite indeed, in whom is no guile."

On the other hand, the young ruler shrunk from the call, and found it a hard saying. "If thou wilt be perfect, go and sell that thou hast, and give to the poor, and thou shalt have treasure in heaven; and come, and follow Me. But when the young man heard that saying, he went away sorrowful, for he had great possessions."[244] Others who seemed to waver, or rather who asked for some little delay from human feeling, were rebuked for want of promptitude in their obedience; for time stays for no one; the word of call is spoken and is gone; if we do not seize the moment, it is lost. Christ was on His road heavenward. He walked by the sea of Galilee;[245] He "passed forth";[246] He "passed by";[247] He did not stop; all men must join Him, or He would be calling on others beyond them.[248] "He said to another, Follow Me. But he said, Lord, suffer me first to go and bury my father. Jesus said unto him, Let the dead bury their dead: but go thou and preach the kingdom of God. And another also said, Lord, I will follow Thee: but let me first go bid them farewell, which are at home at my house. And Jesus said unto him, No man, having put his hand to the plow, and looking back, is fit for the kingdom of God."[249]

Not unlike these last instances are the circumstances of the call of the great prophet Elisha, though he does not seem to have incurred blame from Elijah for his lingering on the thoughts of what he was leaving. "He found Elisha, the son of Shaphat, who was plowing. . . . Elijah passed by him, and cast his mantle over him." He did not stay; he passed on, and Elisha was obliged to run after him. "And he left the oxen, and ran after Elijah, and said, Let me, I pray thee, kiss my father and my mother, and then I will follow thee." This the prophet allowed him to do, and after that "he arose and followed Elijah, and ministered unto him."

Or once more consider the circumstances of the call of Abraham, the father of all who believe. He was called from his father's house, but was not told whither. St. Paul was bid go to Damascus, and there he was to receive further directions. In like manner Abraham left his home for a land "that I *will* show thee,"²⁵⁰ says Almighty God. Accordingly he went out, "not knowing whither he went." "Abram departed as the Lord had spoken unto him."

Such are the instances of Divine calls in Scripture, and their characteristic is this; to require instant obedience, and next to call us we know not to what; to call us on in the darkness. Faith alone can obey them.

But it may be urged, How does this concern us now? We were all called to serve God in infancy, before we could obey or disobey; we found ourselves called when reason began to dawn; we have been called to a state of salvation, we have been living as God's servants and children, all through our time of trial, having been brought into it in infancy through Holy Baptism, by the act of our parents. Calling is not a thing future with us, but a thing past.

This is true in a very sufficient sense; and yet it is true also that the passages of Scripture which I have been quoting do apply to us still, do concern us, and may warn and guide us in many important ways; as a few words will show.

For in truth we are not called once only, but many times; all through our life Christ is calling us. He called us first in Baptism; but afterwards also; whether we obey His voice or not, He graciously calls us still. If we fall from our Baptism, He calls us to repent; if we are striving to fulfill our calling, He calls us on from grace to grace, and from holiness to holiness, while life is given us. Abraham was called from his home, Peter from his nets, Matthew from his office, Elisha from his farm, Nathanael from his retreat; we are all in course of calling, on and on, from one thing to another, having no resting place, but mounting towards our eternal rest, and obeying one command only to have another put upon us. He calls us again and again, in order to justify us again and again—and again and again, and more and more, to sanctify and glorify us.

It were well if we understood this; but we are slow to master the great truth, that Christ is, as it were, walking among us, and by His hand, or eye, or voice, bidding us follow Him. We do not understand that His call is a thing which takes place now. We think it took place in the Apostles' days; but we do not believe in it, we do not look out for it in our own case. We have not eyes to see the Lord; far different from the beloved Apostle, who knew Christ even when the rest of the disciples knew Him not. When he stood on the shore after His Resurrection, and bade them cast the net into the sea, "that disciple whom Jesus loved saith unto Peter, It is the Lord."[251]

Now what I mean is this: that they who are living religiously, have from time to time truths they did not know before, or had no need to consider, brought before them forcibly; truths which involve duties, which are in fact precepts, and claim obedience. In this and suchlike ways Christ calls us now. There is nothing miraculous or extraordinary in His dealings with us. He works through our natural faculties and circumstances of life. Still what happens to us in Providence is in all essential respects what His voice was to those whom He addressed when on earth: whether He commands by a visible presence, or by a voice, or by our consciences, it matters not, so that we feel it to be a command. If it is a command, it may be obeyed or disobeyed; it may be accepted as Samuel or St. Paul accepted it, or put aside after the manner of the young man who had great possessions.

And these Divine calls are commonly, from the nature of the case, sudden now, and as indefinite and obscure in their consequences as in former times. The accidents and events of life are, as is obvious, one special way in which the calls I speak of come to us; and they, as we all know, are in their very nature, and as the word *accident* implies, sudden and unexpected. A man is going on as usual; he comes home one day, and finds a letter, or a message, or a person, whereby a sudden trial comes on him, which, if met religiously, will be the means of advancing him to a higher state of religious excellence, which at present he as little comprehends as the unspeakable words heard by St. Paul in paradise. By a trial we commonly mean a something which if encountered well, will confirm a man in his present way; but I am speaking of something more than this; of what will not only confirm him, but raise him into a high state of knowledge and holiness. Many persons will find it very striking on looking back on their past lives, to observe what different notions they entertained at different periods, of what Divine Truth was, what was the way of pleasing God, and what things were allowable or not, what excellence was, and what happiness. I do not scruple to say, that these differences may be as great as that which may be supposed to have existed between St. Peter's state of mind when quietly fishing on the lake, or Elisha's when driving his oxen, and that new state of mind of each of them when called to be Apostle or Prophet. Elisha and St. Peter indeed were also called to a new mode of life; that I am not speaking of. I am not speaking of cases when persons change their condition, their place in society, their pursuit, and the like; I am supposing them to remain pretty much the same as before in outward circumstances; but I say that many a man is conscious to himself of having undergone inwardly great changes of view as to what truth is and what happiness. Nor, again, am I speaking of changes so great, that a man reverses his former opinions and conduct. He may be able to see that there is a connection between the two; that his former has led to his latter; and yet he may feel that after all they differ in kind; that he has got into a new world of thought, and measures things and persons by a different rule.

Nothing, indeed, is more wonderful and strange than the different views which different persons take of the same subject. Take any single fact, event, or existing thing which meets us in the world; what various remarks will be made on it by different persons! For instance, consider the different lights in which any single action, of a striking nature, is viewed by different persons; or consider the view of wealth or a wealthy man, taken by this or that class in the community; what different feelings does it excite—envy, or respect, or ridicule, or angry opposition, or indifference, or fear and compassion; here are states of mind in which different parties may regard it. These are broad differences; others are quite as real, though more subtle. Religion, for instance, may be reverenced by the soldier, the man of literature, the trader, the statesman, and the theologian; yet how very distinct their modes of reverencing it, and how separate the standard which each sets up in his mind! Well, all these various modes of viewing things cannot one and all be the best mode, even were they all good modes; but this even is not the case. Some are contrary to others, some are bad. But even of those that are on the whole good, some are but in part good, some are imperfect, some have much bad mixed with them; and only one is best. Only one is the truth and the perfect truth; and which that is, none know but those who are in possession of it, if even they. But God knows which it is; and towards that one and only Truth He is leading us forward. He is leading forward His redeemed, He is training His elect, one and all, to the one perfect knowledge and obedience of Christ; not, however, without their cooperation, but by means of calls which they are to obey, and which if they do not obey, they lose place, and fall behind in their heavenly course. He leads them forward from strength to strength, and from glory to glory, up the steps of the ladder whose top reacheth to heaven. We pass from one state of knowledge to another; we are introduced into a higher region from a lower, by listening to Christ's call and obeying it.

Perhaps it may be the loss of some dear friend or relative through which the call comes to us; which shows us the vanity of things below, and prompts us to make God our sole stay. We through grace do so in a way we never did before; and in the course of years, when we look back on our life, we find that that sad event has brought us into a new state of faith and judgment, and that we are as though other men from what we were. We thought, before it took place, that we were serving God, and so we were in a measure; but we find that, whatever our present infirmities may be, and however far we be still from the highest state of illumination, then at least we were serving the world under the show and the belief of serving God.

Or again, perhaps something occurs to force us to take a part for God or against Him. The world requires of us some sacrifice which we see we ought not to grant to it. Some tempting offer is made us; or some reproach or discredit threatened us; or we have to determine and avow what is truth and what is error. We are enabled to act as God would have us act; and we do so in much fear and perplexity. We do not see our way clearly; we do not see what is to follow from what we have done, and how it bears upon our general conduct and opinions: yet perhaps it has the most important bearings. That little deed, suddenly exacted of us, almost suddenly resolved on and executed, may be as though a gate into the second or third heaven—an entrance into a higher state of holiness, and into a truer view of things than we have hitherto taken.

Or again, we get acquainted with someone whom God employs to bring before us a number of truths which were closed on us before; and we but half understand them, and but half approve of them; and yet God seems to speak in them, and Scripture to confirm them. This is a case which not unfrequently occurs, and it involves a call "to follow on to know the Lord."[252]

Or again, we may be in the practice of reading Scripture carefully, and trying to serve God, and its sense may, as if suddenly, break upon us, in a way it never did before. Some thought may suggest itself to us, which is a key to a great deal in Scripture, or which suggests a great many other thoughts. A new light may be thrown on the precepts of our Lord and His Apostles. We may be able to enter into the manner of life of the early Christians, as recorded in Scripture, which before was hidden from us, and into the simple maxims on which Scripture bases it. We may be led to understand that it is very different from the life which men live now. Now knowledge is a call to action: an insight into the way of perfection is a call to perfection.

Once more, it may so happen that we find ourselves, how or why we cannot tell, much more able to obey God in certain respects than heretofore. Our minds are so strangely constituted, it is impossible to say whether it is from the growth of habit suddenly showing itself, or from an unusual gift of Divine grace poured into our hearts, but so it is; let our temptation be to sloth, or irresolution, or worldly anxiety, or pride, or to other more base and miserable sins, we may suddenly find ourselves possessed of a power of self-command which we had not before. Or again, we may have a resolution grow on us to serve God more strictly in His house and in private than heretofore. This is a call to higher things; let us beware lest we receive the grace of God in vain. Let us beware of lapsing back; let us avoid temptation. Let us strive by quietness and caution to cherish the feeble flame, and shelter it from the storms of this world. God may be bringing us into a higher world of religious truth; let us work with Him.

To conclude. Nothing is more certain in matter of fact, than that some men do feel themselves called to high duties and works, to which others are not called. Why this is we do not know; whether it be that those who are not called, forfeit the call from having failed in former trials, or have been called and have not followed; or that though God gives baptismal grace to all, yet He really does call some men by His free grace to higher things than others; but so it is; this man sees sights which that man does not see, has a larger faith, a more ardent love, and a more spiritual understanding. No one has any leave to take another's lower standard of holiness for his own. It is nothing to us what others are. If God calls us to greater renunciation of the world, and exacts a sacrifice of our hopes and fears, this is our gain, this is a mark of His love for us, this is a thing to be rejoiced in. Such thoughts, when properly entertained, have no tendency to puff us up; for if the prospect is noble, yet the risk is more fearful. While we pursue high excellence, we walk among precipices, and a fall is easy. Hence the Apostle says, "Work out your own salvation with fear and trembling, for it is God that worketh in you."[253] Again, the more men aim at high things, the more sensitive perception they have of their own shortcomings; and this again is adapted to humble them especially. We need not fear spiritual pride then, in following Christ's call, if we follow it as men in earnest. Earnestness has no time to compare itself with the state of other men; earnestness has too vivid a feeling of its own infirmities to be elated at itself. Earnestness is simply set on doing God's will. It simply says, "Speak, Lord, for Thy servant heareth." "Lord, what wilt Thou have me to do?" Oh that we had more of this spirit! Oh that we could take that simple view of things, as to feel that the one thing which lies before us is to please God! What gain is it to please the world, to please the great, any, even to please those whom we love, compared with this? What gain is it to be applauded, admired, courted, followed, compared with this one aim, of not being disobedient to a heavenly vision? What can this world offer comparable with that insight, into spiritual things, that keen faith, that heavenly peace, that high sanctity, that everlasting righteousness, that hope of glory, which they have who in sincerity love and follow our Lord Jesus Christ?

Let us beg and pray Him day by day to reveal Himself to our souls more fully; to quicken our senses; to give us sight and hearing, taste and touch of the world to come; so to work within us that we may sincerely say, "Thou shalt guide me with Thy counsel, and after that receive me to glory. Whom have I in heaven but Thee? and there is none upon earth that I desire in comparison of Thee: my flesh and my heart faileth; but God is the strength of my heart, and my portion forever."

[VIII, 2]

Chapter 34

CURIOSITY A TEMPTATION TO SIN

Enter not into the path of the wicked, and go not in the way of evil men.
Avoid it, pass not by it, turn from it, and pass away.
— PROV. 4:14, 15

One chief cause of the wickedness which is everywhere seen in the world, and in which, alas! each of us has more or less his share, is our curiosity to have some fellowship with darkness, some experience of sin, to know what the pleasures of sin are like. I believe it is even thought unmanly by many persons (though they may not like to say so in plain words), unmanly and a thing to be ashamed of, to have no knowledge of sin by experience, as if it argued a strange seclusion from the world, a childish ignorance of life, a simpleness and narrowness of mind, and a superstitious, slavish fear. Not to know sin by experience brings upon a man the laughter and jests of his companions: nor is it wonderful this should be the case in the descendants of that guilty pair to whom Satan in the beginning held out admittance into a strange world of knowledge and enjoyment, as the reward to disobedience to God's commandment. "When the woman saw that the tree was good for food, and that it was pleasant to the eyes, and a tree to be desired to make one wise, she took of the fruit thereof, and did eat, and gave also unto her husband with her, and he did eat."[254] A discontent with the abundance of blessings which were given, because something was withheld, was the sin of our first parents: in like manner, a wanton roving after things forbidden, a curiosity to know what it was to be as the heathen, was one chief source of the idolatries of the Jews; and we at this day inherit with them a like nature from Adam.

I say, curiosity strangely moves us to disobedience, in order that we may have experience of the pleasure of disobedience. Thus we "rejoice in our youth, and let our heart cheer us in the days of our youth, and walk in the ways of our heart, and in the sight of our eyes."[255] And we thus intrude into things forbidden, in various ways; in reading what we should not read, in hearing what we should not hear, in seeing what we should not see, in going into company whither we should not go, in presumptuous reasonings and arguings when we should have faith, in acting as if we were our own masters where we should obey. We indulge our reason, we indulge our passions, we indulge our ambition, our vanity, our love of power; we throw ourselves into the society of bad, worldly, or careless men; and all the while we think that, after having acquired this miserable knowledge of good and evil, we can return to our duty, and continue where we left off; merely going aside a moment to shake ourselves, as Samson did, and with an ignorance like his, that our true heavenly strength is departed from us.

Now this delusion arises from Satan's craft, the father of lies, who knows well that if he can get us once to sin, he can easily make us sin twice and thrice, till at length we are taken captive at his will.[256] He sees that curiosity is man's great and first snare, as it was in paradise; and he knows that, if he can but force a way into his heart by this chief and exciting temptation, those temptations of other kinds, which follow in life, will easily prevail over us; and, on the other hand, that if we resist the beginnings of sin, there is every prospect through God's grace that we shall continue in a religious way. His plan of action then lies plain before him— to tempt us violently, while the world is new to us, and our hopes and feelings are eager and restless. Hence is seen the Divine Wisdom, as well as the merciful consideration, of the advice contained in so many parts of Scripture, as in the text, "Enter not into the path of the wicked, and go not into the way of evil men. Avoid it, pass not by it, turn from it, and pass away."

Let us, then, now for a few moments give our minds to the consideration of this plain truth, which we have heard so often that for that very reason we are not unlikely to forget it—that the great thing in religion is to set off well; to resist the beginnings of sin, to flee temptation, to avoid the company of the wicked. "Enter not into the path of the wicked. . . . Avoid it, pass not by it, turn from it, and pass away."

1. And for this reason, first of all, because it is hardly possible to delay our flight without rendering flight impossible. When I say, resist the beginnings of evil, I do not mean the first act merely, but

the rising thought of evil. Whatever the temptation may be, there may be no time to wait and gaze, without being caught. Woe to us if Satan (so to say) sees us first; for, as in the case of some beast of prey, for him to see us is to master us. Directly we are made aware of the temptation, we shall, if we are wise, turn our backs upon it, without waiting to think and reason about it; we shall engage our mind in other thoughts. There are temptations when this advice is especially necessary; but under all it is highly seasonable.

2. For consider, in the next place, what must in all cases be the consequence of allowing evil thoughts to be present to us, though we do not actually admit them into our hearts. This, namely, we shall make ourselves familiar with them. Now our great security against sin lies in being shocked at it. Eve gazed and reflected when she should have fled. It is sometimes said, "Second thoughts are best": this is true in many cases; but there are times when it is very false, and when, on the contrary, first thoughts are best. For sin is like the serpent, which seduced our first parents. We know that some serpents have the power of what is called "fascinating." Their eye has the power of subduing—nay, in a strange way, of alluring—their victim, who is reduced to utter helplessness, cannot flee away, nay, rather is obliged to approach, and (as it were) deliver himself up to them; till in their own time they seize and devour him. What a dreadful figure this is of the power of sin and the devil over our hearts! At first our conscience tells us, in a plain straightforward way, what is right and what is wrong; but when we trifle with this warning, our reason becomes perverted, and comes in aid of our wishes, and deceives us to our ruin. Then we begin to find, that there are arguments available in behalf of bad deeds, and we listen to these till we come to think them true; and then, if perchance better thoughts return, and we make some feeble effort to get at the truth really and sincerely, we find our minds by that time so bewildered that we do not know right from wrong.

Thus, for instance, everyone is shocked at cursing and swearing when he first hears it; and at first he cannot help even showing that he is shocked; that is, he looks grave and downcast, and feels uncomfortable. But when he has once got accustomed to such profane talking, and been laughed out of his strictness, and has begun to think it manly, and has been persuaded to join in it, then he soon learns to defend it. He says he means no harm by it; that it does no one any harm; that it is only so many words, and that everybody uses them. Here is an instance in which disobedience to what we know to be right makes us blind.

Again, this same confusion frequently happens in the case of temptations from the world. We fear worldly loss or discredit; or we hope some advantage; and we feel tempted to act so as to secure, at any rate, the worldly good, or to avoid the evil. Now in all such cases of conduct there is no end of arguing about right or wrong, if we once begin; there are numberless ways of acting, each of which may be speciously defended by argument, but plain, pure-hearted common sense, generally speaking, at the very first sight decides the question for us without argument; but if we do not listen promptly to this secret monitor, its light goes out at once, and we are left to the mercy of mere conjecture, and grope about with but second-best guides. Then seeming arguments in favor of deceit and evil compliance with the world's wishes, or of disgraceful indolence, urge us, and either prevail, or at least so confuse us, that we do not know how to act. Alas! in ancient days it happened in this way, that Christians who were brought before their heathen persecutors for punishment, because they were Christians, sometimes came short of the crown of martyrdom, "having loved this present world,"[257] and so lost their way in the mazes of Satan's crafty arguments.

Temptations to unbelief may also be mentioned here. Speculating wantonly on sacred subjects, and jesting about them, offend us at first; and we turn away; but if in an evil hour we are seduced by the cleverness or wit of a writer or speaker, to listen to his impieties, who can say where we shall stop? Can we save ourselves from the infection of his profaneness? we cannot hope to do so. And when we come to a better mind (if by God's grace this be afterwards granted to us), what will be our state? like the state of men who have undergone some dreadful illness, which changes the constitution of the body. That ready and clear perception of right and wrong, which before directed us, will have disappeared, as beauty of person, or keenness of eyesight in bodily disorders; and when we begin to try to make up our minds which way lies the course of duty on particular trials, we shall bring enfeebled, unsteady powers to the examination; and when we move to act, our limbs (as it were) will move the contrary way, and we shall do wrong when we wish to do right.

3. But there is another wretched effect of sinning once, which sometimes takes place; not only the sinning that once itself, but being so seduced by it, as forthwith to continue in the commission of it ever afterwards, without seeking for arguments to meet our conscience withal; from a mere brutish, headstrong, infatuate greediness after its bad pleasures. There are beasts of prey which are said to abstain from blood till they taste it, but once tasting it, ever seek it: and, in like manner, there is a sort of thirst for sin which is born with us, but which grace quenches, and which is thus kept under *till* we, by our own act, rouse it again; and which, when once aroused, never can be allayed. We sin, while we confess the wages of sin to be death.

4. Sometimes, I say, this is the immediate effect of a first transgression; and if not the immediate effect, yet it is always the tendency and the end of sinning at length, viz. to enslave us to it. Temptation is very powerful, it is true, when it comes first; but, then, its power lies in its own novelty; and, on the other hand, there is power in the heart itself, divinely given, to resist it; but when we have long indulged sin, the mind has become sinful in its habit and character, and the Spirit of God having departed, it has no principle within it of strength sufficient to save it from spiritual death. What being can change its own nature? that would be almost ceasing to be itself: fire cannot cease to burn; the leopard changes not its spots, and ceases not to rend and devour; and the soul which has often sinned, cannot help sinning; but in this respect awfully differing from the condition of the senseless elements or brute animals, that its present state is all its own fault; that it might have hindered it, and will have one day to answer for not having hindered it.

Thus, easy as it is to avoid sin first of all, at length it is (humanly speaking) impossible. "Enter not into its path," saith the wise man; the two paths of right and wrong start from the same point, and at first are separated by a very small difference, so easy (comparatively) is it to choose the right instead of the wrong way: but wait awhile, and pursue the road leading to destruction, and you will find the distance between the two has widened beyond measurement, and that between them a great gulf has been sunk, so that you cannot pass from the one to the other, though you desire it ever so earnestly.[258]

Now to what do considerations such as these lead us, but to our Lord's simple and comprehensive precept, which is the same as Solomon's, but more impressively and solemnly urged on us by the manner and time of His giving it? "Watch and pray, lest ye enter into temptation." To enter not the path of the wicked, to avoid it, and pass by it, what is this but the exercise of *watching*? Therefore He insists upon it so much, knowing that in it our safety lies. But now, on the other hand, consider *how* many are there among us who can be said to watch and pray? Is not the utmost we do to offer on Sunday some kind of prayer in church to God; or sometimes some short prayer morning and evening in the week; and then go into the world with the same incaution and forgetfulness as if we had never entertained a serious thought? We go through the business of the day, quite forgetting, to any practical purpose, that all business has snares in it, and therefore needs caution. Let us ask ourselves this question, "How often do we think of Satan in the course of the day as our great tempter?" Yet surely he does not cease to be active because we do not think of him; and surely, too, his powers and devices were revealed to us by Almighty God for the very purpose, that being not ignorant of them, we might watch against them. Who among us will not confess, that many is the time that he has mixed with the world, forgetting who the god of this world is? or rather, are not a great many of us living in habitual forgetfulness that this world is a scene of trial; that is, that this is its *chief* character, that all its employments, its pleasures, its occurrences, even the most innocent, the most acceptable to God, and the most truly profitable in themselves, are all the while so handled by Satan as may be the most conducive to our ruin, if he can possibly contrive it? There is nothing gloomy or superstitious in this, as the plain words of Scripture will abundantly prove to every inquirer. We are told "that the devil, our adversary, as a roaring lion walketh about, seeking whom he may devour";[259] and therefore are warned to "be sober, be vigilant." And assuredly our true comfort lies, not in disguising the truth from ourselves, but in knowing something more than this—that though Satan is against us, God is for us; that greater is He that is in us, than he that is in the world;[260] and that He in every temptation will make a way for us to escape, that we may be able to bear it.[261]

God does His part most surely; and Satan too does his part; we alone are unconcerned. Heaven and hell are at war for us and against us, yet we trifle, and let life go on at random. Heaven and hell are before us as our own future abode, one or other of them; yet our own interest moves us no more than God's mercy. We treat sin, not as an enemy to be feared, abhorred, and shunned, but as a misfortune and a weakness; we do not pity and shun sinful men, but we enter into their path so far as to keep company with them; and next, being tempted to copy them, we fall almost without an effort.

Be not you thus deceived and overcome, my brethren, by an evil heart of unbelief. Make up your minds to take God for your portion, and pray to Him for grace to enable you so to do. Avoid the great evils of leisure, avoid the snare of having time on your hands. Avoid all bad thoughts, all corrupt or irreligious books, avoid all bad company: let nothing seduce you into it. Though you may be laughed at for your strictness; though you may lose thereby amusements which you would like to partake of; though you may thereby be ignorant of much which others know, and may appear to disadvantage when they are talking together; though you appear behind the rest of the world; though you be called a coward, or a child, or narrow-minded, or superstitious; whatever insulting words be applied to you, fear not, falter not, fail not; stand firm, quit you like men; be strong. They think that in the devil's service there are secrets worthy our inquiry, which you share not: yes, there are secrets, and such that it is a shame even to speak of them; and in like manner you have a secret which they have not, and which far surpasses theirs. "The secret of the Lord is with them that fear Him." Those who obey God and follow Christ have secret gains, so great, that, as well might we say heaven were like hell, as that these are like the gain which sinners have. They have a secret gift given them by their Lord and Savior in proportion to their faith and love. They cannot describe it to others; they have not possession of it all at once; they cannot have the enjoyment of it at this or that time when they will. It comes and goes according to the will of the Giver. It is given but in small measure to those who begin God's service. It is not given at all to those who follow Him with a divided heart. To those who love the world, and yet are in a certain sense religious, and are well contented with such a religious state, to them it is not given. But those who give themselves up to their Lord and Savior, those who surrender themselves soul and body, those who honestly say, "I am Thine, new-make me, do with me what thou wilt," who say so not once or twice merely, or in a transport, but calmly and habitually; these are they who gain the Lord's secret gift, even the "white stone, and in the stone a new name written which no man knoweth, saving he that receiveth it."[262] Sinners think that they know all that religion has to give, and over and above that, they know the pleasures of sin too. No, they do not, cannot, never will know the secret gift of God, till they repent and amend. They never will know what it is to see God, till they obey; nay, though they are to see Him at the last day, even that will be no true sight of Him, for the sight of that Holy One will then impart no comfort, no joy to them. They never will know the blessedness which He has to give. They do know the satisfaction of sinning, such as it is; and, alas! if they go on as they are going, they will know not only what sin is, but what hell is. But they never will know that great secret which is hid in the Father and in the Son.

Let us not then be seduced by the Tempter and his promises. He can show us no good. He has no good to give us. Rather let us listen to the gracious words of our Maker and Redeemer, "Call unto Me, and I will answer thee, and show thee great and mighty things, which thou knowest not."[263]

[VIII, 5]

Chapter 35

RELIGIOUS JOY

(CHRISTMAS DAY)

And the angel said unto them, Fear not: for behold, I bring you good tidings
of great joy, which shall be to all people. For unto you is born this day in the
city of David a Savior, which is Christ the Lord.
— Luke 2:10,11

There are two principal lessons which we are taught on the great
Festival which we this day celebrate, lowliness and joy. This
surely is a day, of all others, in which is set before us the heavenly
excellence and the acceptableness in God's sight of that state
which most men have, or may have, allotted to them, humble or
private life, and cheerfulness in it. If we consult the writings of
historians, philosophers, and poets of this world, we shall be led to
think great men happy; we shall be led to fix our minds and
hearts upon high or conspicuous stations, strange adventures,
powerful talents to cope with them, memorable struggles, and
great destinies. We shall consider that the highest course of life is
the mere pursuit, not the enjoyment of good.

But when we think of this day's Festival, and what we commemorate upon it, a new and very different scene opens upon us.
First, we are reminded that though this life must ever be a life of
toil and effort, yet that, properly speaking, we have not to seek
our highest good. It is found, it is brought near us, in the descent
of the Son of God from His Father's bosom to this world. It is
stored up among us on earth. No longer need men of ardent
minds weary themselves in the pursuit of what they fancy may be
chief goods; no longer have they to wander about and encounter
peril in quest of that unknown blessedness to which their hearts
naturally aspire, as they did in heathen times. The text speaks to
them and to all, "Unto you," it says, "is born this day in the city of
David a Savior, which is Christ the Lord."

Nor, again, need we go in quest of any of those things which
this vain world calls great and noble. Christ altogether dishon-

ored what the world esteems, when He took on Himself a rank and station which the world despises. No lot could be more humble and more ordinary than that which the Son of God chose for Himself.

So that we have on the Feast of the Nativity these two lessons—instead of anxiety within and despondence without, instead of a weary search after great things, to be cheerful and joyful; and, again, to be so in the midst of those obscure and ordinary circumstances of life which the world passes over and thinks scorn of.

Let us consider this more at length, as contained in the gracious narrative of which the text is part.

1. First, what do we read just before the text? that there were certain shepherds keeping watch over their flock by night, and Angels appeared to them. Why should the heavenly hosts appear to these shepherds? What was it in them which attracted the attention of the Angels and the Lord of Angels? Were these shepherds learned, distinguished, or powerful? Were they especially known for piety and gifts? Nothing is said to make us think so. Faith, we may safely say, they had, or some of them, for to him that hath more shall be given; but there is nothing to show that they were holier and more enlightened than other good men of the time, who waited for the consolation of Israel. Nay, there is no reason to suppose that they were better than the common run of men in their circumstances, simple, and fearing God, but without any great advances in piety, or any very formed habits of religion. Why then were they chosen? for their poverty's sake and obscurity. Almighty God looks with a sort of especial love, or (as we may term it) affection, upon the lowly. Perhaps it is that man, a fallen, dependent, and destitute creature, is more in his proper place when he is in lowly circumstances, and that power and riches, though unavoidable in the case of some, are unnatural appendages to man, as such. Just as there are trades and callings which are unbecoming, though requisite; and while we profit by them, and honor those the more who engage in them, yet we feel we are glad that they are not ours; as we feel grateful and respectful towards a soldier's profession, yet do not affect it; so in God's sight greatness is less acceptable than obscurity. It becomes us less.

The shepherds, then, were chosen on account of their lowliness, to be the first to hear of the Lord's Nativity, a secret which none of the princes of this world knew.

And what a contrast is presented to us when we take into account who were our Lord's messengers to them! The Angels who excel in strength, these did His bidding towards the shepherds. Here the highest and the lowest of God's rational creatures are brought together. A set of poor men, engaged in a life of hardship, exposed at that very time to the cold and darkness of the night, watching their flocks, with the view of scaring away beasts of prey or robbers; they—when they are thinking of nothing but earthly things, counting over the tale of their sheep, keeping their dogs by their side, and listening to the noises over the plain, considering the weather and watching for the day—suddenly are met by far other visitants then they conceived. We know the contracted range of thought, the minute and ordinary objects, or rather the one or two objects, to and fro again and again without variety, which engage the minds of men exposed to such a life of heat, cold, and wet, hunger and nakedness, hardship and servitude. They cease to care much for anything, but go on in a sort of mechanical way, without heart, and still more without reflection.

To men so circumstanced the Angel appeared, to open their minds, and to teach them not to be downcast and in bondage because they were low in the world. He appeared as if to show them that God had chosen the poor in this world to be heirs of His kingdom, and so to do honor to their lot. "Fear not," he said, "for behold I bring you good tidings of great joy, which shall be to all people. For unto you is born this day in the city of David a Savior, which is Christ the Lord."

2. And now comes a second lesson, which I have said may be gained from the Festival. The Angel honored a humble lot by his very appearing to the shepherds; next he taught it to be joyful by his message. He disclosed good tidings so much above this world as to equalize high and low, rich and poor, one with another. He said, "Fear not." This is a mode of address frequent in Scripture, as you may have observed, as if man needed some such assurance to support him, especially in God's presence. The Angel said, "Fear not," when he saw the alarm which his presence caused among the shepherds. Even a lesser wonder would have reasonably startled them. Therefore the Angel said, "Fear not." We are

naturally afraid of any messenger from the other world, for we have an uneasy conscience when left to ourselves, and think that his coming forebodes evil. Besides, we so little realize the unseen world, that were Angel or spirit to present himself before us we should be startled by reason of our unbelief, a truth being brought home to our minds which we never apprehended before. So for one or other reason the shepherds were sore afraid when the glory of the Lord shone around about them. And the Angel said, "Fear not." A little religion makes us afraid; when a little light is poured in upon the conscience, there is a darkness visible; nothing but sights of woe and terror; the glory of God alarms while it shines around. His holiness, the range and difficulties of His commandments, the greatness of His power, the faithfulness of His word, frighten the sinner, and men seeing him afraid, think religion has made him so, whereas he is not yet religious at all. They call him religious, when he is merely conscience-stricken. But religion itself, far from inculcating alarm and terror, says, in the words of the Angel, "Fear not"; for such is His mercy, while Almighty God has poured about us His glory, yet it is a consolatory glory, for it is the light of His glory in the Face of Jesus Christ.[264] Thus the heavenly herald tempered the too dazzling brightness of the Gospel on that first Christmas. The glory of God at first alarmed the shepherds, so he added the tidings of good, to work in them a more wholesome and happy temper. Then they rejoiced.

"Fear not," said the Angel, "for behold I bring you good tidings of great joy, which shall be to all people. For unto you is born this day in the city of David a Savior, which is Christ the Lord." And then, when he had finished his announcement, "suddenly there was with the Angel a multitude of the heavenly host, praising God and saying, Glory to God in the highest, and on earth peace, goodwill towards men." Such were the words which the blessed Spirits who minister to Christ and His Saints spoke on that gracious night to the shepherds, to rouse them out of their cold and famished mood into great joy; to teach them that they were objects of God's love as much as the greatest of men on earth; nay more so, for to them first He had imparted the news of what that night was happening. His Son was then born into the world. Such events are told to friends and intimates, to those whom we love, to those who will sympathize with us, not to strangers. How could Almighty God be more gracious, and show His favor more impressively to the lowly and the friendless, than by hastening (if I may use the term) to confide the great, the joyful secret to the shepherds keeping watch over their sheep by night?

The Angel then gave the first lesson mingled humility and joyfulness; but an infinitely greater one was behind in the event itself, to which he directed the shepherds, in that birth itself of the Holy Child Jesus. This he intimated in these words: "Ye shall find the babe wrapped in swaddling clothes, lying in a manger." Doubtless, when they heard the Lord's Christ was born into the world, they would look for Him in kings' palaces. They would not be able to fancy that He had become one of themselves, or that they might approach Him; therefore the Angel thus warned them where to find Him, not only as a sign, but as a lesson also.

"The shepherds said one to another, Let us now go even unto Bethlehem, and see this thing which is come to pass, which the Lord hath made known to us." Let us too go with them, to contemplate that second and greater miracle to which the Angel directed them, the Nativity of Christ. St. Luke says of the Blessed Virgin, "She brought forth her firstborn Son, and wrapped Him in swaddling clothes, and laid Him in a manger." What a wonderful sign is this to all the world, and therefore the Angel repeated it to the shepherds: "Ye shall find the babe wrapped in swaddling clothes, lying in a manger." The God of heaven and earth, the Divine Word, who had been in glory with the Eternal Father from the beginning, He was at this time born into this world of sin as a little infant. He, as at this time, lay in His mother's arms, to all appearance helpless and powerless, and was wrapped by Mary in an infant's bands, and laid to sleep in a manger. The Son of God Most High, who created the worlds, became flesh, though remaining what He was before. He became flesh as truly as if He had ceased to be what He was, and had actually been changed into flesh. He submitted to be the offspring of Mary, to be taken up in the hands of a mortal, to have a mother's eye fixed upon Him, and to be cherished at a mother's bosom. A daughter of man became the Mother of God—to her, indeed, an unspeakable gift of grace; but in Him what condescension! What an emptying of His glory to become man! and not only a helpless infant, though that were humiliation enough, but to inherit all the infirmities and imperfections of our nature which were possible to a sinless soul. What were His thoughts, if we may venture to use such language or admit such a reflection concerning the Infinite, when human feelings, human sorrows, human wants, first became His? What a mystery is there from first to last in the Son of God becoming man! Yet in proportion to the mystery is the grace and mercy of it; and as is the grace, so is the greatness of the fruit of it.

Let us steadily contemplate the mystery, and say whether any consequence is too great to follow from so marvelous a dispensation; any mystery so great, any grace so overpowering, as that which is already manifested in the incarnation and death of the Eternal Son. Were we told that the effect of it would be to make us as Seraphim, that we were to ascend as high as He descended low—would that startle us after the Angel's news to the shepherds? And this indeed is the effect of it, so far as such words may be spoken without impiety. Men we remain, but not mere men, but gifted with a measure of all those perfections which Christ has in fullness, partaking each in his own degree of His Divine Nature so fully, that the only reason (so to speak) why His Saints are not really like Him is that it is impossible—that He is the Creator, and they His creatures; yet still so, that they are all but Divine, all that they can be made without violating the incommunicable majesty of the Most High. Surely in proportion to His glory is His power of glorifying; so that to say that through Him we shall be made *all but* gods—though it is to say, that we are infinitely below the adorable Creator—still is to say, and truly, that we shall be higher than every other being in the world; higher than Angels or Archangels, Cherubim or Seraphim—that is, not here, or in ourselves, but in heaven and in Christ: Christ, already the first fruits of our race, God and man, having ascended high above all creatures, and we through His grace tending to the same high blessedness, having the earnest of His glory given here, and (if we be found faithful) the fullness of it hereafter.

If all these things be so, surely the lesson of joy which the Incarnation gives us is as impressive as the lesson of humility. St. Paul gives us the one lesson in his epistle to the Philippians: "Let this mind be in you, which was also in Christ Jesus: who, being in the form of God, thought it not robbery to be equal with God: but made Himself of no reputation, and took upon Him the form of a servant, and was made in the likeness of men":[265] and St. Peter gives us the lesson of joyfulness: "whom having not seen, ye love; in whom, though now ye see Him not, yet believing, ye rejoice with joy unspeakable, and full of glory: receiving the end of your faith, even the salvation of your souls."

Take these thoughts with you, my brethren, to your homes on this festive day; let them be with you in your family and social meetings. It is a day of joy: it is good to be joyful—it is wrong to be otherwise. For one day we may put off the burden of our polluted consciences, and rejoice in the perfections of our Savior Christ, without thinking of ourselves, without thinking of our own miserable uncleanness; but contemplating His glory, His righteousness, His purity, His majesty, His overflowing love. We may rejoice in the Lord, and in all His creatures see Him. We may enjoy His temporal bounty, and partake the pleasant things of earth with Him in our thoughts; we may rejoice in our friends for His sake, loving them most especially because He has loved them.

"God has not appointed us unto wrath, but to obtain salvation through our Lord Jesus Christ, who died for us, that whether we wake or sleep, we should live together with Him." Let us seek the grace of a cheerful heart, an even temper, sweetness, gentleness, and brightness of mind, as walking in His light, and by His grace. Let us pray Him to give us the spirit of ever-abundant, ever-springing love, which overpowers and sweeps away the vexations of life by its own richness and strength, and which above all things unites us to Him who is the fountain and the center of all mercy, loving-kindness, and joy.

[VIII, 17]

Selected Prayers, Verses, and Devotions

John Henry Newman's devotional writings profoundly express his sense of the mystical reality of God in his own personal experience. Religious faith for Newman was a matter not of theories and ideas about God but, rather, of a life illuminated by an unwavering trust in the invisible presence of God veiled by the circumstances of ordinary life. Whether Newman was in favor or out of favor with the social and religious currents of his day, his confidence in God's uniquely personal, providential grace bearing on *his* life led him to put his entire trust in this Great Friend, whose unseen hand supported him throughout the seasons of his time on earth.

The contemporary French Oratorian and theologian Louis Bouyer has indicated that Newman's devotional writings convey his adherence both to Scripture and to the sacred liturgy. Together these are the very wellsprings of the patristic spirituality which so impressed him as the authentic source of Christianity. Not only, then, did Newman preach the wisdom of revealed religion but he clung to its truths with all his heart, mind, and soul in his personal piety. These devotions, composed over a long lifetime of prayer, preaching, and service to the people of God, manifest Newman's deep, abiding faith.

In honor of Mary, Mother of Christ, Cardinal Newman wrote meditations for the month of May following the titles given to her in the traditional Litany of Loretto. Newman had preached a sermon while at Oxford on the feast of the Annunciation (March 25, 1832) entitled "The Reverence Due to the Virgin Mary." In that sermon he asked:

> Who can estimate the holiness and perfection of her, who was chosen to be the Mother of Christ? If to him that hath, more is given, and holiness and divine favor go together (and this we are expressly told), what must have been the transcendent purity of her, whom the Creator Spirit condescended to overshadow with His miraculous presence? What must have been her gifts, who was chosen to be the only near earthly relative of the Son of God, the only one

whom He was bound by nature to revere and look up to; the appointed to train and educate Him, to instruct Him day by day, as He grew in wisdom and stature? This contemplation runs to a higher subject, did we dare to follow it; for what, think you, was the sanctified state of that human nature, of which God formed His sinless Son; knowing as we do, that "that which is born of the flesh is flesh," and that "none can bring a clean thing out of an unclean?"

The Loretto meditations are prayerful answers to the questions Newman posed to the congregation when he preached this sermon. Eight have been selected, two each for the four groupings: the Immaculate Conception, the Annunciation, Our Lady's Dolors, and the Assumption.

When John Henry Newman was in Rome in 1846 to study Catholic theology following his conversion, and while casting about as to how to live his vocation in the Church of Rome, he discovered the Oratory of St. Philip Neri, which had been founded in 1575 as a form of community life for secular priests. A group of priests would live together, bound not by vows but by mutual charity, in a town or city where their common life would radiate its influence by their preaching, teaching, and study of the faith. Newman investigated the life of Philip Neri (1515–1595) and found him a most impressive character, a man of serenity, humility, and unaffected love for others. He took Philip as his spiritual friend and model. Consequently, in 1848 Newman was appointed by Pope Pius IX to establish the Oratory in England. Included here is one of Newman's many prayers to St. Philip Neri.

Newman's *Meditations on Christian Doctrine* are deeply personal, confessional, spiritual devotions written in the first person and addressed directly to God. They give voice to praise, thanksgiving, sorrow for sin, faith and confidence, and earnest petitions for grace and perseverance. These meditations express the same fundamental theological themes of the sermons in an ardent, heartfelt fervor that reveals the fire of love burning in Newman's soul for his God and Savior. The examples included here reflect the themes of the selected sermons.

The occasional verses were begun in Newman's youth, starting at age seventeen, and continued through the next fifty years, until

1870. Though he was not a strong poet, these verses frequently express real insight, and they certainly convey his palpable sense of the near and felt presence of unseen spiritual influences.

The Dream of Gerontius was written in January of 1865 and published almost immediately that spring. A meditation on the moment of death, which is followed by judgment and purgatory, this long poem has perdured in its power to give consolation and assurance that Christ does closely abide throughout the sufferings and torment at the end of life to bring the dying soul safely home to the promised serenity and joy of eternal union with Christ and His saints.

The final offering of these selections from the poetry and devotional works of Newman is the lovely "Prayer," excerpted from one of his sermons, "Wisdom and Innocence."

Mary Is the "Domus Aurea," the House of Gold

MAY 6

Why is she called a *House?* And why is she called *Golden?* Gold is the most beautiful, the most valuable, of all metals. Silver, copper, and steel may in their way be made good to the eye, but nothing is so rich, so splendid, as gold. We have few opportunities of seeing it in any quantity; but anyone who has seen a large number of bright gold coins knows how magnificent is the look of gold. Hence it is that in Scripture the Holy City is, by a figure of speech, called Golden. "The City," says St. John, "was pure gold, as it were transparent glass." He means of course to give us a notion of the wondrous beautifulness of heaven, by comparing it with what is the most beautiful of all the substances which we see on earth.

Therefore it is that Mary too is called *golden;* because her graces, her virtues, her innocence, her purity, are of that transcendent brilliancy and dazzling perfection, so costly, so exquisite, that the angels cannot, so to say, keep their eyes off her any more than *we* could help gazing upon any great work of gold.

But observe further, she is a *golden house,* or, I will rather say, a *golden palace.* Let us imagine we saw a whole palace or large church all made of gold, from the foundations to the roof; such, in regard to the number, the variety, the extent of her spiritual excellences, is Mary.

Mary Is "Sancta Maria,"
the Holy Mary

MAY 9

God alone can claim the attribute of holiness. Hence we say in the Hymn, *"Tu solus sanctus,"* "Thou only art holy." By holiness we mean the absence of whatever sullies, dims, and degrades a rational nature; all that is most opposite and contrary to sin and guilt.

We say that God alone is *holy,* though in truth *all* His high attributes are possessed by Him in that fullness, that it may be truly said that He alone has them. Thus, as to goodness, our Lord said to the young man, "None is good but God alone." He too alone is Power, He alone is Wisdom, He alone is Providence, Love, Mercy, Justice, Truth. This is true; but holiness is singled out as His special prerogative, because it marks more than His other attributes, not only His superiority over all His creatures, but emphatically His separation from them. Hence we read in the Book of Job, "Can man be justified compared with God, or he that is born of a woman appear clean? Behold, even the moon doth not shine, and the stars are not pure, in His sight." "Behold, among His saints none is unchangeable, and the heavens are not pure in His sight."

This we must receive and understand in the first place; but secondly we know too, that, in His mercy, He has communicated in various measures His great attributes to His rational creatures, and, first of all, as being most necessary, holiness. Thus Adam, from the time of his creation, was gifted, over and above his nature as man, with the grace of God, to unite him to God, and to make him holy. Grace is therefore called holy grace; and, as being holy, it is the connecting principle between God and man. Adam in paradise might have had knowledge, and skill, and many virtues; but these gifts did not unite him to his Creator. It was holiness that united him, for it is said by St. Paul, "Without holiness no man shall see God."

And so again, when man fell and lost this holy grace, he had various gifts still adhering to him; he might be, in a certain measure, true, merciful, loving, and just; but these virtues did not unite him to God. What he needed was holiness; and therefore the first act of God's goodness to us in the Gospel is to take us out of our *un*holy state by means of the sacrament of Baptism, and by the grace then given us to reopen the communications, so long closed, between the soul and heaven.

We see then the force of our Lady's title, when we call her "*Holy* Mary." When God would prepare a human mother for His Son, this was why He began by giving her an immaculate conception. He began, not by giving her the gift of love, or truthfulness, or gentleness, or devotion, though according to the occasion she had them all. But He began His great work before she was born; before she could think, speak, or act, by making her *holy,* and thereby, while on earth, a citizen of heaven. "*Tota* pulchra es, Maria!" Nothing of the deformity of sin was ever hers. Thus she differs from all Saints. There have been great missionaries, confessors, bishops, doctors, pastors. They have done great works, and have taken with them numberless converts or penitents to heaven. They have suffered much, and have a superabundance of merits to show. But Mary in this way resembles her Divine Son, viz. that, as He, being God, is separate by holiness from all creatures, so she is separate from all Saints and Angels, as being "*full of grace.*"

On the Annunciation

Mary Is the "*Regina Angelorum,*" the Queen of Angels

MAY 10

This great title may be fitly connected with the Maternity of Mary, that is, with the coming upon her of the Holy Ghost at Nazareth after the Angel Gabriel's annunciation to her, and with the consequent birth of our Lord at Bethlehem. She, as the Mother of our Lord, comes nearer to Him than any Angel; nearer even than the Seraphim who surround Him, and cry continually, "Holy, Holy, Holy."

The two Archangels who have a special office in the Gospel are St. Michael and St. Gabriel—and they both of them are associated in the history of the Incarnation with Mary: St. Gabriel, when the

Holy Ghost came down upon her; and St. Michael, when the Divine Child was born.

St. Gabriel hailed her as "full of grace," and as "blessed among women," and announced to her that the Holy Ghost would come down upon her, and that she would bear a Son who would be the Son of the Highest.

Of St. Michael's ministry to her, on the birth of that Divine Son, we learn in the Apocalypse, written by the Apostle St. John. We know our Lord came to set up the kingdom of heaven among men; and hardly was He born when He was assaulted by the powers of the world who wished to destroy Him. Herod sought to take His life, but he was defeated by St. Joseph's carrying His Mother and Him off into Egypt. But St. John in the Apocalypse tells us that Michael and his Angels were the real guardians of Mother and Child, then and on other occasions.

First, St. John saw in vision "a great sign in heaven" (meaning by "heaven" the Church, or kingdom of God), a woman clothed with the sun, and with the moon under her feet, and on her head a crown of twelve stars"; and when she was about to be delivered of her Child there appeared "a great red dragon," that is, the evil spirit, ready "to devour her Son" when He should be born. The Son was preserved by His own Divine Power, but next the evil spirit persecuted her; St. Michael, however, and his Angels came to the rescue and prevailed against him.

"There was a great battle," says the sacred writer; "Michael and his Angels fought with the dragon, and the dragon fought and his angels; and that great dragon was cast out, the old serpent, who is called the devil." Now, as then, the Blessed Mother of God has hosts of Angels who do her service; and she is their Queen.

Mary Is the "Speculum Justitiæ," the Mirror of Justice

MAY 11

Here first we must consider what is meant by *justice,* for the word as used by the Church has not that sense which it bears in ordinary English. By *justice* is not meant the virtue of fairness, equity, uprightness in our dealings; but it is a word denoting all virtues at once, a perfect, virtuous state of soul—righteousness, or moral perfection; so that it answers very nearly to what is meant by *sanctity*. Therefore when our Lady is called the "Mirror of Justice," it is meant to say that she is the mirror of sanctity, holiness, supernatural goodness.

Next, what is meant by calling her a *mirror?* A mirror is a surface which reflects, as still water, polished steel, or a looking glass. What did Mary reflect? She reflected our Lord—but *He* is infinite *Sanctity*. She then, as far as a creature could, reflected His Divine sanctity, and therefore she is the *Mirror* of Sanctity, or, as the Litany says, of *Justice*.

Do we ask how she came to reflect His Sanctity?—it was by living with Him. We see every day how like people get to each other who live with those they love. When they live with those whom they don't love, as, for instance, the members of a family who quarrel with each other, then the longer they live together the more unlike each other they become; but when they love each other, as husband and wife, parents and children, brothers with brothers or sisters, friends with friends, then in course of time they get surprisingly like each other. All of us perceive this; we are witnesses to it with our own eyes and ears—in the expression of their features, in their voice, in their walk, in their language, even in their handwriting, they become like each other; and so with regard to their minds, as in their opinions, their tastes, their pursuits. And again doubtless in the state of their souls, which we do not see, whether for good or for bad.

Now, consider that Mary loved her Divine Son with an unutterable love; and consider too she had Him all to herself for thirty years. Do we not see that, as she was full of grace *before* she conceived Him in her womb, she must have had a vast incomprehensible sanctity when she had lived close to God for thirty years?—a sanctity of an angelical order, reflecting back the attributes of God with a fullness and exactness of which no saint upon earth, or hermit, or holy virgin, can even remind us. Truly then she is the *Speculum Justitiæ,* the *Mirror* of Divine *Perfection*.

OUR LADY'S DOLORS

Mary Is the "Regina Martyrum," the Queen of Martyrs*

MAY 17

Why is she so called?—she who never had any blow, or wound, or other injury to her consecrated person. How can she be exalted over those whose bodies suffered the most ruthless violences and the keenest torments for our Lord's sake? She is, indeed, Queen of all Saints, of those who "walk with Christ in white, for they are worthy"; but how of those "who were slain for the Word of God, and for the testimony which they held"?

To answer this question, it must be recollected that the pains of the soul may be as fierce as those of the body. Bad men who are now in hell, and the elect of God who are in purgatory, are suffering only in their souls, for their bodies are still in the dust; yet how severe is that suffering! And perhaps most people who have lived long can bear witness in their own persons to a sharpness of distress which was like a sword cutting them, to a weight and force of sorrow which seemed to throw them down, though bodily pain there was none.

What an overwhelming horror it must have been for the Blessed Mary to witness the Passion and the Crucifixion of her Son! Her anguish was, as Holy Simeon had announced to her, at the time of that Son's Presentation in the Temple, a sword piercing her soul. If our Lord Himself could not bear the prospect of what was before Him, and was covered in the thought of it with a bloody sweat, His soul thus acting upon His body, does not this show how great mental pain can be? and would it have been wonderful though Mary's head and heart had given way as she stood under His Cross?

Thus is she most truly the Queen of *Martyrs*.

*From this day to the end of the month, being the Novena, and Octave of St. Philip, the meditations are shorter than the foregoing.—J.H.N.

Mary Is the "Consolatrix Afflictorum," the Consoler of the Afflicted

MAY 21

St. Paul says that his Lord comforted him in all his tribulations, that he also might be able to comfort them who are in distress, by the encouragement which he received from God. This is the secret of true consolation: those are able to comfort others who, in their own case, have been much tried, and have felt the need of consolation, and have received it. So of our Lord Himself it is said: "In that He Himself hath suffered and been tempted, He is able to succor those also that are tempted."

And this too is why the Blessed Virgin is the comforter of the afflicted. We all know how special a mother's consolation is, and we are allowed to call Mary our Mother from the time that our Lord from the Cross established the relation of mother and son between her and St. John. And she especially can console us because she suffered more than mothers in general. Women, at least delicate women, are commonly shielded from rude experience of the highways of the world; but she, after our Lord's Ascension, was sent out into foreign lands almost as the Apostles were, a sheep among wolves. In spite of all St. John's care of her, which was as great as was St. Joseph's in her younger days, she, more than all the Saints of God, was a stranger and a pilgrim upon earth, in proportion to her greater love of Him who *had* been on earth, and had gone away. As, when our Lord was an Infant, she had to flee across the desert to the heathen Egypt, so, when He had ascended on high, she had to go on shipboard to the heathen Ephesus, where she lived and died.

O ye who are in the midst of rude neighbors or scoffing companions, or of wicked acquaintance, or of spiteful enemies, and are helpless, invoke the aid of Mary by the memory of her own sufferings among the heathen Greeks and the heathen Egyptians.

ON THE ASSUMPTION

Mary is the "Turris Davidica," the Tower of David

MAY 27

A tower in its simplest idea is a fabric for defense against enemies. David, King of Israel, built for this purpose a notable tower; and as he is a figure or type of our Lord, so is his tower a figure denoting our Lord's Virgin Mother.

She is called the *Tower* of David because she had so signally fulfilled the office of defending her Divine Son from the assaults of His foes. It is customary with those who are not Catholics to fancy that the honors we pay to her interfere with the supreme worship which we pay to Him; that in Catholic teaching she eclipses Him. But this is the very reverse of the truth.

For if Mary's glory is so very great, how cannot His be greater still who is the Lord and God of Mary? He is infinitely above His Mother; and all that grace which filled her is but the overflowings and superfluities of His incomprehensible Sanctity. And history teaches us the same lesson. Look at the Protestant countries which threw off all devotion to her three centuries ago, under the notion that to put her from their thoughts would be exalting the praises of her Son. Has that consequence really followed from their profane conduct towards her? Just the reverse—the countries, Germany, Switzerland, England, which so acted, have in great measure ceased to worship Him, and have given up their belief in His Divinity; while the Catholic Church, wherever she is to be found, adores Christ as true God and true Man, as firmly as ever she did; and strange indeed would it be, if it ever happened otherwise. Thus Mary is the "Tower of David."

Mary Is the "Stella Matutina," the Morning Star—After the Dark Night, but Always Heralding the Sun

MAY 31

What is the nearest approach in the way of symbols, in this world of sight and sense, to represent to us the glories of that higher world which is beyond our bodily perceptions? What are the truest tokens and promises here, poor though they may be, of what one day we hope to see hereafter, as being beautiful and rare? Whatever they may be, surely the Blessed Mother of God may claim them as her own. And so it is; two of them are ascribed to her as her titles, in her Litany—the stars above, and flowers below. She is at once the *Rosa Mystica* and the *Stella Matutina*.

And of these two, both of them well suited to her, the Morning Star becomes her best, and that for three reasons.

First, the rose belongs to this earth, but the star is placed in high heaven. Mary now has no part in this netherworld. No change, no violence from fire, water, earth, or air, affects the stars above; and they show themselves, ever bright and marvelous, in all regions of this globe, and to all the tribes of men.

And next, the rose has but a short life; its decay is as sure as it was graceful and fragrant in its noon. But Mary, like the stars, abides forever, as lustrous now as she was on the day of her Assumption; as pure and perfect, when her Son comes to judgment, as she is now.

Lastly, it is Mary's prerogative to be the *Morning* Star, which heralds in the sun. She does not shine for herself, or from herself, but she is the reflection of her and our Redeemer, and she glorifies Him. When she appears in the darkness, we know that He is close at hand. He is Alpha and Omega, the First and the Last, the Beginning and the End. Behold He comes quickly, and His reward is with Him, to render to everyone according to his works. "Surely I come quickly. Amen. Come, Lord Jesus."

From **FOUR PRAYERS TO ST. PHILIP**

PRAYER 2

O my dear and holy Patron, Philip, I put myself into thy hands, and for the love of Jesus, for that love's sake, which chose thee and made thee a Saint, I implore thee to pray for me, that, as He has brought thee to heaven, so in due time He may take me to heaven also.

And I ask of thee especially to gain for me a true devotion such as thou hadst to the Holy Ghost, the Third Person in the Ever-blessed Trinity; that, as He at Pentecost so miraculously filled thy heart with his grace, I too may in my measure have the gifts necessary for my salvation.

Therefore I ask thee to gain for me those His seven great gifts, to dispose and excite my heart towards faith and virtue.

Beg for me the gift of Wisdom, that I may prefer heaven to earth, and know truth from falsehood:

The gift of Understanding, by which I may have imprinted upon my mind the mysteries of His Word:

The gift of Counsel, that I may see my way in all perplexities:

The gift of Fortitude, that with bravery and stubbornness I may battle with my foe:

The gift of Knowledge, to enable me to direct all my doings with a pure intention to the glory of God:

The gift of Religion, to make me devout and conscientious:

And the gift of Holy Fear, to make me feel awe, reverence, and sobriety amid all my spiritual blessings.

Sweetest Father, Flower of Purity, Martyr of Charity, pray for me.

From MEDITATIONS ON CHRISTIAN DOCTRINE
God with Us

(1)
The Familiarity of Jesus

1. The Holy Baptist was separated from the world. He was a
Nazarite. He went out from the world, and placed himself over
against it, and spoke to it from his vantage ground, and called it to
repentance. Then went out all Jerusalem to him into the desert,
and he confronted it face to face. But in his teaching he spoke of
One who should come to them and speak to them in a far different way. He should not separate Himself from them, He should
not display Himself as some higher being, but as their brother, as
of their flesh and of their bones, as one among many brethren, as
one of the multitude and amidst them; nay, He was among them
already. *"Medius vestrum stetit, quem vos nescitis"*—"there hath
stood in the midst of you, whom you know not." That greater one
called Himself the Son of Man—He was content to be taken as
ordinary in all respects, though He was the Highest. St. John and
the other Evangelists, though so different in the character of their
accounts of Him, agree most strikingly here. The Baptist says,
"There is in the midst of you One whom you know not." Next we
read of his pointing Jesus out privately, not to crowds, but to one
or two of his own religious followers; then of their seeking Jesus
and being allowed to follow Him home. At length Jesus begins to
disclose Himself and to manifest His glory in miracles; but
where? At a marriage feast, where there was often excess, as the
architriclinus implies. And how? in adding to the wine, the
instrument of such excess, when it occurred. He was at that marriage feast not as a teacher, but as a guest, and (so to speak) in a
social way, for He was with His Mother. Now compare this with
what He says in St. Matthew's Gospel of Himself: "John came
neither eating nor drinking—The Son of Man came eating and

drinking, and they say: Behold a man that is a glutton and wine drinker." John might be hated, but he was respected; Jesus was despised. See also Mark 1:22, 27, 37, 3:21, for the astonishment and rudeness of all about Him. The objection occurs *at once,* 2:16. What a marked feature it must have been of our Lord's character and mission, since two Evangelists, so independent in their narrations, record it! The Prophet had said the same (Isai. 53. "He shall," et cetera).

2. This was, O dear Lord, because Thou so lovest this human nature which Thou hast created. Thou didst not love us merely as Thy creatures, the work of Thy hands, but as men. Thou lovest all, for Thou hast created all; but Thou lovest man more than all. How is it, Lord, that this should be? What is there in man, above others? *Quid est homo, quod memor es ejus? yet, nusquam Angelos apprehendit*—"What is man, that Thou art mindful of him?". . . "nowhere doth he take hold of the Angels." Who can sound the depth of Thy counsels and decrees? Thou hast loved man more than Thou hast loved the Angels: and therefore, as Thou didst not take on Thee an angelic nature when Thou didst manifest Thyself for our salvation, so too Thou wouldest not come in any shape or capacity or office which was above the course of ordinary human life—not as a Nazarene, not as a Levitical priest, not as a monk, not as a hermit, but in the fullness and exactness of that human nature which so much Thou lovest. Thou camest not only a perfect man, but as proper man; not formed anew out of earth, not with the spiritual body which Thou now hast, but in that very flesh which had fallen in Adam, and with all our infirmities, all our feelings and sympathies, sin expected.

3. O Jesu, it became Thee, the great God, thus abundantly and largely to do Thy work, for which the Father sent Thee. Thou didst not do it by halves—and, while that magnificence of Sacrifice is Thy glory as God, it is our consolation and aid as sinners. O dearest Lord, Thou art more fully man than the holy Baptist, than St. John, Apostle and Evangelist, than Thy own sweet Mother. As in Divine knowledge of me Thou are beyond them all, so also in experience and personal knowledge of my nature. Thou are my elder brother. How can I fear, how should I not repose my whole heart on one so gentle, so tender, so familiar, so

unpretending, so modest, so natural, so humble? Thou art now, though in heaven, just the same as Thou wast on earth: the mighty God, yet the little child—the all-holy, yet the all-sensitive, all-human.

(2)

Jesus the Hidden God

Noli incredulus esse, sed fidelis.
Be not faithless, but believing.

1. I adore Thee, O my God, who are so awful, because Thou art hidden and unseen! I adore Thee, and I desire to live by faith in what I do not see; and considering what I am, a disinherited out-cast, I think it has indeed gone well with me that I am allowed, O my unseen Lord and Savior, to worship Thee anyhow. O my God, I know that it is sin that has separated between Thee and me. I know it is sin that has brought on me the penalty of igno-rance. Adam, before he fell, was visited by Angels. Thy Saints, too, who keep close to Thee, see visions, and in many ways are brought into sensible perception of Thy presence. But to a sinner such as I am, what is left but to possess Thee without seeing Thee? Ah, should I not rejoice at having the most extreme mercy and favor of possessing Thee at all? It is sin that has reduced me to live by faith, as I must at best, and should I not rejoice in such a life, O Lord my God? I see and know, O my good Jesus, that the only way in which I can possibly approach Thee in this world is the way of faith, faith in what Thou hast told me, and I thank-fully follow this only way which Thou hast given me.

2. O my God, Thou dost overabound in mercy! To live by faith is my necessity, from my present state of being and from my sin; but Thou hast pronounced a blessing on it. Thou hast said that I am more blessed if I believe on Thee, than if I saw Thee. Give me to share that blessedness, give it to me in its fullness. Enable me to believe as if I saw; let me have Thee always before me as if Thou wert always bodily and sensibly present. Let me ever hold communion with Thee, my hidden, but my living God. Thou art in my innermost heart. Thou art the life of my life. Every breath I breathe, every thought of my mind, every good

desire of my heart, is from the presence within me of the unseen God. By nature and by grace Thou are in me. I see Thee not in the material world except dimly, but I recognize Thy voice in my own intimate consciousness. I turn round and say Rabboni, O be ever thus with me; and if I am tempted to leave *Thee,* do not Thou, O my God, leave *me!*

3. O my dear Savior, would that I had any right to ask to be allowed to make reparation to Thee for all the unbelief of the world, and all the insults offered to Thy Name, Thy Word, Thy Church, and the Sacrament of Thy Love! But, alas, I have a long score of unbelief and ingratitude of my own to atone for. Thou art in the Sacrifice of the Mass, Thou art in the Tabernacle, verily and indeed, in flesh and blood; and the world not only disbelieves, but mocks at this gracious truth. Thou didst warn us long ago by Thyself and by Thy Apostles that Thou wouldest hide Thyself from the world. The prophecy is fulfilled more than ever now; but *I* know what the world knows not. O accept my homage, my praise, my adoration!—let me at least not be found wanting. I cannot help the sins of others—but one at least of those whom Thou hast redeemed shall turn around and with a loud voice glorify God. The more men scoff, the more will I believe in Thee, the good God, the good Jesus, the hidden Lord of life, who hast done me nothing else but good from the very first moment that I began to live.

(3)
Jesus the Light of the Soul

Mane nobiscum, Domine, quoniam advesperascit.
Stay with us, because it is towards evening.

1. I adore Thee, O my God, as the true and only Light! From Eternity to Eternity, before any creature was, when Thou wast alone, alone but not solitary, for Thou hast ever been Three in One, Thou wast the Infinite Light. There was none to see Thee but Thyself. The Father saw that Light in the Son, and the Son in the Father. Such as Thou wast in the beginning, such Thou art now. Most separate from all creatures in this Thy uncreated Brightness. Most glorious, most beautiful. Thy attributes are so

many separate and resplendent colors, each as perfect in its own purity and grace as if it were the sole and highest perfection. Nothing created is more than the very shadow of Thee. Bright as are the Angels, they are poor and most unworthy shadows of Thee. They pale and look dim and gather blackness before Thee. They are so feeble beside Thee, that they are unable to gaze upon Thee. The highest Seraphim veil their eyes, by deed as well as by word proclaiming Thy unutterable glory. For me, I cannot even look upon the sun, and what is this but a base material emblem of Thee? How should I endure to look even on an Angel? and how could I look upon Thee and live? If I were placed in the illumination of Thy countenance, I should shrink up like the grass. O most gracious God, who shall approach Thee, being so glorious, yet how can I keep from Thee?

2. How can I keep from Thee? For Thou, who are the Light of Angels, art the only Light of my soul. Thou enlightenest every man that cometh into this world. I am utterly dark, as dark as hell, without Thee. I droop and shrink when Thou art away. I revive only in proportion as Thou dawnest upon me. Thou comest and goest at Thy will. O my God, I cannot keep Thee! I can only beg of Thee to stay. *"Mane nobiscum, Domine, quoniam advesperascit."* Remain till morning, and then go not without giving me a blessing. Remain with me till death in this dark valley, when the darkness will end. Remain, O Light of my soul, *jam advesperascit!* The gloom, which is not Thine, falls over me. I am nothing. I have little command of myself. I cannot do what I would. I am disconsolate and sad. I want something, I know not what. It is Thou that I want, though I so little understand this. I say it and take it on faith; I partially understand it, but very poorly. Shine on me, *O Ignis semper ardens et nunquam deficiens!*— "O fire ever burning and never failing"—and I shall begin, through and in Thy Light, to see Light, and to recognize Thee truly, as the Source of Light. *Mane nobiscum;* stay, sweet Jesus, stay forever. In this decay of nature, give more grace.

3. Stay with me, and then I shall begin to shine as Thou shinest: so to shine as to be a light to others. The light, O Jesus, will be all from Thee. None of it will be mine. No merit to me. It will be Thou who shinest through me upon others. Oh let me thus praise Thee, in the way which Thou dost love best, by shin-

ing on all those around me. Give light to them as well as to me; light them with me, through me. Teach me to show forth Thy praise, Thy truth, Thy will. Make me preach Thee without preaching—not by words, but by my example and by the catching force, the sympathetic influence, of what I do—by my visible resemblance to Thy Saints, and the evident fullness of the love which my heart bears to Thee.

God Alone Unchangeable

Quo ego vado, non potes Me modo sequi, sequeris autem postea.
Whither I go, thou canst not follow Me now, but thou shalt follow hereafter.

1. Thou alone, O my God, are what Thou ever hast been! Man changes. Thou art unchangeable; nay, even as Man Thou hast ever been unchangeable, for Jesus is yesterday and today Himself, and forever. Thy word endureth in heaven and earth. Thy decrees are fixed; Thy gifts are without repentance. Thy Nature, Thy Attributes, are ever the same. There ever was Father, ever Son, ever Holy Ghost. I adore Thee in the peace and serenity of Thy unchangeableness. I adore Thee in that imperturbable heaven, which is Thyself. Thou wast perfect from the first; nothing couldest Thou gain, and nothing mightest Thou lose. There was nothing that could touch Thee, because there was nothing but what Thou didst create and couldst destroy. Again, I adore Thee in this Thy infinite stability, which is the center and stay of all created things.

2. Man on the contrary is ever changing. Not a day passes but I am nearer the grave. Whatever be my age, whatever the number of my years, I am ever narrowing the interval between time and eternity. I am ever changing in myself. Youth is not like age; and I am continually changing, as I pass along out of youth towards the end of life. O my God, I am crumbling away, as I go on! I am already dissolving into my first elements. My soul indeed cannot die, for Thou hast made it immortal; but my bodily frame is continually resolving into that dust out of which it was taken. All below heaven changes: spring, summer, autumn, each has its

turn. The fortunes of the world change; what was high lies low; what was low rises high. Riches take wings and flee away; bereavements happen. Friends become enemies, and enemies friends. Our wishes, aims, and plans change. There is nothing stable but Thou, O my God! And Thou art the center and life of all who change, who trust Thee as their Father, who look to Thee, and who are content to put themselves into Thy hands.

3. I know, O my God, I must change, if I am to see Thy face! I must undergo the change of death. Body and soul must die to this world. My real self, my soul, must change by a true regeneration. None but the holy can see Thee. Like Peter, I cannot have a blessing now, which I shall have afterwards. "Thou canst not follow Me now, but thou shalt follow hereafter." Oh, support me, as I proceed in this great, awful, happy change, with the grace of Thy unchangeableness. My unchangeableness here below is perseverance in changing. Let me day by day be molded upon Thee, and be changed from glory to glory, by ever looking towards Thee, and ever leaning on Thy arm. I know, O Lord, I must go through trial, temptation, and much conflict, if I am to come to Thee. I know not what lies before me, but I know as much as this. I know, too, that if Thou art not with me, my change will be for the worse, not for the better. Whatever fortune I have, be I rich or poor, healthy or sick, with friends or without, all will turn to evil if I am not sustained by the Unchangeable; all will turn to good if I have Jesus with me, yesterday and today the same, and forever.

THE PROVIDENCE OF GOD

1. I adore Thee, my God, as having laid down the ends and the means of all things which Thou hast created. Thou hast created everything for some end of its own, and Thou dost direct it to that end. The end, which Thou didst in the beginning appoint for man, is Thy worship and service, and his own happiness in paying it; a blessed eternity of soul and body with Thee forever. Thou hast provided for this, and that in the case of every man. As Thy hand and eye are upon the brute creation, so are they upon us.

Thou sustainest everything in life and action for its own end. Not a reptile, not an insect, but Thou seest and makest to live, while its time lasts. Not a sinner, not an idolater, not a blasphemer, not an atheist lives, but by Thee, and in order that he may repent. Thou art careful and tender to each of the beings that Thou hast created, as if it were the only one in the whole world. For Thou canst see every one of them at once, and Thou lovest every one in this mortal life, and pursuest every one by itself, with all the fullness of Thy Attributes, as if Thou wast waiting on it and ministering to it for its own sake. My God, I love to contemplate Thee, I love to adore Thee, thus the wonderful worker of all things every day in every place.

2. All Thy acts of Providence are acts of love. If Thou sendest evil upon us, it is in love. All the evils of the physical world are intended for the good of Thy creatures, or are the unavoidable attendants on that good. And Thou turnest that evil into good. Thou visitest men with evil to bring them to repentance, to increase their virtue, to gain for them greater good hereafter. Nothing is done in vain, but has its gracious end. Thou dost punish, yet in wrath Thou dost remember mercy. Even Thy justice when it overtakes the impenitent sinner, who had exhausted Thy loving providences towards him, is mercy to others, as saving them from his contamination, or granting them a warning. I acknowledge with a full and firm faith, O Lord, the wisdom and goodness of Thy Providence, even in Thy inscrutable judgments and Thy incomprehensible decrees.

3. O my God, my whole life has been a course of mercies and blessings shown to one who has been most unworthy of them. I require no faith, for I have had long experience, as to Thy Providence towards me. Year after year Thou hast carried me on— removed dangers from my path—recovered me, recruited me, refreshed me, borne with me, directed me, sustained me. Oh forsake me not when my strength faileth me. And Thou never wilt forsake me. I may securely repose upon Thee. Sinner as I am, nevertheless, while I am true to Thee, Thou wilt still and to the end, be superabundantly true to me. I may rest upon Thy arm; I may go to sleep in Thy bosom. Only give me, and increase in me, that true loyalty to Thee, which is the bond of the covenant

between Thee and me, and the pledge in my own heart and conscience that Thou, the Supreme God, wilt not forsake me, the most miserable of Thy children.

GOD COMMUNICATED TO US

1. Thou hast, O Lord, an incommunicable perfection, but still that Omnipotence by which Thou didst create, is sufficient also to the work of communicating Thyself to the spirits which Thou hast created. Thy Almighty Life is not for our destruction, but for our living. Thou remainest ever one and the same in Thyself, but there goes from Thee continually a power and virtue, which by its contact is our strength and good. I do not know how this can be; my reason does not satisfy me here; but in nature I see intimations, and by faith I have full assurance of the truth of this mystery. By Thee we cross the gulf that lies between Thee and us. The Living God is life-giving. Thou art the Fount and Center, as well as the Seat, of all good. The traces of Thy glory, as the many-colored rays of the sun, are scattered over the whole face of nature, without diminution of Thy Perfections, or violation of Thy transcendent and unapproachable Essence. How it can be, I know not; but so it is. And thus, remaining one and sole and infinitely removed from all things, still Thou are the fullness of all things, in Thee they consist, of Thee they partake, and into Thee, retaining their own individuality, they are absorbed. And thus, while we droop and decay in our own nature, we live by Thy breath; and Thy grace enables us to endure Thy presence.

2. Make me then like Thyself, O my God, since, in spite of myself, such Thou canst make me, such I can be made. Look on me, O my Creator, pity the work of Thy hands, *ne peream in infirmitate meâ*—"that I perish not in my infirmity." Take me out of my natural imbecility, since that is possible for me, which is so necessary. Thou hast shown it to be possible in the face of the whole world by the most overwhelming proof, by taking our created nature on Thyself, and exalting it in Thee. Give me in my own self the benefit of this wondrous truth, now it has been so publicly ascertained and guaranteed. Let me have in my own per-

son, what in Jesus Thou hast given to my nature. Let me be partaker of that Divine Nature in all the riches of its Attributes, which in fullness of substance and in personal presence became the Son of Mary. Give me that life, suitable to my own need, which is stored up for us all in Him who is the Life of men. Teach me and enable me to live the life of Saints and Angels. Take me out of the languor, the irritability, the sensitiveness, the incapability, the anarchy, in which my soul lies, and fill it with Thy fullness. Breathe on me, that the dead bones may live. Breathe on me with that Breath which infuses energy and kindles fervor. In asking for fervor, I ask for all that I can need, and all that Thou canst give; for it is the crown of all gifts and all virtues. It cannot really and fully be, except where all are at present. It is the beauty and the glory, as it is also the continual safeguard and purifier of them all. In asking for fervor, I am asking for effectual strength, consistency, and perseverance; I am asking for deadness to every human motive, and simplicity of intention to please Thee: I am asking for faith, hope, and charity in their most heavenly exercise. In asking for fervor I am asking to be rid of the fear of man, and the desire of his praise; I am asking for the gift of prayer, because it will be so sweet; I am asking for that loyal perception of duty, which follows on yearning affection; I am asking for sanctity, peace, and joy all at once. In asking for fervor, I am asking for the brightness of the Cherubim and the fire of the Seraphim, and the whiteness of all Saints. In asking for fervor, I am asking for that which, while it implies all gifts, is that in which I signally fail. Nothing would be a trouble to me, nothing a difficulty, had I but fervor of soul.

3. Lord, in asking for fervor, I am asking for Thyself, for nothing short of Thee, O my God, who hast given Thyself wholly to us. Enter my heart substantially and personally, and fill it with fervor by filling it with Thee. Thou alone canst fill the soul of man, and Thou hast promised to do so. Thou art the living Flame, and ever burnest with love of man: enter into me and set me on fire after Thy pattern and likeness.

From VERSES ON VARIOUS OCCASIONS

ANGELIC GUIDANCE

Are these the tracks of some unearthly Friend,
   His footprints, and his vesture-skirts of light,
   Who, as I talk with men, conforms aright
Their sympathetic words, or deeds that blend
With my hid thought—or stoops him to attend
   My doubtful-pleading grief—or blunts the might
   Of ill I see not—or in dreams of night
Figures the scope, in which what is will end?
Were I Christ's own, then fitly might I call
That vision real; for to the thoughtful mind
That walks with Him, He half unveils His face;
But, when on earth-stain'd souls such tokens fall,
These dare not claim as theirs what there they find,
Yet not all hopeless, eye His boundless grace.

Whitchurch
December 3, 1832

SUBSTANCE AND SHADOW

They do but grope in learning's pedant round,
   Who on the fantasies of sense bestow
   An idol substance, bidding us bow low
Before those shades of being which are found,
Stirring or still, on man's brief trial-ground;
   As if such shapes and moods, which come and go,
   Had aught of Truth or Life in their poor show,
To sway or judge, and skill to sane or wound.
Son of immortal seed, high-destined Man!
Know they dread gift—a creature, yet a cause:
Each mind is its own center, and it draws

Home to itself, and molds in its thought's span
All outward things, the vassals of its will,
Aided by heaven, by earth unthwarted still.

Falmouth
December 7, 1832

MELCHIZEDEK
*Without father, without mother, without descent; having
neither beginning of days, nor end of life.*

Thrice bless'd are they, who feel their loneliness;
    To whom nor voice of friends nor pleasant scene
    Brings aught on which the sadden'd heart can lean;
Yea, the rich earth, garb'd in her daintiest dress
Of light and joy, doth but the more oppress,
    Claiming responsive smiles and rapture high;
    Till, sick at heart, beyond the veil they fly,
Seeking His presence, who alone can bless.
Such, in strange days, the weapons of heaven's grace;
When, passing o'er the high-born Hebrew line,
He molds the vessel of His vast design;
Fatherless, homeless, reft of age and place,
Sever'd from earth, and careless of its wreck,
Born through long woe His rare Melchizedek.

Corfu
January 5, 1833

THE PILLAR OF THE CLOUD

Lead, Kindly Light, amid the encircling gloom
        Lead Thou me on!
The night is dark, and I am far from home—
        Lead Thou me on!
Keep Thou my feet; I do not ask to see

The distant scene—one step enough for me.
I was not ever thus, nor pray'd that Thou
      Shouldst lead me on.
I loved to choose and see my path, but now
      Lead Thou me on!
I loved the garish day, and, spite of fears,
Pride ruled my will: remember not past years.

So long Thy power hath blest me, sure it still
      Will lead me on,
O'er moor and fen, o'er crag and torrent, till
      The night is gone;
And with the morn those angel faces smile
Which I have loved long since, and lost awhile.

                          At sea
                      June 16, 1833

CONSOLATION
It is I; be not afraid.

When I sink down in gloom or fear,
   Hope blighted or delay'd,
Thy whisper, Lord, my heart shall cheer.
   " 'Tis I; be not afraid!"

Or, startled at some sudden blow,
   If fretful thoughts I feel,
"Fear not, it is but I!" shall flow,
   As balm my wound to heal.

Nor will I quit Thy way, though foes
   Some onward pass defend;
From each rough voice the watchword goes,
   "Be not afraid! . . . a friend!"

And oh! when judgment's trumpet clear
   Awakes me from the grave,

Still in its echo may I hear,
   "'Tis Christ; He comes to save."

At sea
June 23, 1833

ADVENT — VESPERS
Creator alme siderum.

Creator of the starry pole,
   Savior of all who live,
And light of every faithful soul,
   Jesu, these prayers receive.

Who sooner than our foe malign
   Should triumph, from above
Didst come, to be the medicine
   Of a sick world, in love;

And the deep wounds to cleanse and cure
   Of a whole race, didst go,
Pure Victim, from a Virgin pure,
   The bitter Cross unto.

Who hast a Name, and hast a Power,
   The height and depth to sway,
And Angels bow, and devils cower,
   In transport or dismay;

Thou too shalt be our Judge at length;
   Lord, in Thy grace bestow
Thy weapons of celestial strength,
   And snatch us from the foe.

Honor and glory, power and praise,
   To Father, and to Son,
And Holy Ghost, be paid always,
   The Eternal Three in One.

St. Philip in His God

Philip, on thee the glowing ray
　　Of heaven came down upon thy prayer,
To melt thy heart, and burn away
　　All that of earthly dross was there.

Thy soul became as purest glass,
　　Through which the Brightness Incarnate
In undimm'd majesty might pass,
　　Transparent and illuminate.

And so, on Philip when we gaze,
　　We see the image of his Lord;
The Saint dissolves amid the blaze
　　Which circles round the Living Word.

The Meek, the Wise, none else is here,
　　Dispensing light to men below;
His awful accents fill the ear,
　　Now keen as fire, now soft as snow.

As snow, those inward pleadings fall,
　　As soft, as bright, as pure, as cool,
With gentle weight and gradual,
　　And sink into the feverish soul.

The Sinless One, He comes to seek,
　　The dreary heart, the spirit lone,
Tender of natures proud or weak,
　　Not less than if they were His own.

He takes and scans the sinner o'er,
　　Handling His scholars one by one,
Weighing what they can bear, before
　　He gives the penance to be done.

Jesu, to Philip's sons reveal
　　That gentlest wisdom from above,

To spread compassion o'er their zeal,
   And mingle patience with their love.

The Oratory
1850

GUARDIAN ANGEL

My oldest friend, mine from the hour
   When first I drew my breath;
My faithful friend, that shall be mine,
   Unfailing, till my death;

Thou hast been ever at my side;
   My Maker to thy trust
Consign'd my soul, what time He framed
   The infant child of dust.

No beating heart in holy prayer,
   No faith, inform'd aright.
Gave me to Joseph's tutelage,
   Or Michael's conquering might.

Nor patron Saint, nor Mary's love,
   The dearest and the best,
Has known my being, as thou hast known,
   And blest, as thou hast blest,

Thou wast my sponsor at the font;
   And thou, each budding year,
Didst whisper elements of truth
   Into my childish ear.

And when, ere boyhood yet was gone,
   My rebel spirit fell,
Ah! thou didst see, and shudder too,
   Yet bear each deed of hell.

And then in turn, when judgments came,
    And scared me back again,
Thy quick soft breath was near to soothe
    And hallow every pain.

Oh! who of all thy toils and cares
    Can tell the tale complete,
To place me under Mary's smile,
    And Peter's royal feet!

And thou wilt hang about my bed,
    When life is ebbing low;
Of doubt, impatience, and of gloom,
    The jealous sleepless foe.

Mine, when I stand before the Judge;
    And mine, if spared to stay
Within the golden furnace, till
    My sin is burn'd away.

And mine, O Brother of my soul,
    When my release shall come;
Thy gentle arms shall lift me then,
    Thy wings shall waft me home.

                                    The Oratory
                                    1853

THE DREAM OF GERONTIUS

I.

GERONTIUS

Jesu, Maria—I am near to death,
    And Thou art calling me; I know it now.
Not by the token of this faltering breath,
    This chill at heart, this dampness on my brow.
(Jesu, have mercy! Mary, pray for me!)
    'Tis this new feeling, never felt before

(Be with me, Lord, in my extremity!)
    That I am going, that I am no more.
'Tis this strange innermost abandonment
    (Lover of souls! great God! I look to Thee)
This emptying out of each constituent
    And natural force, by which I come to be.
Pray for me, O my friends; a visitant
    Is knocking his dire summons at my door,
The like of whom, to scare me and to daunt,
    Has never, never come to me before;
'Tis death—O loving friends, your prayers!—'tis he! . . .
    As though my very being had given way,
    As though I was no more a substance now,
And could fall back on naught to be my stay,
    (Help, loving Lord! Thou my sole Refuge, Thou)
And turn no whither, but must needs decay
    And drop from out the universal frame
Into that shapeless, scopeless, blank abyss,
    That utter nothingness, of which I came:
This is it that has come to pass in me:
    Oh, horror! this it is, my dearest, this;
So pray for me, my friends, who have not strength to pray.

ASSISTANTS

Kyrie eleison, Christe eleison, Kyrie eleison.
Holy Mary, pray for him.
All holy Angels, pray for him.
Choirs of the righteous, pray for him.
Holy Abraham, pray for him.
St. John Baptist, St. Joseph, pray for him.
St. Peter, St. Paul, St. Andrew, St. John,
    All Apostles, all Evangelists, pray for him.
All holy Disciples of the Lord, pray for him.
All holy Innocents, pray for him.
All holy Martyrs, all holy Confessors,
    All holy Hermits, all holy Virgins.

GERONTIUS

Rouse thee, my fainting soul, and play the man;
    And through such waning span
Of life and thought as still has to be trod,
    Prepare to meet thy God.
And while the storm of that bewilderment
    Is for a season spent.
And, ere afresh the ruin on me fall,
    Use well the interval.

ASSISTANTS

Be merciful, be gracious; spare him, Lord.
Be merciful, be gracious; Lord, deliver him.
From the sins that are past;
    From Thy frown and Thine ire;
      From the perils of dying;
      From any complying
      With sin, or denying
      His God, or relying
On self, at the last;
    From the nethermost fire;
From all that is evil;
From power of the devil;
Thy servant deliver,
For once and forever.

By Thy birth, and by Thy Cross,
Rescue him from endless loss;
By Thy death and burial,
Save him from a final fall;
By Thy rising from the tomb,
    By Thy mounting up above,
    By the Spirit's gracious love,
Save him in the day of doom.

GERONTIUS

Sanctus fortis, Sanctus Deus,
    De profundis oro te,
Miserere, Judex meus,
    Parce mihi, Domine.
Firmly I believe and truly
    God is three, and God is One;
And I next acknowledge duly
    Manhood taken by the Son.
And I trust and hope most fully
    In that Manhood crucified;
And each thought and deed unruly
    Do to death, as He has died.
Simply to His grace and wholly
    Light and life and strength belong,
And I love, supremely, solely,
    Him the holy, Him the strong.
Sanctus fortis, Sanctus Deus,
    De profundis oro te,
Miserere, Judex meus,
    Parce mihi, Domine.
And I hold in veneration,
    For the love of Him alone,
Holy Church, as His creation,
    And her teachings, as His own.
And I take with joy whatever
    Now besets me, pain or fear,
And with a strong will I sever
    All the ties which bind me here.
Adoration aye be given,
    With and through the angelic host,
To the God of earth and heaven,
    Father, Son, and Holy Ghost.
Sanctus fortis, Sanctus Deus,
    De profundis oro te,
Miserere, Judex meus,
    Mortis in discrimine.

I can no more; for now it comes again,
That sense of ruin, which is worse than pain.
That masterful negation and collapse
Of all that makes me man; as though I bent
Over the dizzy brink
Of some sheer infinite descent;
Or worse, as though
Down, down forever I was falling through
The solid framework of created things,
And needs must sink and sink
Into the vast abyss. And, crueler still,
A fierce and restless fright begins to fill
The mansion of my soul. And, worse and worse,
Some bodily form of ill
Floats on the wind, with many a loathsome curse
Tainting the hallow'd air, and laughs, and flaps
Its hideous wings,
And makes me wild with horror and dismay.
O Jesu, help! pray for me, Mary, pray!
Some Angel, Jesu! such as came to Thee
In Thine own agony. . . .
Mary, pray for me. Joseph, pray for me. Mary, pray for me.

ASSISTANTS

Rescue him, O Lord, in this his evil hour,
As of old so many by Thy gracious power—
          (Amen.)
Enoch and Elias from the common doom;
          (Amen.)
Noe from the waters in a saving home;
          (Amen.)
Abraham from th' abounding guilt of Heathenesse;
          (Amen.)
Job from all his multiform and fell distress;
          (Amen.)
Isaac, when his father's knife was raised to slay;
          (Amen.)

Lot from burning Sodom on its judgment day;
     (Amen.)
Moses from the land of bondage and despair;
     (Amen.)
Daniel from the hungry lions in their lair;
     (Amen.)
And the Children Three amid the furnace-flame;
     (Amen.)
Chaste Susanna from the slander and the shame;
     (Amen.)
David from Golia and the wrath of Saul;
     (Amen.)
And the two Apostles from their prison-thrall;
     (Amen.)
Thecla from her torments;
     (Amen.)
                —so to show Thy power,
Rescue this Thy servant in his evil hour.

GERONTIUS

Novissima hora est; and I fain would sleep.
The ping has wearied me . . . Into Thy hands,
O Lord, into Thy hands. . . .

THE PRIEST

Proficiscere, anima Christiana, de hoc mundo!
Go forth upon thy journey, Christian soul!
Go from this world! Go, in the Name of God
The Omnipotent Father, who created thee!
Go, in the Name of Jesus Christ, our Lord,
Son of the Living God, who bled for thee!
Go, in the Name of the Holy Spirit, who
Hath been pour'd out on thee! Go, in the name
Of Angels and Archangels; in the name
Of Thrones and Dominations; in the name
Of Princedoms and of Powers; and in the name

Of Cherubim and Seraphim, go forth!
Go, in the name of Patriarchs and Prophets;
And of Apostles and Evangelists,
Of Martyrs and Confessors; in the name
Of holy Monks and Hermits; in the name
Of Holy Virgins; and all Saints of God,
Both men and women, go! Go on thy course;
And may thy place today be found in peace,
And may thy dwelling be the Holy Mount
Of Zion—through the Same, through Christ, our Lord.

2.

SOUL OF GERONTIUS

I went to sleep; and now I am refresh'd,
A strange refreshment: for I feel in me
An inexpressive lightness, and a sense
Of freedom, as I were at length myself,
And ne'er had been before. How still it is!
I hear no more the busy beat of time,
No, nor my fluttering breath, nor struggling pulse;
Nor does one moment differ from the next.
I had a dream; yes—someone softly said
"He's gone"; and then a sigh went round the room.
And then I surely heard a priestly voice
Cry "Subvenite"; and they knelt in prayer.
I seem to hear him still; but thin and low,
And fainter and more faint the accents come,
As at an ever-widening interval.
Ah! whence is this? What is this severance?
This silence pours a solitariness
Into the very essence of my soul;
And the deep rest, so soothing and so sweet,
Hath something too of sternness and of pain.
For it drives back my thoughts upon their spring
By a strange introversion, and perforce
I now begin to feed upon myself,
Because I have nought else to feed upon—

Am I alive or dead? I am not dead,
But in the body still; for I possess
A sort of confidence which clings to me,
That each particular organ holds its place
As heretofore, combining with the rest
Into one symmetry, that wraps me round,
And makes me man; and surely I could move,
Did I but will it, every part of me.
And yet I cannot to my sense bring home
By very trial, that I have the power.
'Tis strange; I cannot stir a hand or foot,
I cannot make my fingers or my lips
By mutual pressure witness each to each,
Nor by the eyelid's instantaneous stroke
Assure myself I have a body still.
Nor do I know my very attitude,
Nor if I stand, or lie, or sit, or kneel.

So much I know, not knowing how I know,
That the vast universe, where I have dwelt,
Is quitting me, or I am quitting it.
Or I or it is rushing on the wings
Of light or lightning on an onward course,
And we e'en now are million miles apart.
Yet . . . is this peremptory severance
Wrought out in lengthening measurements of space
Which grow and multiply by speed and time?
Or am I traversing infinity
By endless subdivision, hurrying back
From finite towards infinitesimal,
Thus dying out of the expansive world?

Another marvel: someone has me fast
Within his ample palm; 'tis not a grasp
Such as they use on earth, but all around
Over the surface of my subtle being,
As though I were a sphere, and capable
To be accosted thus, a uniform

And gentle pressure tells me I am not
Self-moving, but borne forward on my way.
And hark! I hear a singing; yet in sooth
I cannot of that music rightly say
Whether I hear, or touch, or taste the tones.
Oh, what a heart-subduing melody!

ANGEL

My work is done,
My task I o'er
And so I come,

Taking it home,
For the crown is won,
Alleluia,
Forevermore.

My Father gave
In charge to me
This child of earth
E'en from its birth,
To serve and save,
Alleluia,
And saved is he.

This child of clay
To me was given,
To rear and train
By sorrow and pain
In the narrow way,
Alleluia,
From earth to heaven.

SOUL

It is a member of that family
Of wondrous beings, who, ere the worlds were made,

Millions of ages back, have stood around
The throne of God—he never has known sin
But through those cycles all but infinite,
Has had a strong and pure celestial life,
And bore to gaze on the unveil'd face of God.
And drank from the everlasting Fount of truth,
And served Him with a keen ecstatic love.
Hark! he begins again.

ANGEL

O Lord, how wonderful in depth and height,
	But most in man, how wonderful Thou art!
With what a love, what soft persuasive might
	Victorious o'er the stubborn fleshly heart,
	Thy tale complete of saints Thou dost provide,
	To fill the thrones which angels lost through pride!

He lay a groveling babe upon the ground,
	Polluted in the blood of his first sire,
With his whole essence shatter'd and unsound,
	And coil'd around his heart a demon dire,
	Which was not of his nature, but had skill
	To bind and form his op'ning mind to ill.

Then I was sent from heaven to set right
	The balance in his soul of truth and sin,
And I have waged a long relentless fight,
	Resolved that death-environ'd spirit to win,
	Which from its fallen state, when all was lost,
	Had been repurchased at so dread a cost.

Oh, what a shifting particolor'd scene
	Of hope and fear, of triumph and dismay,
Of recklessness and penitence, has been
	The history of that dreary, lifelong fray!
	And oh, the grace to nerve him and to lead,
	How patient, prompt, and lavish at his need!

O man, strange composite of heaven and earth!
    Majesty dwarf'd to baseness! fragrant flower
Running to poisonous seed! and seeming worth
    Cloking corruption! weakness mastering power!
    Who never art so near to crime and shame,
    As when thou hast achieved some deed of name—

How should ethereal natures comprehend
    A thing made up of spirit and of clay,
Were we not task'd to nurse it and to tend,
    Link'd one to one throughout its mortal day?
    More than the Seraph in his height of place,
    The Angel-guardian knows and loves the ransom'd race.

SOUL

Now I know surely that I am at length
Out of the body; had I part with earth,
I never could have drunk those accents in,
And not have worship'd as a god the voice
That was so musical; but now I am
So whole of heart, so calm, so self-possess'd,
With such a full content, and with a sense
So apprehensive and discriminant,
As no temptation can intoxicate.
Nor have I even terror at the thought
That I am clasp'd by such a saintliness.

ANGEL

All praise to Him, at whose sublime decree
    The last are first, the first become the last;
By whom the suppliant prisoner is set free,
    By whom proud firstborns from their thrones are cast;
Who raises Mary to be Queen of heaven,
While Lucifer is left, condemn'd and unforgiven.

3.

SOUL

I will address him. Mighty one, my Lord,
My Guardian Spirit, all hail!

ANGEL

All hail, my child!
My child and brother, hail! what wouldest thou?

SOUL

I would have nothing but to speak with thee
For speaking's sake. I wish to hold with thee
Conscious communion; though I fain would know
A maze of things, were it but meet to ask,
And not a curiousness.

ANGEL

You cannot now
Cherish a wish which ought not to be wish'd.

SOUL

Then I will speak. I ever had believed
That on the moment when the struggling soul
Quitted its mortal case, forthwith it fell
Under the awful Presence of its God,
There to be judged and sent to its own place.
What lets me now from going to my Lord?

ANGEL

Thou are not let; but with extremest speed
Art hurrying to the Just and Holy Judge:
For scarcely art thou disembodied yet.
Divide a moment, as men measure time,
Into its million-million-millionth part,
Yet even less than the interval

Since thou didst leave the body; and the priest
Cried "Subvenite," and they fell to prayer;
Nay, scarcely yet have they begun to pray.

For spirits and men by different standards mete
The less and greater in the flow of time.
By sun and moon, primeval ordinances—
By stars which rise and set harmoniously—
By the recurring seasons, and the swing,
This way and that, of the suspended rod
Precise and punctual, men divide the hours,
Equal, continuous, for their common use.
Not so with us in the immaterial world;
But intervals in their succession
Are measured by the living thought alone,
And grow or wane with its intensity.
And time is not a common property;
But what is long is short, and swift is slow,
And neat is distant, as received and grasp'd
By this mind and by that, and everyone
Is standard of his own chronology.
And memory lacks its natural resting-points
O years, and centuries, and periods.
It is thy very energy of thought
Which keeps thee from thy God.

SOUL

Dear Angel, say,
Why have I now no fear at meeting Him?
Along my earthly life, the thought of death
And judgment was to me most terrible.
I had it aye before me, and I saw
The Judge severe e'en in the Crucifix.
Now that the hour is come, my fear is fled;
And at this balance of my destiny,
Now close upon me, I can forward look
With a serenest joy.

ANGEL

It is because
Then thou didst fear, that now thou dost not fear.
Thou hast forestall'd the agony, and so
For thee the bitterness of death is past.
Also, because already in thy soul
The judgment is begun. That day of doom,
One and the same for the collected world—
That solemn consummation for all flesh,
Is, in the case of each anticipate
Upon his death; and, as the last great day
In the particular judgment is rehearsed,
So now, too, ere thou comest to the Throne,
A presage falls upon thee, as a ray
Straight from the Judge, expressive of thy lot.
That calm and joy uprising in thy soul
Is first-fruit to thee of thy recompense,
And heaven begun.

4.

SOUL

But hark! upon my sense
Comes a fierce hubbub, which would make me fear
Could I be frighted.

ANGEL

We are now arrived
Close on the judgment-court; that sullen howl
Is from the demons who assemble there.
It is the middle region, where of old
Satan appeared among the sons of God,
To cast his jibes and scoffs at holy Job.
So now his legions throng the vestibule,
Hungry and wild, to claim their property,
And gather souls for hell. Hist to their cry.

SOUL

How sour and how uncouth a dissonance!

DEMONS

Lowborn clods
      Of brute earth
          They aspire
To become gods,
      By a new birth,
And an extra grace,
      And a score of merits,
          As if aught
Could stand in place
              Of the high thought,
          And the glance of fire
Of the great spirits,
The powers blest,
      The lords by right,
          The primal owners,
              Of the proud dwelling
      And realm of light—
Dispossess'd
Aside thrust,
                  Chuck'd down
      By the sheer might
Of a despot's will,
          Of a tyrant's frown.
          Who after expelling
          Their hosts, gave,
      Triumphant still,
And still unjust,
                  Each forfeit crown
      To psalm-droners,
      And canting groaners,
              To every slave,
      And pious cheat,
              And crawling knave,

Who lick'd the dust
    Under his feet.

ANGEL

It is the restless panting of their being;
Like beasts of prey, who, caged within their bars,
In a deep hideous purring have their life,
And an incessant pacing to and fro.

DEMONS

The mind bold
    And independent,
        The purpose free,
So we are told,
Must not think
    To have the ascendant.
            What's a saint?
One whose breath
    Doth the air taint
Before his death;
      A bundle of bones,
Which fools adore,
        Ha! Ha!
When life is o'er;
Which rattle and stink,
    E'en in the flesh.
We cry his pardon!
    No flesh hath he;
    Ha! Ha!
    For it hath died,
    'Tis crucified
    Day by day,
Afresh, afresh,
    Ha! Ha!
    That holy clay,
    Ha! Ha!

This gains guerdon,
So priestlings prate,
Ha! Ha!
Before the Judge,
And pleads and atones
For spite and grudge,
And bigot mood,
And envy and hate,
And greed of blood.

SOUL

How impotent they are! and yet on earth
They have repute for wondrous power and skill;
And books describe, how that the very face
Of the Evil One, if seen, would have a force
Even to freeze the blood, and choke the life
Of him who saw it.

ANGEL

In thy trial-state
Thou hadst a traitor nestling close at home,
Connatural, who with the powers of hell
Was leagued, and of thy senses kept the keys,
And to that deadliest foe unlock'd thy heart.
And therefore is it, in respect of man,
Those fallen ones show so majestical.
But, when some child of grace, Angel or Saint,
Pure and upright in his integrity
Of nature, meets the demons on their raid,
They scud away as cowards from the fight.
Nay, oft hath holy hermit in his cell,
Not yet disburden'd of mortality,
Mock'd at their threats and warlike overtures;
Or, dying, when they swarm'd, like flies, around,
Defied them, and departed to his Judge.

DEMONS

Virtue and vice,
  A knave's pretense,
    'Tis all the same;
    Ha! Ha!
      Dread of hell fire,
    Of the venomous flame,
       A coward's plea.

Give him his price,
       Saint though he be,
Ha! Ha!
   From shrewd good sense
      He'll slave for hire
    Ha! Ha!
     And does but aspire
To the heaven above
    With sordid aim.
And not from love.
     Ha! Ha!

SOUL

I see not those false spirits; shall I see
My dearest Master, when I reach His Throne?
Or hear, at least, His awful judgment-word
With personal intonation, as I now
Hear thee, not see thee, Angel? Hitherto
All has been darkness since I left the earth;
Shall I remain thus sight-bereft all through
My penance-time? If so, how comes it then
That I have hearing still, and taste, and touch,
Yet not a glimmer of that princely sense
Which binds ideas in one, and makes them live?

ANGEL

Nor touch, nor taste, nor hearing hast thou now;
Thou livest in a world of signs and types,
The presentations of most holy truths,
Living and strong, which now encompass thee.
A disembodied soul, thou hast by right
No converse with aught else beside thyself;
But, lest so stern a solitude should load
And break thy being, in mercy are vouchsafed
Some lower measures of perception,
Which seem to thee, as though through channels brought,
Through ear, or nerves, or palate, which are gone.
And thou art wrapp'd and swathed around in dreams,
Dreams that are true, yet enigmatical;
For the belongings of thy present state,
Save through such symbols, come not home to thee.
And thus thou tell'st of space, and time, and size,
Of fragrant, solid, bitter, musical,
Of fire, and of refreshment after fire;
As (let me use similitude of earth,
To aid thee in the knowledge thou dost ask)—
As ice which blisters may be said to burn.
Nor hast thou now extension, with its parts
Correlative—long habit cozens thee—
Nor power to move thyself, nor limbs to move.
Hast thou not heard of those, who after loss
Of hand or foot, still cried that they had pains
In hand or foot, as though they had it still?
So is it now with thee, who hast not lost
Thy hand or foot, but all which made up man.
So will it be, until the joyous day
Of resurrection, when thou wilt regain
All thou hast lost, new-made and glorified.
How, even now, the consummated Saints
See God in heaven, I may not explicate;
Meanwhile, let it suffice thee to possess
Such means of converse as are granted thee,
Though, till that Beatific Vision, thou are blind;

For e'en thy purgatory, which comes like fire,
Is fire without its light.

SOUL

        His will be done!
I am not worthy e'er to see again
The face of day; far less His countenance,
Who is the very sun. Natheless in life,
When I looked forward to my purgatory,
It ever was my solace to believe,
That, ere I plunged amid the avenging flame,
I had one sight of Him to strengthen me.

ANGEL

Nor rash nor vain is that presentiment;
Yes—for one moment thou shalt see thy Lord.
Thus will it be: what time thou art arraign'd
Before the dread tribunal, and thy lot
Is cast forever, should it be to sit
On His right hand among His pure elect,
Then sight, or that which to the soul is sight,
As by a lightning-flash, will come to thee,
And thou shalt see, amid the dark profound,
Whom thy soul loveth, and would fain approach—
One moment; but thou knowest not, my child,
What thou dost ask: that sight of the Most Fair
Will gladden thee, but it will pierce thee too.

SOUL

Thou speakest darkly, Angel; and an awe
Falls on me, and a fear lest I be rash.

ANGEL

There was a mortal, who is now above
In the mid glory: he, when near to die,
Was given communion with the Crucified—
Such, that the Master's very wounds were stamp'd
Upon his flesh; and, from the agony
Which thrill'd through body and soul in that embrace,
Learn that the flame of the Everlasting Love
Doth burn ere it transform. . . .

5.

. . . Hark to those sounds!
They come of tender beings angelical,
Least and most childlike of the sons of God.

FIRST CHOIR OF ANGELICALS

Praise to the Holiest in the height,
    And in the depth be praise;
In all His words most wonderful;
    Most sure in all His ways!

To us His elder race He gave
    To battle and to win,
Without the chastisement of pain,
    Without the soil of sin.

The younger son He will'd to be
    A marvel in His birth:
Spirit and flesh his parents were;
    His home was heaven and earth.

The Eternal bless'd His child, and arm'd,
    And sent him hence afar,
To serve as champion in the field
    Of elemental war.

To be His Viceroy in the world
    Of matter, and of sense;
Upon the frontier, towards the foe
    A resolute defense

ANGEL

We now have pass'd the gate, and are within
The House of Judgment; and whereas on earth
Temples and palaces are form'd of parts
Costly and rare, but all material,
So in the world of spirits naught is found,
To mold, withal, and form into a whole,
But what is immaterial; and thus
The smallest portions of this edifice,
Cornice, or frieze, or balustrade, or stair,
The very pavement is made up of life—
Of holy, blessed, and immortal beings,
Who hymn their Maker's praise continually.

SECOND CHOIR OF ANGELICALS

Praise to the Holiest in the height,
    And in the depth be praise;
In all His words most wonderful;
    Most sure in all His ways!

Woe to thee, Man! for he was found
    A recreant in the fight;
And lost his heritage of heaven,
    And fellowship with light.

Above him now the angry sky,
    Around the tempest's din;
Who once had Angels for his friends,
    Had but the brutes for kin.

O man! a savage kindred they;
    To flee that monster brood
He scaled the seaside cave, and clomb
    The giants of the wood.

With now a fear, and now a hope,
    With aids which chance supplied,
From youth to eld, from sire to son,
    He lived, and toil'd, and died.

He dreed his penance age by age;
    And step by step began
Slowly to doff his savage garb,
    And be again a man.

And quicken'd by the Almighty's breath,
    And chasten'd by His rod,
And taught by angel-visitings,
    At length he sought his God;

And learn'd to call upon His Name,
    And in His faith create
A household and a fatherland,
    A city and a state.

Glory to Him who from the mire,
    In patient length of days,
Elaborated into life
    A people to His praise!

SOUL

The sound is like the rushing of the wind—
The summer wind—among the lofty pines;
Swelling and dying, echoing round about,
Now here, now distant, wild and beautiful;
While, scatter'd from the branches it has stirr'd,
Descend ecstatic odors.

THIRD CHOIR OF ANGELICALS

Praise to the Holiest in the height,
    And in the depth be praise:
In all His words most wonderful;
    Most sure in all His ways!

The Angels, as beseemingly
    To spirit-kind was given,
At once were tried and perfected,
    And took their seats in heaven.

For them no twilight or eclipse;
    No growth and no decay:
'Twas hopeless, all-engulfing night,
    Or beatific day.

But to the younger race there rose
    A hope upon its fall;
And slowly, surely, gracefully,
    The morning dawn'd on all.

And ages, opening out, divide
    The precious, and the base,
And from the hard and sullen mass
    Mature the heirs of grace.

O man! albeit the quickening ray,
    Lit from his second birth,
Makes him at length what once he was.
    And heaven grows out of earth;

Yet still between that earth and heaven—
    His journey and his goal—
A double agony awaits
    His body and his soul.

A double debt he has to pay—
    The forfeit of his sins:

The chill of death is past, and now
　　The penance-fire begins.

Glory to Him, who evermore
　　By truth and justice reigns;
Who tears the soul from out its case,
　　And burns away its stains!

ANGEL

They sing of thy approaching agony,
Which thou so eagerly didst question of:
It is the face of the Incarnate God
Shall smite thee with that keen and subtle pain;

And yet the memory which it leaves will be
A sovereign febrifuge to heal the wound;
And yet withal it will the wound provoke,
And aggravate and widen it the more.

SOUL

Thou speakest mysteries; still methinks I know
To disengage the tangle of they words:
Yet rather would I hear the angel voice,
Than for myself be thy interpreter.

ANGEL

When then—if such thy lot—thou seest thy Judge,
The sight of Him will kindle in thy heart
All tender, gracious, reverential thoughts.
Thou wilt be sick with love, and yearn for Him,
And feel as though thou couldst but pity Him,
That one so sweet should e'er have placed Himself
At disadvantage such, as to be used
So vilely by a being so vile as thee.
There is a pleading in His pensive eyes
Will pierce thee to the quick, and trouble thee.

And thou wilt hate and loathe thyself; for, though
Now sinless, thou wilt feel that thou hast sinn'd,
As never thou didst feel; and wilt desire
To slink away, and hide thee from His sight:
And yet wilt have a longing aye to dwell
Within the beauty of His countenance.
And these two pains, so counter and so keen—
The longing for Him, when thou seest Him not;
The shame of self at thought of seeing Him—
Will be thy veriest, sharpest purgatory.

SOUL

My soul is in my hand: I have no fear—
In His dear might prepared for weal or woe.
But hark! a grand, mysterious harmony:
It floods me like the deep and solemn sound
Of many waters.

ANGEL

We have gain'd the stairs
Which rise towards the Presence-chamber; there
A band of mighty Angels keep the way
On either side, and hymn the Incarnate God.

ANGELS OF THE SACRED STAIR

Father, whose goodness none can know, but they
          Who see Thee face to face,
By man hath come the infinite display
          Of Thy victorious grace;
But fallen man—the creature of a day—
          Skills not that love to trace.
It needs, to tell the triumph Thou hast wrought,
And Angel's deathless fire, an Angel's reach of thought.

It needs that very Angel, who with awe,
          Amid the garden shade,

The great Creator in His sickness saw,
  Soothed by a creature's aid,
And agonized, as victim of the Law
  Which He Himself had made;
For who can praise Him in His depth and height,
But he who saw Him reel amid that solitary fight?

SOUL

Hark! for the lintels of the presence-gate
Are vibrating and echoing back the strain.

FOURTH CHOIR OF ANGELICALS

Praise to the Holiest in the height,
  And in the depth be praise:
In all His words most wonderful;
  Most sure in all His ways!

The foe blasphemed the Holy Lord,
  As if He reckon'd ill,
In that He placed His puppet man
  The frontier place to fill.

For, even in his best estate,
  With amplest gifts endued
A sorry sentinel was he,
  A being of flesh and blood.

As though a thing, who for his help
  Must needs possess a wife,
Could cope with those proud rebel hosts
  Who had angelic life.

And when, by blandishment of Eve,
  That earth-born Adam fell,
He skriek'd in triumph, and he cried,
  A sorry sentinel;

"The Maker by His word is bound,
   Escape or cure is none;
He must abandon to his doom,
   And slay His darling son."

ANGEL

And now the threshold, as we traverse it,
Utters aloud its glad responsive chant.

FIFTH CHOIR OF ANGELICALS

Praise to the Holiest in the height
   And in the depth be praise:
In all His words most wonderful;
   Most sure in all His ways!

O loving wisdom of our God!
   When all was sin and shame,
A second Adam to the fight
   And to the rescue came.

O wisest love! that flesh and blood
   Which did in Adam fail,
Should strive afresh against the foe,
   Should strive and should prevail;

And that a higher gift than grace
   Should flesh and blood refine,
God's Presence and His very Self,
   And Essence all-divine.

O generous love! that He who smote
   In man for man the foe,
The double agony in man
   For man should undergo;

And in the garden secretly,
    And on the cross on high,
Should teach His brethren and inspire
    To suffer and to die.

6.

ANGEL

Thy judgment now is near, for we are come
Into the veilèd presence of our God.

SOUL

I hear the voices that I left on earth.

ANGEL

It is the voice of friends around thy bed,
Who say the "Subvenite" with the priest.
Hither the echoes come; before the Throne
Stands the great Angel of the Agony,
The same who strengthen'd Him, what time He knelt
Lone in that garden shade, bedew'd with blood.
That Angel best can plead with Him for all
Tormented souls, the dying and the dead.

ANGEL OF THE AGONY

Jesu! by that shuddering dread which fell on Thee;
Jesu! by that cold dismay which sicken'd Thee;
Jesu! by that pang of heart which thrill'd in Thee;
Jesu! by that mount of sins which crippled Thee;
Jesu! by that sense of guilt which stifled Thee;
Jesu! by that innocence which girdled Thee;
Jesu! by that sanctity which reign'd in Thee;
Jesu! by that Godhead which was one with Thee;
Jesu! spare these souls which are so dear to Thee;
Souls, who in prison, calm and patient, wait for Thee;
Hasten, Lord, their hour, and bid them come to Thee.
To that glorious Home, where they shall ever gaze on Thee.

SOUL

I go before my Judge. Ah! . . .

ANGEL

. . . Praise to His Name!
The eager spirit has darted from my hold,
And, with the intemperate energy of love,
Flies to the dear feet of Emmanuel;
But, ere it reach them, the keen sanctity,
Which with its effluence, like a glory, clothes
And circles round the Crucified, has seized,
And scorch'd, and shrivel'd it; and now it lies
Passive and still before the awful Throne.
O happy, suffering soul! for it is safe,
Consumed, yet quicken'd, by the glance of God.

SOUL

Take me away, and in the lowest deep
          There let me be.
And there in hope the lone night-watches keep,
          Told out for me.
There, motionless and happy in my pain,
          Lone, not forlorn—
There will I sing my sad perpetual strain,
          Until the morn.
There will I sing, and soothe my stricken breast,
          Which ne'er can cease
To throb, and pine, and languish, till possest
          Of its Sole Peace.
There will I sing my absent Lord and Love—
          Take me away,
That sooner I may rise, and go above,
And see Him in the truth of everlasting day.

7.

ANGEL

Now let the golden prison ope its gates,
Making sweet music, as each fold revolves
Upon its ready hinge. And ye, great powers,
Angels of Purgatory, receive from me
My charge, a precious soul, until the day,
When, from all bond and forfeiture released,
I shall reclaim it for the courts of light.

SOULS IN PURGATORY

1. Lord, Thou hast been our refuge: in every generation;
2. Before the hills were born, and the world was: from age to age Thou art God.
3. Bring us not, Lord, very low: for Thou hast said, Come back again, ye sons of Adam.
4. A thousand years before Thine eyes are but as yesterday: and as a watch of the night which is come and gone.
5. The grass springs up in the morning: at evening tide it shrivels up and dies.
6. So we fail in Thine anger: and in Thy wrath are we troubled.
7. Thou hast set our sins in Thy sight: and our round of days in the light of Thy countenance.
8. Come back, O Lord! how long: and be entreated for Thy servants.
9. In Thy morning we shall be filled with Thy mercy: we shall rejoice and be in pleasure all our days.
10. We shall be glad according to the days of our humiliation: and the years in which we have seen evil.
11. Look, O Lord, upon Thy servants and on Thy work: and direct their children.
12. And let the beauty of the Lord our God be upon us: and the work of our hands, establish Thou it.

Glory be to the Father, and to the Son: and to the Holy Ghost.

As it was in the beginning, is now, and ever shall be: world
    without end. Amen.

ANGEL

Softly and gently, dearly ransom'd soul,
    In my most loving arms I now enfold thee,
And, o'er the penal waters, as they roll,
    I poise thee, and I lower thee, and hold thee.

And carefully I dip thee in the lake,
    And thou, without a sob or a resistance,
Dost through the flood thy rapid passage take,
    Sinking deep, deeper, into the dim distance.
Angels, to whom the willing task is given,
    Shall tend, and nurse, and lull thee, as thou liest;
And masses on the earth, and prayers in heaven,
    Shall aid thee at the Throne of the Most, Highest.

Farewell, but not forever! brother dear,
    Be brave and patient on thy bed of sorrow;
Swiftly shall pass thy night of trial here,
    And I will come and wake thee on the morrow.

                          The Oratory
                          January 1865

PRAYER

O Lord, support us all the day long, until the shadows
lengthen and the evening comes, and the busy world is
hushed, and the fever of life is over, and our work is done.
Then in Thy mercy grant us a safe lodging, and a holy rest,
and peace at the last. Amen.

1844

1. Rev. 7:15, 17, 21:23, 24.
2. Heb. 6:4–6, 10:26–29. Vide also 2 Pet. 2:20, 22.
3. Pet. 4:18.
4. Phil. 2:12, 18.
5. 1 Cor. 8:5.
6. Rom. 2:20.
7. Eph. 5:14–17.
8. Isa. 26:3, 4.
9. *Christian Year,* Sixth Sunday after Trinity.
10. Acts 10:3.
11. 2 Cor. 5:14, 17; Gal. 2:20; Col. 3:12–16; Gal. 4:6; Luke 9:23.
12. John 14:1.
13. Gal. 6:15.
14. Gal. 6:15.
15. Ps.2:11.
16. John 14:6.
17. Gen. 24:63.
18. John 21:21, 22.
19. Hooker on Justification.
20. 1 Pet. 2:7, 8.
21. Vide Mark 4:11–25, etc.
22. John 6:53–68.
23. Matt. 6:25, 26.
24. Eccles. 12:12, 13.
25. Luke 14:25–33.
26. Matt. 12:39, 21:23–27.
27. John 10:30–37.
28. Matt. 19:16–22; Mark 10:17–22; Luke 18:18–23.
29. Mark 9:23.
30. Matt. 13:11; John 14:15.
31. John 21:12.

32. Mark 16:7.
33. Ps. 119:131.
34. Ezek. 3:14.
35. Luke 14:23.
36. John 14:18.
37. Matt. 17:4, 18:1, 20:20; John 14:8.
38. Acts 1:6.
39. Dan. 1:4.
40. Deut. 33:25–27.
41. Heb. 1:6.
42. Rev. 8:1.
43. Tim. 3:16; 2 Cor. 5:19; Isa. 9:6; Rom. 9:5; John 20:28; Rev. 1:8; Heb. 1:2, 3.
44. John 3:6.
45. Exod. 16:8; 1 Thess. 4:8.
46. Acts 19:12.
47. Rom. 1:4; Acts 2:24.
48. Pet. 1:4.
49. Exod. 3:2; Acts 7:35–38; Exod. 19:3, 20:1.
50. 1 John 4:7, 12, 16.
51. Ps. 16:10; Acts 2:24, 27, τὸν ὅσιον.
52. Acts 4:27, τὸν ἅγιον.
53. Gen. 5:3.
54. Rom. 6:9.
55. Rom. 1:4.
56. 1 Cor. 15:47.
57. Isa. 9:6.
58. Heb. 7:25.
59. John 5:26, 14:10.
60. Gen. 2:17; 1 Cor. 15:22, 45, 47.
61. John 6:33–54.

62. Luke 6:19; Mark 5:30. Vide Knox on the Eucharist. *Remains,* vol. 2.
63. Rom. 8:39.
64. Rev. 20:4.
65. Matt. 6:34.
66. Acts 17:27.
67. Eph. 1:17, 18; Col. 3:10; 2 Pet. 1:2; John 18:3.
68. John 14:15; 1 John 2:6; Col. 3:1.
69. Rev. 16:15.
70. Acts 10:41.
71. Matt. 10:3.
72. Ps. 15:1, 2, 24:4.
73. Ps. 31:19, 34:12–14, 18–22.
74. Isa. 26:2, 3.
75. Prov. 16:6; Dan. 4:27; Neh. 13:14; Hab. 2:4.
76. Mark 9:23.
77. Matt. 25:40.
78. Acts 10:2.
79. Acts 16:31.
80. Matt. 16:27; 2 Cor. 5:10; Acts 10:42; James 2:24; Rev. 22:14.
81. John 14:15.
82. Mic. 6:6–8.
83. Matt. 9:13; Rom. 5:6; 1 Tim. 1:15.
84. Matt. 22:13.
85. Heb. 3:7–15.
86. Exod. 33:11.
87. Isa. 54:13.
88. 2 Cor. 4:6.
89. Ps. 139:2.
90. John 6:70, 13:4, 5.
91. Matt. 26:24, 25, 50; Luke 22:48.
92. Mark 10:21, 8:12, 3:5.
93. Vide also Matt. 19:26; Luke 22:61; Mark 3:34, 1:41.
94. 1 Cor. 7:22, 23; Col. 3:22, 24; Rom. 1:1; 1 Cor. 9:21.
95. Eph. 4:22.
96. 2 Cor. 10:5.
97. Rom. 8:1–4; James 2:10; Matt. 5:19, 20; Mark 10:21, 24.
98. Isa. 40:31.
99. Josh. 6, 8, 10.
100. Pet. 3:20.
101. John 14:21, 23.
102. Ps. 104:30.
103. Preached on Whitsunday.
104. Cant. 1:7, 8.
105. Rev. 4:4.
106. Ps. 149:5–9.
107. 1 John 4:20.
108. Ps. 31:24.
109. Rom. 5:2; Phil. 4:4; 1 Thess. 5:16–18; James 5:13.
110. Phil. 3:20.
111. Isa. 26:3.
112. 1 John 2:20, 21, 27, 3:9.
113. 1 John 3:1.
114. Ps. 69:8.
115. John 3:2.
116. Wisd. 5:1–5.
117. ἀγρυπνεῖτε.
118. Mark 13:35–37, γρηγορεῖτε.
119. Luke 12:39.
120. Matt. 25:13.
121. Luke 21:36.
122. Mark 14:37.
123. Rom. 13:11, 12.
124. 1 Cor. 16:13.
125. Eph. 6:10–13.
126. 1 Thess. 5:6.
127. 1 Pet. 4:7, νήψατε, v.8.
128. Rev. 16:15.
129. Rom. 8:17–23; 1 Cor. 1:7; 2 Cor. 4:10; Phil. 3:10; Col. 3:4, 1:24.
130. Hab. 2:1.
131. Luke 12:37, 38.
132. Job 19:26, 27; Num. 24:17; Luke 21:28; Matt. 26:64;

Rev. 1:7; 1 John 3:2; 1 Cor.
13:12; Rev. 22:4.

133. 2 Cor. 5:10; Rom. 14:10–12;
Matt. 25:31, 32.

134. 1 Thess. 5:2, 3; Matt. 25:5, 6.

135. Luke 5:8; Rev. 1:17.

136. Dan. 10:8.

137. Exod. 19:10–12; 2 Cor. 7:1.

138. Col. 3:15, 16; Eph. 5:19, 20;
Phil. 4:6; Thess. 5:18.

139. Phil. 4:4, 11, 18; 1 Tim.
1:12–14.

140. 2 Sam. 23:1.

141. 1 Chron. 29:9–14.

142. Rom. 9:13; Ps. 78:68–71; 1
Cor. 15:8.

143. Second Sunday after Christmas.

144. Gen. 28:20, 21.

145. Gen. 43:36, 38, 43:14, 37:35,
45:26, 27.

146. Gen. 32:9, 10, 35:3, 47:9,
48:3, 7, 15, 16, 21,
49:29–31.

147. Deut. 26:5–10.

148. Job 1:21.

149. Isa. 41:8, 14, 43:1–3.

150. 1 Pet. 1:16; Matt. 5:48.

151. Rom. 7:10.

152. Gen. 3:10.

153. Rom. 8:7, 8, 7:14, 15, 18, 3:20;
Isa. 64:6.

154. Ps. 51:6, 7, 10, 12, 26:6,
119:30, 40, 143:10.

155. Dan. 9:24; Mal. 3:3; Isa. 51:7,
32:15, 16, 17; Jer. 31:31;
Ezek. 36:26, 27; Isa. 61:10;
Rev. 19:7, 8.

156. Luke 24:11; Gal. 1:20; Acts
4:19; Luke 1:19; Rev. 8:2,
1:5; Rom. 3:19; Mic. 6:8;
Luke 1:74, 75; Gen. 7:1;
Dan. 6:22; Luke 1:6; Acts
10:4; 1 Tim. 2:3; Heb.

13:21; 1 Pet. 3:4; 1 John
3:22; Rev. 3:2; Heb. 11:4.

157. 1 Cor. 6:11; 2 Cor. 3:8, 9; Gal.
4:5, 6; Rom. 8:26, 27,
5:18–21.

158. Rom. 15:16, 12:1; Tit. 3:5;
Col. 1:10.

159. Rom. 8:27.

160. Rom. 4:24, 25.

161. Gal. 5:5.

162. Rom. 10:3.

163. Rom. 4:5.

164. Eph. 2:8–10.

165. Rom. 11:6.

166. Rom. 11:30–32.

167. Hooker on Justification, sec.
9.

168. Col. 1:10.

169. Rom. 7:24.

170. 2 Cor. 7:12.

171. 2 Cor. 6:6; Rom. 12:9; Pet.
1:22; James 3:17.

172. Heb. 4:12, 13.

173. Ps. 139:1, 2, 4, 113:8, 31:5,
37:5, 6, 51:4, 17:1–3,
73:24–26.

174. 1 John 3:20, 21, 1:5–9, 2:8,
3:24, 5:10; Rom. 8:16.

175. Luke 16:13.

176. Eph. 5:13.

177. John 3:21.

178. 1 Sam. 13:12.

179. Isa. 37:14.

180. Matt. 14:30.

181. 2 Sam. 24:14.

182. Ps. 90:8.

183. Ps. 16:8.

184. Mal. 3:18.

185. Matt. 16:22.

186. Gal. 2:20.

187. Matt. 6:17.

188. John 16:22, 14:27; Cor. 2:9,
14.

189. Matt. 9:15.

190. Pet. 1:8, 9.
191. Rom. 5:2; Eph. 2:6; Col. 3:3; Phil. 3:20; 2 Cor. 4:6; Gal. 3:27; John 14:21–23, 18–20.
192. Matt. 28:20, 18:20.
193. Eph. 2:22; 1 Cor. 3:16; Eph. 3:17; 1 Cor. 6:15, 7:13, 27; 2 Cor. 13:5; Col. 1:27, 1 John 5:12; John 15:4, 5, 14:19.
194. Acts 9:4, 5.
195. Acts 22:14.
196. 1 Cor. 9:1.
197. Cor. 15:8.
198. Acts 1:21, 22, 10:40, 41.
199. Zech. 14:5–7.
200. Ps. 46:4, 5, 10, 11.
201. John 13:18.
202. John 6:11; Luke 22:19; Matt. 14:19; Matt. 26:26; Matt. 15:36; Luke 24:30; Acts 27:35.
203. Easter.
204. Deut. 32:13, 33:13–15.
205. Gen. 21:10.
206. Matt. 11:19; Luke 7:34.
207. Gen. 14:18.
208. Cor. 10:20.
209. Ezek. 47:12.
210. Rev. 22:2.
211. Hos. 2:21–23.
212. Joel 3:18.
213. Amos 9:13.
214. Isa. 25:6, 62:8, 9, 65:13.
215. Jer. 31:12–14.
216. Zech. 9:17.
217. Mal. 1:11.
218. Ps. 23:5, 26:6, 36:7–9, 43:3, 65:4, 63:6–8.
219. Prov. 9:1–5.
220. Isa. 55:1.
221. Cant. 2:13, 4:6, 5:1.
222. Ezek. 33:11; Isa. 5:4.
223. Eccles. 24:21.
224. Isa. 25:6.
225. Isa. 61:1–3.
226. Hos. 14:5–7.
227. Ps. 81:13–16.
228. Ps. 4:7.
229. Ps. 16:6.
230. Ps. 19:10.
231. Ps. 28:7.
232. Ps. 65:4.
233. Easter.
234. 1 John 3:2.
235. Rev. 1:14–16.
236. Wisd. 5:2–5.
237. 1 Sam. 1:11.
238. Ps. 84:4.
239. Luke 18:13.
240. Acts 9:6.
241. Rom. 8:29.
242. Acts 22:10.
243. Matt. 4:18–20.
244. Matt. 19:21, 22.
245. Matt. 4:18.
246. Matt. 9:9.
247. Mark 2:14.
248. Matt. 20:6, 7.
249. Luke 9:59–62.
250. Gen. 12:1.
251. John 21:7.
252. Hos. 6:3.
253. Phil. 2:12,13.
254. Gen. 3:6.
255. Eccles. 11:9.
256. 2 Tim. 2:26.
257. 2 Tim. 4:10.
258. Luke 16:26.
259. 1 Pet. 5:8.
260. 1 John 4:4.
261. 1 Cor. 10:13.
262. Rev. 2:17.
263. Jer. 33:3.
264. 2 Cor. 4:6.
265. Phil. 2:5–7; 1 Pet. 1:8, 9.

SUGGESTIONS FOR
FURTHER READING

BLEHL, VINCENT. *The White Stone: The Spirituality of John Henry Newman.* Petersham, Mass.: St. Bede's, 1993.

BOUYER, LOUIS. *Newman's Vision of Faith.* San Francisco: Ignatius Press, 1986.

DESSAIN, C. S. *John Henry Newman.* New York: Oxford University Press, 1980.

FABER, GEOFFREY. *Oxford Apostles: A Character Study of the Oxford Movement.* New York: Charles Scribner's Sons, 1934.

FFINCH, MICHAEL. *Newman: Towards the Second Spring.* San Francisco: Ignatius Press, 1992.

GILLEY, SHERIDAN. *Newman and His Age.* Westminister, Md.: Christian Classics, 1991.

JAKI, STANLEY L., ed. *Newman Today.* San Francisco: Ignatius Press, 1989.

KER, IAN. *The Achievement of John Henry Newman.* Notre Dame, Ind.: University of Notre Dame Press, 1991.

———. *John Henry Newman: A Biography.* New York: Oxford University Press, 1990.

———. *Newman and Conversion.* Edinburgh, Scotland: T. and T. Clark, 1993.

———. *Newman and the Fulness of Christianity,* Edinburgh, Scotland: T. and T. Clark, 1993.

———. *Newman on Being a Christian.* Notre Dame, Ind.: University of Notre Dame Press, 1990.

———. *Newman the Theologian: A Reader.* Notre Dame, Ind.: University of Notre Dame Press, 1990.

NEWMAN, JOHN HENRY. *Apologia Pro Vita Sua*. New York: Penguin Books, 1995.

———. *An Essay on the Development of Christian Doctrine*. Notre Dame, Ind.: University of Notre Dame Press, 1990.

———. *The Idea of a University*. New Haven, Conn.: Yale University Press, 1996.

———. *Parochial and Plain Sermons*. San Francisco: Ignatius Press, 1987; reset edn., 1997.

———. *Prayers, Verses, and Devotions*. San Francisco: Ignatius Press, 1989.

PRZYWARA, ERICH. *The Heart of Newman*. San Francisco: Ignatius Press, 1997.

ROBBINS, WILLIAM. *The Newman Brothers*. Cambridge, Mass.: Harvard University Press, 1966.

ZENO, DR. *John Henry Newman: His Inner Life*. San Francisco: Ignatius Press, 1987.